CITIZENSHIP, CRIME AND COMMUNITY IN THE EUROPEAN UNION

Over the past 20 years the European Union has been increasingly active in the area of criminal law. Meanwhile, the status of European Union citizenship has been progressively developed and strengthened. Adopting an expressive and communitarian perspective of the criminal law, this book considers EU criminal law in light of EU citizenship with a view to revealing the structure of the EU's political community as expressed in its criminal law. It argues that while national communities remain dominant, through transnational processes certain features of a supranational community can be said to emerge. The book will be of interest to scholars of EU citizenship, EU criminal law and EU law and integration more generally.

Volume 93 in the Series Modern Studies in European Law

Modern Studies in European Law

Recent titles in this series:

The Division of Competences between the EU and the Member States: Reflections on the Past, the Present and the Future
Edited by Sacha Garben and Inge Govaere

Unity in Adversity: EU Citizenship, Social Justice and the Cautionary Tale of the UK
Charlotte O'Brien

The Use of Force and Article 2 of the ECHR in Light of European Conflicts
Hannah Russell

Environmental Crime in Europe
Edited by Andrew Farmer, Michael Faure and Grazia Maria Vagliasindi

Questioning EU Citizenship: Judges and the Limits of Free Movement and Solidarity in the EU
Edited by Daniel Thym

The European Union under Transnational Law: A Pluralist Appraisal
Matej Avbelj

Illegally Staying in the EU: An Analysis of Illegality in EU Migration Law
Benedita Menezes Queiroz

Social Legitimacy in the Internal Market: A Dialogue of Mutual Responsiveness
Jotte Mulder

The EU Better Regulation Agenda: A Critical Assessment
Edited by Sacha Garben and Inge Govaere

Administrative Regulation Beyond the Non-Delegation Doctrine: A Study on EU Agencies
Marta Simoncini

The Interface Between EU and International Law: Contemporary Reflections
Edited by Inge Govaere and Sacha Garben

The Rise and Decline of Fundamental Rights in EU Citizenship
Adrienne Yong

The Court of Justice and European Criminal Law: Leading Cases in a Contextual Analysis
Edited by Valsamis Mitsilegas, Alberto di Martino and Leandro Mancano

The EU as a Global Regulator for Environmental Protection: A Legitimacy Perspective
Ioanna Hadjiyianni

For the complete list of titles in this series, see 'Modern Studies in European Law' link at www.bloomsburyprofessional.com/uk/series/modern-studies-in-european-law

Citizenship, Crime and Community in the European Union

Stephen Coutts

•HART•
OXFORD • LONDON • NEW YORK • NEW DELHI • SYDNEY

HART PUBLISHING

Bloomsbury Publishing Plc

Kemp House, Chawley Park, Cumnor Hill, Oxford, OX2 9PH, UK

First published in Great Britain 2019

A catalogue record for this book is available from the British Library.

Library of Congress Cataloging-in-Publication data

Names: Coutts, Stephen, author.

Title: Citizenship, crime and community in the European Union / Stephen Coutts.

Description: Oxford, UK ; Chicago, Illinois : Hart Publishing, 2019. | Series: Modern studies in European law ; volume 93 | Based pm author's thesis (doctoral - European University Institute, 2015). | Includes bibliographical references and index.

Identifiers: LCCN 2019015481 (print) | LCCN 2019018324 (ebook) | ISBN 9781509915354 (EPub) | ISBN 9781509915361 (hardback)

Subjects: LCSH: Criminal law—European Union countries. | Citizenship—European Union countries. | BISAC: LAW / International. | POLITICAL SCIENCE / Civics & Citizenship.

Classification: LCC KJE7975 (ebook) | LCC KJE7975 .C68 2019 (print) | DDC 345.24—dc23

LC record available at https://lccn.loc.gov/2019015481

ISBN: HB: 978-1-50991-536-1
ePDF: 978-1-50991-534-7
ePub: 978-1-50991-535-4

Typeset by Compuscript Ltd, Shannon

TABLE OF CONTENTS

PART II
SOCIAL INTEGRATION AND CRIME: INCLUSION AND EXCLUSION

PART III
AN AREA OF JUSTICE: SHARED ENFORCEMENT AND SHARED RECOGNITION OF NATIONAL WRONGS

TABLE OF CASES

European Court of Justice Judgments

National Judgments

European Court of Human Rights Judgments

European Free Trade Association Court Judgments

TABLE OF LEGISLATION

European Union Legislation

Directive 93/109/EC laying down detailed arrangements for the exercise of the right to vote and stand as a candidate in elections to the European Parliament for citizens of the Union residing in a Member State of which they are not nationals [1993] OJ L 329/34 .... 19, 96

Directive 93/96/EEC on the right of residence for students [1993] OJ L 317/59 .... 15, 27

International Treaties

Non-Legislative Documents

1

Citizenship, Crime and Community in the European Union

Introduction

Criminal law is concerned with responsibilities. However, responsibility is a relational concept; we are responsible *to* someone *for* something. That relationship is found in the notion of citizenship; we are responsible *to* each other as citizens of the same political community. And we are responsible *for* our actions that offend against the norms, values and interests of that community. The criminal law therefore reflects aspects of citizenship and political community. It involves responsibilities, corresponding rights and a moral relationship between co-members of the community. Through the criminal law the community lays down the norms that govern relations between its members and expresses the values inherent to that particular community. Through this expressive dimension it can be said to contribute to the formation of the identity of the community.

Citizenship and community are useful as means of explaining criminal law. The converse is also true; a communitarian account of the criminal law can be a useful means of exploring hitherto unexamined aspects of citizenship and the community and can help complement and enrich our understanding of these concepts. This is precisely the approach adopted in this book concerning EU citizenship. An examination of EU citizenship in light of a moral and communitarian account of the criminal law rooted in citizenship can, it is hoped, provide important insights concerning Union citizenship and the political community of the European Union.

This chapter serves as a general introduction to the subjects of this book, EU criminal law and EU citizenship, and develops a communitarian account of the criminal law based on the theory of RA Duff that links the concepts of citizenship and criminal law and which provides concepts used throughout the remainder of this book. The first part presents an account of the criminal law based on an understanding of crimes as public wrongs and as reflecting responsibilities by individuals to other individuals *qua* citizens under the common values and norms of their particular community. The second part briefly introduces the role of the European Union in criminal law. The third part provides a history of EU citizenship while outlining some of its main features. A conclusion provides an outline of the remainder of the book and the main argument.

Citizenship, Crime and Community: A Communitarian Account of the Criminal Law

The criminal law prohibits certain conduct. Through it the state claims authority to declare certain norms of conduct and to insist on their respect. More than any other area of law the criminal law carries the implication of '"ought not to do" and enforces these prohibitions through the use of physical force. It is the censure contained in the criminal law and the exercise of physical force to enforce it that marks out its special social significance'[1] and calls for heightened justification. These simple statements immediately raise a number of questions of the criminal law and in particular the legitimacy of the polity to declare and enforce such norms on supposedly free individuals. To put the question another way: what conduct can the community legitimately require individuals to refrain from and how can punishment be justified?[2] A classic instrumentalist perspective, rooted in the rationalism of the Enlightenment and particularly influential in Anglo-American criminal law,[3] would justify the imposition of criminal liability according to the harm principle, famously articulated by Mill, according to which '*the only* purpose for which power can be rightfully exercised over any member of a civilised community, against his will, is to prevent harm to others'.[4] Feinberg has provided the most comprehensive modern restatement of such a liberal conception of the criminal law through a detailed elaboration of the harm principle based around the concept of a 'setback to interests'.[5] This he has supplemented with an 'offence principle', with very limited application.[6]

However, although the harm principle can be a useful starting point for determining which actions are to be labelled crimes, it is not sufficient in itself to capture what are commonly understood to be crimes. As pointed out by Simester and von Hirsch (who base their view on an updated version of Feinberg's thesis), the criminal law has a moral and condemnatory quality that distinguishes it from tort

[1] Andrew Ashworth, *Principles of Criminal Law*, 2 edn (Clarendon Press, 1995) 1.

[2] There are some crimes of omission, requiring not that an individual refrain from a particular action but take positive steps. However, this category is relatively minor, particularly in the Anglo-American tradition, and only operates under certain circumstances, normally when a pre-existing relationship of a certain quality exists establishing a particular duty to act. See Alan Norrie, *Crime, Reason and History: A Critical Introduction to Criminal Law*, 1 edn (Weidenfeld & Nicolson, 1993) ch 6.

[3] ibid, ch 1.

[4] John Stewart Mill, *On Liberty and Other Essays* [1859] (Oxford University Press, 1991) 15. For a discussion of Mill's but also other versions of the harm principle, see Antony Duff, *Answering for Crime: Responsibility and Liability in the Criminal Law* (Hart Publishing, 2007) 123ff. For a modern restatement of Mill's harm principle, see Joel Feinberg, *The Moral Limits of the Criminal Law: Harm to Others*, vol I (Oxford University Press, 1984).

[5] Feinberg (n 4).

[6] Joel Feinberg, *The Moral Limits of the Criminal Law: Offense to Others*, vol 2 (Oxford University Press, 1985).

and other regulatory forms of law.[7] Instead, Duff, amongst others, has proposed applying a moral rather than harm-based approach to the question of criminalisation, defining crimes as public wrongs.[8]

Duff has pointed out that the harm principle is both under- and over-inclusive. It is under-inclusive in that it fails to capture the moral, in addition to the material or physical, nature of a criminal attack.[9] Thus, the violation of personal privacy and space, in addition to simply deprivation of material goods, occasioned by burglary is not captured by all but the most wide-ranging harm principle. Equally we consider rape to be criminal not simply by virtue of the physical and emotional harm caused to the victim but also by its blatant disregard for the respect due him or her as a morally autonomous individual. Furthermore, it is difficult to reconcile the harm principle with situations where individuals willingly submit to what might otherwise be considered a harmful situation such as polygamy or sadomasochism.[10] The criminal law reserves the right to criminalise conduct regardless of whether the 'victim' considers it harmful. It is true that these situations might be captured by a sufficiently broad definition of 'harm'; however, to do so would stretch the underlying concept of the harm principle and ultimately leave it so broad as to be meaningless.[11] It would certainly fail in its stated purpose of providing clear guidance on what may or may not be criminalised by the state.

The harm principle is also over-inclusive in two ways. Firstly, it would criminalise harm that we would normally consider private and outside the purview of the criminal law, such as emotional or even financial harm caused by the breakdown of a relationship. Secondly, a proper application of the harm principle requires not simply the criminalisation of directly harmful conduct, but criminalisation of conduct that poses a mere *risk* of harm, such as reckless driving or failure to follow safety rules in a high-risk industry. Therefore, for this reason also 'it is hard to see how [the harm principle] can set tight or determinate limits on the scope of the criminal law'.[12]

[7] AP Simester and Andreas von Hirsch, *Crimes, Harms and Wrongs: On the Principles of Criminalisation* (Hart Publishing, 2011) ch 1.

[8] Most famously articulated by Lord Devlin in response to the Wolfenden Report advocating, amongst other issues, the decriminalisation of homosexual acts in the UK. For an account and HLA Hart's response, see HLA Hart, *Law, Liberty and Morality* (Oxford University Press, 1962). For one of the more prominent moral theories of criminalisation, see Michael Moore, *Placing Blame: A Theory of Criminal Law* (Oxford University Press, 1997).

[9] Although it should be noted that Feinberg's formulation of the harm principle only prohibits wrongful harms, ie harms that violate an individual's rights. See also Simester and von Hirsch (n 7) ch 2. However, it is unlikely that Feinberg's notion of a violation of a right properly articulates Duff's conception of a moral wrong. That conception is closer (although still certainly distinct) to the more clearly moralist position of Moore, based on emotions and sense of violation. See Moore (n 8).

[10] Duff gives the example of the famous UK House of Lords decision of *R v Brown* [1994] 1 AC 212 involving consensual sadomasochistic sexual encounters between groups of adult men.

[11] With the further result that it would cease 'to set substantial independent constraints on the scope of criminal law', Duff (n 4) 135.

[12] ibid, 137.

Instead of the harm principle, Duff proposes a broader and explicitly moral basis for the criminal law: crimes as wrongs.[13] Unlike torts, the remedy of which is to undo the harm caused, crimes are *wrongs*, and conviction of a crime involves punishment and condemnation.[14] It involves a retributive element independent from deterrence or restoration. The harm principle can still play a role in identifying at least some, if not all, of those criminal wrongs, particularly as a constraint on a liberal criminal law. However, even if harm is used as a criterion for identifying a crime, in the eyes of the criminal law it cannot be disassociated from its wrongful character.[15] Defining crimes as wrongs necessarily abandons the pursuit of any master principle capable of identifying the content of the criminal law once and for all. The concept of a wrong is not a closed or fixed category and there is no

> single concept or value that will capture *the* essence of crime, or *the* essential characteristic in virtue of which crimes are properly punished. … [R]ather we should resist this desire in favour of a pluralism that recognises a diversity of reasons for criminalisation, matching the diversity of kinds of wrong which can legitimately be the criminal law's business.[16]

The criminal law and the wrongs it embodies can therefore vary from time to time and from place to place depending on the prevailing moral consensus of a particular society or community.

This is not to say that there are no limits on the criminal law. There is an inherent limitation in the public nature of the criminal law. Crimes are not only wrongs, they are *public* wrongs and individuals can only be punished for wrongs that concern the broader community in a sufficiently serious manner to warrant retribution and condemnation. In the words of Blackstone, crimes

> are breach and violation of the public rights and duties, due to the whole community, considered as community, in its social aggregate capacity.… [B]esides the injury done to individuals, [crimes] strike at the very being of society, which cannot possibly subsist, where actions of [that] sort are suffered to escape with impunity. In all cases the crime includes an injury: every public offence is also a private wrong, and somewhat more; it affects the individual and it likewise affects the community.[17]

This is not to say that criminal law should confine itself to acts that directly affect the public space or institutions such as public order offences or terrorism.

[13] It should be pointed out that Feinberg also considers the criminal law to contain a moral element, in his version of the harm principle it is *wrongful* harms (ie those setbacks to interest that violate another person's rights) that constitute by far the largest categories of acts that can be legitimately criminalised. See Feinberg, *The Moral Limits of the Criminal Law: Harm to Others* (n 4) ch 3.

[14] See Joel Feinberg, 'The Expressive Function of Punishment' (1965) 49 *The Monist* 397, who considers the condemnatory aspect the defining characteristic of punishment.

[15] 'A moralised version of the Harm Principle does not aim to identify harms independently of the wrongs that generate them.' See Duff (n 4) 139.

[16] ibid, 139 (emphasis in original). See also Anthony Duff, 'Theorizing Criminal Law: A 25th Anniversary Essay' (2005) 25 *OJLS* 353.

[17] As quoted in Duff (n 4) 52.

Nor should we attempt to construe crimes against individuals as crimes directed against the social order per se. Duff rightly points out that to do so would 'distract us from the wrong done to the direct victims of such crimes, which surely should be central to our understanding of their criminal character'.[18] Rather than being wrongs done directly *to* the community, crimes are wrongs that *concern* the community for reasons of their seriousness and their affront to deeply held normative values of the community. They are wrongs in which the community shares.[19] More recently, Duff has restated and expanded on the definition of public wrong, linking it to the notion of 'civil order'.[20] We are collectively engaged in a practice of living together as members of a political community; public is anything which is relevant to that practice, however it may be defined by the community.[21]

Several characteristics of the criminal law, and in particular criminal procedure, underline its public quality. Criminal prosecution is brought by a public body, a prosecutor or judge, in the name of the state, or even more tellingly 'the people'. Unlike in civil claims, the individual victim has a minimal role in both initiating and conducting the action. These procedural aspects reflect the underlying characteristic of the crime as a public wrong. It involves 'an authoritative, communal declaration of… wrongs' that, through the criminal trial, merit 'a public, communal response'.[22] The criminal trial is a means of publicly calling the transgressing member of society to account for his actions, that he or she may possibly justify or excuse.[23] Similarly, punishment can be seen, not simply or even primarily, as a means of deterrence, but in combining deterrence with a retributive and rehabilitative purpose, as a form of 'secular penance' towards the community.[24]

We therefore move away from a simple Austinian 'command and control' conception of the criminal law based on a relationship between sovereign and subjects to one in which individuals as members of a community have a relationship of responsibility to each other and the broader community by virtue of their membership. It is an inherently community-based account of the criminal law. In the criminal trial the individual is called to account for his or her actions before the community. He or she is required to answer for his or her conduct deemed wrongful. The criminal law is a set of responsibilities on the basis of which we can

[18] RA Duff, *Punishment, Communication and Community* (Oxford University Press, 2001) 61.

[19] Duff (n 4) 52. See also SE Marshall and RA Duff, 'Criminalization and Sharing Wrongs' (1998) 11 *Canadian Journal of Law and Jurisprudence* 7.

[20] RA Duff and SE Marshall, 'Crimes, Public Wrongs, and Civil Order' (2010) 13 *Criminal Law and Philosophy* 27.

[21] ibid, 1.

[22] Duff (n 18) 61.

[23] See also Christopher Bennett, *The Apology Ritual: A Philosophical Theory of Punishment* (Cambridge University Press, 2008) for whom the criminal trial is a means of simulating the making of amends on the part of the offender vis-à-vis the community.

[24] Duff (n 18) ch 3. See also Bennett (n 23) ch 7, for whom punishment can serve the purpose of restoring relations that have been ruptured between the individual and the community through the commission of crime.

be called to give an account. However, calling to account implies a relationship between the caller and the called that pre-exists the calling.[25] Responsibility, and therefore criminal law itself, is a relational concept. A is responsible *to* B *for* C. Moreover, the content of the responsibility of A to B depends on the type of relationship that exists between A and B. Given the public character of criminal law, it is in our capacities as *citizens* that we owe responsibilities to each other under the criminal law and may be called to account in the context of the community. 'As citizens who are both bound and protected by the values of our polity, we have both rights and responsibilities: we are answerable to each other for our conduct as citizens.'[26] Furthermore, both the status of the offender and the victim as citizens explains and justifies the interest the community as a whole takes in the wrong; it renders a private wrong public and hence criminal. Even those wrongs that are directed at individuals

> count as 'our' wrongs because they violate our public values and because we share them with the victim: our concern for the victim as our fellow citizen makes them our business. As does our recognition of the wrongdoer as a fellow citizen: what is done by one of us, when it impinges on our shared values, is our business.[27]

Basing criminal law on citizenship raises three questions: firstly the position of non-citizens;[28] secondly, the question of those individuals who, while *de jure* citizens, do not consider themselves such, or at least do not consider themselves bound by the norms of the polity of which they are nominal members, what Duff calls 'recussants';[29] and thirdly, the effect of criminal activity, particularly persistent and egregious, on the citizenship status of offenders.[30]

Citizenship is an exclusive status whereas the criminal law both protects victims of crime and condemns offenders regardless of citizenship.[31] Although this may seem problematic it can be explained by conceiving of non-citizens as visitors to the polity who enjoy the status of guests. As guests they enjoy the protection but must also respect the normative values of the host society as expressed in its criminal law and must conduct themselves accordingly.[32] With some consideration for the position of 'guests', Duff's theory can therefore accommodate non-citizens on the territory of the state.[33]

[25] RA Duff, 'Responsibility, Citizenship and Criminal Law' in RA Duff and Stuart P Green (eds), *Philosophical Foundations of Criminal Law* (Oxford University Press, 2011) 132.

[26] Duff (n 4) 50.

[27] Duff (n 25) 139.

[28] For an alternative view, see Alejandro Chehtman, 'Citizenshp v Territory: Explaining the Scope of the Criminal Law' (2010) 13 New Criminal Law Review 427.

[29] Duff and Marshall (n 20) 16–18.

[30] Duff (n 25) 141ff.

[31] There are a small number of crimes that are citizenship specific, such as voter fraud or treason.

[32] Duff (n 4) 142.

[33] See most recently the more developed account in RA Duff, *The Realm of Criminal Law* (Oxford University Press, 2018) ch 3, s 3.

Can an individual in effect consider him or herself *not* bound by the criminal law of the state? In answer to this question Duff notes that associative obligations, such as those embodied in the criminal law, can, depending on the association, exist regardless of whether the individual concerned assented.[34] Relations, and the obligations that arise from them, can exist in a variety of circumstances, only some of which depend on the individual's willingness to be bound by them. Political association generates certain obligations regardless of consent.[35]

Finally, there is the question of the impact serious breaches of the criminal law may have on the membership status of convicted citizens. Do such individuals by persistent and particularly serious transgressions of the normative values of the community, or even by direct attack on the interests or institutions of the state, forfeit either some of their rights of membership or indeed the status entirely? Although there is certainly a case to be made for such a view,[36] in the liberal polity favoured by Duff, an inclusive rather than exclusive approach to convicted citizens would be taken.[37] Nonetheless, '[a]ny determinate answer to the question of whether, and to what extent, those who commit crimes should be taken to have forfeited their standing and their rights as citizens must depend on a normative account of political community and of criminal law's role in it'.[38] This does raise particular issues in the context of a plural polity, such as the European Union, where citizenship rights are primarily exercised on a transnational basis and the possibility of expulsion remains.[39] This question is explored further in Chapter 5. Suffice to say at this point that expulsion from the host Member State does in fact constitute a suspension of citizenship rights vis-à-vis a particular part of the broader Union polity, one moreover that is endorsed by EU law and that reflects a certain feature of EU citizenship: its necessarily contingent nature vis-à-vis the host society.[40]

[34] Duff and Marshall (n 20) 16.

[35] See Dudley Knowles, *Political Obligation: A Critical Introduction* (Routledge 2010) for a discussion of the question of political obligation and ch 7 specifically for the problems of consent as its basis.

[36] For a debate on the question, see Audrey Macklin and Rainer Bauböck, 'The Return of Banishment: Do the New Denationalisation Policies Weaken Citizenship?' (2015) EUI Working Papers, RSCAS 2015/14.

[37] Duff (n 33) ch 3, s 5.

[38] ibid, ch 3, sec 5.

[39] See Mancano's characterisation of the expulsion regime for EU citizens as 'enemy' criminal law following Jakobs in Leandro Mancano, 'Punishment and Rights in European Union Citizenship: Persons or Criminals?' (2018) 24 *ELJ* 206.

[40] It is important to point out that although this possibility exists under EU law we should not overstate its significance for the status of citizenship, as Mancano possibly does. Firstly, a heightened protection for EU citizens exists, particularly those who are long-term residents. Secondly, that heightened protection is guaranteed by supranational law, which enjoys primacy over national law, thereby reducing pure national discretion in this field, including in procedural matters. Thirdly, and perhaps most importantly, what we are concerned with is a limited suspension of citizenship rights in two ways. Firstly, it is limited in time; all entry bans by Member States must be reviewable at the latest after three years in accordance with Directive 2004/38/EC on the right of citizens of the Union and their family members to move and reside freely within the territory of the Member States [2004] OJ L158/77, Art 29. Secondly, it is limited in geographic scope, to the Member State that adopted the order. An entry ban cannot constitute grounds for exclusion from the European Union as a whole. See Case C-503/03 *Commission v Spain* EU: C:2006:74, [2006] ECR I-1097 in the context of the Schengen area.

A crime is therefore a wrong that properly concerns the community as a whole rather than simply the individual victim(s). It is an act that the community has recognised as wrongful in light of its shared values. The precise content of the criminal law will therefore necessarily vary between communities depending on their particular understandings of wrongfulness and the proper scope of matters of public concern.[41] The criminal law declares or recognises certain wrongs deemed publicly wrongful in light of the shared values and normative understandings of that community and prescribes the appropriate public reaction. It is therefore expressive or declarative: it declares certain actions to be wrongs and attaches formal censure and condemnation to them.[42] In a sense it is the 'common law' par excellence, which is not

> imposed on a people by a sovereign, which they must receive and obey as subjects. Rather it is the law of the community itself. It embodies the shared values and normative understandings of the community. It flows not from the will of a separate sovereign but from the traditions and practices of the community.[43]

Such a vision of criminal law, as declaring certain acts to be wrongful in the eyes of the community and to be of concern to the community, presupposes a group of individuals sufficiently bound by ties of affection or affiliation and sharing a collective identity and political life in common, and moreover a common understanding of what properly concerns the community as a whole. This not to say that such a criminal law requires a community based on a thick, ethno-cultural identity; while it does presuppose some element of community, it does not necessarily require a heavily communitarian perspective of the state, emphasising the needs of the community and the commonly defined 'good' over the interests of individuals. Indeed, the fundamental principles and tenets of modern criminal law developed out of a major period of reform originating in Enlightenment thinking and characterised by a liberalist philosophy.[44] Duff himself proposes

[41] Duff (n 18) 63.

[42] Either by virtue of some pre-legal wrongfulness or by virtue of the place they occupy in a wider system of regulation necessary to maintain certain goods. Thus *mala in se*, such as murder, rape, assault or physical endangerment, are wrongful by their very nature and are deemed to be wrongful independent of regulation. They are 'wrongful harms'. On the other hand, *mala prohibitata*, such as driving on the wrong side of the road or various financial crimes, are wrong by operation of the law rather than some pre-legal wrongfulness. Nonetheless once a system is established to coordinate conduct and deviation from which undermines the system and gives rise to harm or the danger of harm, that in turn may generate a wrong. In contrast to *mala in se*, *mala prohibita* are harmful wrongs. See Duff (n 4) 153ff.

[43] Duff (n 18) 59. Lacey, on the other hand, while also subscribing to a communitarian view of the criminal law, identifies the content of the criminal law as those acts that threaten the 'values considered to be most fundamental in that society' which are related to its fundamental interests, which include 'the preservation of society itself, protecting the environment, the maintenance of some degree of public order and ultimately the upholding of its framework of shared understandings and common values' See Nicola Lacey, *State Punishment: Political Principles and Community Values* (Routledge, 1987) 100–01.

[44] Norrie (n 2) ch 2.

a liberal community as the context within which his theory would apply,[45] and notes that a relatively modest degree of consensus, perhaps of a Rawlsian overlapping kind, may be all that is necessary to underpin shared understandings of what is wrongful and of public concern sufficient to ground criminal law in a liberal polity.[46]

Criminal law has developed principally in the context of the nation-state, a relatively homogeneous unit that combines the strong, historically founded affective ties of 'the imagined community'[47] with the institutions of the modern state and its monopoly over the use of force. In such a context, where individuals are presumed to identify as equal members of the wider community and share the basic values of that community, the criminal law as representing ties of civic responsibilities between citizens and a minimum shared normative understanding can be rationalised and justified. This purely national picture of criminal law has begun to change somewhat. One development that lies outside the scope of this book is the growth and increasing institutionalisation of international criminal law. Whether this represents a proto-cosmopolitan community encompassing all of humanity to which all persons are potentially accountable is open to question.[48] The power to legislate on criminal matters also exists at a sub-state level and can be rationalised as shifts in the understanding of community within a federal context. Nonetheless, it remains the case that both citizenship and criminal law are typically considered within the context of a national community.

The European Union is not a national community but does possess both a meaningful citizenship status and a substantial body of criminal law. And yet both citizenship and criminal law are inherently community-based concepts. This does not, however, exclude the possibility of applying a communitarian view of the criminal law to the European Union. In fact, given the ambiguities surrounding the exact nature of the Union as a political community and the novel nature of its citizenship in a post-national setting, an analysis of EU citizenship in the light of such a view of the criminal law may reveal important features concerning both the status of Union citizenship and the broader community to which it relates. However, before we embark on such a task, the remainder of this chapter will provide a brief introduction to both criminal law and citizenship in the European Union.

[45] Duff (n 18) ch 2.

[46] Duff and Marshall (n 20) 21.

[47] Benedict Anderson, *Imagined Communities*, 2nd edn (Verso, 2006). Although it should be pointed out that increasing multiculturalism in Western states has called for a reappraisal of the values underpinning our political communities and the need for an adequately pluralistic framework. See, for example, Will Kymlicka, *Multi-Cultural Citizenship: A Liberal Theory of Rights* (Oxford University Press, 1995).

[48] Duff (n 4) 55.

The Role of the European Union in Criminal Law

The European Union affects criminal law in three main ways. Firstly, EU law, as a law that enjoys primacy over national law requiring any conflicting national law be set aside, has in certain circumstances prevented Member States from either criminalising certain conduct or applying certain sanctions. Even when Member States are permitted to use criminal law within the scope of EU law, national criminal law remains subject to Union law principles of fundamental rights and proportionality. Secondly, EU law must be implemented by Member States and must be done so in an effective manner. In a pair of cases the Court of Justice recognised a general competence on the part of the Union to oblige Member States to adopt criminal sanctions in order to more effectively implement EU law. Both of these situations – where EU law affects national law negatively, by proscribing the use of criminal law, and positively, by prescribing the use of criminal law – were developed in what was known as the European Community. The third, final area where the European Union affects criminal law was initially located in the ex-Third Pillar of the Treaty on European Union, known as Justice and Home Affairs, and allowed for approximation of national criminal law, judicial and police cooperation and the establishment of a number of criminal law enforcement agencies. The Treaty of Lisbon finally 'communitarised' this area of law, applying the general institutional and legal framework of EU law to this area (albeit with some particularities).[49] As a result we can speak of a qualitative shift in the nature of EU criminal law and in effect its constitutionalisation.[50]

Firstly, the European Union can affect national criminal law in a negative sense, preventing its application. As with all reserved national competences, national criminal law must be exercised in conformity with EU law. In practice this means that national criminal law may be set aside in the event that it conflicts with EU law.[51] Given the far-reaching potential impact of free-movement provisions in the internal market, it is this area that has perhaps been the clearest in setting aside national criminal law. Union law might operate as outright *defence*, setting aside the prohibition contained in national criminal law.[52] Similarly, Union law, and in particular the operation of the principle of proportionality, can call into question the application of criminal sanctions where a fundamental freedom is at stake.[53]

[49] See Valsamis Mitsilegas, 'European Criminal Law and Resistance to Communautarisation after Lisbon' (2010) 1 *New Journal of European Criminal Law* 458.

[50] Valsamis Mitsilegas, *EU Criminal Law after Lisbon* (Hart Publishing, 2016) ch 2.

[51] See Estella Baker, 'Taking European Criminal Law Seriously' [1998] *Crim LR* 361.

[52] Such as the case of *Bordessa* in which a Spanish law criminalising currency export was set aside: see Joined Cases 358/93 and C-416/93 *Criminal proceedings against Aldo Bordessa, Vicente Marí Mellado and Concepción Barbero Maestre* EU: C:1995:54, [1995] ECR I-361. For an account see Baker (n 51).

[53] Case C-193/94 *Criminal proceedings against Sofia Skanavi and Konstantin Chryssanthakopoulos* EU: C:1996:70, [1996] ECR I-929 in which the application of criminal sanctions for failure to comply with a regulation requiring exchange of foreign driving licences was deemed to be disproportionate. See further Baker (n 51).

Thus, even when national criminal law that frustrates a fundamental freedom is permitted under EU law, its exercise is conditioned by the general principles of EU law, including fundamental rights and proportionality. One of the most extensive areas in which national criminal law interacts with EU law is in the free movement of persons, where national criminal law can be used to justify the expulsion of EU citizens but only under certain conditions. The treatment of this residual power of the Member States is dealt with in further detail in Chapter 5.

EU law has also impacted on national criminal law in a more positive sense, namely *obliging* Member States to enact criminal legislation to ensure to effective implementation of EU law.[54] Based on a duty of sincere cooperation and the general principle of effectiveness of EU law, the European Union has long obliged Member States to ensure the effective implementation of EU law.[55] In *Greek Maize* the Court of Justice established an obligation to impose sanctions for the breach of EU law under conditions that were effective and equivalent to similar national breaches.[56] In a controversial set of judgments and following much inter-institutional wrangling, this was later developed into a fully fledged doctrine permitting the Union to oblige Member States to adopt *criminal* sanctions for the effective implementation of EU law.[57] Since the Treaty of Lisbon, this competence has been formalised in Article 83(2) TFEU, allowing the Union to adopt measures requiring Member States to criminalise certain acts, if necessary for the effective enforcement of other EU policies.[58]

Both of the above instances where EU law affects criminal law, both negatively and positively, flow from the fact that in these instances Member States are acting within the field of EU law, either by breaching rights of free movement or in implementing Union law. Both were implicit in the old Community competence and both are ancillary to other EU law policies. The Union has also adopted a more autonomous criminal law policy, generally focused around the issue of cross-border crime and criminal law enforcement.[59] Initially established as a

[54] Note this was originally termed the 'Community's' competence in criminal law rather than the Union in distinction to the competence exercised under the ex-Third Pillar of the TEU. For the sake of clarity, the terms EU law and the (European) Union shall be used unless specific considerations require otherwise.

[55] See Michael Dougan, 'From Velvet Glove to the Iron Fist: Criminal Sanctions for the Enforcement of Union Law' in Marise Cremona (ed), *Compliance and the Enforcement of EU Law* (Oxford University Press, 2012).

[56] Case 68/88 *Commission v Greece* EU: C:1989:339, [1989] ECR 2968.

[57] Case C-176/03 *Commission v Council (Environmental Crimes)* EU: C:2005:542, [2005] ECR I-7879 and Case C-440/05 *Commission v Council (Ship Source Pollution)* EU: C:2007:625, [2007] ECR I-9097. For an account, see Anthony Dawes and Orla Lynskey, 'The Ever-Longer Arm of EC Law: The Extension of Community Competence into the Field of Criminal Law' (2008) 45 *CML Rev* 131; and Steve Peers, 'The European Community's Criminal Law Competence: The Plot Thickens' (2008) 33 *EL Rev* 399.

[58] See Steve Peers, *EU Justice and Home Affairs Law*, vol II: *EU Criminal Law, Policing and Civil Law*, 4 edn (Oxford University Press, 2016) 174–82.

[59] Although as is explored elsewhere, this criminal law competence was frequently justified as necessary to compensate for potential negative effects of free movement and the abolition of border controls. See Jörg Monar, 'The Dynamics of Justice and Home Affairs: Laboratories, Driving Factors and Costs' (2001) 39 *Journal of Common Market Studies* 747. See also Wenceslas de Lobkowicz, 'L'Europe et la sécurité intérieure: Une elaboration par étapes' (décembre 2001) La Documentation française, no 5144–45.

system of quasi-international law under the Treaty of Maastricht under a separate pillar of the European Union, it was partially 'communitarised' under the Treaty of Amsterdam before being incorporated within the main body of EU law under the Treaty of Lisbon.[60] Following the Treaty of Lisbon the European Union can now be said to exercise criminal law competence in three areas.[61]

Firstly, the Union can adopt approximation measures to effectively harmonise national criminal legislation in a number of key areas, mostly linked with cross-border crime.[62] The harmonisation or approximation must be of a minimum nature and is limited in scope to a closed list but nonetheless reflects a real, independent normative presence in the field. Under the institutional regime operating following the Treaty of Amsterdam the European Union adopted a number of such approximating instruments (then known as Framework Decisions) in fields such as terrorism, drug trafficking, human trafficking, computer crime and organised crime, amongst others.[63] This substantive criminal law competence of the European Union in cross-border crimes, known as 'Euro-crimes', now sits alongside the competence of the Union described above to adopt harmonising measures for the effective enforcement of other EU policies.[64]

Secondly, the Union enjoys a competence to facilitate judicial cooperation and in particular the mutual recognition of various judgments and orders adopted by national authorities including courts, prosecutors and other judicial bodies.[65] This 'mutual recognition' competence was implicit in the pre-Lisbon framework but has since been elevated to a specific legal basis[66] and given priority by political institutions.[67] Mutual recognition is now the main tool in the Union's criminal law policy and in the creation of what has been termed an area of justice and a whole range of mutual recognition instruments, most notably the European Arrest Warrant Framework Decision (EAW FD),[68] have been adopted by the Union.[69] Mutual recognition is to be based on what has been termed 'mutual trust' between national authorities. In an effort to provide some basis for such trust the Union has also been entrusted with a competence to adopt harmonising instruments in the

[60] For an institutional history of justice and home affairs in the EU, see Peers (n 58) ch 2.

[61] Albeit subject to specific institutional constraints: see Jörg Monar, 'The Area of Freedom, Security and Justice' in Jurgen Bast and Armin von Bogdandy (eds), *Principles of European Constitutional Law*, 2 edn (Hart Publishing, Verlag CH Beck, 2010); and Stephen Coutts, 'The Lisbon Treaty and the Area of Freedom, Security and Justice as an Area of Legal Integration' (2011) 7 *Croation Yearbook of European Law* 87. See also Mitsilegas (n 49).

[62] Art 83(1) TFEU.

[63] For a comprehensive account, see Peers (n 58) ch 5.

[64] Now contained in Art 83(2) TFEU.

[65] Art 82(1) TFEU.

[66] Art 83(1) TFEU.

[67] See 'The Stockholm Programme: An Open and Secure Europe Serving and Protecting Citizens' [2010] OJ C115/01.

[68] Framework Decision 2002/584/JHA on the European arrest warrant and the surrender procedures between Member States (EAW FD) [2002] OJ L190/1.

[69] For a list, see Peers (n 58) 187ff.

area of procedural rights. Since the Treaty of Lisbon an incremental approach has been taken in this field with the adoption of a number of specific instruments[70] following a roadmap on procedural rights.[71]

Finally, a number of EU agencies and information systems exist to facilitate cross-border cooperation in criminal law enforcement.[72] Europol is an agency established under EU law and provides an institutional basis for information sharing and analysis and a framework for joint investigations through joint investigation teams. Europol is assisted in its task by the Europol Information System and through access to a number of other databases.[73] Eurojust consists of national prosecutors, judges and senior police officers tasked with criminal investigations and prosecutions. Its role is to facilitate information exchange and cooperation between national agencies in situations of cross-border crimes. The Treaty of Lisbon also provides for the establishment of a European Public Prosecutors Office (EPPO).[74] Initially to be tasked with prosecuting crimes against the Union's financial interests, its scope may be extended by Member States. After an initial proposal by the Commission met with Member State resistance, a regulation was adopted in 2017 establishing the EPPO.[75] Although characterised by its limited scope[76] and decentralised nature,[77] it remains an important instance of a Union body involved in the prosecution of crime.[78]

Finally, a word should be said regarding the Schengen Agreement signed between a select number of Member States in 1984 and now extended to cover most, but not all, of the Union and some non-Union states such as Norway and Iceland.[79] Those states, Ireland and the United Kingdom, that remain outside the main body of the agreement, may nonetheless opt-in on a case-by-case basis to specific measures.[80] The Schengen Agreement was an agreement to abolish

[70] Directive 2013/48/EU on the right of access to a lawyer in criminal proceedings and in European arrest warrant proceedings and on the right to have a third party informed upon deprivation of liberty and to communicate with thrid persons and with consular authorities while deprived of liberty [2013] OJ L294/1; Directive 2012/13/EU on the right to information in criminal proceedings [2013] OJ L142/1; Directive 2010/64/EU on the right to interpretation and translation in criminal proceedings [2010] OJ L280/1; and Directive 2016/343/EU on the strengthening of certain aspects of the presumption of innocence and of the right to be present at the trial in criminal proceedings [2016] OJ L65/1.

[71] Resolution of the Council on a Roadmap for strengthening procedural rights of suspected or accused persons in criminal proceedings [2009] OJ C295/1.

[72] See generally Peers (n 58) chs 6 and 7, also dealing with issues of jurisdiction and police cooperation.

[73] ibid, 325ff.

[74] Art 86 TFEU.

[75] Regulation 2017/1939/EU implementing enhanced cooperation on the establishment of the European Public Prosecutor's Office ('the EPPO') [2017] OJ L283/1.

[76] The EPPO is limited to investigating and directing prosecution for crimes concerning the Union's own resources and related crimes. See ibid, Art 4.

[77] Mitsilegas (n 50) 104–09.

[78] See further Chapter 8.

[79] Steve Peers, *EU Justice and Home Affairs Law*, vol I: *EU Immigration and Asylum Law* (Oxford University Press, 2016) ch 1.

[80] Protocol 21, TFEU.

border controls and primarily concerns borders, visas and immigration control. Nonetheless, there are implications for criminal law and a number of elements concerned criminal law enforcement and recognition of judgments in a borderless area. There also exists a Schengen Information System containing details of criminal offences of third-country nationals seeking entry into the European Union. Of particular concern to any study of EU citizenship and criminal law is Article 54 of the Convention Implementing the Schengen Agreement (CISA), addressed in Chapter 7, preventing an individual from being prosecuted in more than one Member State for the same act. The Schengen Agreement was incorporated within the European Union in the Treaty of Amsterdam and involved a complex process of dividing it between its criminal law and immigration, borders and asylum components when allocating it to different pillars of the Treaties.[81]

Citizenship in the Union – A Short History

European citizenship appeared on the political agenda in the early 1970s. A legal form of citizenship was long considered implicit in the free movement of persons, while a 'political' vision of citizenship, closely tied to the notion of identity formation and loyalty, was explicit in a number of political statements and policies throughout the 1970s and 1980s. European Council meetings in Paris and Copenhagen in the early 1970s called for reports on a 'European Union', resulting in the Tindemanns Report of 1976, which in turn contained a chapter on a 'Citizens' Europe'. At the same time the European Parliament became directly elected, laying the foundations for a pan-European democratic citizenship. From the perspective of identity and symbolism various measures were adopted such as a uniform passport, an anthem and flag. The Adonnoio reports in 1984 continued this work, stressing in particular possible voting rights in other Member States and presenting free movement as contributing towards the construction of a European citizenship.[82]

Alongside the political, identity-based, discourse, legal commentators noted the potential for a rights-based European citizenship rooted in European law. The rights accorded to economically active individuals under the rules of the internal market were identified by Plender as an incipient form of European citizenship as early as 1976.[83] This conclusion was only strengthened by the subsequent expansive jurisprudence of the Court of Justice granting directly enforceable rights of free movement and non-discrimination to individuals, interpreting both the

[81] Peers (n 79) ch 1.

[82] Epsen DH Olsen, 'Transnational European Citizenship: Tracing Conceptions of Citizenship in the European Integration Process' (PhD thesis, European University Institute, Florence 2008) ch 5.

[83] Richard Plender, 'An Incipient Form of European Citizenship' in Francis Jacobs (ed), *European Law and the Individual* (North-Holland, 1976).

material and personal scope of such rights expansively.[84] Furthermore, although lawyers are prone to pay close attention to the actions of Courts, it would be negligent to ignore the important role of the European legislature in developing free-movement rights for individuals.[85] Legislation adopted on the free movement of workers and the self-employed contained not only expansive economic rights of employment but also were careful to include a social and human dimension with equal treatment in social benefits and strong rights of family reunification. Indeed, a stated goal of the legislation was to promote the social integration of Community nationals. Finally, three directives, adopted at the beginning of the 1990s, extended some of these rights, particularly rights of residence, to non-economically active individuals, albeit under conditions of self-sufficiency.[86]

The citizenship that politically remained a discourse and was legally only implicit was rendered explicit in the Treaty of Maastricht. In response to Spanish demands in particular, in 1992 the Treaty of Maastricht inserted a new Part Two on Citizenship of the Union into the revised Treaty establishing a European Community.[87] Citizenship of the Union was to be conferred on nationals of the Member States who were to 'enjoy the rights conferred by this Treaty and … be subject to the duties imposed thereby'.[88] Citizens were granted rights to free movement and residence 'subject to the limitations and conditions laid down in [the] Treaty and the measures adopted to give it effect'. Citizens also had the right to consular protection of another Member State in a third country where his or her own Member State was not represented. Article 8(c) granted a right to petition the ombudsperson. Finally, citizens of the Union were granted active and passive voting rights in relation to local and European elections in other Member States.

The initial reaction to this potentially bold development was a mixture of disappointment and hope. Most of the legal rights, particularly those of free movement and residence, were either already in existence and/or subject to further measures and especially limitations contained in the treaty, implying a simple repackaging of existing rights spread across the internal market and residence directives under

[84] See, for example, Case 53/81 *DM Levin v Staatssecretaris van Justitie* EU: C:1982:105, [1982] ECR 1035 and Case 139/85 *RH Kempf v Staatssecretaris van Justitie* [1986] ECR 1741 regarding a relatively wide definition of 'worker'. For a comprehensive overview of the caselaw of the Court of Justice over the decades in the area of free movement of persons, see Thomas Burri, *The Greatest Possible Freedom: Interpretive Formulas and their Spin in Free Movement caselaw* (Nomos, 2015).

[85] See Niamh Níc Shuibhne, 'The Third Age of EU Citizenship' in Phil Syrpis (ed), *The Juriciary, the Legislature and the EU Internal Market* (Cambridge University Press, 2012), describing the development of free movement of persons as 'Court fueled but legislature led' (334).

[86] Directive 90/364/EEC on the right of residence [1990] OJ L180/26; Directive 90/365/EEC on the right of residence for employees and self-employed persons who have ceased their occupational activity [1990] OJ L180/28; and Directive 93/96/EEC on the right of residence for students [1993] OJ L317/59.

[87] Pt 2 TEC, Treaty on European Union, together with the complete text of the Treaty Establishing the European Community [1992] OJ C224/1.

[88] Art 8 TEC [1992]. For the genesis of the provision, see Síofra O'Leary, The Evolving Concept of Community Citizenship: From the Free Movement of Persons to Union Citizenship (Kluwer 1996) ch 1.

the guise of 'citizenship'. While voting rights for EU citizens in second Member States, allowing non-nationals to participate for the first time in the democratic life of the nation, was a significant step for some Member States and required constitutional amendment,[89] the failure to cover the most meaningful elections, namely national elections, significantly reduced its impact both from a symbolic and practical point of view. The failure of the new Union to develop a clear bill of fundamental rights and to associate this with the new status of citizenship was also seen as a failure.[90] Other commentators were more hopeful and pointed to the *potential* of European citizenship.[91] In their view it could provide the language and legal basis on which a meaningful status could be developed either by judicial interpretation or legislative action. At a conceptual level the introduction of citizenship of the Union was potentially significant not only from the point of view of the European Union in equipping it with a core concept of political legitimacy but also for the very concept of citizenship, introducing as it did a new form of post-national citizenship.[92]

After a short few years the Court of Justice appeared to confirm the basic hope of the optimists. Initially the Court of Justice made few references to citizenship and continued to decide cases on the free movement of persons provisions contained in the internal market. However, in *Sala* the Court relied directly on then Article 6 TEC to establish a right of non-discrimination, independent of the internal market through a combined reading of citizenship of the Union and the general prohibition on grounds of nationality found in Article 6 TEC (now Article 18 TFEU).[93] This combined reading of the citizenship provisions and non-discrimination on the grounds of nationality was later used to considerable effect in extending the duties of solidarity owed by Member States to EU citizens,[94] most notably in the cases of *Grzelczyk*,[95] *Baumbast*[96] and *Bidar*.[97]

[89] Specifically France and Spain, see O'Leary (n 88) ch 6.

[90] ibid, Conclusion.

[91] See Dora Kostakopoulou, 'Ideas, Norms and European Citizenship: Explaining Institutional Change' [2005] 68 *MLR* 233, 233ff and citations therein.

[92] 'European citizenship is also a conceptual challenge; that is, it has the capacity to change our understanding of citizenship and membership with a view to opening up new forms of political community.' Dora Kostakopoulou, 'European Citizenship: Writing the Future' 13 *ELJ* 623, 642.

[93] Case C-85/96 *Maria Martinez Sala and Freistaat Bayern* EU: C:1998:217, [1998] ECR I-2694.

[94] See for example Case C-224/98 *Marie-Nathalie D'Hoop v Office national de l'emploi* [2002] ECR I-6191 and Case C-456/02 *Michel Trojani v Centre public d'aide sociale de Bruxelles (CPAS)* EU: C:2004:488, [2004] ECR I-7573. For a critical account, see Kay Hailbronner, 'Union Citizenship and Access to Social Benefits' (2005) 42 *CML Rev* 1245.

[95] Case C-184/99 *Rudy Grzelczyk v Centre public d'aide sociale d'Ottignies-Louvain-la-Neuve* EU:C:2001:458, [2001] ECR I-6193.

[96] Case C-413/99 *Baumbast and R v Secretary of State for the Home Department* EU: C:2002:493, [2002] ECR I-7091.

[97] Case C-209/03 *The Queen (on the application of Dany Bidar) v London Borough v Ealing, Sec of State for Education and Skills EU*: C:2005:169, [2005] ECR I-2119.

However, it would be a mistake to view the development of EU citizenship as exclusively the handiwork of the Court of Justice.[98] The legislature has also played a role, at times in tension, but mostly complementary to the Court. The thicket of legislative measures on the free movement of persons, some recent, some with a more vintage quality, and case-law of the Court of Justice on citizenship was simplified, codified and complemented by the passing of Directive 2004/38/EC or the 'Citizenship Directive'.[99] The Citizenship Directive codified and reformed the law of the free movement of persons. It brought the disparate statuses of worker, self-employed, self-sufficient and student under the rubric of 'citizenship' and applied common administrative procedures and rights of family reunification. Nonetheless, while ostensibly under the same status of 'citizen' within the text, important differences of substance remained. The exact range of rights enjoyed by citizens and the limitations those rights could be subject to, were differentiated according to the type of activity in which an individual was engaged. The concept of a progressively strengthened status, visible in *Bidar*,[100] was also reflected in the structure of the Directive. Not only were rights differentiated according to the activity of the migrant worker but also according to his length of residence. The longer a migrant was resident, a period that reflected his level of integration, the greater his right to equal treatment, the fewer conditions could be applied to his right of residence and the greater his protection from expulsion.

Since the passage and implementation of the Citizenship Directive, the case-law of the Court has focused on interpreting and elaborating certain provisions of the Directive and in particular details around the acquisition and enjoyment of the right to permanent residence.[101] It has also revisited the question of equal treatment and social rights and in some cases adapted its stance in light of the Directive. Recent years have seen a decidedly restrictive trend on the part of the Court. Starting with *Dano*,[102] the Court has limited the instances in which individuals may benefit from the right of equal treatment, specifically with regard to social benefits, through a strict application of the conditions and limitations

[98] Níc Shuibhne (n 85) claiming that the development has been 'Court fuelled but legislature led' (334). For a more recent analysis of the interaction between the Court and the legislature in the area of citizenship, see Michael Dougan, 'The Bubble that Burst: Exploring the Legitimacy of the Case Law on the Free Movement of Union Citizens' in Maurice Adams et al (eds), *Judging Europe's Judges: The Legitimacy of the Case law of the European Court of Justice* (Hart Publishing, 2013).

[99] Citizenship Directive (n 39). See Philippe de Bruycker, 'La Libre Circulation des Citoyens Europeens Entre Codification et Reforme' in Jean-Yves Carlier and Elspeth Guild (eds), *L'Avenir de la libre circulation des personnes dans l'UE/ The Future of Free Movemenet of Persons in the EU* (Bruylant, 2006).

[100] *Bidar* (n 97).

[101] Ex Case C-162/09 *Secretary of State for Work and Pensions v Taous Lassal* EU:C:2010:592, [2010] ECR I-9217 and Joined Cases C-424/10 and C-425/10 *Tomasz Ziolkowski and Barbara Szeja and Others v Land Berlin* EU:C:2011:866, [2011] ECR I-14035.

[102] Case C-333/13 *Elisabeta Dano & Florin Dano v Jobcenter Leipzig* EU:C:2014:2358, followed by Case C-67/14 *Jobcenter Berlin Neukölln v Nazifa Alimanovic and Others* EU:C:2015:597, Case C-299/14 *Vestische Arbeit Jobcenter Kreis Recklinghausen v Jovanna García-Nieto and Others* EU:C:2016:114 and Case C-308/14 *Commission v UK* EU:C:2016:436.

contained in the Directive and a consequent limiting of the role an individualised proportionality assessment.[103]

Independently of the Directive,[104] the Court has also developed a set of rights for *non-mobile* based on the *status* of EU citizenship. In a short and cryptic decision of 2011 the Court of Justice ruled that Member States cannot take measures that would deprive citizens of the European Union of the genuine enjoyment of the substance of the rights conferred by virtue of their status as citizens of the Union'.[105] This right was enforceable against the Member State of nationality or one's 'own' Member State, implying that the status of EU citizenship was somehow independent of free movement and having potential implications for the constitutional structure of the Union itself.[106] The follow-up to this ground-breaking decision was hesitant, seemingly limiting its application to the very exceptional situations where a Union citizen was either deprived entirely of his status as citizen[107] or where he would be forced to leave the territory of the European Union entirely.[108] More recently, the '*Zambrano* doctrine' has been revitalised in a number of cases,[109] and has been linked with the rights of free movement and residence, implying a close relationship between the status of EU citizenship located in Article 20 TFEU and the core rights of free movement and residence located in Article 21 TFEU.

[103] The shift in the Court's case-law is well documented. See, for example, Niamh Níc Shuibhne, 'Limits Rising, Duties Ascending: The Changing Legal Shape of Union Citizenship' (2015) 52 *CML Rev* 889; Eleanor Spaventa, 'Earned Citizenship: Understanding Union Citizenship through its Scope' in Dimitry Kochenov (ed), *EU Citizenship and Federalism: The Role of Rights* (Cambridge University Press, 2017); and the contributions in Daniel Thym (ed), *Questioning EU Citizenship: Judges and the Limits of Free Movement and Solidarity in the EU* (Hart Publishing, 2017). For a somewhat contrary view on nature (or even existence) of this shift, see Gareth Davies, 'Has the Court changed, or Have the Cases? The Deservingness of Litigants as an Element in Court of Justice Citizenship Adjudication' (2018) 25 *Journal of European Public Policy* 1442. For an analysis linking this to the question of social integration, see Stephen Coutts, 'The Absence of Integration and the Responsibilisation of Union Citizenship' (2018) 3 *European Papers* 761. The issue is explored in further detail in Chapter 2.

[104] While drawing on its provisions and case-law based on the Directive in some cases. See Case C-165/14 *Alfredo Rendón Marín v Administración del Estado* EU:C:2016:675, paras 82–86, applying the case-law relating to expulsion under Directive 2004/38/EC to situations falling within Art 20 TFEU.

[105] Case C-34/09 *Gerardo Ruiz Zambrano v Office national de l'emploi (ONEm)* EU: C:2011:124, [2011] ECR I-1177 para 42.

[106] See, for example, the potential envisaged by Dimitry Kochenov, 'On Tiles and Pillars: EU Citizenship as a Federal Denominator' in Dimitry Kochenov (ed), *EU Citizenship and Federalism: The Role of Rights* (Cambridge University Press, 2017). See also Armin von Bogdandy et al, 'Reverse Solange – Protecting the Essence of Fundamental Rights against EU Member States' (2012) 49 *CML Rev* 489 finding in the status of EU citizenship a possible jurisdiction for a generalised fundamental rights competence for the Union, regardless of any free movement. For a contrary perspective, see Martijn van den Brink, 'EU Citizenship and Fundamental Rights: Empirical, Normative and Conceptual Problems' (2019) 25 *ELJ* 21.

[107] Case C-135/08 *Janko Rottmann v Freistaat Bayern* EU: C:2010:104, [2010] ECR I-1449.

[108] Case C-434/09 *Shirley McCarthy v Secretary of State for the Home Dept* EU: C:2011:277, [2011] ECR I-3375, Case C-256/11 *Murat Dereci and Others v Bundesministerium für Inneres* EU: C:2011:734, [2011] ECR I-11315, Case C-87/12 *Ymeraga v Minstre du Travail, de l'Emploi et de l'Immigration* EU:C:2013:291.

[109] See Rendón Marín (n 104), Case C-304/14 *Secretary of State for the Home Department v CS* EU:C:2016:674 and in particular Case C-133/15 *Chavez-Vilchez and Others v Raad van bestuur van de Sociale verzekeringsbank and Others* EU:C:2017:354.

Although most of the developments of EU citizenship have taken place on a legal level, focusing on the rights of free movement, residence and non-discrimination of individuals, particularly (although not exclusively) in cross-border situations, there have also been moves, particularly in the Treaty of Lisbon, to inject a democratic element into the status of EU citizenship. As mentioned above, the European Parliament has been directly elected since 1979;[110] however, it was not until *Delvigne*[111] that the Court of Justice, assisted by reference to the Charter, explicitly found a right to vote in the European Parliament that attached to EU citizenship, regardless of movement. The right to vote and to stand as a candidate in a *second* Member State in the European Parliament and local elections were explicitly rights of EU citizenship and were introduced in the Treaty of Maastricht. These were later elaborated upon in a set of Directives providing for the conditions under which migrant citizens could vote in European[112] and local elections,[113] and harmonising to some extent the modalities of European parliamentary elections.[114] Finally, in the Treaty of Lisbon there was an effort to broaden the range of political participation and introduce forms of participatory democracy, through representative institutions and civil society,[115] and direct democracy through the innovative 'citizenship initiative', requiring the Commission to respond to a request by a minimum of one million citizens from a number of Member States to legislate on a particular matter.[116] This innovative measure has been introduced along with more traditional means of increasing democratic input such as increasing the powers and role of the European Parliament and through involving national parliaments more closely in European governance matters.[117]

[110] Act concerning the election of the representatives of the Assembly by direct universal suffrage [1976] OJ L278/5.

[111] Case C-650/13 *Thierry Delvigne v Commune de Lesparre Médoc and Préfet de la Gironde* EU:C:2015:648. For an analysis, see Stephen Coutts, 'Delvigne: A Multi-Levelled Political Citizenship' (2017) 42 *EL Rev* 867. Prior to this, in the judgments of Joined Cases C-300/04 *Eman and Sevinger v College van Burgemeester en Wethouders van Den Haag* EU:C:2006:545, [2006] ECR I-8055 and Case C-145/04 *Spain v UK* EU: C:2006:543, [2004] ECR I-7902, the Court had been ambiguous as to whether a right to vote in European Parliamentary elections attached to EU citizenship.

[112] Council Directive 93/109/EC laying down detailed arrangements for the exercise of the right to vote and stand as a candidate in elections to the European Parliament for citizens of the Union residing in a Member State of which they are not nationals [1993] OJ L329/34.

[113] Council Directive 94/80/EC laying down detailed arrangements for the exercise of the right to vote and to stand as a candidate in municipal elections by citizens of the Union residing in a Member State of which they are not nationals [1994] OJ L 368/38 as amended by Council Directive 96/30/EC [1996] OJ L 122/14.

[114] Uniform Election Procedure (n 112).

[115] See Joana Mendes, 'Participation and the Role of Law after Lisbon: A Legal View on Article 11 TEU' (2011) 48 *CML Rev* 1849.

[116] Art 11 TEU. Regulation 211/2011/EU on the citizens' initiative [2011] OJ L65/1 has also been adopted at 'breakneck speed'. For an analysis, see Michael Dougan, 'What Are We to Make of the Citizens' Initiative' (2011) 48 *CML Rev* 1807 and Luis Bouza Garcia, 'The European Citizen's Initiative: A New Institution for Empowering Europe's Citizens?' in Michael Dougan, Niamh Nic Shuibhne and Eleanor Spaventa (eds), *Empowerment and Disempowerment of the European Citizen* (Hart Publishing, 2012).

[117] See Gavin Barrett, 'Introduction – A New Improved Formula? The Treaty of Lisbon and National Parliaments' in Gavin Barrett (ed), *National Parliaments and the European Union: the Consitutional Challenge for the Oireachtas and other Member State legislatures* (Clarus Press, 2008).

At this stage the basic shape and role of EU citizenship in the European Union can be discerned. Union citizenship is a status that is dependent on national citizenship – it is derivative in nature. Moreover it is exercised primarily (although not exclusively) vis-à-vis *other* EU Member States, and is primarily concerned with the situation of cross-border movement. Arising out of the internal market, it provides the holder with a series of rights, primarily of free movement and non-discrimination when travelling to other Member States. Political rights exist, including the right to participate in local and European elections in a *second* Member State. EU citizenship is less important as a status vis-à-vis the European Union itself, either directly at a Union level, or as a supranational guarantee or protection against national abuses. A nascent set of rights based on the status of EU citizenship is still developing, while the Court has in *Delvigne*[118] developed a supranational right to vote in European parliamentary elections. If citizenship is a relational concept, linking an individual to a political community, then EU citizenship is a multi-level status, establishing links with various political units within the broader structure of the European Union and is strongest in establishing *horizontal* relations with other Member States, and distinctly less developed in establishing *vertical* relations with the Union. In this sense it resembles early federal citizenships.[119] This basic structure of a multilevel, interstate citizenship is elaborated in more detail in Part I and is used as a framework for an analysis of the effect of criminal law on EU citizenship in the rest of this book.

Conclusion: Method and Structure

The goal of this book is to determine what the operation of criminal law in the European Union can reveal about EU citizenship and the political community of the Union more generally. It is therefore primarily a book about EU citizenship and how it is affected by EU law, rather than attempting to provide a comprehensive explanatory or justificatory account of EU criminal law. Certainly, certain aspects of citizenship and of how it interacts with criminal law can contribute to a better explanation of the nature and structure of EU criminal law and may provide a framework of legitimacy for some of the more controversial aspects of EU criminal law, such as mutual recognition. To the extent that this book touches on these issues they are noted. However, that is not the perspective or goal of this book. It is primarily concerned with the potential impact of criminal law and the treatment of criminal law by the Court and the Union legislature on EU citizenship and the political community of the European Union.

[118] *Delvigne* (n 111).

[119] Christopher Schönberger, 'European Citizenship as Federal Citizenship: Some Citizenship Lessons of Comparative Federalism' (2007) 19 *European Review of Public Law* 61. See also van den Brink (n 107) 12–13.

To that end this book adopts a communitarian view of the criminal law theory and draws on key concepts and ideas of RA Duff based on the links between citizenship, crime and community. His is an explanatory and a justificatory theory for criminal law through an examination of the structure of responsibility that lies behind the criminal law. Other analytical and normative theories of criminal law attempt to synthesise and explain the criminal law, or alternatively lay down criteria for justifying punishment or identifying those acts that can be properly the subject of criminalisation.[120] Duff's theory addresses both of these questions but has the added advantage for present purposes of approaching the criminal law from a relational perspective and in particular the relationship of citizen and polity.[121] The choice of Duff's theory is therefore a methodological one. It addresses the question of criminal law from the perspective of the individual located in a community and holding a particular status in that community and, through its explicitly relational approach, allows us to trace links of responsibility between individuals and different political communities. Its communitarian dimension also allows us to identify the source of particular values as embodied in the criminal law and to map this onto the current structure of the European Union as a political community. It therefore provides particularly useful tools and concepts to explore the interaction between citizenship and criminal law in the European Union and the implications this might have for the broader, multi-level and plural polity that is the European Union. It also has a certain explanatory value, with much, although certainly not all,[122] of the legal practice in this field capable of being described in terms deriving from Duff's work.

[120] For an overview, see Anthony Duff, 'Theories of Criminal Law' in *The Stanford Encyclopedia of Philosophy* (Summer 2013 edition) (n 14). Reviews of the theory of criminal law can be found in Lacey (n 43) ch 2 and Victor Tadros, *The Ends of Harm: Moral Foundations of the Criminal Law* (Oxford University Press, 2011) ch 2 and John Braithwaite and Philip Pettit, *Not Just Deserts: A Republican Theory of Criminal Justice* (Oxford University Press, 1992), Introduction.

[121] Bennett (n 23) likewise focuses on the relationship between the individual and the political community as the basis for his explanation and justification for punishment.

[122] As Mancano (n 39) points out and as is emphasised in Chapter 5 below, certain features of the Court's case-law in the area of expulsion demonstrate an exclusive tendency, which would run contrary to Duff's *preference* for inclusive responses to crime in a 'decent' polity. Although it is open to debate as to whether the Court is in fact rendering citizens 'enemies' in these cases, more importantly, such a practice does not *necessarily* contradict a communitarian account of the criminal law and can certainly be accommodated within it depending on the underlying principles of that political community and the manner in which it regulates its membership. In fact, it is plausible that a communitarian approach to the criminal law could, under certain conceptions, in fact *justify* exclusion (see in this vein Stephen Coutts, 'Union Citizenship as Probationary Citizenship: *Onuekwere*' (2015) 52 *CML Rev* 531). An inclusive approach to criminals in this sense is a desideratum for Duff and part of his understanding of a 'decent' polity, but it is not central to his account of the criminal law as based on citizenship (see Duff (n 33) ch 3, s 5). Finally, even if such an approach of the Court in a particular area of the law was not compatible with a particular aspect of Duff's understanding of the criminal law, this would not imply that the entire approach developed by Duff based on the relationship of citizenship in a political community can be discarded; a theory need not (and perhaps cannot) explain *all* instances of a given practice in order to be useful.

Duff's theory uses the concept of citizenship and community to explain and justify criminal law. This book adopts the reverse approach, using the concept of criminal law, seen in a communitarian light and based on the notion of membership and citizenship, to explain certain aspects of citizenship and the political community in a particular polity: the European Union. The criminal law is presented as a set of wrongs, based in the particular values of a community and criminal responsibility is seen as being founded on the concept of membership or citizenship. The criminal law has an expressive quality and punishment has a communicative purpose. Finally, being prosecuted, tried and punished involves a process of being called to account for one's actions before the community in a public dialogue involving accusation, justification, excuse and condemnation.

This book looks specifically at the possible links between the status of EU citizenship and criminal law. In order to provide a framework for this analysis Part I breaks EU citizenship into separate components, namely a transnational dimension and a supranational dimension. The transnational dimension addressed in Chapter 2 is subsequently divided into two sub-dimensions, social integration and autonomy, that can be discerned as two, at times opposing and at times complementary, principles that drive much of the legal practice in EU citizenship. Chapter 3 addresses the supranational dimension of EU citizenship, which while present, is less well developed than transnational citizenship. However, while presented as distinct, the two dimensions – transnational and supranational – can be said to be connected and to mutually influence each other. Through a combination of the right to social integration in other Member States and a right to move freely throughout the Union, EU citizenship gives rise to a single area of movement to which a certain supranational reference for EU citizenship can be said to emerge. Thus EU citizenship and the political community it represents is a complex interaction of national, transnational and supranational that combined form a multi-levelled, composite political community.

Part II, consisting of Chapters 3 and 4, considers the impact of criminal law in the context of the social integration dimension of EU citizenship. A brief section introduces these two chapters and relates the concept of social integration in criminal law to EU citizenship. In criminal law social integration arises in two instances. Firstly, social integration is seen as a goal of punishment, namely the social rehabilitation of the offender. This use of social integration is analysed in Chapter 4. Secondly, criminal activity is said to constitute a rejection of the norms of society and a failure to integrate into society. This aspect of social integration is analysed in Chapter 5. The Court has used both of these criminological understandings of social integration and has integrated them within the social integration dimension of EU citizenship, altering it and leading to both the greater inclusion and greater exclusion of EU citizens in host Member States.

Part III, consisting of Chapters 6 and 7, considers the construction of an Area of Justice through two instruments in particular, the European Arrest Warrant Framework Decision (EAW FD) and Article 54 of the Convention Implementing the Schengen Agreement (CISA). A brief section introduces these two chapters and considers the links between an area of movement associated with the autonomy dimension of citizenship and the Area of Justice. Chapter 6 characterises the European Arrest Warrant as a system of shared enforcement of national criminal law. Chapter 7 details how the Court of Justice has constructed a single status for individuals in a single area through a free-movement-driven interpretation of the *ne bis in idem* principle contained in Article 54 CISA.

Part IV consists of a single chapter, Chapter 8, which considers the possibility of a community at a supranational level arising from the adoption of substantive criminal law by the European Union itself. It is seen that the Union's ability to directly bind individuals and identify supranational wrongs is limited, mirroring the weaker supranational dimension of EU citizenship. Nonetheless, in certain areas it does appear to be capable of expressing supranational values or identifying supranational public goods capable of engaging the Union's interest as a whole. However, the most important role of supranational criminal law is not to provide an autonomous expression of supranational values at a Union level but rather to frame national criminal law and facilitate transnational legal processes involving criminal law. There is therefore an interaction between the supranational and national *through* transnational processes. A normative community does emerge at a supranational level but arising from various interacting national communities.

A conclusion draws the different elements of the book together and discusses the consequences for our understanding of EU citizenship and the political community of the European Union. The ways in which a communitarian analysis of the criminal law can complement our understanding of citizenship are outlined, including its contribution to understandings of rights, responsibilities and values. Finally, the main conclusion of this book is presented, namely that it is primarily through a complex interaction of national, transnational and supranational processes that a plural political community can be said to emerge at the level of the European Union.

PART I

EU Citizenship: Between Transnational and Supranational

To recall, according to Duff, criminal law governs the relations between the individual and the community, or more accurately the relations between individuals in their capacity as members of the community. It regulates behaviour according to the core values and norms of the community, which in contemporary liberal democracies include first and foremost, but not exclusively, individual freedom. Following the premise that core individual interests must be protected from undue interference in the interests of maximising liberty for all, the harm principle provides a basic but not a comprehensive principle for the criminal law. It forms the basis of many, if not most, wrongs but is supplemented by other wrongs done either to the community as a whole or other individuals as members of that community. The result is a moral and contextualised account of the criminal law based on the particular community in which it is applied and where the exact content of the criminal law varies from time to time and from place to place. The responsibilities contained in the criminal law flow from the relationship between individuals in the civic community, ie as co-citizens. We are called to account as citizens by the political community for wrongs done to other citizens. From this brief sketch of Duff's theory emerges the broad outline of a criminal justice system that is based on the idea of public wrongs, defined according to the prevailing norms and values of a particular community and justified by ties of responsibility between individuals in their capacity as members of that community.[1]

The question arises of what this model of a citizen-centred account (both normative and descriptive) of criminal law can reveal concerning the links between EU citizenship and criminal law and relatedly what an analysis of EU criminal law in light of this model can reveal about the nature of the European Union as a political community. Before we can answer these questions we must look at the specificities of the European Union as a political community and the particular form and structures of its membership status, namely EU citizenship. Citizenship can be said to be a microcosm of the broader constitutional subject,[2] reflecting in

[1] See Antony Duff, *Punishment, Communication and Community* (Oxford University Press, 2003); Antony Duff, *Answering for Crime: Responsibility and Liability in the Criminal Law* (Hart Publishing, 2007); and the account provided in Chapter 2.

[2] See Michel Rosenfeld, *The Identity of the Constitutional Subject: Selfhood, Culture and Community* (Routledge, 2010) ch 7.

the various rules relating to its acquisition and loss a certain self-understanding and political identity of the community. It is also a relational concept, establishing civic links between individuals and between the individual and the community as a whole. These links are reflected primarily in the rights (and obligations) afforded individuals by virtue of that status. By analysis of the rights granted individual citizens and more importantly the legal relations reflected in those rights, we can begin to discern the structure of the political community itself.

These next two chapters explore the rights of EU citizenship with an eye to describing the nature of the links established by that status between individuals and Member States and between individuals and the European Union as a whole. The relationship between EU citizens and Member States is analysed first in Chapter 3. This relationship is governed by two principles, autonomy and integration, that combined create a transnational status allowing individuals to enjoy the opportunities offered by a broader geographical space spread over a number of national communities. Legally social integration is primarily based on the principle of non-discrimination contained in Article 18 TFEU, whereas autonomy tends to rely to a greater extent on the rights of free movement and residence found in Article 21 TFEU. The separation between these two sets of rights however should not be considered rigid. Rather, as has long been acknowledged, their operation is mutually interdependent and interactive.

The relationship between individuals and the Union itself – or the supranational dimension to EU citizenship – is less developed and is analysed in chapter 4. Initially established in the cases of *Rottmann*[3] and *Zambrano*[4] on the basis of Article 20 TFEU and the status of EU citizenship, it emphasised that EU citizens were not to be deprived of the genuine enjoyment of the rights associated with EU citizenship.[5] The impact of this rather nebulous test was, for many years, limited.[6] However, in a number of recent judgments[7] that test has been revived and developed. In doing so the Court of Justice has underlined that the rights at stake in the 'genuine enjoyment' test are precisely the rights to free movement and residence, but this time linked to the territory of the Union as a whole.[8] It is therefore *through* the rights of free movement and residence and the transnational dimension to EU citizenship that a broader right to the territory of the European Union as a whole and a supranational dimension to EU citizenship emerges. The resulting

[3] Case C-135/08 *Janko Rottmann v Freistaat Bayern* EU:C:2010:104, [2010] ECR I-1449.

[4] Case C-34/09 *Gerardo Ruiz Zambrano v Office national de l'emploi (ONEm)* EU:C:2011:124, [2011] ECR I-1177.

[5] ibid, para 45.

[6] See, for example, Case C-256/11 *Murat Dereci and Others v Bundesministerium für Inneres* EU:C:2011:734, [2011] ECR I-11315, Case C-86/12 *Alokpa et al v Minstre du Travail de l'Emploi et de l'Immigration* EU:C:2013:645, and Case C-40/11 *Yoshikazu Iida v Stadt Ulm* EU:C:2012:691.

[7] Case C-165/14 *Alfredo Rendón Marín v Administración del Estado* EU:C:2016:675 and Case C-133/15 *Chavez-Vilchez and Others v Raad van bestuur van de Sociale verzekeringsbank and Others* EU:C:2017:354.

[8] See, for example, *Zambrano* (n 4) para 45 and *Chavez-Vilchez* (n 7) para 65.

picture is of a nested membership status,[9] establishing links primarily with a set of national communities on the basis of social integration and autonomy and the presence of a discernible but weaker overarching community at a supranational level. Furthermore, the concept of the territory of the Union operates as a key reference for this overarching community.

The argument of these two chapters is not that the shaping of EU citizenship into these separate elements has been by conscious design or that it reflects distinct lines of case-law or legal practice adopted explicitly by either the Court of Justice or the EU legislature. The history of EU citizenship is a status that grew out of the internal market in a relatively organic fashion,[10] instituted as a political stratagem in the Treaty of Maastricht[11] and gradually shedding its economic legacy through incremental steps taken by the Court of Justice[12] and complemented by legislative activity.[13]

EU citizenship, like citizenship generally, can be viewed from a variety of perspectives[14] and a number of political and legal forces, not always acting in harmony, have contributed to its fashioning.[15] The purpose of the chapters

[9] For a similar view of Union citizenship as representing a nested membership status, see Rainer Bauböck, 'Why European Citizenship? Normative Approaches to Supranational Union' (2007) 8 *Theoretical Inquiries in Law* 453.

[10] At least in its legal sense. For an analysis of EU citizenship as a political practice inter alia, see Epsen DH Olsen, 'Transnational European Citizenship: Tracing Conceptions of Citizenship in the European Integration Process' (PhD thesis, European University Institute, Florence, 2008). See also Antje Weiner, *European Citizenship Practice* (Westview Press, 1998).

[11] Síofra O'Leary, *The Evolving Concept of Community Citizenship: From the Free Movement of Persons to Union Citizenship* (Kluwer, 1996) ch 1. See also Luuk van Middelaar, *Passage to Europe: How a Continent became a Union*, trans Liz Waters (Yale University Press, 2013) 258–59.

[12] See, in particular, the paradigm-shifting cases of Case C-85/96 *Maria Martinez Sala and Freistaat Bayern* EU:C:1998:217, [1998] ECR I-2694, Case C-459/99 *Mouvement contre le racisme, l'antisémitisme et la xénophobie ASBL (MRAX) v Belgian State* EU:C:2002:461, [2002] ECR I-6591, and Case C-209/03 *The Queen (on the application of Dany Bidar) v London Borough v Ealing, Sec of State for Education and Skills* EU:C:2005:169, [2005] ECR I-2119. Although note the role played by economic conditions in the enjoyment of rights under the Citizenship Directive, recently revived in Case C-333/13 *Elisabeta Dano & Florin Dano v Jobcenter Leipzig* EU:C:2014:2358 and subsequent cases (see further Chapter 3).

[13] Initially the 'residence directives': Directive 90/364/EEC on the right of residence [1990] OJ L180/26; Directive 90/365/EEC on the right of residence for employees and self-employed persons who have ceased their occupational activity [1990] OJ L180/28 and Directive 93/96/EEC on the right of residence for students [1993] OJ L317/59. These later being replaced and consolidated with other legislation on the free movement of persons into Directive 2004/38/EC on the right of citizens of the Union and their family members to move and reside freely within the territory of the Member States [2004] OJ L158/77 (Citizenship Directive). See Niamh Níc Shuibhne, 'The Third Age of EU Citizenship' in Phil Syrpis (ed), *The Juriciary, the Legislature and the EU Internal Market* (Cambridge University Press 2012) for a history of EU citizenship taking into account the interaction between the legislature and the judiciary.

[14] A particular distinction might be made between a political perspective and a legal perspective. For an alternative early account of different elements of EU citizenship, see Jo Shaw, 'Citizenship of the Union – Towards Post-National Membership' (1997) Jean Monnet Working Papers 06/97, http://centers.law.nyu.edu/jeanmonnet/archive/papers/97/97-06-.html (accessed 14 March 2013).

[15] For a superb account of the early years of EU citizenship up to and in the years after its introduction as a formal status in the Treaty of Maastricht, see Paul Magnette, *La Citoyennéte Européenne* (Editions de l'Université de Bruxelles, 1999).

contained in this part is to deconstruct and reconstruct the case-law and legislative practice of citizenship in order to provide some rationality to the multiple strands of legal practice[16] and to provide a framework for the analysis conducted in the rest of the book. It divides EU citizenship into different elements – social integration, autonomy and a supranational community – to provide headings in order to better investigate the interaction of EU citizenship and criminal law. These elements interact and combine in different ways, and are interconnected; any clean distinction is likely to be somewhat artificial and to miss an important point regarding the whole that is more than these component parts. In particular, social integration and autonomy together offer individual EU citizens a broader space of movement: the EU territory as composed of Member States that in turn is linked to the supranational status of citizenship and in particular the right to the EU territory as echoed in *Zambrano*[17] and developed further in *Rendón Marín*[18] and *Chavez Vilchez*.[19] There is therefore an interaction between the transnational and the supranational, in which certain supranational phenomena emerge from transnational processes and transnational processes are framed, justified and facilitated by supranational phenomenon. This interaction between the transnational and the supranational is a strong theme in this book and is evident throughout the study of criminal law in light of the concepts of social integration, autonomy and a supranational community.

The vision of EU citizenship presented here therefore primarily serves a methodological purpose, namely to break EU citizenship into its component parts to provide a framework for an analysis of its interaction with criminal law. The choice of specific components serves an additional methodological purpose related to both EU citizenship and Duff's theory. Duff's theory is specifically community based, describing and justifying the criminal law as an expression of a particular community. A related goal of this book is to demonstrate how the treatment of criminal law in the European Union can contribute to our understanding of the structure of the Union as a political community. Thus the dimensions of social integration, autonomy and supranational are selected with an eye to the different links that EU citizenship forges with different component parts – national and supranational – of the Union's political community and hence to indirectly characterise that political community.

[16] In this sense it is an exercise in rational reconstruction as described in Neil MacCormick, 'Reconstruction after Deconstruction: A Response to CLS' (1990) 10 *OJLS* 539.

[17] *Zambrano* (n 4).

[18] *Rendón Marín* (n 7).

[19] *Chavez-Vilchez* (n 7).

2

The Transnational Dimension of EU Citizenship

Introduction

EU citizenship emerged from the internal market, and in particular the free movement of the economically active – principally workers and the self-employed – and the economically self-sufficient. The market origins of EU citizenship attracted the particular criticism of Everson, who denounced the instrumentalist and instrumentalised individual that arose from such a historical context.[1] It is arguable whether EU citizenship has evolved significantly beyond its market origins. Commentators have pointed out that in one of the first meaningful citizenship cases, *Martinez Sala*,[2] the Court of Justice divorced free movement from the condition of economic activity, to eventually give rise to a 'fifth fundamental freedom'.[3] However, more recently O'Brien has pointed out the differentiated nature of EU citizenship and the various 'rights cliffs' that arise from the continued importance of economic activity in claiming rights under EU law.[4] Recent years have seen a decidedly reactive turn by the Court of Justice, restricting the welfare rights of mobile EU citizens and emphasising the capacities of Member States to impose limits on those rights.[5]

Regardless of the role economic activity per se plays in activating and sustaining EU citizenship rights, what is undeniable is the structural legacy that the internal market has bestowed on EU citizenship. Níc Shuibhne is particularly

[1] Michelle Everson, 'The Legacy of the Market Citizen' in Jo Shaw and Gillian More (eds), *New Legal Dynamics of European Union* (Clarendon Press, 1995). See more recently Dimitry Kochenov, 'On Tiles and Pillars: EU Citizenship as a Federal Denominator' in Dimitry Kochenov (ed), *EU Citizenship and Federalism: The Role of Rights* (Cambridge University Press, 2017).

[2] Case C-85/96 *Maria Martinez Sala and Freistaat Bayern* EU:C:1998:217, [1998] ECR I-2694.

[3] Ferdinand Wollenschläger, 'A New Fundamental Freedom beyond Market Integration: Union Citizenship and its Dynamics for Shifting the Economic Paradigm of European Integration' (2011) 17 *ELJ* 1.

[4] Charlotte O'Brien, 'I Trade, therefore I Am: Legal Personhood in the European Union' (2013) 50 *CML Rev* 1643 and Charlotte O'Brien, '"Civis Captialist Sum": Class as the new Guiding Princple of EU Free Movement Rights' (2016) 53 *CML Rev* 937.

[5] The broad development has been extensively explored in the literature. See, for example, Niamh Níc Shuibhne, 'Limits Rising, Duties Ascending: The Changing Legal Shape of Union Citizenship'

clear in pointing out the enduring transnational and cross-border nature of EU citizenship.[6] While this is presented as the continuing importance of 'market citizenship', many of the case-studies provided by Níc Shuibhne point not to the economic importance of EU citizenship as an individual status in a constitutionalised market, but rather the transnational character of EU citizenship,[7] a character that clearly originates in the nature of the internal market.[8] A supranational dimension to EU citizenship, not related to crossing borders, is developing and is explored in greater detail in the next chapter. However, for the time being the core of EU citizenship remains the rights it grants its holders in Member States other than those of which they are nationals.

The core rights of EU citizenship remain free movement and non-discrimination. These two principles reflect two distinct dimensions of EU citizenship as a transnational status: autonomy and integration. An emphasis on free movement tends to privilege autonomy and non-discrimination social integration; however, this is not to say that non-discrimination is irrelevant to autonomy or that free movement is irrelevant to integration. Both principles interact and reinforce each other; it is the manner of their combination that reveals an emphasis on autonomy or social integration. These two concepts of autonomy and integration infuse the case law on EU citizenship both separately and within the same judgments.

In many ways they are largely complementary; the autonomy that EU citizenship grants individuals to enjoy a wider space of movement and opportunity facilitates precisely the integration in other Member States. However, on a more abstract level and if pushed to extremes they reveal two visions of EU citizenship that can be in tension, if not downright opposition, that can crudely be categorised as a communitarian/liberal divide.[9] On the one hand an emphasis on autonomy may be said to lead to a particularly individualistic notion of EU citizenship, independent of communal ties of affection, cultural and solidarity.[10]

(2015) 52 *CML Rev* 889, Eleanor Spaventa, 'Earned Citizenship: Understanding Union Citizenship through its Scope' in Kochenov (n 1) and the various contributions in Daniel Thym (ed), *Questioning EU Citizenship: Judges and the Limits of Free Movement and Solidarity in the EU* (Hart Publishing, 2017).

[6] Niamh Níc Shuibhne, 'The Resilience of EU Market Citizenship' (2010) 47 *CML Rev* 1597.

[7] The account of EU citizenship as a transnational status overlaps somewhat with that offered by Iliopoulou Penot; see Anastasia Iliopoulou Penot, 'The Transnational Character of Union Citizenship' in Michael Dougan, Niamh Níc Shuibhne and Eleanor Spaventa (eds), *The Empowerment and Disempowerment of the European Citizen* (Hart Publishing, 2012).

[8] Indeed, Níc Shuibhne sees this as an advantage, given the constitutionalised nature and status of the market in EU law: 'While it seems counter-intuitive, a theory of market citizenship actually takes seriously the call to put the person at the centre of the EU project. … [I]t is not that market citizenship must inherently fall short, but rather that we tend artificially to constrain the capacity of the market and to overlook the normative as well as economic capacity of a constitutional market.' Níc Shuibhne (n 6) 1609.

[9] For a discussion of the two political philosophies (and the limited differences between them) see Simon Caney, 'Liberalism, Communitarianism: a Misconceived Debate' (1992) 40 *Political Studies* 273.

[10] For a critique of such a vision of EU citizenship, and in particular its tendencies to exacerbate economic inequalities, see Michelle Everson, 'A Very Cosmopolitan Citizenship: But Who Pays the Price?' in Dougan et al (n 7).

On the other hand an emphasis on integration might justify the imposition of a duty of assimilation into the host society and an acceptance of its social, economic and political values. At the very least it implies the adoption of a social identity and the preservation of national ties of identity, albeit with the important proviso that they are open to other EU citizens.[11] The next section explores what is termed the autonomy dimension of EU citizenship that rests principally on the right to free movement. The following section addresses EU citizenship as a status of integration. A conclusion considers these two dimensions – autonomy and integration – together and their larger contribution to the nature of EU citizenship as a transnational citizenship status.

Free Movement and Transnational Citizenship as a Status of Autonomy

As the name suggests, free movement can easily be understood as liberating for individuals. In its legal operation it is largely concerned with the removal of *barriers* that individuals face, not simply in moving but in participating in a whole host of activities with a cross-border impact. Indeed, the condition of cross-border effect is so easily met that in the internal market the rights of free movement can be convincingly presented as a freedom from unwarranted interference with the exercise of an economic activity.[12] Tryfonidou has recently argued that recent expansive readings of the free-movement provisions can in fact be justified in light of EU citizenship.[13] Thus free movement can be seen as providing a supranational guarantee of freedom and choice for individuals. While initially limited to non-discrimination on the grounds of nationality, EU citizenship, as with other fundamental freedoms, came to include the right to be free from unjustified barriers to free movement.[14] In the context of EU citizenship the principle takes on a more expansive role, being linked to the various and virtually unlimited facets

[11] In this sense it is important not to overstate the exclusive character of a form of citizenship privileging social integration as its main operative principle. EU citizenship has inherent inclusive and (bounded) cosmopolitan characteristics (see the work of Kostakopoulou in particular on the possibilities of EU citizenship, eg Dora Kostakopoulou, 'Ideas, Norms and European Citizenship: Explaining Institutional Change' [2005] 68 *MLR* 233). It is probably more accurate to characterise it as representing a liberal nationalist rather than harder communitarian political philosophy. For an account of liberal nationalism within EU law, see Elke Cloots, *National Identity in EU law* (Oxford University Press, 2015) ch 4.

[12] Eleanor Spaventa, *Free Movement of persons in the European Union: Barriers to Movement in their Constitutional Context* (Kluwer Law International, 2007).

[13] Alina Tryfonidou, *The Impact of Union Citizenship on the EU's Market Freedoms* (Hart Publishing, 2016).

[14] The breakthrough occurred in Case C-224/02 *Heikki Antero Pusa v Osuuspankkien Keskinäinen Vakuutusyhtiö* [2004] ECR I-5763, Case C-192/05 *K Tas-Hagen and RA Tas v Raadskamer WUBO van de Pensioen- en Uitkeringsraad* [2006] ECR I-10451 and Case C-403/03 *Egon Schempp v Finanzamt München V* [2005] ECR I 6421. See also Wollenschläger (n 3) 25ff.

of an individual's personal and social life. To simplify somewhat, free movement in the context of EU citizenship has been deployed to protect an individual's right to pursue a life in various Member States. Member States must facilitate and recognise the right to move between various national communities within the Union. Legally, this implies a right to carry rights and civil status acquired in one Member State throughout the Union. While initial cases tended to somewhat awkwardly fit this right into a discrimination-based analysis ('discrimination against movers'), later cases properly recognised the free-movement basis for this right. This tendency can be seen in two areas in particular, names and family life. In both areas not only must *host* Member States facilitate migrants but also *home* Member States. This has been mirrored by legislation, particularly in the field of private international law, which emphasises the free movement of individuals and the portability of a civil status.[15] A similar argument could be made in relation to the transfer of social security benefits and contributions.[16] When migrants move, Member States must recognise and facilitate the rights acquired under the law of other Member States. It is not therefore a right of integration, to move to and settle permanently in another Member State, but rather a right of migration back and forth, to build one's life on the basis of that migration and to enjoy the broader range of possibilities that EU citizenship offers. The result is a wider space of free movement, choice and autonomy.

Names and Civil Status

In *Garcia Avello* Belgium was required to recognise the double-barrelled name of dual-national Belgian–Spaniard children, despite the fact that Belgian naming rules required children to be named after their father alone.[17] Mr Garcia-Avello was not asking that his children be treated the same as other Belgians; on the contrary he was asking to be treated differently. The Court granted this wish by employing a somewhat tortuous discrimination analysis that in the end was nonetheless based on a movement rationale. According to the Court of Justice, the Garcia-Avello children, as dual Spanish–Belgian nationals, were not in the same position as single-national Belgian children. In later life they may move to Spain and would there encounter various professional, educational and personal

[15] See, for example, Regulation 2201/2003/EC concerning jurisdiction and the recognition and enforcement of judgments in matrimonial matters and the matters of parental responsibility [2003] OJ L338/23. For an analysis of civil status in EU law in this vein, see Etienne Pataut, 'A Family Status for the European Citizen' in Loïc Azoulai, Ségolène Barbou des Places and Etienne Pataut (eds), *Constructing the Person in EU Law: Rights, Roles and Identities* (Hart Publishing, 2016).

[16] See Regulation 883/2004 on the coordination of social security systems [2004] OJ L166/1. For an overview of the interpretation of the regulation (alongside summaries of all case-law on free movement of persons), see Thomas Burri, *The Greatest Possible Freedom: Interpretive Formulas and their Spin in Free Movement Caselaw* (Nomos, 2015).

[17] Case C-148/02 *Carlos Garcia Avello v Belgian State* EU:C: 2003:539,[2003] ECR I-11613.

difficulties due to the discrepancy between their Belgian-registered name and their Spanish-registered name. The principle of non-discrimination required that like situations be treated similarly and that unlike situations be treated differently. As the Garcia-Avello family were unlike other Belgian children it would be discriminatory to treat them in the same way when it came to naming rules. The Belgian practice therefore constituted a breach of then Article 12 TEC (now Article 18 TFEU). However, while on the face of it the case was an exercise in the application of the principle of non-discrimination, it was because of potential future movement, and the barriers to that movement that might arise as a consequence of their names, that they constituted a different class and accordingly faced discrimination. Through a creative construction of the comparator the Court was able to shoehorn what was essentially a free-movement analysis into a non-discriminatory framework. The ethos behind the case was that the Garcia-Avello family, and children in particular, should not be disadvantaged by the possibility of them building transnational life with links to both countries and to some extent autonomous of at least one of their home states.

The free-movement rationale and the implications for transnational autonomy were rendered explicit in the case of *Grunkin Paul*.[18] Leonard Matthias was born of German parents in Denmark who gave him a double-barrelled surname, as was permitted under Danish law. Upon return to Germany, however, the relevant authorities refused to register the name Grunkin-Paul, the use of double-barrelled names being generally prohibited in Germany. In contrast to *Garcia Avello*, the Court found that there was no discrimination on the grounds of nationality; both parents and the child were German and sought to register the child's name in Germany and objected to the application of German rules. Instead of an analysis based on discrimination, the Court focused on free movement. A difference in an individual's name on various official documents could represent a serious inconvenience for Leonard Matthias in later life. In particular the Court was concerned to facilitate his life in both his state of residence and his state of nationality, recognising the cross-border and transnational nature of his life.[19] Member States in short would have to adapt their regulations, even those that were not discriminatory, to take into account the transnational life choices made by EU citizens. Union citizenship facilitates not simply movement to another Member State and integration into a new host society, but a right to participate to varying extents in different national communities and to be free from restrictions in pursuing such a transnational life. The key point to take from *Grunkin Paul* is the obligation on the part of the 'home' Member State to recognise the rights and personal situation acquired by the EU citizen under the law of another Member State.

However, the right associated with this autonomy is not absolute. It can, in specific circumstances, be opposed by the particular interests, needs and indeed

[18] Case C-353/06 *Stefan Grunkin and Dorothee Regina Paul* [2008] ECR I-7639.
[19] ibid, para 26.

constitutional values of a Member State. In *Sayn-Wittgenstein* the Austrian applicant sought to retain a title of Princess (*Fürstin*) acquired in Germany following her adoption by a German prince and under which she had operated a business selling castles and other stately homes for a period of fifteen years.[20] The Court noted that her situation was comparable with *Grunkin-Paul*. In fact, given her professional life and the use to which she put her title, the inconveniences presented by a change in name would be even more direct and apparent in her case.[21] Where *Sayn-Wittgenstein* differed from *Grunkin-Paul* was in the justification presented by the Member State. The abolition of titles of nobility represented a key feature of the establishment of the Austrian Republic. It had constitutional status and was linked to the political identity of the state, an identity that could be understood in terms of public policy[22] and that was respected in EU law by virtue of Article 4(2) TEU.[23] The law abolishing titles, and therefore the measure disallowing Ms Sayn-Wittgenstein from using *Fürstin* in her official documents, was a justified restriction on her right of free movement and proportionate to the goal of preserving the constitutional identity of the Federal Republic of Austria.

In the case of *Vardyn*, the Court of Justice accepted the possibility that a discrepancy between the spelling of a husband's surname and a part of his wife's double-barrelled surname arising from the application of national spelling rules could cause serious inconveniences and constitute a restriction on their rights under Article 21 TFEU.[24] It also accepted that such a restriction could be justified in light of the need to protect the official national language in order to 'safeguard national unity and preserve social cohesion'. Moreover the national language in question, Lithuanian, was claimed to be 'a constitutional asset which preserves the nation's identity, contributes to the integration of citizens and ensures the expression of national sovereignty, the indivisibility of the State and the proper functioning of the services of the State'.[25] At the same time it recognised the individual right to identity and privacy inherent in an individual's choice of name. Ultimately, it left the question of the balance to be struck between the general public interest in the constitutional and political identity of the state and the individual interest in privacy and autonomy to be determined by the national court through an assessment of the proportionality of the restriction.[26]

More recent case-law has tended to confirm this balancing act between general and individual interests and the tension between individual personal identity and

[20] Case C-208/09 *Ilonka Sayn-Wittgenstein v Landeshauptmann von Wein* EU:C:2010:806, [2010] ECR I-13693.

[21] ibid, para 63.

[22] ibid, para 84.

[23] ibid, para 92.

[24] Case C-391/09 *Malgožata Runevič-Vardyn and Łukasz Paweł Wardyn v Vilniaus miesto savivaldybės administracija and Others* EU:C:2011:291; [2011] ECR I-3787, paras 75–78.

[25] ibid, para 84.

[26] Hinting that in light of the national practice of allowing Mr Wardyn to register his surname in the Polish manner, the refusal to allow Mrs Runevič-Vardyn to do so may be disproportionate (ibid, paras 92–93).

national constitutional identity. In both *von Wolffersdorff*[27] and *Frietag*[28] German nationals were returning to Germany after a period spent abroad and after voluntarily acquiring a different name in another Member State. Mr von Wolffersdorf had moved to the UK, there acquired British nationality and changed his name to include various words indicating noble titles.[29] Mr Frietag, on the other hand, had been adopted in Germany by a German national and both acquired German nationality and took the name of his adoptive father (Mr Frietag). He then returned to Romania, the Member State in which he and both his parents were born, and entered his name on the civil register as Pavel, the name of his birth father. Subsequently he sought the recognition of his reacquired Romanian name in Germany.

In both cases the Court of Justice ultimately left the final determination to be made by the German authorities. In *von Wolffersdorff* the national court was obliged to make the assessment balancing, on the one hand, the interests of the individual including the fundamental right to a name and the close links this right has to the right to privacy,[30] against, on the other hand, the legitimate interest of the state in preventing the use of public titles and respecting the constitutional identity of the German Republic and upholding the principle of equality.[31] In *Freitag* the national court was obliged to ensure that national administrators exercised their discretion in deciding on an application for recognition of a name change in such a manner as to respect the right to recognition of a name duly acquired in another Member State. In doing so the national administrative authorities were obliged to take into account the ties enjoyed by Mr Frietag in his state of nationality, namely Romania, and that this must constitute a 'compelling reason' under the relevant German legislation.[32]

The overall message arising from the name cases is that EU citizenship facilitates the choice and autonomy of individuals to pursue a transnational life, an autonomy that Member States must recognise and facilitate up to certain limits. Those limits relate not to administrative convenience[33] or the needs of social assimilation[34] but a desire to protect the linguistic and national identity of the state.

[27] Case C-438/14 *von Wolffersdorff v Standesamt der Stadt Karlsruhe* EU:C:2016:401.

[28] Case C-541/15 *Mircea Florian Freitag* EU:C:2017:432.

[29] They were not recognised as noble titles as such in the United Kingdom, as they were not granted by the sovereign but merely inserted through a change of name by deed poll. See Case C-438/14 *von Wolffersdorff v Standesamt der Stadt Karlsruhe* (Opinion of AG Wathelet) EU:C:2016:11, para 94.

[30] See, in particular, *von Wolffersdorff* (ibid) para 35, where the Court speaks of a person's forename and surname as 'a constituent element of his identity and his private life, the protection of which is enshrined in Article 7 of the Charter of Fundamental Rights of the European Union'.

[31] ibid, para 80.

[32] *Frietag* (n 28) paras 43–46.

[33] See, in particular, the systematic rejection by the Court of a number of justifications raised by German authorities relating to administrative convenience, length of names and issues of continuity of names in *von Wolffersdorff* (n 27) paras 50–60.

[34] Although note the reference to the role of the national language in the integration of citizens as raised by the Member States in *Vardyn* (n 24) para 84.

They demonstrate that the particular situations of cross-border individuals and families must be accommodated, both in a host Member State, as in the case in *Garcia Avello* and upon movement to another Member State, including the state of nationality as in *Grunkin Paul*. While the judgements are phrased in terms of the transportability of civil status acquired in a particular Member State and the elimination of obstacles, the question of cultural identity also lies in the background, of both the individuals and of host community, and has become particularly marked in recent cases. If *Garcia Avello* simply concerned the issue of national discrepancies in an individual's official name, an alternative would simply have been to oblige Spain to adapt its laws. Indeed, this would have arguably been a more appropriate solution given the reality of the children's actual lives in Belgium rather than the hypothetical of their future life in Spain. Instead, the solution chosen by the Court privileges the parent's right to make a choice regarding the cultural identity of their children, emphasising their transnational roots in opposition to the local culture. Interestingly, a justification raised by both the Belgian and Danish governments in *Garcia Avello* was that an obligation to conform to the national regulations would in fact facilitate integration – a clear indication of a preference for assimilation and a rejection of multiculturalism as a social policy for dealing with migration.[35] This policy choice was undermined by the Court, who read in EU citizenship precisely a right to be treated differently rather than the same. If anything, *Grunkin Paul* is also remarkable in upholding the choice of the individual, this time employing a technique that bears striking resemblance to a mutual recognition framework. Mutual recognition as a technique is designed to preserve Member State autonomy while at the same time facilitating the creation of a single legal space with multiple interoperable legal systems. Thus, as this decision was based on a free-movement rationale and portability of an official name and civil status, *Grunkin Paul* obliges the home Member State to accept the consequences of EU citizens' transnational lives and to recognise the rights they have acquired under the laws of other Member States. The motif of mutual recognition is even more apparent in the area of family reunification rights. Finally, in *Freitag* the German authorities are obliged to take into account the connections an individual enjoys in other Member States.[36]

However, if the desire of a state to ensure social integration and assimilation is insufficient to trump an individual's or a family's right to maintain the rights they enjoy as transnational citizens, upholding the state's political identity framed in linguistic or constitutional terms[37] *does* appear to be a legitimate goal that can be opposed to an individual's right to 'passport' his or her status and identity.

[35] *Garcia Avello* (n 17) paras 40–41.

[36] *Frietag* (n 28), para 46.

[37] Echoing perhaps Habermas's 'constitutional patriotism' based on civil and political values rather than ethnic or cultural identities. Jurgen Habermas, 'The Postnational Constellation and the Future of Democracy' in Jurgen Habermas (ed), *The Postnational Constellation* (Polity Press, 2001).

Thus the Court does not deny the continued importance of Member States as national communities, indeed it notes that their identities are protected under EU law, but endorses only certain manifestations of that community, namely political rather than social or cultural.

Family Reunification

Family reunification has been the subject of much litigation in the area of EU citizenship and on the issue of reverse discrimination in particular.[38] Two factors may explain this large volume of litigation. On the one hand, family life is of fundamental importance for an individual and migration has the potential to cause significant disruption to family life. On the other hand, there is a significant gap between the sometimes restrictive national law in relation to family reunification and the generous EU law on the matter.[39] The combination of these two circumstances creates a very real incentive for an individual to place himself within the scope of EU law when seeking to be joined by non-national family members. Given the sometimes restrictive national practices, this incentive applies both in a host Member State but also in the citizen's 'home' Member State.

The generous family reunification provisions in EU law arise from an early recognition of human side of migration and the social importance of the family to an individual who may wish to move, on the one hand, and the importance of family life for the integration of an individual into a host society, on the other.[40] Regulation 1612/68/EEC established a virtually automatic right for mobile EU workers to be joined by their immediate family in a Member State to which they move and moreover, granted extensive rights of residence, education and access to benefits to these family members. Moreover, in addition to family members who were EU nationals, the family reunification provisions of Regulation 1612/68/EEC also covered non-Community nationals or third-country nationals (TCNs). Regulation 1612/68/EEC has since been replaced and updated

[38] For an overview, see Peter van Elsuwege and Stanislas, 'EU Citizenship and the Federal Challenge through the Prism of Family Reunification' in Kochenov (n 1).

[39] See, for example, the case of Case C-165/16 *Toufik Lounes v Secretary of State for the Home Department* EU:C:2017:862 in which a dual Spanish–UK national sought to rely on her rights as an EU citizen (and indirectly on her Spanish nationality) while seeking residence rights for her TCN spouse.

[40] 'Whereas the right of freedom of movement, in order that it may be exercised, by objective standards, in freedom and dignity, requires that equality of treatment shall be ensured in fact and in law in respect of all matters relating to the actual pursuit of activities as employed persons and to eligibility for housing, and also that obstacles to the mobility of workers shall be eliminated, in particular as regards the worker's right to be joined by his family and the conditions for the integration of that family into the host country', Preamble, Regulation 1612/68/EEC on freedom of movement for workers within the Community [1968] OJ L257/2. This language was retained word for word in recital 6 of the replacement legislation, Regulation 492/2011/EU on freedom of movement for workers within the Union (codification) [2011] OJ L141/1.

by Regulation 492/2011/EU[41] and Directive 2004/38/EC,[42] which retain and expand rights of family members and of family reunification.

The interpretation of these provisions by the Court of Justice reduced significantly the discretion that Member States enjoyed in relation to migration matters in the sphere of family members of EU nationals. In *MRAX* the Court of Justice underlined the limitations on Member State competence to control such immigration, finding that the right to family reunification stemmed directly from EU law.[43] EU law laid down the conditions for enjoying those rights and Member States could not impose further conditions and requirements of proof. In *Akrich*, however, the Court appeared to backtrack on its position and shield the competence Member States have in immigration matters, particularly with regard to 'first entry' into the Union (rather than secondary movement from *within* the Union).[44] *Akrich* permitted Member States to impose a condition of prior lawful residence on family reunification. Member States could require that a TCN family member was lawfully resident in the Union before granting a right to join the mobile EU national. Perhaps influenced by the competence argument advanced by the Advocate General,[45] the Court reasoned according to a limited vision of the right of free movement based on a narrow, deterrence-based logic. Family reunification rights were granted under EU law to remove obstacles to free movement and in particular the deterrent that might arise if an individual was to be separated from his or her family upon movement to another Member State.[46] If, however, that EU citizen did not enjoy the company of his or her family before moving, so the logic went, then there could be no deterrence if his or her family was not allowed entry into the new Member State.[47]

While no doubt welcomed by national administrations, *Akrich* attracted considerable academic criticism.[48] The case left certain questions open, such as the problematic definition of 'prior lawful residence', and made a strange and out-of-place reference to Article 8 of the European Convention on Human Rights (ECHR).[49] Furthermore, its treatment of the question of competences, presenting

[41] Regulation 492/2011/EU (n 40).

[42] Directive 2004/38/EC on the right of citizens of the Union and their family members to move and reside freely within the territory of the Member States [2004] OJ L158/77.

[43] Case C-459/99 *Mouvement contre le racisme, l'antisémitisme et la xénophobie ASBL (MRAX) v Belgian State* EU:C:2002:461, [2002] ECR I-6591.

[44] Case C-109/01 *Secretary of State for the Home Department v Hacene Akrich* EU:C:2003:491, [2003] ECR I-9607.

[45] Case C-109/01 *Secretary of State for the Home Department v Hacene Akrich* (Opinion of AG Geelhoed) EU:C:2003:112 paras 1–9.

[46] *Akrich* (n 44) paras 51–52.

[47] ibid, paras 53–54.

[48] For a selection, see Chistopher Schiltz, '*Akrich*: A Clear Delimitation without Limits' (2005) 12 *Maastrict Journal of European and Comparative Law* 241; Eleanor Spaventa, 'Case C-109/01 *Secretary of State for the Home Department v H Akrich*' (2005) 42 *CML Rev* 225; and Robin CA White, 'Conflicting Competences: Free Movement Rules and Immigration Laws' (2004) 29 *EL Rev* 385.

[49] The situation was deemed to fall outside the scope of EU law and so there was simply no jurisdiction for the Court of Justice to intervene and apply any fundamental rights to the situation in question.

national immigration competences as something reserved to Member States and insulated entirely from the scope of EU law, did not appear to correspond with the traditional view of reserved national competences, according to which Member States must still exercise such competences in compliance with their obligations under EU law.[50]

These matters were addressed in *Metock*[51] in which, in an unusual move, the Court of Justice explicitly reversed its position.[52] *Metock* concerned Irish regulations adopted following the Court's judgment in *Akrich*, requiring TCN family members to have prior lawful residence in the Union before they would be granted a right of residence under EU law. In reversing *Akrich* the Court corrected its approach to national immigration competences and, more importantly for present purposes, broadened its understanding of free movement. Rather than the narrow deterrence-based logic deployed in *Akrich*, focusing on the notion of less favourable treatment, in *Metock* the Court employed a far broader vision of what free movement entails, in particular the right of the citizen to install him or herself in the Member State of his or her choosing and to provide the appropriate conditions, including 'a normal family life', under which this could occur.[53] In particular, the Court focused on how discrepancies between national immigration rules could impact on the choice of a citizen to install him/herself in a particular Member State.[54] This element of choice was even more explicit in the opinion of the Advocate General who found that:

> [T]he fact that Union citizens established in Ireland are unable to have their spouses join them from outside the Community is such as to undermine their *free choice to reside in that Member State* since it will tend to induce them to leave Ireland and to go to a State, whether a Member State or not, where they will be able to live together with their spouse.[55]

EU citizenship therefore creates the optimal conditions under which an individual can exercise his right of mobility and moreover exercise that right in the

[50] See Koen Lenaerts, 'Constitutionalism and the Many Faces of Federalism' (1990) 38 *American Journal of Comparative Law* 205, 220ff for a discussion of the absence of any reserved area of national competence entirely shielded from EU law influence.

[51] Case C-127/08 *Metock v Minister for Justince Equality and Law Reform* EU:C:2008:449, [2008] ECR I-6241. For a commentary, see Catherine Costello, '*Metock*: Free Movement and "Normal Family Life" in the Union' (2009) 46 *CML Rev* 587.

[52] *Metock* (n 51) para 58.

[53] ibid, paras 62–64.

[54] See especially ibid, paras 63–65: 'The refusal of the host Member State to grant rights of entry and residence to the family members of a Union citizen is such as to discourage that citizen from moving to or residing in that Member State, even if his family members are not already lawfully resident in the territory of another Member State. It follows that the Community legislature has competence to regulate the entry and residence of nationals of non-member countries who are family members of a Union citizen in the Member State in which that citizen has exercised his right of freedom of movement, including where the family members were not already lawfully resident.'

[55] ibid, para 9 (emphasis added).

fullest possible degree of choice. Those conditions include the right to lead a 'normal family life'.[56] It is important to point out that this is not a question of discrimination.[57] The EU citizens involved in *Metock* were not seeking equal treatment with Irish nationals, instead they were asking the Court to provide a special EU law regime, facilitating their choice and autonomy to move within the Union unhindered by restrictive national regulations on family reunification. It was this aspect of EU citizenship, based on free movement and choice, that founded a right for the Union to harmonise rules on family reunification for mobile EU citizens.

An additional reason for Member States' concern in this matter was the possibility of citizens exercising this right not only in a host Member State but vis-à-vis their home Member State upon returning. This possibility arose following the case of *Singh* in which the Court held that a returning EU worker must enjoy 'at least the same rights of entry and residence as would be granted to him or her under [Union] law if his or her spouse chose to enter and reside in another Member State'.[58] Member States were concerned of an erosion of their immigration competence not only in relation to EU citizens from other Member States but in relation to their own nationals who could, by temporarily exercising their right of free movement, circumvent restrictive national regulations on family reunification. Indeed, this is precisely the situation that occurred in *Akrich*. Mrs Akrich had moved to Ireland from the United Kingdom with the stated intention of being joined by her husband and returning to the UK, carrying with her a right to be accompanied by her husband and circumventing more restrictive UK provisions.

It may be argued, as it was by the Court in *Akrich*, that the EU national is not in fact disadvantaged if he is not granted the right to be accompanied by his spouse upon return to the home Member State; he cannot lose a right he never enjoyed in the first place. However, what is protected in the case of returning migrants is the right of the EU citizen to maintain the rights he or she gains in a second Member State and not to be faced with the uncertainty of not knowing whether particular rights and situations acquired and developed in the host Member State can be retained upon return to the home Member State. To provide otherwise would introduce an element of instability and uncertainty that would deter individuals from exercising their freedom of movement. This reasoning was made especially clear in the case of *Eind* in which a Dutch man was joined by his Surinamese daughter while working in the UK.[59] He then returned to the Netherlands and the Court found he was entitled to be accompanied by his daughter. The logic of the

[56] ibid, para 62.

[57] Indeed, the Court had already held that family reunification was classified as a social benefit within the meaning of Regulation 1612/68/EEC and hence was covered by the principle of equal treatment. See Case 59/85 *Netherlands v Ann Florence Reed* [1986] ECR 1283 for the case of equal treatment of unmarried partners.

[58] Case C-370/90 *The Queen v Immigration Appeal Tribunal and Surinder Singh* EU:C:1992:296, [1992] ECR I-4265, para 23.

[59] Case C-291/05 *Minister voor Vreemdelingenzaken en Integratie v RNG Eind* EU:C:2007:771, [2007] ECR I-10719.

Court was clear: Mr Eind must be allowed to retain rights he acquired in another Member State and if necessary exercise them against his own Member State. His choice to pursue a cross-border life and the social situation that might arise from living in various Member States must be protected from undue interference in both the host *and* the home Member State. Indeed, the same logic would presumably protect his family life in any Member State.

This line of case-law has been confirmed and expanded by the Court of Justice in the cases of *O & B* and *S & G*.[60] Both *O & B* and *S & G* concerned the third-country spouses of Dutch nationals seeking residence in the Netherlands. In *O & B* two Dutch nationals had resided temporarily (for a couple of months in the case of *O*) and sporadically (at weekends in the case of *B*) in other Member States with their TCN spouses. They returned to their home Member State after a limited period of time abroad and sought to bring their spouses with them. In *S & G* the Dutch nationals resided in the Netherlands but worked and performed services in another Member State. They were variations on the 'frontier worker': one a frontier worker as commonly understood, living in the Netherlands but working for a Belgian company in Belgium; the other a part-time cross-border service provider, living and employed in the Netherlands but spending approximately a third of his working time in Belgium as part of his job. Thus while all four were Dutch nationals living in the Netherlands, they all claimed some cross-border connection through either temporary stays abroad or through exercising a cross-border economic activity.

In *O & B* the Court restated its position that free movement includes the freedom to return to the host Member State.[61] It was firm in upholding its findings in *Singh* and *Eind* and in extending this reasoning to the situation of non-economically active EU citizens relying on Article 21(1) TFEU. In particular, it emphasised the need to guarantee that an EU citizen will be able to 'continue the family life which he created or strengthened in the host Member State'.[62] However, this only referred to family life that was created or strengthened in the context of 'genuine', 'settled' residence in the second Member State, to be determined by analogy to the categories of residence found in Directive 2004/38/EC.[63] The Court therefore excluded the possibility of a family life being created or strengthened on the basis of mere temporary residence. In *S & G* the Court confirmed the possibility that cross-border economic activity could entail certain rights of family reunification, while at the same time indicated that this would only arise in limited circumstances.[64] Furthermore, given the facts of the case, it felt able to limit its

[60] Case C-456/12 *O v Minister voor Immigratie, Integratie en Asiel and Minister voor Immigratie, Integratie en Asiel v B* EU:C:2014:135 and Case C-457/12 *S & G v Minister voor Immigratie, Integratie en Asiel* EU:C:2014:136.

[61] *O & B* (n 60) paras 47–59.

[62] ibid, para 49.

[63] ibid, para 56.

[64] Thus upholding the central finding of Case C-60/00 *Mary Carpenter v Secretary of State for the Home Department* EU:C:2002:434, [2002] ECR I-06279 while limiting its application in practice.

reasoning to workers under Article 45 TFEU and declined to rule on the impact of EU citizenship under Article 21 TFEU. Restrictions on an EU citizen worker's family life must be such as to discourage 'the worker from effectively exercising his rights'.[65] However, the *desirability* of a particular familial arrangement, such as childcare by a mother-in-law, is not sufficient in itself to establish a right of residence for a family member.[66]

O & B and *S & G* represent the reality of modern migration as a circulatory phenomenon whereby individuals move back and forth between Member States over the course of their lives, or even during the course of their working day, as in the case of frontier workers. They present EU citizenship as a status facilitating this form of migration and the choice to pursue lives across various borders at different stages of life, not simply in migrating from one state to another but in enjoying a broader choice across the territory of the European Union, unhindered by differences in national laws. This implies not only the right to move from one state to another, but back again and indeed the positive choice and freedom of where to live. This right is particularly apparent in the more recent case of *McCarthy* in which the Court found that the United Kingdom, despite it being outside the Schengen system, was not entitled to impose visa requirements on the TCN spouse of a dual UK–Irish national resident in Spain but returning regularly to the UK where the couple owned a residence.[67] The recognition of the couple's transnational life with various ongoing connections to different Member States was particularly strong in the opinion of AG Szpunar who noted that:

> In today's European Union, a citizen's origins may lie in a Member State of which he is a national of one (or of several) Member State(s) in which he has never lived. He may also have several nationalities, or indeed live in two or more Member States, while retaining genuine links, both occupational and personal, with all those states.[68]

As with the 'name' cases, the family reunification cases also clearly demonstrate that free movement is not simply a question of a right to move to and settle definitively in another Member State, but also implies a general right, spread over the course of a lifetime, to move around the territory of the Union and to avail of the expanded possibilities offered in various Member States. Firstly, as *Metock* demonstrates, it is a choice that is offered to the EU citizen as an inherent part of that status and that choice must be facilitated by the creation of optimal conditions, especially conditions of 'normal family life'. Note that this is only partially, and secondarily, an integration or non-discrimination based logic. The reasoning of the Court in *Metock* is based almost entirely on free movement. It is the choice contained in EU citizenship, and the need to facilitate that choice, that grants EU law the competence to regulate family reunification, even instances of so called

[65] *S & G* (n 60) paras 42–43.
[66] ibid, para 43.
[67] Case C-202/13 *McCarthy v Secretary of State for the Home Department* EU:C:2014:2450.
[68] Case C-202/13 *McCarthy v Secretary of State for the Home Department* (Opinion of AG Szpunar) EU:C:2014:345, para 62.

'first entry'. Secondly, *Singh*, *Eind* and *O & B* provide that those situations that arise in one Member State must be accommodated in other Member States, including the Member State of origin. As with a name or civil status, a family life 'strengthened or created' in one Member State must be portable. Family reunification for EU citizens is not a mutual-recognition regime as we traditionally understand it, indeed that is exactly what was at stake in *Akrich* and *Metock*, in the sense that it is based not on national rights or national laws but on EU rights created on foot of the harmonisation contained in the Treaty articles on free movement and implemented in Directive 2004/38/EC. Nonetheless, the result of *Eind* and *O & B* obliges host Member States to accept the 'vested rights'[69] (albeit this time rights acquired on the basis of EU law) acquired by virtue of free movement. The result points towards a vision of EU citizenship presented by Preuss in 1995:

> [B]y creating the opportunity for the citizens of the Member States of the European Union to engage in manifold economic, social, cultural, scholarly and even political activities irrespective of the traditional territorial boundaries of the European nation-states, European citizenship helps to abolish the hierarchy between the different loyalties … and to allow the individuals a multiplicity of associative relations without binding them to a specific nationality. In this sense, European citizenship is more an amplified bundle of options within a physically broadened and functionally more differentiated space than a definitive legal status.[70]

It will be noted, however, that *O & B* was not so clear-cut as to permit uninhibited movement based on a rootless and continual movement. Rather, it was only family life that was formed on the basis of residence in the host Member State in conformity with conditions of economic activity or self-sufficiency – 'evidence of settling there' – that would be recognised.[71] In other words only family life created or strengthened on the basis of settled or 'genuine' residence could be retained upon return to the host Member State. These considerations point to the other aspect of EU citizenship as a transnational status that is at times in tension with the autonomy of EU citizens: citizenship as a status of integration in the society of the host Member State.

Non-discrimination and Transnational Citizenship as a Status of Integration

EU citizenship offers individuals the right to move around and enjoy the opportunities presented by a variety of economies and cultures. However, perhaps more importantly, it offers EU citizens the right to become part of, to integrate into, the

[69] A term found in private international law; see Jan-Jap Kuipers, 'Cartesio and Grunkin Paul: Mutual Recognition as a Vested Rights Theory based on Party Autonomy in Private Law' (2009) 2 *EJLS* 66.
[70] Ulrich Preuß, 'Problems of a Concept of European Citizenship' (1995) 1 *ELJ* 267, 280.
[71] *O & B* (n 60) para 53.

society of other Member States. It is a status of social integration.[72] This dimension of EU citizenship is intimately bound up with the principle of non-discrimination but is facilitated by free movement. Equal treatment is both the catalyst or the means by which integration takes place and also the consequence of this process.[73] In terms of a legal status this feature of EU citizenship has been developed by both the Court of Justice and by the EU legislature in a largely collaborative endeavour over the past two decades. While for the most part this principle has operated to regulate the position of migrant EU citizens in the host Member State, it has also been used in limited circumstances to strengthen the rights of emigrant EU citizens vis-à-vis their home Member State. In the concept of social integration the Court of Justice and the EU legislature have elaborated a criteria, in addition to that of nationality, for attaching individuals to particular national communities with the European Union and for allocating responsibilities amongst Member States for those individuals.[74] The result has been the establishment of an additional principle of belonging in the context of changing social and economic ties between individuals and societies in a set of political communities.

Union Citizenship and as a Status of Integration and the Court of Justice

EU citizenship as integration is closely tied to the principle of non-discrimination on grounds of nationality now found in Article 18 TFEU. While the principle is of general application across the Treaty and arises in a more specific application in the provisions on the free movement of persons in the internal market,[75] it emerged as a defining component of EU citizenship in the case of *Martiníz Sala*.[76] The relationship between the principle of non-discrimination and EU citizenship is symbiotic. Non-discrimination on the grounds of nationality soon formed the core of EU citizenship and gave rise to the first series of cases that put 'flesh on the bones' of a status whose importance had until then been considered limited.[77] At the same time, the application of the principle of non-discrimination on the

[72] Loïc Azoulai, 'La Citoyenneté Européenne, un Statut d'Intégration Sociale' in Gérard Cohen-Jonathan et al (eds), *Chemins d'Europe: Mélanges en l'honneur de Jean Paul Jacqué* (Dalloz, 2010).

[73] For an excellent overview of the different uses and manner of application of the principle of integration in EU citizenship law, see Ségolène Barbou des Places, 'The Integrated Person in EU Law' in Azoulai et al (n 15).

[74] Indeed, the concept of nationality was first developed in the nineteenth century as a means of allocating individuals to particular states in the German confederation. See Rogers Brubaker, *Citizenship and Nationhood in France and Germany* (Harvard University Press, 1992) 64ff.

[75] Agustín José Mendéz, 'European Citizenship after Martiníz Sala and Baumbast: Has European Law become More Human but Less Social?' in Miguel Poirias Maduro and Loic Azoulai (eds), *The Past and Future of EU Law* (Hart Publishing, 2010).

[76] *Martinez Sala* (n 2).

[77] To borrow an expression from Síofra O'Leary: see Síofra O'Leary, 'Putting Flesh on the Bones of European Union Citizenship' (1999) 24 *EL Rev* 68.

grounds of nationality, in theory limited to the scope of the Treaty, was broadened considerably with the advent of EU citizenship. The personal scope of the principle was widened to include all lawfully resident EU citizens in another Member State.[78] Furthermore, given the expansive range of EU law, it was possible to find some exercise of EU competence in a particular area with increasing ease, thereby bringing the situation within the material scope of the prohibition of non-discrimination on grounds of nationality.[79]

The impact of the principle was particularly felt in the field of social benefits, which were subject to a variety of qualifying conditions determining the personal limits of financial solidarity, generally mapped onto the national community.[80] In a series of cases in the late 1990s and early 2000s the Court began to redraw these boundaries of solidarity based on the concept of EU citizenship and the principle of equal treatment.[81] In time, the extent to which an individual had a 'real link' with the society of a particular Member State became the principle for determining the extent of equal treatment a citizen was entitled to and hence the extent of the financial solidarity owed that citizen by host Member States.[82] In 2004 the legislature codified this jurisprudence in Directive 2004/38/EC, extending the right to equal treatment to mobile EU citizens, while at the same time attempting to provide for limits and conditions, primarily economic activity or self-sufficiency, to that right in the fields of social assistance.[83]

The case-law of the Court of Justice on equal treatment and welfare rights can be broken into two distinct phases. After an initial period in which the Court made little reference and even less use of the citizenship provisions contained in the Treaty of Maastricht, the Court beginning with *Martinez Sala* proceeded to, in the words of O'Leary, put 'flesh on the bones'[84] of EU citizenship over the next two decades by extending the rights to equal treatment enjoyed by EU citizens and restricting the ability of Member States to limit these rights. The past five years have, however, seen a reversal, or perhaps rebalancing of this line of case-law. A number of cases, beginning with *Dano*,[85] have limited the rights of EU citizens to equal treatment in the field of welfare rights and have asserted the rights of Member States to exclude non-economically active mobile EU citizens.

[78] *Martinez Sala* (n 2) paras 46–49.

[79] For a particularly tenuous link, see Case C-60/00 *Mary Carpenter v Secretary of State for the Home Department* EU:C:2002:434, [2002] ECR I-6279.

[80] Michael Dougan, 'The Spatial Restructuring of National Welfare States within the European Union: the contribution of Union Citizenship and the relevance of the Treaty of Lisbon.' in Ulla Neergaard, Ruth Nielson and Lynn Rosebury (eds), *Integrating Welfare Function into EU Law: From Rome to Lisbon* (Djøf Publishing, 2009). See also Maurizio Ferrera, *The Boundaries of Welfare: European Integration and the New Spatial Politics of Social Protection* (Oxford University Press, 2005) chs 1–3.

[81] For the interaction of free movement and national welfare states generally, see Ferrera (n 80).

[82] For a summary of the case-law, see Burri (n 16) pts B.IV.i (the 1990s) and B.V.i (the 2000s).

[83] See, in particular, the limitations contained in Art 24(2) of the Citizenship Directive (n 42).

[84] O'Leary (n 77).

[85] Case C-333/13 *Elisabeta Dano & Florin Dano v Jobcenter Leipzig* EU:C:2014:2358.

Early cases tended to expand the rights of mobile EU citizens who were not economically active to access the welfare systems of host Member States by drawing on the directly effective rights located in primary law. *Martínez Sala* established the principle that all EU citizens lawfully resident in another Member State were entitled to equal treatment in all matters that fell within the scope of EU law.[86] In Mrs Sala's case this included a right to a child-rearing allowance. Mrs Sala enjoyed this right simply by virtue of her status as an EU citizen lawfully resident in another Member State and not as a worker. *Grzelczyk* found that Member States had, through the creation of the status of EU citizenship and by providing that mobile EU citizens must not become an *unreasonable* burden, accepted 'a certain degree of financial solidarity between nationals of a host Member State and nationals of other Member States'.[87] In *Trojani*[88] the Court attempted to balance the rights of individual EU citizens to the enjoyment of that solidarity in other Member States with the need to ensure that non-economically active, mobile EU citizens did not constitute an unreasonable burden on the host Member State. Its response was to provide that whereas an individual's residence could be terminated on the basis that he or she lacked sufficient resources, removal could never be the automatic consequence of an application for social assistance.[89]

The exact extent of this solidarity and its link with social integration was outlined in the case of *Bidar*[90] in which a French student in the UK was found to be discriminated against by a system for awarding subsidised loans for student fees. While excluded from the scope of secondary legislation, Mr Bidar was able to rely on the Treaty directly.[91] The Court accepted that some conditions on the award of such assistance could be justified by the need to limit it 'to students who have demonstrated a certain degree of integration into the society of [the host] State'.[92] However, that link was specifically a *social* one, with the Court excluding the possibility of requiring an economic link or one with the employment market.[93] The application of the conditions necessary to ensure such a link had to be conducted in a proportionate manner, in other words such conditions needed to be both necessary to achieve the objective of ensuring a genuine link with the society of the host Member State and not to go beyond what was necessary. A certain period

[86] *Martinez Sala* (n 2).

[87] Case C-184/99 *Rudy Grzelczyk v Centre public d'aide sociale d'Ottignies-Louvain-la-Neuve* EU:C:2001:458, [2001] ECR I-6193, para 44.

[88] Case C-456/02 *Michel Trojani v Centre public d'aide sociale de Bruxelles (CPAS)* EU:C:2004:488, [2004] ECR I-7573.

[89] ibid, para 45. For a more recent (and more elaborate) statement of this position, see Case C-140/12 *Pensionsversicherungsanstalt v Peter Brey* EU:C:2013:565.

[90] Case C-209/03 *The Queen (on the application of Dany Bidar) v London Borough v Ealing, Sec of State for Education and Skills* EU:C:2005:169, [2005] ECR I-2119.

[91] See also Case C-413/99 *Baumbast and R v Secretary of State for the Home Department* EU:C:2002:493, [2002] ECR I-7091, para 84, finding that Art 21(1) TFEU [then Art 18(1) TEC] contained a directly effective right to residence for mobile EU citizens.

[92] *Bidar* (n 90) para 57.

[93] ibid, para 58.

of residence was indicative of a certain degree of integration but a system, such as that in the case of *Bidar*, whereby it was impossible for a non-UK national to achieve settled status while a student, could not be justified.[94]

Thus, in a series of cases the Court of Justice gradually established a status extending equal treatment to mobile EU citizens, even those not economically active, that was based on the principle of social integration; the more integrated a mobile EU citizen, the less likely any restriction on his or her rights to access social assistance on the same basis as nationals would be considered proportionate. In other words, the degree of equal treatment and access to rights increased in proportion to the extent of the individual's social integration which became a key operative principle in EU citizenship law.[95] Union citizenship became, in the words of Azoulai, 'a status of social integration'.[96] Before refusing equal treatment a Member State needed to make a case-by-case assessment.[97] In carrying out this assessment, Member State authorities had to comply with the principle of proportionality and assess the extent to which a particular EU citizen constituted an unreasonable burden on the social assistance system of the host Member State.[98] This was to be assessed taking into account the extent of his links to the host Member State and whether his difficulty was temporary or permanent. Finally, while a mobile EU citizen's right to residence could be terminated for lack of sufficient resources, an application for social assistance could not automatically lead to removal.[99] While protective of the rights of mobile EU citizens, not least through the application of the principle of proportionality, the system thus established relied on administrative discretion hedged by vague legal rules, a situation that did not lend itself to legal clarity.

Perhaps responding to this criticism and a broader political climate concerned with the effects of migration,[100] the Court has reversed this expansive reading of the rights of mobile Union citizens to the same treatment of nationals in the field of welfare benefits. The Court of Justice has asserted the Directive as the main reference instrument when determining the lawfulness or otherwise of restrictions on the rights of mobile EU citizens to access social assistance and in the process sidelined the principle of proportionality and the need for an individualised

[94] ibid, para 61.

[95] For an overview of the different functions that social integration plays in EU citizenship law, see Barbou des Places (n 73).

[96] Azoulai (n 72).

[97] See, for example, *Brey* (n 89).

[98] ibid, para 64.

[99] *Trojani* (n 88) para 45 and *Brey* (n 89) para 63.

[100] See, for example, the analysis by Urška Šadl and Suvi Sankari, 'Why Did the Citizenship Jurisprudence Change?' in Thym (n 5). Although see Gareth Davies, 'Has the Court Changed, or Have the Cases? The Deservingness of Litigants as an Element in Court of Justice Citizenship Adjudication' (2018) 25 *Journal of European Public Policy* 1442 for an argument that a more straightforward (and therefore convincing) explanation for the change in direction of the Court's jurisprudence is the factual circumstances of the cases.

assessment. *Dano*[101] is widely considered as constituting the turning point in the jurisprudence of the Court. In *Dano* a Romanian national moved to Germany and lived there for a number of years with her son. It would appear that she never worked, or sought work. Her application for a subsistence allowance was refused by the German authorities on the basis that she was not lawfully resident. The right to equal treatment found in Article 24(1) of the Citizenship Directive was conditional on the individual fulfilling the conditions of lawful residence contained in the Directive.[102] In the words of the Court of Justice:

> A Member State must … have the possibility … of refusing to grant social benefits to economically inactive Union citizens who exercise their right to freedom of movement solely in order to obtain another Member State's social assistance although they do not have sufficient resources to claim a right of residence.[103]

In later cases it became clear that the Court was concerned with excluding not simply those without a regular residence status, but all those who are not economically active or self-sufficient from the scope of the equal-treatment guarantee in the Directive and to enable Member States to exclude such individuals from their welfare systems. In *Alimanovich*,[104] the denial of welfare rights was extended to jobseekers. Although Mrs Alimanovic and her daughter were lawfully resident in the host Member State (Germany), their residence was of the wrong kind as they were jobseekers rather than workers. They could therefore legitimately be denied rights to social assistance on the basis of Article 24(2) of the Citizenship Directive without the need for an individual assessment.[105] Similarly, in *Garcia Nieto*[106] the applicants were lawfully resident – being resident in the host Member State for a period of less than three months – but again were denied access to social assistance on the basis of Article 24(2) of the Citizenship Directive. Finally, in *Commission v UK*[107] the Court of Justice extended the denial of equal treatment from social assistance to social benefits.[108]

The Court successfully excluded non-economically active mobile EU citizens from the scope of equal treatment by relying almost exclusively on the wording of the Directive. It set aside the requirement of an individualised assessment and

[101] *Dano* (n 85). For a commentary, see Daniel Thym, 'The Elusive Limits of Solidarity: Residence Rights of and Social Benefits for Economically Inactive Union Citizens' (2014) 52 *CML Rev* 17.

[102] *Dano* (n 85) para 69.

[103] ibid, para 78.

[104] Case C-67/14 *Jobcenter Berlin Neukölln v Nazifa Alimanovic and Others* EU:C:2015:597.

[105] Ibid, para 58.

[106] Case C-299/14 *Vestische Arbeit Jobcenter Kreis Recklinghausen v Jovanna García-Nieto and Others* EU:C:2016:114.

[107] Case C-308/14 *Commission v UK* EU:C:2016:436. For a critical commentary, see Charlotte O'Brien, 'The ECJ Sacrifices EU Citizenship in Vain: *Commission v United Kingdom*' (2017) 51 *CML Rev* 209.

[108] There are various more detailed analysis of these developments. See, for example, the contributions in Thym (n 5). For a broader consideration of these cases in the historical development of EU citizenship, see Dion Kramer, 'From Worker to Self-Entrepeneur: The Transformation of Homo Economicus and the Freedom of Movement in the European Union' (2017) 23 *ELJ* 172.

emphasised the ability of Member States to apply bright-line rules.[109] It upheld the rights of states to impose limits, found in the Directive, over the rights of individuals to access social assistance, derived ultimately from the Treaties. In doing so it has (re)introduced an economic dimension into the extent to which an individual can be said to have a claim on host Member States.

The Court of Justice has not abandoned the integration paradigm but rather has expanded it to include the individual's economic integration and reversed the causal relationship between rights and integration. Economic contributions now constitute preconditions before solidarity is to be extended. For AG Wathelet in *Dano*, provisions in the Citizenship Directive allowing Member States to refuse welfare benefits to the economically inactive 'serve to prevent persons exercising their right to freedom of movement without intending to integrate themselves from becoming a burden on the social assistance system'.[110] The Court remains concerned with balance of rights and obligations between mobile citizens and host Member States, as is evident in its language in *Dano*. The concept of a gradually increasing status, in line with the integration of the mobile citizen and the links he or she has forged with the host society, remains. Only now the Court is content to defer to the choice of the legislature in this matter. Indeed, as explored below, that the Directive itself embodies the integration paradigm, has recently been re-emphasised by the Court.[111] Thus, an individualised assessment is set aside in *Alimanovic* because: 'Directive 2004/38, establishing a gradual system as regards the retention of the status of worker … itself takes into consideration various factors characterising the individual situation of each applicant for social assistance and, in particular the duration of the exercise of any economic activity'.[112]

Finally, it is worth pointing out in passing that the use of the 'real link' and the concept of social integration also operates to a lesser extent in the other direction, enabling individuals to 'export' benefits to other Member States to the extent that they retain sufficient links with the society of the home Member State. In both *Nerkowska*[113] and *Stewart*[114] the Court found that EU citizenship allowed individuals to retain benefits owed them by virtue of their past association with a particular Member State when moving to another Member State, based on the particular characteristics of the benefits in question and the links of those individuals with the home Member State. The result is an example of the complementarity

[109] See, in particular, *Alimanovic* (n 104) para 60.

[110] Case C-333/13 *Elisabeta Dano & Florin Dano v Jobcenter Leipzig* (Opinion of AG Wathelet) EU:C:2014:341, para 131.

[111] See below, and in particular the judgment in *Lounes* (n 39). For a reading of the *Dano* line of case-law in light of the principle of integration, see Stephen Coutts, 'The Absence of Integration and the Responsibilisation of Union Citizenship' (2018) 3 *European Papers* 761.

[112] *Alimanovic* (n 104) para 60.

[113] See Case C-499/06 *Halina Nerkowska v Zakład Ubezpieczeń Społecznych Oddział w Koszalinie* EU:C:2008:300, [2008] ECR I-3993.

[114] Case C-503/09 *Lucy Stewart v Secretary of State for Work and Pensions* EU:C:2011:500, [2011] ECR I-6497.

of the principles of autonomy and integration. Just as family reunification is used to facilitate social integration, the concept of social integration is here used to facilitated further autonomy. EU citizenship therefore not only disrupted the personal boundaries of national welfare systems by allowing non-nationals to gain equal treatment in host Member States[115] but also the territorial boundaries by allowing individuals who retain sufficient links with Member States to maintain rights. The net result is a system whereby individuals are increasingly associated with particular states and communities based not only on ties of nationality but also social and economic connections. This tendency to use the concept of 'social integration', alongside nationality, to allocate responsibility for particular individuals to particular Member States[116] is also found in the area of sentencing, where it is reinforced by the penological principle of rehabilitation, as explored further in Chapter 4.

EU Citizenship and as a Status of Integration and the Legislature

This vision of EU citizenship as a status of integration was taken up by the EU legislature and made the *Leitmotif* of the Citizenship Directive. Indeed, the development of the concept of a 'real link' by the Court of Justice occurred in parallel with the elaboration of the Citizenship Directive.[117] While on one level a unifying instrument, applying a single instrument and certain common principles to all EU citizens in another Member State, the Directive still categorises citizens according to the activity they undertake and the length of time they spend in a host Member State. The major innovation of the Directive is the status of 'permanent resident', which is intended to be 'a genuine vehicle for integration into the society of the host Member State in which the Union citizen resides'.[118] This is achieved by presenting EU citizenship as a progressively strengthened status. Short stays attract a minimum of rights. Initial stays of up to five years are subject to conditions but nonetheless include an extensive right to equal treatment.[119] Stays of more than five years entitle the EU citizen and his family to 'permanent residence'. A permanent resident enjoys almost complete equal treatment and is no longer subject to conditions of residence, such as paid employment or sufficient

[115] Ferrera (n 80).

[116] Barbou des Places (n 73).

[117] Evident from the timing of the *Bidar* judgment, handed down after the adoption of the Citizenship Directive but before its transposition deadline.

[118] Citizenship Directive (n 42) recital 18. For an analysis of the continuity and changes in the Citizenship Directive relative to the preceding law, see Philippe de Bruycker, 'La libre circulation des citoyens européens entre codification et reforme' in Jean-Yves Carlier and Elspeth Guild (eds), *L'Avenir de la libre circulation des personnes dans l'UE / The Future of Free Movement of Persons in the EU* (Bruylant, 2006).

[119] Citizenship Directive (42) Art 24.

resources. This picture of protection and rights increasing in parallel over time is also found in the provisions relating to expulsion. In Article 28 of the Directive the level of threat that needs to be established in order to justify the expulsion of a EU citizen increases with the length of his residence.[120]

The purpose of the Directive is to create a supranationally guaranteed and generous status of migration, with wide-ranging rights of employment, equal treatment, residence and family reunification, explicitly based on the concept of social integration. Integration in immigration law is normally considered a condition to be applied to those individuals who may be granted a right to stay on a more permanent basis.[121] However, the entire Directive is organised along a trajectory of increasing links and rights of the EU citizen with the ultimate goal of the EU citizen's status approaching that of a national and becoming a quasi-member of the community.[122] If it is an immigration status, it is one that is orientated from the very beginning towards virtually full membership of the immigrant over time. This view of the Directive as being organised towards the acquisition of permanent residence, intended to be a 'genuine vehicle of integration in the society of the host Member State', has been endorsed on many occasions by the Court of Justice.[123] Perhaps the most striking affirmation of this logic of the Directive is also one of the more recent. In *Lounes* the Court of Justice underlined the philosophy of the Directive and the Treaty article on which it is based as one of integration into the society of the host Member State, to the point of full naturalisation. Thus, a Spanish national should be able to rely on her EU citizenship rights to family reunification even after she had acquired the nationality of the host Member State (here the UK). To do otherwise would be 'contrary to the underlying logic of gradual integration that informs Article 21(1) TFEU' as it would mean that citizens 'who have acquired rights under that provision as a result of having exercised their freedom of movement must forego those rights … because they have sought, by becoming naturalised in that Member State, to become more deeply integrated in the society of that State'.[124] Their rights would thus be 'reduced in line with their increasing degree of integration in the society of that Member State'.[125]

[120] ibid, Art 16(1).

[121] For a critical analysis of the use of integration as a concept in migration law, see Dora Kostakopoulou, 'The Anatomy of Civic Integration' (2010) 73 *MLR* 933.

[122] In this sense it could be described as a form of denizenship. However, unlike traditional forms of denizenship based on national law, EU citizenship under the Directive is one that is explicitly tailored to this end and indeed forms the overall theme of the Directive. For an analysis of denizenship as it emerged in European states, see Tomas Hammar, *Democracy and the Nation State: Aliens, Denizens and Citizens in a World of International Migration* (Ashgate, 1990). For use of the concept in the context of the EU, see Neil Walker, 'Denizenship and Deterritorialisation in the European Union' in Hans Lindahl (ed), *A Right to Inclusion and Exclusion: Normative Faultlines of the EU's Area of Freedom, Security and Justice* (Hart Publishing, 2009).

[123] Joined Cases C-424/10 and C-425/10 *Tomasz Ziolkowski and Barbara Szeja and Others v Land Berlin* (Opinion of AG Bot) EU:C:2011:575, [2011] ECR I-14035 paras 37ff and citations therein.

[124] *Lounes* (n 39) para 58. For a comment, see Vincent Réveillère, 'Family Rights for Naturalised EU Citizens: *Lounes*' (2018) 55 *CML Rev* 1855.

[125] *Lounes* (n 39) para 59.

In its interpretation of the Directive, the Court has engaged actively with its underlying philosophy, reading it in light of its *telos* of integration, and has drawn on its provisions to inform its own jurisprudence. The Court has consistently interpreted provisions relating to permanent residence in light of its goal of both facilitating and being the objective of a process of integration. In *Lassal* this underlying objective of Article 16 of Directive 2004/38/EC was used as an argument, amongst others, to apply the five-year qualifying period retrospectively, in that case to allow a French woman to count periods of residence that occurred prior to transposition of the Directive when acquiring the right of permanent residence.[126] More harmful for the position of the individual, but still based on the concept of integration, in *Onuekwere* the Court went even further and excluded periods spent in prison from the calculation of the five-year period on the basis that such periods could not be considered periods in which the individual was engaged in a process of integration with the host society.[127] Indeed, the Court of Justice has not only interpreted the award of permanent residence as a form of reward for properly integrated EU citizens, but has also interpreted the residence conditions of the Directive as those that ensure or provide for integration. In *Ziolkowsi* the Court of Justice accepted that while 'legal residence' need not necessarily be residence explicitly based on the Directive, it must comply with the substantive conditions of the Directive, in particular those found in Article 7(1).[128] In *O & B* the Court was even more explicit in characterising the conditions contained in the Directive for periods of more than three months as those under which a Union citizen becomes 'settled' and enjoys 'genuine residence'.[129] Indeed, the *Dano* line of case-law could be read as implicitly reading economic activity as a dimension of the integration of migrants.[130] In *Lounes* the Court notes that individuals resident in accordance with the conditions contained in the Directive indicate an intention to become permanently integrated in the host Member State.[131] Not only does the Directive aim towards the integration of the Union citizen, but it provides the conditions under which such integration can take place.

[126] Case C-162/09 *Secretary of State for Work and Pensions v Taous Lassal* EU:C:2010:592, [2010] ECR I-9217, para 37.

[127] Case C-378/12 *Nnamdi Onuekwere v Secretary of State for the Home Department* EU:C:2014:13. See also Case C-400/12 *Secretary for State for the Home Department v MG* EU:C:2014:9. Although note the recent qualification of this aspect of *Onuekwere* in Joined Cases C-316/16 and C-424/16 *B v Land Baden-Württemberg and Secretary of State for the Home Department v Vomero* EU:C:2018:256. See further Chapter 3.

[128] Joined Cases C-424/10 and C-425/10 *Tomasz Ziolkowski and Barbara Szeja and Others v Land Berlin* EU:C:2011:866, [2011] ECR I-14035 paras 46–47.

[129] *O & B* (n 60).

[130] For this argument, see Coutts (n 111).

[131] *Lounes* (n 39) para 57.

Conclusion: EU Citizenship as a Transnational Status – Between Autonomy and Integration

The defining feature of EU Citizenship as a legal status is therefore the ability of individual EU citizens to enjoy the expanded range of opportunities offered by a wider geographical space containing a plurality of legal systems and political communities.[132] Two features in particular can be discerned in the case-law and the legislation. Individual autonomy is strengthened by an emphasis on free movement in particular. Individuals may move to another Member State, there establish a life, avail of the legal, economic and social advantages available in other Member States, and acquire rights in those Member States. EU citizenship allows these rights and personal situations and civil statuses acquired in one Member State to be carried or, in the words of AG Sharpston, 'passported' to other Member States.[133] In many instances the analogy with mutual recognition is striking and while normally we understand mutual recognition to mean the recognition of national regulations in the case of the internal market or judgments in the case of the Area of Freedom, Security and Justice,[134] in this field it is the mutual recognition of duly acquired rights based on both national and EU law. The result is that bundles of rights and personal situations developed by EU citizens by leading transnational lives must be able to follow them across borders. In this picture the sphere of operation of EU citizenship is the territory of the European Union as a whole, albeit composed of various individual national territories amongst which the EU citizen can effectively pick and choose depending on his personal choices, means and life circumstances.[135]

Another distinct characteristic of EU citizenship, and one that has been more prevalent in the case-law and especially in legislative activity, is EU citizenship as a status of integration in another Member State. The emphasis in this vision is not a footloose, cosmopolitan individual toing and froing throughout the Union, disregarding national regulations and provisions that may hinder him.

[132] See Preuß (n 70).

[133] Joint Opinion of AG Sharpston for Cases C-456/12 and C-457/12 *O v Minister voor Immigratie, Integratie en Asiel and Minister voor Immigratie, Integratie en Asiel v B and S v Minister voor Immigratie, Integratie en Asiel and Minister voor Immigratie, Integratie en Asiel v G* (Opinion of AG Sharpston) EU:C:2013:837, para 95.

[134] See generally Christine Janssens, *The Principle of Mutual Recognition in EU Law* (Oxford University Press, 2013).

[135] '[L]e sujet actif renaît comme sujet *auto-organisé*: acquérant non seulement le droit de s'intégrer d'une manière aussi complète que possible dans les différentes sociétés composant l'Union, mais aussi la faculté d'accéder aux biens communs et aux structures collectives dans les autres Etats membres et, en outré, la liberté de s'organiser et de choisir son style de vie, ses lieux et ses régimes de vie parmi les possibilités offertes sur le territoire de l'Union. L'autonomie se transforme: c'est une capacité d'être en mesure d'organiser sa vie, conformément à une idée de la justice de nature "aspirationnelle"' (emphasis in original). Loïc Azoulai, 'L'autonomie de l'individu européen et la question du statut' (2013/14) EUI Working Papers LAW.

This EU citizen is a more familiar image in the history of migration, an individual who moves to another Member State with the intention of settling there. In this capacity he enjoys a series of rights and a status, progressively strengthened along an axis of social integration. In this field, the Court of Justice and the EU legislature have entered into a fruitful and close collaboration. The central concept of a 'real link' was elaborated almost simultaneously by both institutions, and in subsequent developments the Court has borrowed and exported elements of the Directive to add detail to rights derived directly from the Treaty. Similarly, the notion of social integration has driven its interpretation of key concepts in the Directive, in particular the definition of residence and the acquisition of permanent residence status. The concept of social integration and its use within the context of EU citizenship has established a new principle, alongside the traditional principle of nationality, for allocating individuals to particular political communities. This has been most striking in the field of social benefits but has lately been exported to other areas, including, as we shall see, the field of criminal law and in particular imprisonment.

The two dimensions of transnational EU citizenship are intermingled at various points in the law, and in theory and in practice tend to support and reinforce each other. They are not necessarily mutually exclusive and in certain circumstances they can be considered complementary, particularly in today's world of increased mobility and more changeable life circumstances. Indeed, on a more philosophical level the notion of autonomy can be said to be dependent on the existence of a particular community or society within which options become available to the individual. It is only within a particular social context and broader community that an individual can in fact develop attributes of rationality and make valuable personal choices.[136] Thus in the case-law aspects of the principle of autonomy, such as the right to carry a family life across borders, are sometimes used to strengthen integration. After all, it is in the context of a particular society and necessarily with others that a family life is formed and developed. *O & B* and *S & G* perhaps represent within the same set of judgments the balance between autonomy and integration. Autonomy here is used to facilitate potential integration; rights of return for family members are granted so as not to deter initial free movement to a host Member State for the purposes of settling there, or at least spending more than a nominal period of time. Similarly, both dimensions emerge in *Frietag* where, when assessing the right of the applicant to change his name in Germany, the administrative authorities are to take into account his connections with other Member States, and in particular the state in which he acquired his chosen name.[137]

However, taken individually, the principles of autonomy and integration can be said to be in tension and offer competing visions of the EU citizen and his or her relationship with the societies of Member States; one representing a liberal, cosmopolitan philosophy, the other a rooted, communitarian image.

[136] Caney (n 9) 280, where he states that '[a]utonomy … is facilitated by a culture instantiating a variety of cultural options from which individuals may choose their conception of the good life'.
[137] *Frietag* (n 28) para 46.

They represent competing ideals of both the EU citizen and the notion of community in the European Union. At the level of the individual, EU citizenship as social integration tends to promote a rooted, socially constituted individual, living within and as part of particular society. EU citizenship as autonomy promotes a looser, more individualised character; self-determining and not bound to a particular society, a quasi (and regionally bounded) cosmopolitan citizenship.[138] Individuals are not required, and indeed are protected from, a requirement to choose one particular Member State in which to live their lives and to integrate within the society of that state. On the level of community, the concept of social integration privileges the national. National communities are understood as being the primary location for the development and existence of social life between individuals, and moreover, they are deemed to be quasi-exclusive; one integrates into another particular Member State's society and becomes part of that society, enjoying its rights and cultural space. Note, for example, the stipulation in Article 16(4) of the Citizenship Directive that the status of permanent resident may be lost after an absence of two years from the host Member State.[139] Union citizenship as autonomy tends to privilege a Union-wide existence, in which individuals are 'offered' a broader space of different opportunities and to pick and choose the different components of their life from amongst those opportunities – a kind of eclectic, variable political space. Through the operation of a principle of autonomy in EU citizenship, a certain supranational space emerges occupied by citizens as autonomous and self-constituting individuals.

At times, the tensions between these two visions emerge in the case-law. In *Garcia Avello* there was a direct tension between treating the children as quasi-Belgian or as cosmopolitan Europeans; between the choice of the parents as a transnational family and the equal treatment of the children vis-à-vis Belgian society and between the Union as a collection of individual national communities or as a broader space of movement.[140] In *von Wolffersdorff* a similar tension emerges between the two principles underlying autonomy and social integration. The fact that the name change sought by the applicant was voluntary was held *not* to justify an outright denial of his application,[141] but nonetheless the fact that it was the result of a purely personal preference *was* a relevant factor to be taken into account in the proportionality assessment when balancing the individual right to a change of name with the broader societal interest in respect for the underlying constitutional values of the German Republic.[142] In *O&S*, while the Court tended

[138] See Everson (n 10). See also Alexander Somek, *Individualism: An Essay on the Authority of the European Union* (Oxford University Press, 2008) and Damian Chalmers, 'The Persona of EU Law' in Azoulai et al (n 15).

[139] Citizenship Directive (n 42) Art 16(4).

[140] *Garcia Avello* (n 17).

[141] *von Wolffersdorff* (n 27) para 56 with the Court stressing in the same section that the fact that an individual's name formed part of his personal identity and respect for an individual's choice in that regard was mandated by the fundamental right of privacy (see para 54).

[142] ibid, para 82.

to strike a balance between integration and free movement or autonomy, it was an awkward balance. There is no logical, necessary link between an individual having 'genuine settled' residence of a certain period of time and acquiring rights capable of being passported and enjoyed throughout the Union. What imposing such a requirement does achieve is to compromise the autonomy of EU citizens in leading transnational lives in the political interests of Member States interesting in retaining a certain measure of control over immigration policies and social cohesion.

Both do, however, enable the Union citizen to live across borders, either across multiple and changing borders in the case of citizenship as autonomy or across a single border and entry into the society of another Member State in the case of citizenship as integration. Combined, they reflect EU citizenship as a transnational status. It establishes rights for the individual who moves across borders and enjoys the fruits of multiple national communities and is principally exercised against other Member States and to a limited extent against the Member State of nationality where this is necessary to secure the reality of the transnational life. It is the ability both to move throughout and around the Union *and* to have the option to settle in other Member States that together make-up EU citizenship as a transnational status. In order to be fully achieved it entails both the right to move to, settle in and eventually receive equal treatment as a quasi-full member of the host society *and* the right to carry an ensemble of rights and a civil status throughout the territory of the Union. This capacity remains at the core of EU citizenship, even its supranational dimension, as we shall explore in the next chapter.

3

The Supranational Dimension of EU Citizenship

Introduction

EU citizenship broadens the autonomy of its holders to choose a particular life within the context of particular communities, only now there is a multiplicity of communities from which individuals can draw to develop their own conception of the self and develop their own individual life-plans. However, as pointed out by Preuß, this is not the same thing as developing a corresponding community at a Union-wide level.[1] Indeed, until recently EU citizenship did not establish relations between EU citizens directly, nor did it reflect a 'European' community of citizens at a supranational level independent of national membership.[2]

Recent developments in the jurisprudence of the Court of Justice have questioned this picture of the purely transnational nature of EU citizenship. In a series of cases the Court has established the autonomous character of EU citizenship based on Article 20 TFEU, emphasising not a (direct) relationship between Member States and individuals but a relationship between individuals and the supranational legal order of the European Union itself by virtue of the status of EU citizenship. There does appear to be a supranational reference point for a European community of citizens slowly emerging through the jurisprudence of the Court of Justice, which, it is argued here, reflects an autonomous supranational dimension resulting in a right to place. Importantly, this supranational dimension *emerges from* the transnational rights to free movement and residence, placing them in the context of the European Union as a whole. These two dimensions – supranational and transnational – while conceptually distinct as reflecting two different sets of

[1] See also the sentiment expressed by Ulrich Preuß, 'Problems of a Concept of European Citizenship' (1995) 1 *ELJ* 267, 280.

[2] Indeed, this sentiment might be seen behind the rules of acquisition of EU citizenship and the language used in the Treaty ('Citizenship of the Union shall be *additional to* and not replace national citizenship' [emphasis added]) and in the unilateral declaration of Denmark following the Edinburgh Council Meeting ('Nothing in the Treaty on European Union implies or foresees an undertaking to create a citizenship of the Union in the sense of citizenship of a nation-state'). See Conclusions of the Presidency Edinburgh, 12 December 1992, Annex 3, Unilateral Declaration of Denmark.

relations between citizens and other Member States on the one hand and citizens and the European Union as a whole on the other, are nonetheless intimately connected in that both emerge from the rights of free movement and residence. This development has been hesitant and, in the words of Lenaerts, has proceeded via a 'stone-by-stone' approach.[3] Three phases can be discerned in the case-law of the Court: an initial breakthrough phase establishing a supranational status of EU citizenship conceptually independent from national citizenship and yet remaining insubstantial, a second phase of retrenchment and limitation, and finally a third phase of re-emergence and development.

At the heart of supranational citizenship based on Article 20 TFEU lies the concept of the 'substance of the rights of Union citizenship'. However, it is becoming increasingly apparent that by this phrase the Court of Justice is not referring to a new set of autonomous federal rights[4] but rather, in what might seem a limiting move, back to the rights of Article 21 TFEU – those of free movement and residence. However, in doing so it transforms the scope and import of these rights and casts them in the context of the European Union as a whole. Through the rights to free movement and residence throughout the Union, the Court is fashioning a right to a place and moreover a place of rights: the territory of the European Union as a whole. The notion of the Union as a distinct space occupied by its citizens has special resonance when discussing the Area of Freedom, Security and Justice in particular.

The Establishment of an Autonomous Supranational Status: *Rottmann* and *Zambrano*

In a pair of cases in 2010 and 2011 the Court of Justice outlined a theory of EU citizenship that included an autonomous status, linking the individual directly with the European Union legal order. This stemmed directly from Article 20(1) TFEU establishing EU citizenship itself.

EU citizenship is a derived status. It is acquired through holding the nationality of a Member State, the acquisition of which is determined solely by that Member State.[5] Nationality laws, defining who is and who is not a member of the national

[3] Koen Lenaerts, 'EU Citizenshp and the European Court of Justice's 'stone-by-stone' approach' (2015) 1 *International Comparative Jurisprudence* 1.

[4] These rights may emerge in some limited circumstances and we should be mindful of the use made by the Court of Justice of the Charter of Fundamental Rights in Case C-133/15 *Chavez-Vilchez and Others v Raad van bestuur van de Sociale verzekeringsbank and Others* EU:C:2017:354 to establish a potential denial of the genuine substance of the rights of the child. See below.

[5] Art 20(1) TFEU: 'Every person holding the nationality of a Member State shall be a citizen of the Union. Citizenship of the Union shall be additional to and not replace national citizenship. Conclusions of the Presidency Edinburgh, 12 December 1992, Annex 3, Unilateral Declaration of Denmark.

political community and hence indirectly the community itself, can be said to lie at the heart of national sovereignty.[6] The derived nature of EU citizenship is beyond doubt, as is the exclusive competence of Member States in awarding nationality. However, in *Rottmann* the Court of Justice found that when *withdrawing* nationality from an individual, Member States were required to apply general principles of EU law and in particular undertake a proportionality assessment. This involved taking into account the impact on the individual from the loss of his rights under EU law and the legitimate interests the Member State may have in depriving him of those rights.[7] It arrived at this conclusion by reading EU citizenship as an autonomous status under EU law that generates its own rights. The decision of a Member State to withdraw it must therefore be subject to review under the principles of EU law,[8] in addition to any requirements of national law.

Union citizenship, while linked with nationality in terms of possession, in fact constitutes a separate and parallel status established under EU law and subject to its requirements. It establishes a relationship between Europeans, constituting a new community that builds on national communities at a supranational level. Nationality and EU citizenship 'are both inextricably linked and independent'.[9] The Opinion of AG Maduro in *Rottmann* contains an eloquent exposition of this vision of EU citizenship and its relationship with nationality. Nationality and EU citizenship are linked in their mode of acquisition and indeed loss, and as a consequence in the nature of the forms of membership they represent. Indeed, it is the 'miracle of Union citizenship' that

> it strengthens the ties between us and our States (in so far as we are European citizens precisely because we are nationals of our States) and, at the same time, it emancipates us from them (in so far as we are now citizens beyond our States). Access to European citizenship is gained through nationality of a Member State, which is regulated by national law, but like any form of citizenship, it forms the basis of a new political area from which rights and duties emerge, which are laid down by Community law and do not depend on the State.[10]

It is *through* nationality that one becomes an EU citizen and accordingly it is through membership of a national community of a Member State that one becomes

[6] For an illustration of Member State discretion in this respect, see Case C-192/99 *The Queen and Secretary of State for the Home Department, ex parte: Manjit Kaur* EU:C:2001:106, [2001] ECR I-1252. Indeed, this very insistence on maintaining exclusive national competence in this area has led to knock-on effects for other Member States, ironically limiting their discretion in certain areas, in particular in recognising the underlying nationality of EU citizens once granted by a Member State: see Case C-369/90 *Mario Vicente Micheletti and others v Delegación del Gobierno en Cantabria* EU:C:1992:295, [1992] ECR I-4239; Case C-138/02 *Brian Francis Collins v Secretary of State for Work and Pensions* EU:C:2004:172, [2004] ECR I-2803; and C-200/02 *Kunqian Catherine Zhu, Man Lavette Chen v Secretary of State for the Home Department* EU:C:2004:639, [2004] ECR I-9951.

[7] Case C-135/08 *Janko Rottmann v Freistaat Bayern* EU:C:2010:104, [2010] ECR I-1449, paras 55–56.

[8] ibid, para 48.

[9] ibid.

[10] ibid (Opinion of AG Maduro) para 23.

a member of a supranational European community.[11] Yet once one has become such a member, it is an autonomous and independent status.

The implications of *Rottmann* became apparent in the case of *Zambrano*.[12] *Zambrano* is noted for founding a right of residence for EU citizens and certain members of their families even in their home Member State under certain circumstances. In modifying the so-called 'purely internal rule' and the question of reverse discrimination[13] it can be added to the long list of decisions protecting the family life of EU citizens and transforming family members of even static EU citizens into 'quasi-citizens'.[14] However, for present purposes the real interest in the decision lies in the interpretative technique used by the Court, and in particular its reliance on the independent *status* of EU citizenship, identified in *Rottmann*, to justify its decision. Quickly finding that the rights of free movement and residence found in Article 21 TFEU and the relevant secondary legislation (Directive 2004/38/EC) did not apply in the case of a static EU citizen, the Court moved on to consider the case under Article 20 TFEU and found that Member States could not adopt measures that would 'have the effect of depriving citizens of the Union of the genuine enjoyment of the substance of the rights conferred by virtue of their status as citizens of the Union'.[15] Such deprivation would occur if an EU citizen was obliged to leave the territory of the European Union. In the present case refusal to grant Mr Ruis Zamrano, the father of minor EU citizens entirely dependent upon him, a right of residence and a right to work in the home Member State, Belgium would amount to such a deprivation. In particular it would oblige them to leave 'the territory of the Union'.[16]

While much criticised for the brevity and opacity of its reasoning,[17] *Zambrano* is clear in providing a new paradigm for understanding EU citizenship.[18]

[11] This linkage may in certain circumstances also work in reverse, whereby the status (and exercise of the rights) of EU citizenship provide the basis for the acquisition of the nationality of a Member State. For a description of this 'Europeanisation' of nationality law effected by Case C-165/16 *Toufik Lounes v Secretary of State for the Home Department* EU:C:2017:862, see Vincent Réveillère, 'Family Rights for Naturalised EU Citizens: *Lounes*' (2018) 55 *CML Rev* 1855.

[12] Case C-34/09 *Gerardo Ruiz Zambrano v Office national de l'emploi (ONEm)* EU:C:2011:124, [2011] ECR I-1177.

[13] For an overview of the purely internal rule and its evolution, including in *Zambrano*, see Síofra O'Leary, 'The Past, Present and Future of the Purely Internal Rule in EU Law' in Michael Dougan, Niamh Nic Shuibhne and Eleanor Spaventa (eds), *Empowerment and Disempowerment of the European Citizen* (Hart Publishing, 2012). For a judicial treatment, see in particular Case C-34/09 *Gerardo Ruiz Zambrano v Office national de l'emploi (ONEm)* (Opinion of AG Sharpston) EU:C:2010:560.

[14] Loïc Azoulai, '"Euro-Bonds": The Ruiz Zambrano judgment or the Real Invention of EU Citizenship' (2011) 3 *Perspectives on Federalism* 37.

[15] *Zambrano* (n 12) para 42.

[16] ibid, para 44.

[17] See, in particular, Niamh Nic Shuibhne, 'Seven Questions for Seven Paragraphs' (2011) 36 *EL Rev* 161 and Kay Hailbronner and Daniel Thym, 'Case Note C-34/09: Zambrano v ONEm' (2011) 48 *CML Rev* 1253 (n 19), 1259–60.

[18] See Dimitry Kochenov, 'A Real European Citizenship: A New Jurisdiction Test: A Novel Chapter in the Development of the Union in Europe' (2011) 18 *Columbia Journal of European Law* 55. See also Dimitry Kochenov, 'On Tiles and Pillars: EU Citizenship as a Federal Denominator' in Dimitry Kochenov (ed), *EU Citizenship and Federalism: The Role of Rights* (Cambridge University Press, 2017) in which a much broader role for EU citizenship in the constitution of the Union is envisaged.

Zambrano is not concerned with the wording of the Treaty or the rights of EU citizenship,[19] but develops an autonomous concept of EU citizenship as a status and linking individual holders of that status to the EU legal order.[20] It is this supranational status and the Zambrano children's membership of the broader European community that brings the issue within the scope of EU law. In supplementing the rights contained in Article 21 TFEU and Directive 2004/38/EC with a protection based on Article 20 TFEU and the status of EU citizenship itself, the Court of Justice is in effect supplementing a set of transnational rights with a supranational status, founded in EU law and linking the EU citizen directly with a supranational polity.[21]

Retrenchment: An Ill-Defined and Insubstantial Substance

The ruling in *Zambrano* was confirmed by the Court of Justice on a number of occasions, as was the new 'genuine enjoyment' test based on the supranational status of EU citizenship.[22] However, subsequent cases based on Article 20 TFEU tended to disappoint applicants and commentators alike in refusing to extent the protection offered in the case of the Zambrano family to other applicants in what appeared to be similar situations or in clarifying what exactly was meant by the 'status of Union citizenship' and the 'genuine enjoyment of the substance of the rights' that attached to it.

In the cases of *McCarthy*[23] and *Derici*,[24] decided shortly after *Zambrano*, the Court of Justice appeared to close the door on the potentially revolutionary application of *Zambrano*. Although affirming the existence of the status of EU citizenship found in Article 20 TFEU and the 'genuine enjoyment' test that had been developed in *Zambrano*, the Court appeared to be at pains to limit its possible application, no doubt conscious of the widespread adverse reaction against that judgment on the part of Member States who feared yet another loosening of their control over migration and family reunification in the face of EU citizenship.[25] In these and subsequent cases the true limitations on *Zambrano* became apparent.

[19] Indeed, Hailbronner and Thym have argued that the vision of Union citizenship it entails is radically different from that found in the text of the Treaties. See Hailbronner and Thym (n 17) 1262ff.

[20] ibid, 1263.

[21] ibid, 1262–64.

[22] Case C-434/09 *Shirley McCarthy v Secretary of State for the Home Dept* EU:C:2011:277, [2011] ECR I-3375; Case C-256/11 *Murat Dereci and Others v Bundesministerium für Inneres* EU:C:2011:734, [2011] ECR I-11315; Case C-40/11 *Yoskikazu Iida v Stadt Ulm* EU:C:2012:691; Joined Cases C-356/11 and C-357/11 *O and S v Maahanmuuttovirasto and Maahanmuuttovirasto v L* EU:C:2012:776; Case C-87/12 *Ymeraga v Minstre du Travail, de l'Emploi et de l'Immigration* EU:C:2013:291; and Case C-86/12 *Alokpa et al v Minstre du Travail de l'Emploi et de l'Immigration* EU:C:2013:645.

[23] *McCarthy* (n 22).

[24] *Dereci* (n 22).

[25] See critical comments made by Níc Shuibhne in Niamh Níc Shuibhne '(Some) of the Kids are All Right' (2012) 49 *CML Rev* 349, 378–79.

Article 20 TFEU did not entail the right to live in a Member State of one's choosing but only the right to reside somewhere in the European Union. If one could, through an alternative nationality, reside in another Member State, one did not enjoy the protections contained in Article 20 TFEU.[26] Similarly being *forced* to leave the territory of the Union meant precisely that, the mere *desirability* of having a family member remain was not sufficient to reach the threshold of the denying the genuine enjoyment of the substance of the rights attaching to EU citizenship.[27] Dependence, which became key to determining the application of the 'genuine enjoyment test', was construed narrowly and in particular only referred to financial dependence, emotional and social dependence being excluded.[28] Additionally, it was the EU citizen child who needed to be dependent in the relationship with the TCN family member, not the other way around.[29] Finally, fundamental rights did not appear to be included in the 'substance of the rights' conferred by EU citizenship. While Member States must have regard to their obligations under the ECHR and under the Charter of Fundamental Rights (CFR) in situations that fall within the scope of EU law, breach of a fundamental right, such as the right to family and private life, does not in and of itself amount to a denial of the 'genuine enjoyment' of a right conferred by EU citizenship.[30] Thus, while through a series of cases it became clear what the genuine enjoyment of the substance of the rights of EU citizenship *was not*, it was not apparent what precisely it in fact *was*.

The result was a clear and dramatic narrowing of the application of any test under Article 20 TFEU. The exceptional nature of such an application was underlined by the Court itself, finding in both *Alopka* and *Ymeraga* that it applied only in 'very specific situations'.[31] In these two cases the language and justification of the Court also shifted somewhat, marking a return to more traditional notions. It found that Article 20 TFEU situations, such as that in *Zambrano*, have an 'intrinsic connection with the freedom of movement of a Union citizen'[32] and employed the language of 'effectiveness' when describing the test under Article 20 TFEU. Although the concept of effectiveness has been used to promote the application of EU law in other areas,[33] it does tend to characterise Article 20 TFEU in instrumental terms rather than the inherent protection of the individual as a European conferred by the 'fundamental status' of Union citizenship.

[26] *Alokpa* (n 22) paras 33–35.

[27] *Dereci* (n 22) para 66.

[28] ibid. See also *Alokpa* (n 22) para 25. Although a loosening of the strictures of this test is effected in *O & S* (n 22).

[29] *Ymeraga* (n 22).

[30] *Dereci* (n 22) paras 70–72. For a nuanced commentary on this issue, see Domink Düsterhaus, 'EU Citizenship and Fundamental Rights: Contradictory, Converging of Complementary?' in Kochenov (n 18).

[31] *Alokpa* (n 22) para 32 and *Ymeraga* (n 22) para 36.

[32] *Ymeraga* (n 22) para 37.

[33] See the overview offered by Herlin Karnell in Ester Herlin-Karnell, *The Constitutional Dimension of European Criminal Law* (Hart Publishing, 2012) ch 4.

The Re-emergence of Supranational Citizenship

After having lain dormant for a number of years, recent cases appear to have revitalised the supranational dimension to EU citizenship and in particular the protections offered by Article 20 TFEU, broadening the range of these protections and demanding a more contextualised assessment of the position of individual citizens and their family members in its application. In *Rendón Marín*[34] and *CS*[35] the Court of Justice applied the *Zambrano* test to the situation of family members facing expulsion following criminal convictions and extended the protections developed in its own case-law and secondary legislation. Six months later in *Chavez-Vilchez*[36] the Court extended the protection of Article 20 TFEU to individuals facing removal from the Netherlands, and in doing so indicated a loosening of the test that had been so restrictively interpreted since *Derici*, introducing a more individualised assessment[37] and a prominent place for fundamental rights, in particular the principle of the best interests of the child.[38]

In *Rendón Marín* and *CS* the Court of Justice found that the situation of the applicants fell within the scope of Article 20 TFEU.[39] In both cases the TCN parents of EU citizen children holding the nationality of the state in question had been convicted of crimes and were facing either the non-renewal of a residence permit (the case of *Rendón Marín*) or deportation (the case of *CS*). Both actions – the denial of a residence permit or the actual removal – could have potentially resulted in the EU citizen child also being forced to leave the territory of the Union and hence being denied the genuine enjoyment of the substance of the rights inherent in the status of EU citizenship. Removal of the parents could therefore have the effect of forcing the EU citizen children to leave the territory of the Union and hence would violate their rights under Article 20 TFEU.[40]

However, the Court also found that 'the right … to reside in the territory of the Union is not unconditional but may be subject to the limitations and conditions imposed by the Treaty'.[41] 'Article 20 TFEU does not affect the possibility of Member States relying on an exception linked in particular to upholding the requirements of public policy and safeguarding public security.'[42] However, that

[34] Case C-165/14 *Alfredo Rendón Marín v Administración del Estado* EU:C:2016:675.

[35] Case C-304/14 *Secretary of State for the Home Department v CS* EU:C:2016:674.

[36] *Chavez-Vilchez* (n 4).

[37] ibid, para 71.

[38] ibid, para 70.

[39] Directive 2004/38/EC on the right of citizens of the Union and their family members to move and reside freely within the territory of the Member States [2004] OJ L158/77 (Citizenship Directive). Although in light of the Polish nationality of one of Mr Rendon-Marin's children there was a possibility that he could rely on Art 21 TFEU as the carer of a mobile EU citizen child (see *Rendón Marín* (n 34) paras 51–52). Nonetheless, it is striking that despite this alternative route, the Court still felt the need to progress to an analysis of the situation in light of Art 20 TFEU.

[40] *Rendón Marín* (n 34) paras 77–78 and *CS* (n 35) para 32.

[41] *Rendón Marín* (n 34) para 55.

[42] *CS* (n 35) para 36.

limitation would have to be in compliance with EU law and the principle of proportionality.[43] The Court then effectively applied the body of its case-law developed under Directive 2004/38/EC and its predecessors to the situation of Article 20 TFEU rights.[44] Both the procedural and the substantive protections were engaged. Not only did the Member State in question (Spain in the case of Mr Rendón Marín and the UK with respect to CS) have to demonstrate 'a sufficiently serious threat affecting one of the fundamental interests of society',[45] but that threat had to be of a present and individual nature.[46] Thus a general rule denying TCNs with a criminal conviction renewal of a residence permit or deporting such individuals without taking into account the personal situation of the applicant and the threat he posed, was deemed to result in the removal of the TCN family member and the EU citizen in turn. It therefore represented a potential denial of the genuine enjoyment of the substance of the EU citizen's rights and was precluded by the operation of Article 20 TFEU.[47]

This focus on an individualised assessment emerged also in *Chavez-Vilchez*, not in relation to any assessment of a threat to public security or public order but in assessing the existence or otherwise of a relationship of dependence between the EU citizen and his or her TCN family member. Already in *Rendón Marín* the Court had drawn the national court's attention to the need to assess the extent to which Mr Rendón Marín and his family could 'in fact' return to Poland, the Member State of nationality of one of his children, noting the absence of any social links with Poland and the inability of either Mr Rendón Marín or his daughter to speak Polish.[48] In *Chavez-Vilchez* the Court went further in focusing on the relationship of dependence and demanded a more contextualised assessment of the individual circumstances, of the nature of the relationship between the EU citizen and the family member, and the broader context of that family's situation. The result is a clear move beyond the narrow definition of dependence focused solely on material dependence found in *Derici* and *Alopka* towards a more holistic conception of the social links between an individual, their family and the wider community of which they form a part.[49] Important in *Chavez-Vilchez*, again providing a point of contrast with *Dereci*, is the use made of the CFR. It will be recalled that in *Dereci* the use of

[43] ibid (n 35) paras 34ff and *Rendón Marín* (n 34) paras 81ff.

[44] *Rendón Marín* (n 34) paras 55ff and *CS* (n 35) paras 36ff.

[45] *CS* (n 35) para 36 and *Rendón Marín* (n 34) para 83.

[46] *CS* (n 35) paras 41–42 and *Rendón Marín* (n 34) para 85.

[47] *Rendón Marín* (n 34) para 87 and *CS* (n 35) paras 44–46.

[48] *Rendón Marín* (n 34) para 79. Thereby effectively reversing the finding in *Alokpa* (n 22) that the possession by the EU citizen of the nationality of another Member State would effectively foreclose the possibility of relying on Art 20 TFEU rights. Although note that while this appeared to exclude the application of Art 20 TFEU in the actual case of *Alopka*, the Court did admit in principle the possible application of Art 20 TFEU in transnational situations (ie where the EU citizen was resident in a Member State other than that of nationality). See Chiara Raucea, 'European Citizenship and the Right to Reside: "No One on the Outside has a Right to be Inside"' (2016) 22 *ELJ* 470.

[49] In doing so the Court relies on *O & S* (n 22) which already provided a list of certain factors to be taken into account.

the CFR in establishing a possible denial of the enjoyment of the substance of the rights of EU citizenship, and hence a violation of Article 20 TFEU, was precluded by a traditional reading of the nature of the Charter and its role in the Union's constitutional order.[50] The Charter is a second-order instrument and the situation must fall within the scope of EU law before it can be applied. The Charter itself cannot bring a matter within the scope of EU law.[51] In *Chavez-Vilchez*, however, the Charter *is* to be taken into account in making an assessment of dependence at the initial stage of determining if an individual EU citizen child would be obliged to leave the territory of the European Union as a consequence of a carer parent being removed,[52] ie in determining whether the matter falls within the scope of EU law in the first place. While this is certainly not a finding that a breach of the right to a family life and the best interests of the child themselves bring the matter within the scope of EU law – in the analysis they are ancillary to a finding that the citizen child would be forced to leave the territory of the Union – their inclusion does emphasise the indirect role the Charter can play in bringing a matter within the scope of Union law.[53]

Conclusion: A Right to a Place and a Place of Rights

The final and perhaps most important finding to emerge from *Rendón Marín* and *Chavez-Vilchez* is a clearer picture of precisely what the enigmatic reference to the 'genuine substance of the rights of Union citizenship' actually entails. The answer appears prosaic but is perhaps more fundamental than might be assumed at first glance. The substance of the rights attached to EU citizenship mentioned in *Zambrano* would appear to be none other than the classic rights of EU citizenship of free movement and residence that evolved from the internal market as described at the beginning of this chapter as rights reflecting a transnational citizenship. However, the reference to these rights in the Article 20 TFEU case-law has evolved over time to emerge as a distinct right, independent of movement and transnational citizenship.

The gradual emergence of this link can be traced through the case-law and in particular in the references to free movement and residence. In some of the more

[50] *Dereci* (n 22) para 71.

[51] See Michael Dougan, 'Judicial Review of Member State Action under the General Principles and the Charter: Defining the "Scope of Union Law"' (2015) 52 *CML Rev* 1201.

[52] *Chavez-Vilchez* (n 4) para 70.

[53] A similar movement can be discerned in Case C-650/13 *Thierry Delvigne v Commune de Lesparre Médoc and Préfet de la Gironde* EU:C:2015:648 in which the provision of primary law – Art 14(3) TEU providing that MEPs were to be elected by direct and universal suffrage – was to be interpreted in light of Art 39(2) CFR, with similar wording, but importantly contained in a section of the Charter containing rights for EU citizens. There was therefore a right conferred on EU citizens, *qua* EU citizens, to vote in European Parliamentary elections. For a more detailed note, see Stephen Coutts, 'Delvigne: A Multi-Levelled Political Citizenship' (2017) 42 *EL Rev* 867.

restrictive post-*Zambrano*, judgments, namely *Iida*[54] and *Ymeraga*,[55] the Court of Justice found that Article 20 TFEU cases all had an 'intrinsic connection' with the free movement of EU citizens.[56] This was later expanded in *Rendón Marín* to an 'intrinsic connection with free movement *and residence*' of Union citizens.[57] Finally, in *Chavez-Vilchez*, the Court expanded on the link to free movement and residence by finding that 'the consequence [of the denial of a residence permit to third country national parent of Union citizen] might be a restriction on the rights conferred on their children by their status as Union citizens, in particular the right of residence'.[58]

Note that 'free movement' in *Ymeraga* and *Iida* turns into 'free movement and residence' in *Rendón Marín* and finally simply 'residence' (or rather 'in particular residence') in *Chavez-Vilchez*. Rather than being a simply mirroring of the already existing free-movement and residence rights, the development of these rights in light of Article 20 TFEU appears to have effected a qualitative shift in their operation by separating them. Free movement and residence are no longer considered cumulative – one moves and then resides somewhere – but rather may now to be considered disjunctively as two separate rights – one may move and/or one may reside. There is thus a separate right of residence that applies independently of movement; a stand-alone right of residence, including in a citizen's Member State of nationality, emerges, effectively eliminating the 'purely internal rule' in certain limited circumstances. This indeed is the most plausible reading of the recent case-law and mirrors calls from academics such as Spaventa as far back as 2008[59] and the opinion of AG Sharpston in *Zambrano*.[60] If this is the case there is a real shift in the traditional rights of free movement and residence and move away from a purely transnational scope for EU citizenship. How it is developed in the future and in particular what conditions and limitations may be developed and permitted by the Court is open to question.

On one level, what we are seeing in these cases is a stand-alone right to residence that applies in the Member State of nationality and appears to affect in particular the right of family reunification for minor EU citizens with TCN parents. Important as this new right to family reunification is, we should not lose sight of the (even) broader constitutional question at stake and the implications of this finding. In order to understand this it is necessary to bring back in the reference to the 'territory of the Union as a whole' which featured so prominently and enigmatically in *Zambrano* itself and which continues to be repeated in later

[54] *Iida* (n 22).
[55] *Ymeraga* (n 22).
[56] *Iida* (n 22), para 37 and *Ymeraga* (n 22), para 72.
[57] *Rendón Marín* (n 34) paras 75–77 (emphasis added).
[58] *Chavez-Vilchez* (n 4) para 65.
[59] Eleanor Spaventa, 'Seeing the Woods despite the Trees? On the Scope of Union citizenship and its Constitutional Effects' (2008) 45 *CML Rev* 13.
[60] *Zambrano* (Opinion of AG Sharpston) paras 74ff.

cases,[61] a concept that was described by Azoulai at the time as containing both a geographical and normative reference.[62]

The right established in *Zambrano* and now reaffirmed in *Chavez-Vilchez* is nothing less than a right to a place in the world guaranteed by EU law and attached to EU citizenship.[63] It involves the emplacement of the individual citizen and the concept of EU citizenship within something termed the 'territory of the Union'. This is not a normatively neutral stance nor is it bereft of implications for EU citizenship. Citizenship can be viewed as an institution that emplaces individuals within particular territories and legal orders, and which designates the right place for an individual in a normative and geographic sense.[64] As put by Walker: '[I]t is the link to territory that is deemed to forge the special association that qualifies all individuals as citizens of one polity or another and supplies the citizen with her primary political identity.'[65] The protection offered by a legal order – a protection which is intimately linked to the territory of the state in the context of a Westphalian order of territorially delimited sovereignty – to its citizens is, in certain views, central to the very concept of citizenship. By establishing such a right the European Union is in effect making a determination regarding the 'right' or 'good' place for an individual EU citizen and establishing a link of belonging between the individual EU citizen and the larger space occupied by the Union as a political community.[66] Moreover, it is a common space shared by EU citizens (indeed 'offered' to them)[67] on which their life in common is projected and indeed protected.[68]

However, it is via the 'enjoyment' of the rights of free movement and residence that this broader right to the territory of the Union emerges. The core of EU citizenship remains transnational in a certain sense; it is still the right to move around the different Member States and become part of the different national communities that is at stake. There is a clear link, as enunciated in the case-law, between the transnational rights of free movement and residence and the broader status of EU citizenship. However, the references to free movement and residence refer not to actual, specific instances of the exercise of these transnational rights – hence the

[61] See, for example, *Zambrano* (n 12) para 44; *Dereci* (n 22) para 66; *Rendón Marín* (n 34) para 35; and *Chavez-Vilchez* (n 4) para 65, with the latter two cases speaking of the 'territory of the European Union'.

[62] Azoulai (n 14) 34–35.

[63] See Alison Kesby, *The Right to Have Rights: Citizenship, Humanity and International Law* (Oxford University Press, 2012).

[64] Hans Lindahl, 'Finding a Place for Freedom, Security and Justice: The European Union's Claim to Territorial Unity' (2004) 29 *EL Rev* 461.

[65] Neil Walker, 'The Place of Territory in Citizenship' in Rainer Bauböck et al (eds), *The Oxford Handbook of Citizenship* (Oxford University Press, 2017) 556.

[66] See Lindahl (n 64) also discussing the link between place and collective identity.

[67] See Art 3(1) TEU: 'The Union shall offer its citizens an area of freedom, security and justice.'

[68] See in a somewhat similar vein Editorial Comments, 'EU Law as a Way of Life' (2017) 54 *CML Rev* 357 which speaks of the EU as an area of 'human hope' and 'an area of shelter'.

non-application of Article 21 TFEU and the Directive to the cases – but rather the *potential* exercise of those rights and what they reflect in the abstract; the right to the *enjoyment* of the rights of free movement and residence. These, as analysed in Chapter 3 reflect the transnational right to the Member States, the communities they represent, and the public goods they offer in terms of material resources, opportunities, rights, culture, and indeed social and political contexts for the development of the good life. However, now that is raised to the broader territory of the Union, representing the collective Member States and the combined plural political community they together represent. The transnational and supranational dimensions to EU citizenship are not distinct and independent but rather interdependent and in fact conceptually connected. It is through the transnational rights of autonomy and integration that a unique plural space is generated and offered to EU citizens as *their* place.

In *Rendón Marín* and *Chavez Vilchez* the meaning and the relationship between the concept of territory of the European Union and the rights of free movement and residence and hence the relationship between transnational EU citizenship and the presence of a supranational dimension to this status becomes clearer and reveals a broader understanding of the Union, EU citizenship and the structure of its political community. The (singular) 'territory of the Union as a whole' is one that emerges from the rights of individual citizens to access the various national communities associated with transnational citizenship. It is the potential right to the 'bundle of opportunities' mentioned by Preuß[69] in 1994 that is at stake in *Zambrano* and *Chavez-Vilchez* but one that is seen in its abstract totality rather than a set of distinct options. It is through transnational rights and through the right to the collective set of national communities offered by EU citizenship that the supranational status of a right to place, and indeed the shape of a supranational community, emerges.

[69] Preuß (n 1) 280.

PART II

Social Integration and Crime: Inclusion and Exclusion

The Social Integration Paradigm

EU citizenship is principally, if not exclusively, a status of social integration.[1] In practice this transnational status enables EU citizens to move to and become part of another society in the European Union. EU citizenship confers a right to acquire rights in another Member State and to gain a status that approaches (if never quite equals) national citizenship. The borders of national communities are not eliminated but become more porous, open to other nationals of EU Member States.[2]

Acquiring these rights is not, however, automatic and instantaneous but involves an ongoing process. The main principle developed by the Court of Justice[3] and taken up by the legislature[4] is that of social integration. The relationship between rights and integration is seen as a continuously mutually reinforcing process: rights and the protections offered by rights are seen as a means of enabling the integration of the EU citizen. Further integration in turn leads to more secure rights to residence and equal treatment in particular. The result is a framework for the development of the relationship between the host Member State and the individual, a relationship that develops along an axis of social integration. Focusing on the transnational dimension, the concept of social integration establishes a framework for a relationship between the host society and the individual migrant EU citizen. However, it is a relationship that is lopsided, with most duties, including duties of equal treatment and financial and social solidarity, flowing from the Member State. Beyond certain economic 'conditions' attached to residence,[5] there appears to be little in the way of explicit requirements on the part of the individual.

[1] See Loïc Azoulai, 'La Citoyenneté Européenne, un Statut d'Intégration Sociale' in Gérard Cohen-Jonathan et al (eds), *Chemins d'Europe: Mélanges en l'honneur de Jean Paul Jacqué* (Dalloz, 2010); and Anastasia Iliopoulou Penot, 'The Transnational Character of Union Citizenship' in Michael Dougan, Niamh Nic Shuibhne and Eleanor Spaventa (eds), *The Empowerment and Disempowerment of the European Citizen* (Hart Publishing, 2012).

[2] See Dora Kostakopoulou, 'European Citizenship: Writing the Future' (2007) 13 *ELJ* 623.

[3] Case C-209/03 *The Queen (on the application of Dany Bidar) v London Borough v Ealing, Sec of State for Education and Skills* EU:C:2005:169, [2005] ECR I-2119.

[4] Directive 2004/38/EC on the right of citizens of the Union and their family members to move and reside freely within the territory of the Member States [2004] OJ L158/77 (Citizenship Directive).

[5] See Case C-325/09 *Secretary of State for the Home Department v Maria Dias* EU:C:2011:498, [2011] ECR I-6387.

The Relationship with the Host Society – Inclusion and Exclusion

Developed principally in the field of equal treatment for social benefits, the principle of social integration has been extended to regulate the status of migrant EU citizens in other areas,[6] including in the area of criminal law. Five areas in particular have developed in the field of criminal law: Article 4(6) of the European Arrest Warrant Framework Directive (EAW FD)[7] on the right to remain in a state to serve a sentence; the Transfer of Custodial Sentences Framework Decision; the extension of domestic nationality exemptions to migrant EU citizens; expulsion decisions under Article 28 of the Directive 2004/38/EC (Citizenship Directive);[8] and the question of imprisonment and the calculation of periods of residence under the same Directive.

All five areas are regulated by the concept of social integration. It is a clear extension of the principle from the area of social solidarity and equal treatment to welfare rights to different areas, indicating that the concept of social integration is the key operative principle in regulating the relationship of the EU citizen with the host Member State. However, social integration, once extended to such diverse fields, necessarily engages different concerns that in turn can alter the nature of the social integration paradigm and feedback into our understanding of EU citizenship. This is precisely what has occurred in the field of criminal law, with two issues, particular to the criminal justice system, being incorporated into the social integration test, namely rehabilitation and integration as adherence to the values of the host society.

Chapter 3 details the case-law relating to Article 4(6) EAW FD, the Transfer of Sentences Framework Decision and the extension of the nationality exemption to migrant EU citizens. The two instruments and the Court's case-law have focused on the need to rehabilitate the offender as a widely accepted goal of the criminal justice system. This has been incorporated into the social integration test as reinforcing the 'right' of the migrant EU citizen, who is sufficiently integrated, to remain in the host Member State in order to serve his sentence.[9] Rehabilitation concerns the reintegration of the individual into society, a reintegration that is said to be facilitated by remaining close to family and a social network and being in a familiar environment. Thus while operating within the very different field of penology and criminal justice, the concept of rehabilitation complements the EU law concept of social integration and reinforces the inclusion of the EU citizen in the society of the host Member State. The obligations of the host Member State are therefore extended or reinforced through the use of the concept of rehabilitation.

[6] See Case C-524/06 *Heinz Huber v Bundesrepublik Deutschland* EU:C:2008:724, [2008] ECR I-9705.

[7] Framework Decision 2002/584/JHA on the European arrest warrant and the surrender procedures between Member States (EAW FD) [2002] OJ L190/1.

[8] Citizenship Directive (n 4).

[9] If the Member State has in fact decided to implement the optional provision.

In terms of its operation this is a relatively straightforward application of the principle of social integration: the greater the degree of social integration, the greater the rights of the migrant citizen and the greater his legal inclusion and level of protection. The only difference is that rehabilitation reinforces the traditional operation of the principle of social integration.

Starkly different in effect is the conception of criminal law employed in the other two areas, the expulsion cases and the cases dealing with periods of imprisonment dealt with in Chapter 6. In these cases, a view of the criminal law as wrong-doing emerges. Moreover, it is wrong-doing against society as a whole, the values and norms of which are reflected in the criminal law. Unlike rehabilitation, which is complementary, crime as wrong-doing is inimical to the process of social integration and implicitly justifies the expulsion of the criminal EU citizen. Residence rights, be they permanent residence or enhanced protection against expulsion, are the result of a process of social integration. Criminal acts that result in imprisonment rupture that process of integration, resulting in a loss or a failure to acquire rights relating to EU citizenship. This concept of crime has therefore has resulted in a degree of exclusion for the offending EU citizen.

While it is certainly the case that these two approaches have radically different impacts on the position of the migrant EU citizen – one favouring inclusion, the other exclusion – and a certain tension can be discerned, it is not the case that they are necessarily in opposition or conceptually irreconcilable.[10] Both in fact operate within the communitarian and normative conceptualisation of the criminal law adopted here. As noted by AG Bot in *Onuekwere*, it is precisely because the individual has breached the fundamental values of society, and hence demonstrated the absence of a desire to integrate, that rehabilitation as a practice of social integration makes sense.[11] *Both* sets of concerns – social rehabilitation and criminal acts as a repudiation of the values of society – operate in the case-law of the Court. At different points in the case-law, a different emphasis occurs and one or the other approach predominates; in cases dealing with serving of sentences of sufficiently integrated citizens, rehabilitation dominates, whereas in expulsion cases crime as wrong-doing is the dominant paradigm. A rough division can be discerned between the treatment of 'good' and 'bad' citizens depending on the level of their integration in the host society and the seriousness of their criminal conduct.[12] For the 'good' and, importantly, *already* integrated EU citizen, rehabilitation in the host

[10] See Leandro Mancano, 'Punishment and Rights in European Union Citizenship: Persons or Criminals?' (2018) 24 *ELJ* 206, who argues that an exclusionary approach by the Court of Justice in the expulsion cases indicate an approach towards a criminal law for foreigners or enemies to the detriment of an inclusive communitarian approach. It should be noted that Mancano only deals with expulsion and imprisonment cases in this piece.

[11] Case C-378/12 *Nnamdi Onuekwere v Secretary of State for the Home Department* EU:C:2014:13, paras 54–55, noting the interplay between retribution and rehabilitation.

[12] Following Loïc Azoulai, 'Transfiguring European Citizenship: From Member State Territory to Union Territory' in Dimitry Kochenov (ed), *EU Citizenship and Federalism: The Role of Rights* (Cambridge University Press, 2017).

society is the primary concern and the operative principle within the case-law. For the 'bad' and non-integrated EU citizen, crime as wrong-doing and as repudiating the values of the host society predominates and their exclusion is deemed justified.

B and Vomero in fact demonstrates the joint presence and interaction between these two principles in a single judgment.[13] Mr Vomero had been convicted of manslaughter, burglary, theft, and battery with a blade. He had not acquired permanent residence in his host Member State, the UK, despite having lived there since 1985, and had worked only occasionally. The other part of the case concerned a much more sympathetic individual.[14] B, a troubled youth, had been born in his host Member State (Germany) and lived there his entire life. Furthermore, his links with his Member State of nationality (Greece) were tenuous. He had had psychiatric problems throughout his adolescence and received a custodial sentence only because of his attempt to pay a fine imposed for previous offences by holding up an arcade with a fake firearm.[15]

For Mr Vomero, the discourse adopted by the Court is focused almost exclusively on the absence of the 'qualitative' dimension of social integration, attested to by the fact that he had not, it appeared, acquired permanent residence.[16] For this reason he is denied the heightened level of protection, facilitating his expulsion from the host Member State. Crime as wrong-doing and the demonstration of a lack of integration predominates, leading to reduced protection and possible expulsion.[17]

For B the Court adopts a far more nuanced approach and insists that an overall assessment of his integrative links be taken into account when assessing whether he should benefit from the heightened protection offered in Article 28(3) of the Citizenship Directive. The strengths of his integrative links forged prior to his imprisonment appear such that a period of time spent in prison cannot automatically be taken as having broken those links.[18] Moreover, as part of the overall assessment of his degree of integration *both* the circumstances of the offence and the extent to which it does in fact represent a disconnect with society and the extent to which rehabilitation plays a role in his imprisonment must be taken into account, with the strong implication that in such a case, B may in fact benefit from the heightened protection.[19] For B, both concerns – crime as wrongdoing and rehabilitation – are at play and combined provide a far more individualised

[13] Joined Cases C-316/16 and C-424/16 *B v Land Baden-Württemberg and Secretary of State for the Home Department v Vomero* EU:C:2018:256.

[14] See ibid, paras 28–34.

[15] ibid, paras 12–17. His previous offences had been tried in simplified proceedings before a local court, presumably in light of the extenuating circumstances of his mental health difficulties and antisocial behaviour.

[16] ibid, para 33.

[17] ibid, paras 51–59

[18] ibid, para 71.

[19] ibid, paras 70–74.

assessment of his situation and the possibility of determining the degree to which he deserves to be included, despite his criminal conduct.

Between Transnational and Supranational

The use of criminal law concepts in these series of cases and legislation analysed in these two chapters has tended to alter the relationship between the individual and the host society, leading to both greater inclusion and exclusion. What is similar to both, however, is that it is the national community that remains the social unit and it is the relationship between the migrant EU citizen and the national community that is at stake. These are primarily transnational processes. However, in both rehabilitation and crime as wrong-doing, their inclusion in the social integration paradigm appears to give rise to certain supranational elements. In cases dealing with the rehabilitation of offenders, there does appear to be a Union-wide interest in their reintegration into society, an interest and responsibility that is shared amongst Member States depending on the criteria of nationality on the one hand and social integration on the other. More clear is the supranational element contained in the case of crime as wrong-doing, and its interaction with national and transnational processes. Here, while on its face the duty in question may appear negative and national, it in fact reveals positive and supranational dimensions. On the one hand, there appears to be a clear implication that the individual migrant citizen should adopt a particular attitude of respect towards the host society. On the other hand, while the content of the duty arises from national criminal law, in its nature and consequences it is in fact supranational. It is a duty imposed by EU law and entails the loss of rights of EU citizenship, in addition to whatever consequences may flow from national law. This appears to be confirmed by a certain validation by which national values justifying expulsion are endorsed by EU instruments. What appears to emerge is a duty of respect towards the values of the host society peculiar to EU citizenship, reflecting both a rebalancing of the relationship of integration between the host society and the individual – placing more emphasis on the role of the individual – and also a shift in the quality of that integration from an economic to a normative or indeed moral plane.

4

Social Integration – I. Rehabilitation and Inclusion

Introduction: Rehabilitation and Social Integration

From the external perspective citizenship – or rather its international law corollary, nationality – functions to allocate individuals to particular political units or states.[1] International law aims at a complete and discrete system whereby all individuals are allocated to a state, and only one state.[2] At this stage of the development of EU citizenship it is evident that within the European Union an additional criterion is used to establish a bond or link between an individual and a particular state, that of social integration. Social integration is usually thought of in terms of rights, the rights of the individual. But rights correlate with duties or responsibilities[3] and from the point of view of EU law the concept of social integration is a supplementary means of allocating responsibility between different states for particular individuals. EU citizens from other Member States who are sufficiently integrated into the host society are entitled to a certain degree of solidarity. Equally, so long as a degree of social integration persists, Member States are obliged to continue to extend certain, non-territorially linked, benefits to their own nationals who seek to travel to another Member State.[4] In short, the obligations and responsibilities that Member States hold towards individuals wax and wane with their degree of social integration.

[1] Rogers Brubaker, *Citizenship and Nationhood in France and Germany* (Harvard University Press, 1992) 3ff. See also Alison Kesby, *The Right to Have Rights: Citizenship, Humanity and International Law* (Oxford University Press, 2012) ch 2. See also William Walters, 'Deportation, Expulsion and the International Police of Aliens' (2000) 6 *Citizenship Studies* 265.

[2] Rainer Bauböck, *Transnational Citizenship: Migration and Rights in International Migration* (Edward Elgar Publishing, 1994) 24. In both respect it fails; there are still both de facto and de jure stateless individuals in the world today (see Kesby (n 1) ch 1). At the same time with increasing migration there is an ever-increasing number of individuals with dual or multiple nationality and an ever-increasing number of states that permit such a situation.

[3] It should be noted that the correlativity theory is contested in rights theory. See HLA Hart, 'Are there any Natural Rights?' (1955) 64 *Philosophical Review* 175, 177ff.

[4] See, for example, Case C-503/09 *Lucy Stewart v Secretary of State for Work and Pensions* EU:C:2011:500, [2011] ECR I-6497 or Joined Cases C-11/06 and C-12/06 *Rhiannon Morgan v Bezirksregierung Köln and Iris Bucher v Landrat des Kreises Düren* EU:C:2007:626, [2007] ECR I-9161. See further Chapter 3.

In the context of criminal law, the concept of social integration plays a different role. From a traditional sociological perspective, first presented by Durkheim and echoed by legal moralists such as Lord Devlin, the purpose of the criminal law was to assert the shared values of society, which in turn performed a certain integrative role.[5] Breach of the criminal law emerged from a state of anomie or normlessness, in which individuals from a certain section of society found themselves.[6] The criminal law, and in particular punishment, was society striking back at an action that damaged the normative bonds of society, thereby reasserting its values and coherence.[7] A related concept of social (re)integration exists in the area of penology as one (and at times the principal) purpose of punishment.[8] Starting from the same premise that criminal activity is a symptom of a social alienation on the part of the individual and a lack of integration in the social, economic and perhaps cultural structures of society, the goal of the treatment of offenders should therefore be to 'reintegrate' the individual into society – to rehabilitate him, to render him a 'functioning', law-abiding, member of society.[9]

The two meanings of the concept – in EU law as the means of determining the rights and responsibilities of individuals vis-à-vis particular states, and in criminal law as a symptom of social alienation and rehabilitation as a goal of the penal process – have been integrated by the Court of Justice and by the EU legislature in a series of cases and legislation dealing with where an individual should serve his or her sentence. The result of importing the logic of rehabilitation within the social integration framework of EU citizenship has been the reinforcement of the inclusion of the EU migrant in the society of the host Member State. It has altered the traditional concepts of allocating responsibility for (troublesome) criminal EU citizens, expanding and altering the concept of the national community for these purposes, while at the same time raising the possibility of a pan-European interest in the rehabilitation of the offender and a collective responsibility for communicating the wrongfulness of the conduct. This phenomenon has been highlighted in three areas in particular. Two of these deal with the internal transfer of individuals within the European Union, namely the modified 'nationality exception' in the European Arrest Warrant Framework Decision (EAW FD) and

[5] HLA Hart, *Law, Liberty and Morality* (Oxford University Press, 1962) 48. See also Paul Rock, 'Sociological Theories of Crime' in Robert Reiner, Mike Maguire and Rod Morgan (eds), *The Oxford Handbook of Criminology*, 5 edn (Oxford University Press, 2012) 44–49.

[6] Emile Durkheim, *The Division of Labour in Society*, trans George Simpson (The Free Press, 1933) ch 2.

[7] ibid, ch 2.

[8] Although similar in terms of the underlying sociological view of the causes of crime, the penological focus on rehabilitation reflects an instrumentalist and utilitarian view of punishment, the primary goal of which should be to reduce incidences of wrong-doing. See Peter Raynor and Gwen Robinson, 'Defining Rehabilitation' in Jo Campling (ed), *Rehabilitation, Crime and Justice* (Palgrave Macmillan, 2005) ch 1.

[9] There have been different understandings advanced for rehabilitation from correctional, to social integration properly speaking to a legal form of restoring the individual to a status of citizenship. For a typology of the forms and justification of different understandings of rehabilitation, see ibid, chs 1–2.

the Framework Decision on the Transfer of Sentences. Finally, the question has been raised concerning external transfers, ie transfers of EU citizens to third states and in particular whether non-national EU citizens can nonetheless benefit from protections against extradition enjoyed by a Member State's own nationals and serve their sentence in the home Member State.

The Transformation of the Nationality Exception

A staple of extradition law is the so-called nationality exemption.[10] Under this rule, common in continental legal systems but less so in the common law tradition, individuals who hold the nationality of the particular state are shielded from involuntary extradition to another state for the purposes of placing them on trial or for serving a sentence. The rationale for the exemption has been linked to a mistrust of other criminal justice systems and the particular bond established between the sovereign and its subjects reflected in the status of nationality.[11]

In the effort to secure a more effective system of transfer and a single area of justice,[12] the EAW FD sought to eliminate this exception in surrenders between Member States. Although an abolition was proposed by the Commission with its replacement by a principle on integration,[13] the final text contained a modified 'nationality exemption' in Articles 4(6) and 5(3) EAW FD.[14] Article 4(6) EAW FD is an optional provision, allowing Member States to refuse to surrender their nationals or persons 'resident or staying in' that Member State for the purposes of serving a sentence if they undertake to allow the individual to serve the sentence in that Member State. Similarly, Article 5(3) EAW FD allows Member States to impose a guarantee on the surrender of nationals or residents in cases concerning individuals standing for trial, such that the individual concerned will be able to return to the executing Member State to serve his or her sentence in the event that a custodial sentence is imposed. Thus individuals could serve their sentence in a particular Member State with which they had 'special bonds', including nationality, while at the same time remaining subject to the criminal law of other Member States.

It will be noted that unlike the nationality exemption as traditionally applied, Articles 4(6) and 5(3) EAW FD are designed to ensure that the individual

[10] See Michael Plachta, '(Non-)Extradition of Nationals: A Neverending Story' (1999) 13 *Emory International Law Review* 70.

[11] ibid.

[12] See further Chapter 5.

[13] Proposal for a Council Framework Decision on the European arrest warrant and the surrender procedures between the Member States COM(2001) 522 final [2001] OJ C332 E/18, Art 33.

[14] Framework Decision 2002/584/JHA on the European arrest warrant and the surrender procedures between Member States (EAW FD) [2002] OJ L190/1 (EAW Framework Decision).

concerned does in fact face trial and/or serve her sentence;[15] she is not entitled to escape justice. Moreover, it is the issuing Member State that is entitled to try, prosecute and sentence the individual. *Popławski*[16] expressly found that the rule contained in Article 4(6) EAW FD is not a rule of *aut dedere, aut judicare*, whereby extradition is refused in order to allow prosecution in the home Member State.[17] The individual therefore *must* face trial before the courts of the *issuing* Member State and serve a sentence determined by those courts.[18] *Sut* likewise emphasised that the sentence as determined by the issuing Member State must be served either in the executing or, if this was impossible, in the issuing Member State.[19] Priority is given to the enforcement of the sentence and the effectiveness of the EAW FD.[20] Thus if Belgium was not in a position to enforce a custodial sentence because, for the same crime it only imposed a pecuniary sanction, it could not avail of Article 4(6) and was obliged to surrender the individual to serve his sentence in the executing Member State.[21] Articles 4(6) and 5(3) EAW FD only ensure that she can serve her sentence closer to home and in particular in her 'home' Member State. Note the division of responsibility between the two Member States: the issuing Member State, ie the state against whom the (alleged) crime has been committed, tries, prosecutes and imposes a sentence on the individual; the executing Member State – the state with whom the individual citizen enjoys a bond by virtue of residence or social integration – simply carries out that sentence, if it in a position to do so.

The consequences of this abolition of the nationality exemption and the obligation to serve a sentence imposed by another Member State on the relationship between the nationals of a particular Member State and other Member States in the construction of a single area of justice is analysed in further detail in Chapter 7. This chapter is concerned with the separate matter of the relationship between EU citizens who are not nationals of the executing Member State and the extent to which the Court of Justice has used the concept of social integration to reinforce the inclusion of such citizens in the host society.

Although billed as the replacement to the 'nationality exemption', the rules contained in Articles 4(6) and 5(3) EAW FD, as they have been interpreted by the Court of Justice, are of a fundamentally different nature. Beyond ensuring that the individual concerned must stand trial and suffer punishment in the state

[15] It should be pointed out that frequently non-extradition is combined with extensive extraterritorial jurisdiction allowing the state of nationality to punish the individual for the act under its own criminal law. In such cases clearly the individual does not escape justice.

[16] Case C-579/15 *Openbaar Ministerie v Daniel Adam Popławski* EU:C:2017:503.

[17] ibid, para 45.

[18] Under extradition treaties states sometimes would undertake to surrender or prosecute. See Plachta (n 10). The difference with the EAW system is that it is the issuing Member State who prosecutes and tries the individual.

[19] Case C-514/17 *Ministère public v Marin-Simion Sut* EU:C:2018:1016.

[20] In this sense *Sut* marks a return to the logic of *Wolzenburg*, whereby a limitation on the use of an exception is deemed to enhance the effectiveness of the overall Framework Decision.

[21] *Sut* (n 19) para 37.

against whom crime is (alleged) to have been originally committed, two differences in particular stand out: the subject of the exception and the justification for the exception. The exception is now to be applied not just to nationals but to residents and, in the case of Article 4(6) EAW FD, also those 'staying in' a Member State. Similarly, in its interpretation of those particular terms the Court of Justice has justified the exception not on some essential and traditional bond between an individual and his sovereign but rather on the more modern, and more flexible, concept of rehabilitation. Both changes have been driven by an interpretation based on EU citizenship and social integration.

Subject of the Exception: From Nationals to EU Citizens

The EAW FD itself clearly indicates that the new 'exception' is to apply to both nationals and other individuals sufficiently connected with or integrated into the host society. In addition to nationals, Article 4(6) EAW FD applies to persons 'staying in or resident' in the host society, whereas Article 5(3) EAW FD applies to residents.

In interpreting these terms, the Court has drawn explicitly on EU citizenship, and in particular that part termed in Chapter 3 the social integration dimension, in order to determine the precise contours of these new groups of persons who can benefit from Articles 4(6) and 5(3) EAW FD. In *Kozłowski*,[22] in interpreting the notion of 'staying in', the Court defined the category in terms of 'connections' with the host society and in particular an 'overall assessment of various objective factors characterising the situation of that person which include … the length, nature and conditions of his presence and the family and economic connections which he has with the executing Member State'.[23]

Whereas in *Kozłowski* the link with EU citizenship concepts was implicit, in *Wolzenburg*[24] it is rendered explicit. The Dutch provision in question, requiring a five-year period of residence and a formal residence permit before non-nationals could benefit from the exemption, was deemed to be discriminatory and contrary to Article 20 TFEU and Article 18 TFEU in particular.[25] When justifying such discrimination the Member State was entitled to raise the prospect of reserving the exception for individuals with sufficiently close links to the host society, to be

[22] Case C-66/08 *Proceedings concerning the execution of a European arrest warrant issued against Szymon Kozłowski* EU:C:2008:437, [2008] ECR I-6041.

[23] ibid, para 48.

[24] Case C-123/08 *Dominic Wolzenburg* EU:C:2009:616, [2009] ECR I-9621.

[25] As pointed out by Herlin-Karnell the application of the citizenship provisions, and in particular the prohibition on non-discrimination, is both unsurprising and to be welcomed and may very well be applicable to other aspects of the Framework Decision that may have been implemented in a discriminatory manner. See, for example, the Swedish provision applying the statute barred ground for refusal to Swedish nationals only. Ester Herlin-Karnell, 'The Swedish Supreme Court and the European Arrest Warrant: Comment on the Decision of 21 March 2007, Surrending of Polish National (Ö 430-07)' [2007] *Europarättsligtidskrift* 885.

assessed according to the criteria of social integration and in light of the principle of proportionality.[26]

Finally, in *da Silva*[27] the obligations on Member States to expand the group of persons who may benefit from Article 4(6) EAW FD (and presumably by implication Article 5(3) EAW FD) was brought full circle. If Member States opt to implement Article 4(6) EAW FD in relation to their own nationals, they cannot automatically and categorically exclude nationals of other Member States.[28] In its rejection of the French government's argument that international obligations only allowed it to refuse surrender for its own nationals, the Court, relying on the Commission's submissions, pointed out that for the purposes of those obligations, a state may define the term 'national' to include those resident in that state, an option that has been exercised by a number of states.[29] In effect, the Court implied that a Member State may be required under EU law, and more particularly the duty-to-conform interpretation in combination with EU citizenship, to define, under certain international instruments, as its own nationals EU citizens who are sufficiently integrated.[30]

Nationality remains a key criterion in the operation of Articles 4(6) and 5(3) EAW FD by establishing something of a presumption that the individual enjoys strong links with the society of the Member State of which he is a national.[31] While in *Wolzenburg* the Court found that the Dutch provision automatically preventing the surrender of Netherlands nationals 'does not appear excessive' in light of their presumed strong connections to Dutch society,[32] that conclusion must be reassessed in light of *Popławski*.[33] There, the Court, following earlier pronunciations by AG Bot,[34] found that national implementing legislation should not impose an automatic ban on surrender but rather, if the Member State chose to avail of the exception, it should confer a certain discretion on the national court as to whether surrender is or is not appropriate in light of the need to ensure the subsequent social rehabilitation of the offender.[35] Thus under Article 4(6) EAW FD Member

[26] *Wolzenburg* (n 24), para 67.

[27] Case C-42/11 *Proceedings concerning the execution of a European arrest warrant issued against João Pedro Lopes Da Silva Jorge* EU:C:2012:517.

[28] ibid, para 50.

[29] ibid, paras 47–48.

[30] See also a discussion of the obligation of conform interpretation in applying Art 4(6) EAW FD in *Popławski* (n 16) paras 31ff.

[31] See, for example, Case C-579/15 *Openbaar Ministerie v Daniel Adam Popławski* (Opinion of AG Bot) EU:C:2017:116, para 36, where the Advocate General speaks of the 'very strong connection' with a state which nationality reflects, while stressing that this should not be considered an irrebuttable presumption.

[32] *Wolzenburg* (n 24) para 70.

[33] *Popławski* (n 16).

[34] See *Dominic Wolzenburg* (Opinion of AG Bot) EU:C:2009:183, para 63.

[35] *Popławski* (n 16) paras 21–22. A similar solution has been preferred in the application of the optional ground to refuse surrender in the case of trials in absentia. See Case C-271/17 *Openbaar Ministerie v Sławomir Andrzej Zdziaszek* EU:C:2017:629, paras 106–07 and Case C-270/17 *Openbaar Ministerie v Tadas Tupikas* EU:C:2017:628, paras 96–97.

States are permitted to retain the nation and nationality as a framework for the community, in that it raises a presumption in favour of social integration by including all nationals within the ratio personae of the provision. This is complemented by those with sufficient social connections to the host Member State. Thus, while ensuring that nationality remains a relevant criterion in the operation of the provisions, the Court has reinterpreted it in light of *social* links and connections rather than through some pre-social, ethnocultural notion of belonging, or some idealized link between the sovereign and its subjects. This is particularly the case after *Popławski*.[36] Nationals are presumed to have sufficiently strong connections with the society of the host society that justifies their inclusion within the scope of Article 4(6) EAW FD. However, this must be assessed in light of the individual's chances of successful rehabilitation post-release[37] and therefore, one presumes, in light of the family, economic and social links he actually enjoys in that state. Nationality here is not some form of traditional, quasi-mystical ethnocultural bond but rather a proxy (albeit perhaps in some cases a rather tenuous one) for the social connections an individual enjoys with a particular Member State.

Justification: From Nationality to Rehabilitation

The reason why social connections were deemed relevant for the operation of the exemption is therefore linked to the criminological understanding of social integration identified above. It is not the tie to the sovereign or distrust of other legal systems that justifies Articles 4(6) and 5(3) EAW FD but the more prosaic concept of rehabilitation and social reintegration. The Court first identified rehabilitation and reintegration as one of the goals of the EAW FD in *Kozłowski*. Article 4(6) EAW FD has 'the objective of enabling the executing judicial authority to give particular weight to the possibility of increasing the requested person's chances of reintegrating into society when the sentence imposed on him expires'.[38] This goal of the Framework Decision is also raised in *Wolzenburg* (albeit in tension with the other goal of the Framework Decision to create an effective system of surrender)[39] and is combined with the concept of social integration that regulates the equal treatment of migrant EU citizens.[40]

[36] *Popławski* (n 16).
[37] ibid, para 22.
[38] *Kozłowski* (n 22) para 45.
[39] See criticism in Steve Peers, 'The European Arrest Warrant: The Dilemas of Mutual Recognition, Human Rights and EU Citizenship' in Allan Rosas, Yves Bot and Egils Leits (eds), *The Court of Justice and the Construction of Europe: Analyses and Perspectives on Sixty Years of Case-Law* (Asser Press, 2013).
[40] The question of potential unequal treatment is avoided in *Popławski* on the basis that the underlying Netherlands practice of refusing to surrender only if it was possible to prosecute a foreign national in the Netherlands for the same crime for which that individual was sought for enforcement under Art 4(6) EAW FD, was itself in breach of the Framework Decision and the Charter of Fundamental Rights prohibition on *ne bis in idem*. Hence the question of discriminatory treatment did not arise. See *Popławski* (n 16) paras 45–48.

The use of the EU citizenship concept of social integration and the concept of rehabilitation are complementary. It is precisely because Article 4(6) EAW FD seeks to promote reintegration and rehabilitation that it is particularly appropriate to use the language and the test of social integration in assessing which individuals may benefit from the provision. Those EU citizens who are sufficiently integrated are entitled to equal treatment, including in their chances of rehabilitation in their now 'home' society. Moreover, their chances of rehabilitation are greater in that society because they are deemed to be integrated. The combined logic of equal treatment, EU citizenship, social integration and rehabilitation, therefore serves to reinforce the inclusion of (sufficiently integrated) EU citizens in the host society.

The result of these cases and the interpretation of Article 4(6) of the EAW FD is striking. Rather than renounce the continued importance of national communities and nationality, and abolish altogether the possibility of employing the nationality exemption, the Framework Decision and the Court have allowed Member States discretion in retaining the possibility of refusing to surrender their own nationals, albeit with the proviso that an individual assessment must be made by the executing judicial authority.[41] A distinction does remain between nationals who are presumed to have some strong link with the executing Member State and qualify automatically for consideration under the provision, and non-national EU citizens who do not. However, it is not true that following *Wolzenburg*, and even more so *da Silva*, that 'European citizenship is not yet the basic paradigm for the condition of the individual confronted with a Member State's public power within the EU's AFSJ [Area of Freedom, Security and Justice]'.[42] Such a view ignores the progressive nature of EU citizenship based on social integration, one that is strengthened and deepened over time as a greater degree of integration is reached.[43] What these cases have underlined is the importance that Member States, when operating Article 4(6) EAW FD, leave open the possibility that other EU citizens, those sufficiently integrated, may benefit from it, in effect rendering the borders of national communities for the purposes of determining the responsibility placed on a state with respect of enforcing sentences more porous and open to nationals of other Member States. Although one may agree or disagree with the discretion afforded Member States in applying this rule, it does fit with the concept of EU citizenship as a status that is strengthened as a result of social integration.[44] Furthermore,

[41] ibid, paras 22–23.

[42] Luisa Marin, '"A Spectre is Haunting Europe": European Citizenship in the Area of Freedom, Security and Justice' (2011) 17 *European Public Law* 705, 726.

[43] It is arguably also based on a mistaken understanding of the relationship between EU citizenship and nationality. EU citizenship is additional to and coexists with national citizenship. Indeed, the Court has drawn a link between the social integration dimension of EU citizenship and the national community, arguing that full integration into the national community through naturalisation is in fact the ultimate goal of EU citizenship. See Case C-165/16 *Toufik Lounes v Secretary of State for the Home Department* EU:C:2017:862.

[44] Perhaps allowing the operation which, by any standards, is a form of direct discrimination on the grounds of nationality that is not justified by one of the explicit exceptions would be problematic for internal market purists.

nor is it without interest that this has been achieved by placing the 'nationality' exemption in a more social setting, stressing the importance of social ties to the community and softening the otherwise exclusionary nature of a more traditional ethnocultural view of the national community.[45] While retaining the importance of the national community, Article 4(6) has rendered it less exclusionary and based more on the societal and legal realities inherent in EU citizenship. It has done this by employing the concept of genuine links to the host society and social integration familiar in other areas of EU citizenship law and reinforcing it with the principle of rehabilitation.

Complementing rather than replacing the logic based on a special political bond between national and state with a social bond based on integration and the responsibility of rehabilitation appears to be confirmed by the legislative history of the Framework Decision. In its original proposal the Commission emphasised the importance attached to the principle of integration in the application of the EAW system. Recital 13 of the proposal emphasises that due consideration should be given for the reintegration of criminals and that that fact should be reflected in the place in which they serve their sentence.[46] Furthermore, under Article 33 of the proposal, entitled 'The Principle of Integration', the Commission proposed an optional ground of refusal, refusing surrender and imposing the sentence in the executing state, to take into account the possible 'better possibilities of integration' in the executing state.[47] A comparison with the final version reveals the replacement of this article on the 'Principle of Integration' with more traditional provisions, retaining the category of national but extending it to other persons, namely those 'staying in' or 'resident' deemed to have a particular relationship with the executing state. The express inclusion of nationality as a ground for refusal, while extending it to other sufficiently connected individuals, does not imply a rejection of the principle of integration. Indeed, the Court has subsequently upheld its view in a number of other cases, not directly related to Article 4(6), that the Framework Decision is informed by the concept of social rehabilitation.[48] Furthermore, even in the case of nationals, national courts should retain discretion as to whether refusal to surrender would be appropriate in light of the principle of social rehabilitation.[49] However, it has accommodated the concept of nationality within the principle of social rehabilitation by implicitly accepting that nationals enjoy a particular relationship to their 'home society'

[45] Indeed, we see here echoes of Kymlicka's description of the European Union as an enterprise that 'tames rather than transcends' nationalism. See Will Kymlicka, 'Liberal Nationalism and Cosmopolitan Justice' in Seyla Benhabib (ed), *Another Cosmopolitanism* (Oxford University Press, 2006) 131.

[46] EAW Commission Proposal (n 13) recital 13.

[47] ibid, Art 33(1).

[48] See Case C-306/09 *IB* EU:C:2010:626, [2010] ECR I-10341, para 32 and Case C-192/12 PPU *Melvin West* EU:C:2012:404 (View of AG Cruz-Villalón) para 73.

[49] *Popławski* (n 16). See also the discussion of the key role that rehabilitation plays in the functioning of Art 4(6) EAW FD in *Popławski* (Opinion of AG Bot) (n 31) paras 33–38.

that facilitates reintegration. This pattern is repeated in another complementary piece of legislation, namely the Framework Decision on the Transfer of Sentences, to which we now turn.

The Framework Decision on the Transfer of Sentences

Articles 4(6) and 5(3) EAW FD have been complemented by a Framework Decision on the Transfer of Sentences that applies the principle reflected in those articles: that individuals should serve their sentence in the state with which they enjoy the closest connection and in particular that in which they would enjoy the best chances of reintegration. As with Articles 4(6) and 5(3) EAW FD, the principle of nationality is supplemented by taking into account those with a particular connection to a particular society.

The guiding principle of the Framework Decision on the Transfer of Sentences is that of social rehabilitation and reintegration.[50] Accordingly, the core of the Framework Decision is contained in Article 4, which outlines those circumstances under which a Member State must, or is encouraged to, execute a custodial sentence. As with Articles 4(6) and 5(3) EAW FD, an assessment of a sentenced person's chances of rehabilitation is to be made, taking into account his integration in the executing state and, as with Articles 4(6) and 5(3) EAW FD, the relevant criteria for determining this are nationality on the one hand, and residence with sufficient social connections on the other.

Under the Framework Decision on the Transfer of Sentences a Member State (the issuing Member State), where it considers a person's rehabilitation would be best served by a transfer, may forward a judgment to a second Member State (the executing Member State), where, after consultation with the executing Member State and the individual concerned, it is thought rehabilitation would best be served. In principle, decisions to transfer the sentence are automatically recognised and the executing Member State shall take the necessary measures to enforce it,[51] in accordance with its own laws.[52] The usual grounds for non-recognition of judgments apply, including cases involving minors, statute-barred cases, *ne bis in idem*[53] and residual cases of dual criminality.[54]

As with the Court's interpretation of the relevant provisions of the EAW FD, responsibility for sentenced persons is allocated based on a mixture of

[50] Framework Decision 2008/909/JHA on the application of the principle of mutual recognition to judgments in criminal matters imposing custodial sentences or measures involving deprivation of liberty for the purposes of their enforcement in the European Union [2008] OJ L327/27 (Framework Decision on the Transfer of Custodial Sentences) recital 9.

[51] ibid, Art 8(1).

[52] ibid, Art 17.

[53] ibid, Art 9.

[54] ibid, Art 7(3).

nationality and the social connections a person might have with a particular society. Sentenced persons are divided into three categories for the purposes of the Framework Decision: nationals of the executing state who live in that state; nationals of the executing state who will be deported to that state upon release; and, finally, other individuals. Member States are obliged to accept persons who fall into the first two categories, ie nationals who either live in the executing state or will be deported there upon release. Problematically, the consent of the sentenced person is not required in these cases. The consent of the executing Member State and the sentenced person is required for the final, residual, category. However, it does not appear that Member States may categorically refuse to accept the transfer of persons falling within the final category. Member States are instead obliged to adopt legislation outlining the criteria to be used when deciding whether to accept individuals under the final, residual, category, taking into account the goal of social rehabilitation.[55] Furthermore, they are encouraged, through reciprocal notification, to automatically accept all nationals not covered by the first two categories and residents of five years or more who will retain that right of residence upon release.[56]

In relation to EU citizens, it is arguable that the principle of non-discrimination would apply to the Framework Decision on the Transfer of Sentences in a similar fashion as in the case of Article 4(6) EAW FD. Following the logic of *Wolzenburg*[57] and *da Silva*,[58] Member States could legitimately include their own nationals, who can be assumed under those cases to already have the requisite social connections with the 'home state'. However, they would not be entitled to exclude automatically and categorically all non-national EU citizens from the application of the Framework Decision. Rather, they should ensure that relevant authorities are able 'to assess whether there is a legitimate interest which would justify the sentence imposed in the issuing Member State being enforced within the territory of the executing Member State'.[59]

Aside from the usual ground of effectiveness that drives much of the EU criminal law agenda, one of the main motivations for adopting the Framework Decision was that the international law instruments it replaced only allowed the transfer

[55] ibid, Art 4(6). An analogy may be drawn with Art 3(2) of Directive 2004/38/EC on the right of citizens of the Union and their family members to move and reside freely within the territory of the Member States [2004] OJ L158/77 (Citizenship Directive), requiring that Member States 'facilitate' the entry of a residual category of family members not falling within the more narrow group of family members for whom entry into the host Member State is a right. In Case C-83/11 *Secretary of State for the Home Department v Muhammad Sazzadur Rahman and Others* EU:C:2012:519 the Court found that the provision in question, while not obliging Member States to admit such individuals and granting significant discretion in this area, did create some procedural obligations including a right to a reasoned decision and a right to review the decision.

[56] Transfer of Custodial Sentences Framework Decision (n 50) Art 4(6).

[57] *Wolzenburg* (n 24).

[58] *Da Silva Jorge* (n 27).

[59] ibid, para 51.

of nationals.[60] The Framework Decision therefore establishes a scheme, guided by the principle of social rehabilitation, allocating responsibility to particular Member States for particular individuals. In doing so it extends this responsibility beyond the traditional criteria of nationality to include non-nationals deemed to have a particular relationship with that state. This relationship is determined by the person's social ties to the host society and may be assumed in the case of long-term or permanent residents. In making decisions under the Framework Decision Member States should take into account 'the person's attachment to the executing State, whether he or she considers it the place of family, linguistic, cultural or economic and other links to the executing state'.[61] This connection is also deemed to be established through secure residence. Member States may exercise an option to automatically accept permanent residents. If they do so it is envisaged that 'permanent residence' for the purposes of the Framework Decision refers to residence on the basis of either the status of EU citizen or long-term resident[62] – a form of 'subsidiary' EU citizenship in many respects.[63]

External Transfer and the Principle of Social Integration

More recently the Court of Justice has been faced with the question of the operation of national nationality exemptions vis-à-vis third states and in particular whether EU citizens, by virtue of the principle of non-discrimination found in Article 18 TFEU, should enjoy equal treatment also in this area, with the effect that they too would be shielded from surrender to third states. Although the law here is not yet definitively settled, the Court of Justice does appear to have concluded that a certain category of EU citizens should enjoy equal treatment in this area, namely those who have sufficient connections to the host society. Again, this reading of social integration is arrived at in light of the requirement of social rehabilitation of the offender.

In *Petruhhin*[64] the Court of Justice was faced with an extradition request on the part of an Estonian national, arrested in Latvia on foot of an international arrest warrant issued by the Russian Federation for serious narcotics crimes. Latvian law provided that Latvian nationals could not be extradited[65] but also that Latvia would exercise extraterritorial jurisdiction with respect to its nationals and

[60] Transfer of Custodial Sentences Framework Decision (n 50) recital 4.

[61] ibid, recital 9.

[62] ibid, Art 7(b).

[63] Diego Acosta Arcarazo, *The Long-Term Residence Status as a Subsidiary Form of EU Ctizenship: An Analysis of Directive 2003/109*, vol 23 (Martinus Nijhoff, 2011).

[64] Case C-182/15 *Aleksei Petruhhin v Latvijas Republikas Ģenerālprokuratūra* EU:C:2016:630.

[65] Case C-182/15 *Aleksei Petruhhin v Latvijas Republikas Ģenerālprokuratūra* (Opinion of AG Bot) EU:C:2016:330, para 9.

permanent residents.[66] In contrast, for non-nationals Latvia would not exercise its extraterritorial jurisdiction, unless they were residents.[67] Mr Petruhhin claimed this difference in treatment violated his right to equal treatment under Article 18 TFEU and that he should accordingly also enjoy immunity from extradition under the same conditions as Latvian nationals.

In its judgment the Court of Justice adopted a rather novel solution based on an innovative interpretation of the relevant Treaty articles. The matter fell within the scope of EU law by virtue of Mr Petruhhin's exercise of his rights of free movement.[68] There was a difference in treatment, which amounted to a restriction on Mr Petruhhin's right of free movement.[69] That restriction could be justified by the need to avoid impunity,[70] which, in light of Latvia not exercising extraterritorial jurisdiction with respect to non-nationals and non-residents, would occur if Mr Petruhhin were not extradited.[71] Extradition to the Russian Federation was not, however, the least restrictive option available to the Latvian authorities. Instead, the Court ruled that Latvia should make full use of the instruments of judicial cooperation available in the Area of Freedom, Security and Justice to allow for the Member State of nationality to issue an EAW if possible.[72]

In *Petruhhin* the Court used expansive language and the need for the Union in 'its relations with the wider world … to uphold and promote its values and interests and contribute to the protection of its citizens, in accordance with Article 3(5) TEU'.[73] In the subsequent case of *Pisciotti*, while not repudiating the basic test outline in *Petruhhin*, the Court adopts a much more muted tone as to precisely what this 'protection' involves. In *Pisciotti* an Italian travelling between Nigeria and Rome was apprehended in Frankfurt airport from where he was subsequently extradited to the United States to serve a sentence relating to anti-trust offences.[74] Believing his surrender to be unlawful as a breach of the principle of non-discrimination in light of the fact that Germany does not surrender its own nationals, Mr Pisciotti subsequently took an action for damages against the German state.[75]

[66] ibid, para 7.
[67] ibid, para 7.
[68] *Petruhhin* (n 64) para 31.
[69] ibid, para 32.
[70] ibid, para 37.
[71] ibid, para 39.
[72] ibid, paras 47ff. For a comment, see Martin Böse, 'Mutual Recognition, Extradition to Third Countries and Union Citizenship: *Petruhhin*' (2017) 54 *CML Rev* 1781.
[73] *Petruhhin* (n 64) para 44.
[74] Case C-191/16 *Romano Pisciotti v Bundesrepublik Deutschland* EU:C:2018:222, paras 14–25.
[75] See Christain Ritz and Bernardo Vasconcelos, 'Extradition Discrimination? Pisciotti's Legal Battle Continues as Regional Court of Berlin Refers Questions of Fundamental EU Law Principles to the CJEU' (2016) 37 *European Competition Law Review* 277. Ritz and Vasconcelos also describe in detail the myriad means by which Mr Pisciotti sought to resist his surrender, including challenges through the German court system up to and including review before the Bundesverfassungsgericht, a complaint to the Commission and finally an action against the Commission under Art 265 TFEU for a failure to act, before the General Court (Case T-403/14 *Romano Pisciotti v European Commission* EU:T:2014:692) and the Court of Justice (Case C-411/14 P *Romano Pisciotti v European Commission* EU:C:2015:48).

Despite the fact that an EU-level extradition treaty was in existence between the European Union and the United States (in contrast to the situation obtaining in *Petruhhin*), the Court applied the basic test outlined in *Petruhhin*. The matter therefore fell within the scope of EU law,[76] the difference in treatment amounted to a restriction of Mr Pisciotti's freedom of movement,[77] and that restriction could be justified in light of the need to avoid impunity.[78] However, a more proportionate solution would be informing the Member State of nationality. However, if this took place, which it did in the present case, and if that Member State failed to issue an EAW, then extradition to the third state would be the least restrictive option.[79] Despite the (contested) possibility that German law did allow for extraterritorial jurisdiction with respect to non-nationals in certain circumstances, the Court avoided assessing the extent to which equal treatment vis-à-vis German nationals could be extended to EU citizens in such situations.[80]

Both *Petruhhin* and *Pisciotti* concerned individuals sought for prosecution abroad who moreover were temporary residents or merely in transit. *Raugevicius*,[81] by contrast, concerned an individual who was a permanent resident in the host Member State and was sought for enforcement of a sentence in a third state, a situation more comparable to that obtaining in *Wolzenburg*. Here, as we might expect, the concepts of social rehabilitation and social reintegration come to the fore in resolving the situation, leading to equal treatment being extended to Mr Raugevicius. Mr Raugevicius, a Latvian, was, in contrast to Mr Petruhhin and Mr Pisciotti, a long-term resident in the host Member State, Finland, where he enjoyed a family life and also had two children of Finnish nationality. For the Court, where nationals of other Member States 'demonstrate a certain degree of integration into that State's society'[82] they are in a comparable situation to nationals of the requested Member State for the purposes of the nationality exemption. The Court appears to demonstrate a preference for an interpretation of the relevant domestic and international rules to allow Mr Raugevicius to serve his sentence in Finland.[83] In any event, however, he should enjoy a similar protection from extradition as nationals,[84] the implication being that if it is not possible for Mr Raugevicius to serve his sentence in Finland (eg if the consent of the sentencing state, Russia, is not forthcoming), his extradition may be prevented as it would be for Finnish nationals.

These three cases display an interplay of the supranational and national. In *Petruhhin* there is a general reference to the obligation on the part of the

[76] *Pisciotti* (n 74) para 34.
[77] ibid, para 44.
[78] ibid, para 47.
[79] ibid, paras 51–54.
[80] ibid, paras 49–50.
[81] Case C-247/17 *Oikeusministeriö v Denis Raugevicius* EU:C:2018:898.
[82] ibid, para 46.
[83] ibid, para 42.
[84] ibid, para 47.

European Union to promote its values and protect its citizens.[85] This is to be achieved by ensuring that the individual concerned remains on the territory of the Union. Note that it is less restrictive of an individual's rights of free movement and residence to be prosecuted in his or her Member State of nationality than to be removed to a third state. The reference to the rights of free movement and residence are also intriguing. It was argued in Chapter 3 that a broader right to the territory of the European Union is emerging in Article 20 TFEU cases but via the rights of free movement and residence. It is those rights that, in the opinion of the Court, are restricted to a greater extent by removal from the Union and by being tried and sentenced elsewhere. There is a certain protective role asserted by the Court for the Union's legal order in protecting 'its' citizens.

Importantly, however, this is not achieved via Article 20 TFEU but rather through the transnational rights of Article 21 TFEU; it is via the Member States, through the operation of the principle of equal treatment or the suite of judicial cooperation tools available in the Area of Freedom, Security and Justice, that the right to remain in the European Union is ensured. In *Petruhhin* it was the Member State of nationality which was designated to assume responsibility for the EU citizen. Although one could have considered that Member States other than that of nationality or the host Member State who would be in a position to prosecute may also be under some kind of obligation following *Petruhhin*, *Pisciotti* appeared to confirm that in fact the Member State we are concerned with is in fact the Member State of nationality. In *Pisciotti* the Court does not appear to be concerned with keeping Mr Pisciotti in the Union, or rather it is concerned with keeping Mr Pisciotti in a particular part of the Union, namely Italy. It is sufficient to meet the *Petruhhin* test for Italy to be simply kept informed of the ongoing proceedings to enable it, if it so choses, to exercise any jurisdiction it may have over its nationals. Both *Petruhhin* and especially *Pisciotti* clearly indicate that the right place for such individuals is not in their host societies or elsewhere in the Union, but rather in their Member States of nationality. Nationality is clearly the criterion to allocate such individuals to the appropriate political community; within the Union certainly, but more particularly in their Member State of nationality.

That solution is not preferred in *Raugevicius*. Here, Mr Raugevicius is entitled to equal treatment with Finnish nationals, resulting in him resisting extradition to Russia, preferably to serve his sentence in Finland, but in any event his extradition cannot be ordered. There are a number of differences between *Raugevicius* and the preceding two cases which may contribute to the different outcome. Firstly, *Raugevicius* concerns a request for extradition for enforcement rather than prosecution. Although in both cases the Member State is being asked to exercise its *ius punedi*, it is certainly possible that the Court of Justice is more willing to oblige a Member State to enforce a sentence handed down elsewhere (bearing in mind the

[85] *Petruhhin* (n 64) para 44.

possibility of permitting the Member State to impose a double-criminality requirement) rather than obliging a Member State to prosecute and punish an individual. Secondly, the relevant legal instruments, both at a domestic and at an international level, were pliable on the question of precisely who was to enjoy protection from extradition and who could serve their sentence in Finland. In its domestic law, Finland provided that in addition to nationals, permanent residents could also serve sentences handed down abroad in Finland.[86] Similarly, for the purposes of the European Convention on Extradition, Finland had included domiciled aliens within its definition of nationals.[87]

But perhaps the crucial difference between *Petruhhin* and *Pisciotti* was the position of Mr Raugevicius as a permanent resident of Finland, with, moreover, two Finnish children. We can therefore assume that Mr Raguevicius enjoyed a family and social life in Finland and that he enjoyed, in the words of the Court, 'a certain degree of integration' with host society.[88] Note the difference with *Petruhhin* and *Pisciotti*, which concerned individuals with very tenuous and limited links to the host Member States. For them, the appropriate place was their Member States of nationality. Note also in *Pisciotti* the avoidance of any assessment of non-discrimination or the possibility of prosecution taking place in Germany.[89] In *Pisciotti* the Court was clear: the right place for Mr Pisciotti is Italy, or alternatively extradition. In *Raugevicius*, the opposite is the case: Mr Raugevicius belongs in Finland, regardless of whether he can eventually serve his sentence there or not.

If in *Petruhhin* and *Pisciotti* the difference in treatment and the eventual outcome is justified by the need to avoid impunity, a growing principle in the Area of Freedom, Security and Justice,[90] the principle driving the outcome in *Raugevicius* is that of social rehabilitation, which, in a clear parallel with *Kozłowski*,[91] *Wolzenburg*[92] and *da Silva*,[93] is linked to EU citizenship through the concept of social integration.[94] This is particularly relevant in the Opinion of AG Bot who, after discussing the key role that the concept of social rehabilitation plays in determining where a sentence should be served and that individuals with strong links to the host society are in a comparable situation to nationals, finds that '[t]he rehabilitation function of the sentence thus serves as an equal treatment rule which, as such, is an integral part of the status of Union citizenship'.[95]

[86] *Raugevicius* (n 81) paras 41–42.
[87] ibid, para 7.
[88] ibid, para 46.
[89] *Pisciotti* (n 74) para 50.
[90] First coming to prominence in Case C-129/14 PPU *Criminal proceedings against Zoran Spasic* EU:C:2014:586. See further Chapter 7.
[91] *Kozłowski* (n 22).
[92] *Wolzenburg* (n 24).
[93] *Da Silva Jorge* (n 27).
[94] *Raugevicius* (n 81) paras 36–37 referring to the general logic of allowing individuals to serve sentences in their 'home' society.
[95] Case C-247/17 *Oikeusministeriö v Denis Raugevicius* (Opinion of AG Bot) EU:C:2018:616, para 72.

Azoulai has demonstrated that a dichotomy emerges in relation to EU citizens and the degree of their integration.[96] The 'good citizen' occupies the EU territory and the holds the status EU Union citizen, enabling them to enjoy the rights of EU citizenship, including a right of inclusion in the host societies. The bad citizen, on the other hand, reverts to his status as national and is returned to the national territory. This distinction turns on the concept of social integration, with the good citizen being the integrated and the bad the unintegrated.[97] Nowhere is this clearer than in the cases of *Pisciotti* and *Raugevicius*. In *Pisciotti* – concerning an individual with no links to the host society, one who is literally passing through – the sole concern of the Court is allow Italy to assert its prerogative to prosecute. In *Raugevicius* – concerning a permanent resident and father of two Finnish daughters – the Court is far more clear in assimilating this individual as a Finnish national and imposing an obligation on Finland to refuse his surrender. The two categories of citizen are clearly identified in paragraphs 47 and 48 of *Raugevicius*. The citizen who is a permanent resident 'should benefit from the provision preventing extradition from being applied to Finnish nationals and may, under the same conditions as Finnish nationals, serve their sentences on Finnish territory'.[98] If, however, such an individual 'may not be regarded as residing permanently in the requested Member State, the issue of his extradition is to be settled on the basis of the applicable national or international law'.[99] For the integrated EU citizens, the protection of EU law; for others, domestic and international law.

Conclusion: National Responsibility for a Supranational Interest

The EAW FD and the Framework Decision on the Transfer of Sentences establish a system for allocating responsibility between Member States for the imprisonment and ultimately social rehabilitation of individuals. In *Raugevicius* this has been extended to include those sought by third states for the enforcement of sentences. In this sense it resembles and reflects one of the traditional functions of citizenship, namely the allocation of responsibility for particular individuals to a particular state.[100] And in situations where extradition requests from third states are at stake, it is the Member State of nationality, which in effect gets a right of first refusal in order to prosecute.[101] It is confirmed by the obligation on Member States

[96] See Loïc Azoulai, 'Transfiguring European Citizenship: From Member State Territory to Union Territory' in Dimitry Kochenov (ed), *EU Citizenship and Federalism: The Role of Rights* (Cambridge University Press, 2017).
[97] ibid, 193ff.
[98] *Raugevicius* (n 81) para 47.
[99] ibid, para 48.
[100] See Walters (n 1).
[101] *Pisciotti* (n 74).

to take back those of their nationals who face deportation within the European Union.[102] However, it is complemented by an additional criterion of membership or belonging based on the social ties an individual holds with a particular society. This has been achieved in light of the application of the rules of EU citizenship and in particular the principle of non-discrimination on the grounds of nationality and reflects the general model of EU citizenship as a status of integration that alters the configuration of national communities and the relationship between Member States and nationals of other Member States.

It will, however, be noted that there are limits to this assimilation hinted at in the Framework Decision on the Transfer of Sentences; individuals may only 'benefit' from the Framework Decision if they maintain a right to *remain* a resident of a Member State, a fact that has been echoed in the application of Articles 4(6) and 5(3) EAW FD.[103] Both nationality and social integration operate in tandem to determine the appropriate state of responsibility for an individual. Originally, for the majority of EU citizens, it would be nationality, then after a sufficient period of time and process of integration in another Member State, it would be the criterion of social integration. However, as we shall see in the expulsion cases, treated in the next chapter, and in the residual provisions in the Transfer of Sentences Framework Decision, nationality can resurface as the allocating criterion in situations of particularly serious crimes that undo the process of integration and warrant expulsion.[104] Thus it is not the case that rehabilitation disappears from the set of criminological principles simply because in certain cases of more serious offences deportation is permissible or because in such cases the interests of the host society in excluding the serious criminal predominate.[105] Rather both principles operate, often in tension, within the broader scheme of social integration and EU citizenship; the precise manner of their deployment being a function of the relationship between the mobile EU citizen and the host society. In relation to the 'good citizen', who is socially integrated, rehabilitation appears to play a dominant role. For the 'bad citizen', who has demonstrated his repudiation of the host society's values, on the other hand, an exclusionary principle based on a moralistic approach to the criminal law predominates.[106]

[102] Transfer of Custodial Sentences Framework Decision (n 50), Art 4(1)(b).

[103] Case C-66/08 *Proceedings concerning the execution of a European arrest warrant issued against Szymon Kozłowski* (View of AG Bot) EU:C:2008:253, para 172 where he finds that the commission of criminal offences are only relevant for determining whether an individual is a resident for the purposes of Art 4(6) EAW FD where they lead to the issuing of an expulsion order under the Citizenship Directive. Similarly, in *Wolzenburg* (n 24) the Dutch rule requiring an individual to retain a right of residence in order to benefit from the national legislation implementing the EAW FD, is found to be compatible with EU law.

[104] For a similar view in relation to social integration more broadly and with reference to the territory of the European Union, see Azoulai (n 96).

[105] As suggested in Leandro Mancano, 'Punishment and Rights in European Union Citizenship: Persons or Criminals?' (2018) 24 *ELJ* 206.

[106] Adopting the scheme developed in Azoulai (n 96). See further Chapter 7.

Although it is clear that the shape of the national community has been altered through the use of the concept of social integration, it remains the national, rather than supranational community that is responsible for the rehabilitation of the offender; it is the national social context in which that rehabilitation takes place, and it is the national community of which the individual seeks membership. Clearly, nationality still remains a defining criteria for identifying individuals, a criterion that only makes sense if the relevant unit into which an individual is to be reintegrated is in fact the national community. See, for example, the priority given to Italy in *Pisciotti* as the appropriate state to prosecute and presumably punish Mr Pisciotti.[107] Similarly, the entire logic of both the line of case-law dealing with Article 4(6) EAW FD and the Transfer of Sentences Framework Decision is premised on the fact that it is the national community, or at least a local part of it, with which the individual enjoys certain connections. The economic, social, cultural and perhaps even linguistic connections and efforts at integration are directed at the host (ie national) society. As with the operation of the social integration dimension of EU citizenship generally, its operation in this context serves to preserve and highlight the role of national communities as the site of social existence, while at the same time altering their exclusive character and rendering their borders more porous.

At the same time, there are some indications that there is at least a Union-wide interest in the reintegration and indeed protection of EU citizens, making the Union as a whole a more socially cohesive and, by implication, safer place. Rehabilitation *tout court* is cited as a goal of the EAW FD and indeed the Transfer of Sentences Framework Decision, a view that has been endorsed by the Court,[108] not rehabilitation in the host society specifically. It is simply that an individual is in a better position to be rehabilitated in a place closer to his family connections and one with which he is culturally familiar. In *Raugvicius* the Advocate General notes that 'the social rehabilitation of the Union citizen in the Member State in which he has become genuinely integrated is not only in his interest but also in that of the European Union in general'.[109] Furthermore, the Court itself and AG Bot have stressed in the context of expulsion cases that there is indeed a Union-wide interest in the rehabilitation of offenders. In *Tsakouridis* the Court pointed out that Member States when deciding whether to expel an individual must be cognizant of 'the risk of compromising the social rehabilitation of the Union citizens … which … is not only in his interest but also in that of the European Union in general'.[110] The Advocate General, on whose assessment the finding is based, highlighted the existence of freedom of movement: a circumstance that rendered the

[107] *Pisciotti* (n 74).
[108] Case C-289/15 *Criminal proceedings against Jozef Grundza* EU:C:2017:4, paras 50–51.
[109] *Raugevicius* (Opinion of AG Bot) (n 95), para 67.
[110] Case C-145/09 *Land Baden-Wurttemberg v Panagiotis Tsakouridis* EU:C:2010:708, [2010] ECR I-11979, para 50.

'problem' of the offender and the 'solution' of his rehabilitation of concern not just to the host Member State and/or the state of nationality, but to the Union as a whole.[111]

Finally, we should not ignore the fact that in the operation of both of these instruments a Member State different to that which passes judgment carries out the sentence. Although the calling to account for the wrong is done by the issuing Member State, it is the executing Member State that carries out the sentence. In effect the executing Member State is *acting for* the issuing Member State. In *Popławski* the Court is very clear that prosecution by the home Member State is in no way envisaged by Article 4(6) EAW FD as substitute for prosecution by the executing Member State.[112] The judgment of *Ognyanov*[113] is illustrative of this underlying fact. Contrary to its own law on the enforcement of sentences, Bulgaria in this case was not entitled to discount periods of time spent working while the individual was in prison in Denmark for a crime committed in Denmark. Although the Court restricted itself to a textual interpretation of the Framework Decision, noting a strict temporal division of responsibility between the issuing and executing Member States corresponding to the applicable law, AG Bot was clear that what was at stake was Bulgaria enforcing a wrong committed against Denmark: '[I]t was the public order of the Kingdom of Denmark that Mr Ognyanov offended by his conduct. It is therefore the judicial authorities of that Member State that have the jurisdiction to try him and to sentence him for the offences which he committed.'[114] At the same time, once present on the territory of the executing Member State, it is that Member State that becomes responsible for the enforcement of that sentence and its law that applies from then on. There is a joint responsibility for the enforcement of the sentence on the part of both Member States, the division of which is regulated by the Framework Decision.

For Duff punishment is essentially a communicative enterprise, in which the community expresses its disapproval of the wrongful conduct and attempts to enter into a process of moral education of the offender.[115] By delegating the carrying out of the sentence to the executing Member State, the issuing Member State

[111] Case C-145/09 *Land Baden-Wurttemberg v Panagiotis Tsakouridis* (Opinion of AG Bot) EU:C:2010:322, para 95: 'Even if he is expelled from a Member State and prohibited from returning, when released the offender will be able, as a Union citizen, to exercise his freedom of movement in the other Member States. It is therefore in the general interests that the conditions of his release should be such as to dissuade him from committing crimes and, in any event not risk pushing him back into reoffending.'

[112] *Popławski* (n 16) para 45. See also para 37, which stresses that the criminal liability is imposed by the executing Member State.

[113] C-554/14 *Criminal proceedings against Ognyanov* EU:C:2016:835.

[114] Case C-554/14 *Criminal proceedings against Ognyanov* (Opinion of AG Bot) EU:C:2016:319, para 112.

[115] Antony Duff, *Punishment, Communication and Community* (Oxford University Press, 2003) 88ff. For the classic statement of this position, see Joel Feinberg, 'The Expressive Function of Punishment' (1965) 49 *The Monist* 397. See also Christopher Bennett, *The Apology Ritual: A Philosophical Theory of Punishment* (Cambridge University Press, 2008).

delegates the communicative task of punishment to the executing Member State. The result is that the Member States share the calling to account and punishment of the individual concerned. The implication is that not only is there a collective, Union-wide interest in the rehabilitation of the offender but that there is a collective, Union-wide process of communicating disapproval.

It is not therefore simply a national matter, but in addition there is a supranational dimension to this exercise. It is transnational processes, free movement and social integration, that render a criminal a supranational concern, that give rise to the possibility of an EU interest and goal in the rehabilitation of individuals and a collective Union-wide exercise in communication of disapproval for wrongful conduct. Responsibility for that rehabilitation is shared amongst the national communities of the Member States according to criteria linking an individual to a particular community – both nationality and social integration. It is the concept of rehabilitation, combined with the logic of social integration, that has reshaped and reordered the traditional system of allocating responsibility for individuals to particular states, rendered the borders of national communities more porous, and operated to reinforce the inclusion of a certain group of migrant EU citizens. At the same time, it has also, indirectly, given rise to a shared goal amongst the Member States for the rehabilitation of individuals, both in their own interests and in the interest of the European Union as a whole, and a shared exercise in communicating disapproval through punishment.

5

Social Integration – II. Wrongdoing and a Supranational Duty of Respect

Introduction: Integration, Rights and Duties

As described in Chapter 3, the concept of social integration determines the relationship between the host Member State and the citizen. The rights of EU citizenship are intended to facilitate integration; in turn, the more integrated an individual becomes, the more rights he or she is entitled to. The goal is to firmly root an individual as a member in the society of another Member State. The operation of a broad principle of non-discrimination in particular is intended to facilitate integration,[1] but other aspects of EU citizenship, including free-movement-based rights such as family reunification, are concerned with facilitating the social inclusion of an individual.[2] This occurs in a material sense in allowing individuals to participate fully in the economic, social and even political life of the host society.[3] It also operates in a symbolic fashion, by reducing instances where difference manifests between EU citizens and nationals.[4] Social integration, in conjunction with the operation of a principle of proportionality and the principle of

[1] See, for example, the rights of equal access to social services, labour rights and other welfare benefits guaranteed to migrant workers as early as 1968. See Regulation 1612/68/EEC on freedom of movement for workers within the Community [1968] OJ L257/2, since replaced by Regulation 492/11/EU on freedom of movement for workers within the Union [2011] OJ L141/1.

[2] See Case C-127/08 *Metock v Minister for Justince Equality and Law Reform* EU:C:2008:449, [2008] ECR I-6241.

[3] See Council Directive 94/80/EC laying down detailed arrangements for the exercise of the right to vote and to stand as a candidate in munipal elections by citizens of the Union residing in a Member State of which they are not naionals [1994] OJ L368/38 as amended by Council Directive 96/30/EC [1996] OJ L122/14 and Council Directive 93/109/EC laying down detailed arrangements for the exercise of the right to vote and stand as a candidate in elections to the European Parliament for citizens of the Union residing in a Member State of which they are not nationals [1993] OJ L329/34.

[4] Case C-524/06 *Heinz Huber v Bundesrepublik Deutschland* EU:C:2008:724, [2008] ECR I-9705. The logic being that in their interactions with officials of Member States, EU citizens are not to be classified as somehow 'other' and therefore more suspicious. See, in particular, the sentiments expressed by AG Maduro: '[T]he idea underlying the EU law provisions on citizenship and the right of entry and residence is that individuals should be able to integrate into the society of the host Member State and enjoy the same treatment as nationals, the system in question perpetuates the distinction between "us" – the natives – and "them" – the foreigners.' See Case C-524/06 *Heinz Huber v Bundesrepublik Deutschland* (Opinion of AG Poiares Maduro) EU:C:2008:194, para 15.

non-discrimination, has become the axis along which the extent of an individual's membership in the host society, and hence the responsibilities of that society towards him or her, is measured.[5]

The relationship between rights and social integration is typically mutually reinforcing and progressive. Rights of free movement, residence and non-discrimination, access to the labour market, and family reunification are granted to individuals in order to allow them to move to and engage in a process of integration into the host society. EU citizenship, and in particular the status of permanent residence, is therefore intended to be 'a genuine vehicle for integration into the society of the host Member State',[6] a fact recently underlined by the Court of Justice in the judgment in *Lounes*.[7] In turn, the more integrated an individual becomes, the more rights he or she is entitled to. Or to put it more accurately, the less ability a Member State will have to legitimately discriminate against him or her in increasing areas of economic and social life. As well as being reinforcing, the relationship was, until recent years,[8] seen as operating exclusively in a progressive manner; rights and integration increase with each other. EU citizenship can therefore be seen as the basis of an impressive set of transnational rights vis-à-vis other Member States; national rights guaranteed by supranational law[9] and operating according to a logic of integration. Like other forms of citizenship, it is a membership status complete with rights, but it is one that operates within a unique political entity and one that functions primarily on a transnational basis.

EU citizenship therefore determines a set of rights and responsibilities between EU citizens and the host Member State. However, that relationship is curiously lop-sided with rights held primarily by the EU citizen and the responsibilities in turn held by the host Member State. What EU citizenship conspicuously appears to lack is a set of duties. Although the Treaty proudly declares that 'Citizens of the Union shall enjoy the rights and be subject to the duties provided for in the Treaties',[10] the subsequent list contains no duties, and commentators

[5] Case C-209/03 *The Queen (on the application of Dany Bidar) v London Borough v Ealing, Sec of State for Education and Skills* EU:C:2005:169, [2005] ECR I-2119. See further Chapter 1. Although there is a separate strand of case-law that bases a citizen's inclusion on mere residence [see Gareth Davies, '"Any Place I Hang my Hat?" or: Residence is the New Nationality' (2005) 11 *ELJ* 43] this has been losing out to an increasingly 'qualitative' understanding of social integration as a means of regulating the boundaries of national communities and responsibilities of host Member States. See Daniel Thym, 'The Elusive Limits of Solidarity: Residence Rights of and Social Benefits for Economically Inactive Union Citizens' (2014) 52 *CML Rev* 17, citing in particular the judgment in Case C-333/13 *Elisabeta Dano & Florin Dano v Jobcenter Leipzig* EU:C:2014:2358.

[6] Directive 2004/38/EC on the right of citizens of the Union and their family members to move and reside freely within the territory of the Member States [2004] OJ L158/77 (Citizenship Directive) preamble point (18).

[7] Case C-165/16 *Toufik Lounes v Secretary of State for the Home Department* EU:C:2017:862.

[8] See, in particular, the line of case-law associated with *Dano* (n 5). This turn in the case-law of the Court has been extensively analysed. For a variety of perspectives, see the contributions in Daniel Thym (ed), *Questioning EU Citizenship: Judges and the Limits of Free Movement and Solidarity in the EU* (Hart Publishing, 2017).

[9] Paul Magnette, *La Citoyennéte Européenne* (Editions de l'Université de Bruxelles 1999).

[10] Treaty on the Functioning of the European Union, Art 20(2).

have struggled to find any other set of EU-citizenship-specific duties.[11] The decline of citizenship duties is also apparent at a national level[12] but at an EU level it is even more striking. Duties that may be considered 'citizenship-like' at a national level, such as paying taxes, jury service, voting and military service, do not have any analogy at an EU level.[13]

However, perhaps attempting to locate the duties of EU citizenship at a supranational level is misguided. EU citizenship is a transnational status and it is through transnational processes that duties are most likely to be created. A series of cases dealing with the effect of criminal activity on EU rights have challenged both assumptions regarding EU citizenship: the progressive relationship between rights and integration and in turn the absence of duties on the part of EU citizens. Two areas in particular have been instrumental in this development: the interpretation of the new concept of 'imperative reason of public security' in expulsion cases, and the effect of imprisonment on qualifying periods for residence rights under the Citizenship Directive. In assessing the effect of criminal activities on the integration process of particular individuals and the impact this may have on their rights under the Citizenship Directive, the Court has fashioned a general duty of respect for the host society of the Member State. Social integration is therefore maintained as the principle by which the relationship between the individual and the host Member State is regulated but – combined with a particular reading of criminal law – is also used to rebalance this relationship and impose obligations on EU citizens. Although in appearance a duty under national law, this is in fact a supranational duty or rather has a supranational dimension, imposed by EU law and with consequences in EU law for the rights of EU citizenship and reflecting supranational values; it is a supranational duty of respect for national communities.

[11] See Dmitry Kochenov, 'EU Citizenship without Duties' (2014) 20 *ELJ* 482. Eleftheriadis does attempt to justify obligations individual citizens may have towards the Union and hence obedience to its laws as forming part of a general cosmopolitan duty to respect the legitimate moral creations (states and international organisations) of others. See Pavlos Eleftheriadis, 'Citizenship and Obligation' in Julie Dickson and Pavlos Eleftheriadis (eds), *Philosophical Foundations of European Union Law* (Oxford University Press, 2012).

[12] Kochenov (n 11).

[13] There is an argument that the Union levies taxes indirectly, in particular through its own resources. Similarly, whether the ability to vote in European parliamentary elections could be considered an EU duty is open to question. It is unclear whether the European Parliament does in fact represent a European people or is simply an aggregation of representatives of national peoples. See Case C-145/04 *Spain v UK* EU:C:2006:543, [2004] ECR I-7902 and Joined Cases C-300/04 *Eman and Sevinger v College van Burgemeester en Wethouders van Den Haag* EU:C:2006:545, [2006] ECR I-8055 and comment by Jo Shaw, 'The Political Representation of Europe's Citizens: Developments' (2008) 4 *European Constitutional Law Review* 162. More recently, however, *Delvigne*, confirming a direct right conferred on EU citizens to vote in European parliamentary elections even in the absence of movement, appears to confirm the emergence of a single European demos (at least formally) for the purposes of the EP elections. See Case C-650/13 *Thierry Delvigne v Commune de Lesparre Médoc and Préfet de la Gironde* EU:C:2015:648 and comment in Stephen Coutts, 'Delvigne: A Multilevelled Political Citizenship' (2017) 42 *EL Rev* 867.

Crime as Wrongdoing: Expulsion

In a number of cases, interpreting the concepts of public policy and public security, the Court has in fact reorientated the interpretation of the public policy and public security exception towards a normative perspective. This is even more apparent given the clear wording and expectations attached to Article 28(3) of the Citizenship Directive that speak of threats to public security only.

The Traditional View: Public Policy as Risk Minimisation

Member States have always had the ability to expel EU citizens[14] for having committed sufficiently serious crimes. The residual and exceptional power on the part of Member States to expel unwanted individuals was based on a catch-all public policy and public security derogation. For the most part considered synonymous, the terms are best understood as corresponding to the French term *ordre public* – public order, or more accurately public policy.[15] The criminal law, as a set of imperative rules designed to secure the rights and freedoms of individuals,[16] is necessarily a part of public policy.[17] All criminal laws are therefore rules of public policy,[18] even if not all public policy rules are necessarily reflected in the criminal law;[19] criminal law is a subset of public policy rules, but a significant subset. That the public policy and public security derogation contained in EU citizenship covers criminal acts is beyond doubt.[20] Most of the instances of expulsion are

[14] And before 1992 nationals of other Member States exercising rights as workers, self-employed or some other status. See Directive 64/221/EEC on the co-ordination of special measures concerning the movement and residence of foreign nationals which are justified on grounds of public policy, public security or public health [1964] OJ L117, since replaced by Citizenship Directive (n 6) ch VI.

[15] Perhaps not directly translatable: see Case C-554/13 *Z, Zh & O v Staatssecretaris van Veiligheid en Justie* (Opinion of AG Sharpston) EU:C:2015:94 para 33. For an overview of the use of the concept in EU law, see Georges Karydis, 'L'ordre public dans l'ordre juridique communautaire: un concept à contenu variable' [2002] *Revue trimestrielle de droit européen* 1.

[16] For such an account of *ordre public*, see Etienne Picard, 'La Fonction de l'Ordre Public dans l'Ordre Juridique' in Marie-Joëlle Redor (ed), *L'ordre public: Ordre public ou ordres publics? Ordre public et droits fondamentaux* (Bruylant, 2001).

[17] Agnes Cerf, 'Ordre Public, Droit Pénal et Droits Fondamentaux' in Marie-Joëlle Redor (ed), *L'ordre public: Ordre public ou ordres publics? Ordre public et droits fondamentaux* (Bruylant, 2001).

[18] See Case C-554/13 *Z, Zh & O v Staatssecretaris van Veiligheid en Justie* EU:C:2015:377 (n 15): 'The rules of criminal law are all [public order] rules in the sense that they are imperative rules … a breach of a Member State's criminal law therefore equates to an act contrary to [public order]' (paras 61–62).

[19] See Case 41/74 *van Duyn v Home Office* EU:C:1974:133, [1974] ECR 1337 concerning a public policy related to limitations on the Church of Scientology. More recently, see the EFTA Court case of Case E-15/12 *Jan Anfinn Wahl v the Icelandic State* [2013] EFTA Ct Rep 534 relating to a similar policy with respect of the Hell's Angels Motorcycle group. Note that although not relating to directly criminalised acts or organisations, there must be some objective evidence of a stated policy on the part of the Member State concerned.

[20] Although note not all threats to public order and hence not all crimes will fall within the derogation; threats need to reach a certain level of seriousness. See *Z, ZH & O* (Opinion of AG Sharpston) (n 15).

based on criminal conduct of individuals. As the Commission pithily puts it, the Citizenship Directive 'allows Member States to expel criminals'.[21]

Although a prerogative of the Member States and a residue of the traditionally unlimited discretionary powers of the sovereign in this area,[22] this power has always been circumscribed in EU law. In particular, the principle of proportionality, in combination with the concept of social integration, has come to play an important role in its operation.[23] The more integrated an individual, the more his or her interests would be harmed by expulsion and a greater risk would be required in order to justify his or her expulsion.[24] The use of the proportionality principle in this fashion draws explicitly and extensively from the case-law of the European Court of Human Rights (ECtHR) on the right to respect for family and private life found in Article 8 of the ECHR.[25] It is also coherent with the general view of EU citizenship based on social integration and the mutually reinforcing and progressive relationship between social integration and the rights of an individual migrant; the more integrated, the more links, familial, social, economic, etc, one has established with the society of the host Member State, the more disproportionate an expulsion decision would be and the greater protection one enjoys from expulsion. The use of proportionality in this context therefore neatly dovetails with the overall operation of EU citizenship as a transnational status of social integration.

[21] Report from the Commission to the European Parliament and the Council on the application of Directive 2004/38/EC on the right of citizens of the Union and their family members to move and reside freely within the territory of the Member States COM(2008) 840 final 7.

[22] See Gérard Lyon-Caen, 'La réserve d'ordre public en matiere de liberé d'etablissement et de libre circulation' (1966) *Revue trimestrielle de droit européen* 693.

[23] Another important limitation is the definition of what constitutes public policy or public security. Although it is a national concept to be defined in terms of national laws it must comply with a general EU law condition that it be a 'genuine and sufficiently serious threats to the requirements of public policy affecting one of the fundamental interests of society'. See Case 30/77 *Regina v Pierre Bouchereau* EU:C:1977:172, [1977] ECR 1999, para 35. See also Citizenship Directive (n 6) Art 27(2).

[24] The inclusion of the proportionality principle within the law on expulsion of EU citizens was contained in the Opinion of AG Pergola in Case C-348/96 *Criminal Proceedings against Donatella Calfa* EU:C:1999:6, [1999] ECR I-11 and could be said to be implicit in the Court's judgment. It was explicitly and in a detailed fashion outlined by the Court in Joined Cases C-482/01 and C-493/01 *Georgios Ofanopoulos et al and Raffaele Oliveri v Land Baden-Würtemberg* EU:C:2004:262, [2004] ECR I-5257 in which the Court stated that: '[T]he necessity of observing the principle of proportionality must be emphasized. To assess whether the interference envisaged is proportionate to the legitimate aim pursued, in this instance the protection of public policy, account must be taken, particularly of the nature and seriousness of the offences committed by the person concerned, the length of his residence in the host Member State, the period which has elapsed since the commission of the offence, the family circumstances of the person concerned and the seriousness of the difficulties which the spouse and any of their children risk facing in the country of origin of the person concerned' (para 99). For a recent statement of the need to respect the principle of proportionality and its link with Art 7 CFR, see Joined Cases C-331/16 and C-366/16 *K v Staatssecretaris van Veiligheid en Justitie and HF v Belgische Staat* EU:C:2018:296, paras 61–63.

[25] See *Boultif v Switzerland* ECHR 2001-IX. See also *Maslov v Austria* App no 1683/03 (ECtHR, 23 June 2008). For a critical discussion of the ECtHR's case-law in the area, see Colin Harvey, 'Promoting Insecurity: Public Order Explusion and the ECHR' in Elspeth Guild and Paul Minderhoud (eds), *Security of Residence and Expulsion: Protection of Aliens in Europe* (Kluwer International, 2001).

It is important to note that in this view the criminal law, and in particular breaches of the criminal law, are seen primarily as *risks* to public policy or public order; it is a harm-based and future-orientated assessment. Criminal activity is seen as disturbing public order and the security and safety of citizens. Sufficiently serious breaches of the criminal law are seen as manifesting threats on the part of the individual concerned to public policy and public security. It is the present *threat* posed (threat being a future and probability-orientated assessment) rather than the past conduct that is important. The previous criminal convictions of an individual are relevant, but only insofar as they indicate a propensity to commit crimes in the future.[26] The Court speaks of the 'danger which the person represents'.[27] Under this version of the proportionality assessment, the social integration and the risk posed by the individual are balanced against each other as competing interests. To borrow from the ECtHR's jurisprudence on which the Court of Justice draws:

> The Court's task consists in ascertaining whether in the circumstances the refusal to renew the applicant's residence permit struck a fair balance between the relevant interests, namely the applicant's right to respect for his family life, on the one hand, and the prevention of disorder or crime, on the other.[28]

Social integration, and in particular the bonds created between the migrant individual and the host society, be they familial, social or economic, are not undone or negated by the criminal act or the perceived threat to public policy and public security. Rather the threat or harm to one outweighs the harm to the other; it is simply a balancing exercise.

The operation of public policy, and in particular the executive discretion it is associated with, is one of the main areas in which nationals differ from aliens.[29] Indeed, for some, expulsion or deportation is constitutive of citizenship, in the sense that the possibility or impossibility of removal from the national territory effective defines the status of citizenship.[30] One could therefore be forgiven for thinking that with the advent of EU citizenship – in theory a legally reinforced and politically symbolic membership status different in kind from alienship – the discretion afforded Member States with respect to EU citizens would be even further restricted and circumscribed.[31] This was the Commission's perspective,

[26] Although the past conduct may be relevant in assessing the present threat: see *Bouchereau* (n 22) para 29.

[27] *Calfa* (n 24) para 26.

[28] *Boultif v Switzerland* (n 25) para 47.

[29] Lyon-Caen (n 21) 693–94.

[30] Bridget Anderson, Matthew J Gibney and Emanuela Paoletti, 'Citizenship, Deportation and the Boundaries of Beloning' (2011) 15 *Citizenship Studies* 547.

[31] The separate question of extending the protections offered by Directive 221/64/EEC to all EU citizens and not simply the economically active was addressed by the Court in Case C-50/06 *Commission v Netherlands* EU:C:2007:325, [2007] ECR I-4383, which did in fact extend the scope of the Directive.

even before the adoption of the new Citizenship Directive,[32] as noted in a Communication of 1999:

> The new concept of citizenship of the Union should play a role in the overall assessment of the position of a Union citizen in case national authorities consider his/her expulsion or non-admission for reasons of public order, public security or public health. Article 18 of the EC Treaty [now Article 21 TFEU] should be accorded its full weight by national authorities when they contemplate the application of Directive 64/221/EEC to a Union citizen.[33]

Indeed, in its comparison with TCNs, and in particular Turkish nationals, the Court did appear to recognise a new paradigm in expulsion cases instituted by the introduction of the concept of EU citizenship,[34] and in one case immediately before the transposition of the Citizenship Directive it invoked the oft-repeated formula of EU citizenship as the fundamental status of nationals of Member States.[35]

This new, increased protection by virtue of the nature of EU citizenship appeared to be also reflected in legislative developments with the Citizenship Directive introducing a new, graduated and improved system of protection for EU citizens, in particular those of longer residence in the host society. This new system reflected the principle of proportionality and its application in light of the concept of social integration.[36] Three groups of EU citizens were established: a general category could be expelled for reasons of public policy and public security;[37] a second category that held permanent residence could be expelled only for 'serious reasons of public policy and public security';[38] and a final category consisting of EU citizens resident for ten years or more and minors could be expelled only for 'imperative reasons of public security'.[39] It will be noted that for the final category the EU legislature differentiated both in terms of degree and kind; the threat was

[32] Citizenship Directive (n 6).

[33] European Commission, *Communication on the Special Measures concerning the Movement and Residence of Citizens of the Union which are Justified on Grounds of Public Policy, Public Security or Public Health* COM(1999) 372 final, 1999. With the implication, perhaps, that similar considerations would not apply to other individuals covered by the Directive, notably family members of EU citizens.

[34] Case C-371/08 *Nural Ziebell v Land Baden-Wurtenmburg* EU:C:2011:809, [2011] ECR I-12735: 'It thus follows from the substantial differences to be found not only in their wording but also in their object and purpose between the rules relating to the EEC-Treaty Association and European Union law concerning citizenship that the two legal schemes in question cannot be considered equivalent' (para 73). More recently the Court has stressed the differences, and also the similarities, between the public security regimes relevant to TCNs and EU citizens in Case C-544/15 *Sahar Fahimian v Bundesrepublik Deutschland* EU:C:2017:255.

[35] *Ofanopoulous and Oliveri* (n 24) para 65.

[36] Citizenship Directive (n 6) preamble point 23.

[37] Ibid, Art 28(1).

[38] Ibid, Art 28(2).

[39] Ibid, Art 28(3).

to be more serious ('imperative') and it was also to be restricted to threats to public security, excluding reasons of public policy. The Commission for its part emphasised this distinction in its guidance on the implementation of the Directive, stressing as follows:

> It is crucial that Member States define clearly the protected interests of society, and make a clear distinction between public policy and public security. The latter cannot be extended to measures that should be covered by the former. *Public security* is generally interpreted to cover both internal and external security along the lines of preserving the integrity of the territory of the Member State and its institutions. *Public policy* is generally interpreted along the lines of preventing disturbance of social order.[40]

Thus while public policy might, in certain circumstances, refer to the public morality of a Member State,[41] it would appear that public security would not. However, in its interpretation of the provision, the Court of Justice has taken a remarkably different approach.

Public Security as Values

In three cases, the Court of Justice has interpreted the concept of public security in a strikingly different manner to that suggested by the Commission or a plain reading of the text.[42] In a nutshell, it has interpreted public security in normative terms, allowing it to be defined as reflecting the fundamental interests of the society of a Member State based on its particular values and has allowed a moral assessment of the individual's conduct to be used as a basis for his or her expulsion. In *Tsakouridis* the individual in question had been resident in Germany since birth with the exception of two brief periods during which he returned to Greece, the country of his nationality. After a number of convictions for petty crimes he was convicted for six years for drug possession and membership of a criminal organisation.[43] In *PI* an expulsion order was made following Mr I's conviction for continuous sexual abuse of his young stepdaughter over a seven-year period.[44] In both cases what was at stake was the interpretation of a new formula, 'imperative reasons of public security' as distinct from simply 'public policy and public security'. In *K and HF* an EU citizen, on the one hand, and a family member of

[40] *Communication from the Commission to the European Parliament and the Council on guidance for better transposition and application of Directive 2004/38/EC on the right of citizens of the Union and their family members to move and reside freely within the territory of the Member States* COM(2009) 313 final, 10 (emphasis in original).

[41] See, for example, *van Duyn* (n 19) and Joined Cases 115/81 and 116/81 *Adoui and Cornuaille v Belgium* EU:C:1982:183, [1982] ECR 1665.

[42] See Georgios Anagnostaras, 'Enhanced Protection of EU Nationals against Expulsion and Concept of Internal Public Security: Comment on the PI Case' (2012) 37 *EL Rev* 627.

[43] Case C-145/09 *Land Baden-Wurttemberg v Panagiotis Tsakouridis* EU:C:2010:708, [2010] ECR I-11979.

[44] Case C-348/09 *PI v Oberburgermeisterin der Stadt Remscheid* EU:C:2012:300.

an EU citizen, on the other, had been excluded from refugee status on the basis of having been suspected of having committed war crimes.[45] On the basis of this decision of the asylum authorities the two individuals were denied residence in the Netherlands and Belgium, respectively. Through its judgments, and in particular in a number of shifts between *Tsakouridis* and *PI*, the Court of Justice has interpreted imperative reasons of public security in terms of the host society's values: it has focused not on potential harm to the integrity of the Member State and its institutions or its territorial integrity but rather on the wrongness and blameworthiness of the individual's actions. *K and HF*, dealing with the value-loaded language of war crimes and crimes against humanity, confirmed this trend in unambiguous language.

Three shifts between *Tsakouridis* and *PI* contribute to this new understanding of 'public security': the collapse of any distinction between the concepts of public security and public policy and the consequential extension of the definition of public security to cover public policy; the definition of seriousness in terms of the blameworthiness of the act rather than any threatened harm; and finally the individualised rather than systemic nature of the threat, a harm and wrong that while directly experienced by the individual is nonetheless shared by the host society. Together they point to a reorientation of the understanding of the expulsion power of Member States from a security measure aimed at future harms to a technique for imposing a general duty of respect for the host society's values.

Firstly, in *PI* the Court abandons any attempt to make a conceptual distinction between the notions of public policy and public security, instead defining both as reflecting the 'fundamental interests of society' as arising from the particular values of the Member State in question. As noted above, Article 28(3) of the Citizenship Directive appears to make a distinction in both degree and kind between public policy and public security, on the one hand, and imperative reasons of public security, on the other. In *Tsakouridis* the Court appears to endorse this difference in kind, noting that public security specifically refers to 'the functioning of institutions and essential public services and the survival of the population'.[46] However, in its application to the threat in question – drug trafficking – the Court gives the definition of an imperative threat to public security a particularly wide scope, noting the systemic economic and social threats that drug trafficking (along with organised crime) poses to the 'population as a whole or a large part of it'.[47] In *PI*, however, the Court abandons any attempt to maintain a definitional distinction between its previous definition of public policy and public security, and public security *simpliciter*. An imperative threat to public security is simply one that threatens a fundamental interest of society and the calm and physical security of the population (note how the caveat 'as a whole or a large part' is dropped).[48]

[45] *K & HF* (n 24).
[46] *Tsakouridis* (n 43) para 44.
[47] ibid, para 47.
[48] *PI* (n 44) para 28.

In *K and HF* the Court of Justice describes how a 'direct threat to the peace of mind … of the population' can constitute a threat to internal security.[49] A threat to a 'fundamental interest of society' is the classic formula employed by the Court over decades in the context of expulsions for reasons of public policy.[50] One would have expected a ground for expulsion based on public security alone to be different. The result is that a threat to 'public security' is to be defined as a threat to the social order of the host society, including its values. The only difference is that in order to invoke Article 28(3) of the Citizenship Directive, a Member State must establish 'a particularly serious' threat, something flowing from the imperative quality of such a reason.

That seriousness, however, appears to be defined in terms of the moral blameworthiness of the individual and his act rather than the degree of harm or threat he may pose. An ambiguity existed in *Tsakouridis* on this point: on the one hand, the Court noted that 'drug addiction represents a serious evil for the individual';[51] on the other hand, there was a concerted effort on the part of the Court to present drug trafficking (again linked to organised crime) as an activity that presented serious harms both to individuals and society at large.[52] That ambiguity diminishes significantly in *PI*. In *PI* conduct of the individual in question is regarded as particularly serious for a variety of reasons that stem more from the abhorrent and wrongful nature of the crime rather than the physical harm or certainly the future threat posed. The sexual exploitation of children is noted as a serious violation of the rights of children, as was the fact that the crime was committed against a minor and the fact that the perpetrator of the crime was in a position of responsibility.[53] In its description of the case, relying on the referral from the national court, the Court of Justice notes the continuous suffering endured, the brutal nature of the crime and the perpetrator's apparent lack of remorse.[54] Some of these factors may be construed as elements pointing to the potential threat that Mr I continues to pose to the safety of other young girls and women. However, they are principally used to determine the blameworthiness of the crime in terms of past harm caused and moral culpability. There is an undeniable moralistic undertone in

[49] *K & HF* (n 24) para 42.

[50] *Bouchereau* (n 22) para 35. For an account, see Niamh Níc Shuibhne, 'Derogating from the Free Movement of Persons. When Can EU Citizens Be Deported?' (2005–06) 8 *Cambridge Yearbook of European Legal Studies* 187, 188–93.

[51] *Tsakouridis* (n 43) para 44.

[52] ibid, para 46 with the Court referring to the preamble of the Framework Decision on Drug Trafficking which in turn notes the threat posed by drug trafficking to 'health, safety and the quality of life of citizens of the Union and to the legal economy, stability and security of the Member States'. See Framework Decision 2004/757/JHA laying down minimum provisions on the constituent elements of criminal acts and penalties in the field of illicit drug trafficking [2004] OJ L335/8, preamble point (1).

[53] *PI* (n 44) paras 26–27. Recently reaffirmed in Case C-193/16 *E v Subdelegación del Gobierno en Álava* EU:C:2017:542, paras 20–21.

[54] *PI* (n 44) paras 11–13.

the Court's consideration of Mr I's conduct throughout the judgment. The seriousness appears to be related to the blameworthiness of Mr I's actions – his mental state and culpability – rather than to any propensity for future harm. The suffering of the victim was indeed great and the culpability of Mr I clear. These point to the seriousness of the act certainly, but in terms of blameworthiness, rather than potential harm to the broader population.

The third shift from *Tsakouridis* to *PI* is the individualised nature of the threat; the threat only impacted on a single individual rather than society as a whole.[55] It would appear that Mr I was not part of a broader network, nor is there any evidence to suggest that he committed similar crimes outside the confines of the family home. The implication is that Mr I did not, nor would not, pose any threat outside that rather narrow context.[56] In *Tsakouridis* the Court appears at pains to stress the systemic nature of drug trafficking as a crime, one with wide-ranging economic and social consequences beyond the immediate victims; a 'diffuse crime'.[57] In *PI*, on the other hand, as noted by AG Bot, the crime did not present similar characteristics. Mr I was not part of a broader network, it was not an instance of the sexual abuse of children linked to the broader phenomenon of human trafficking, nor was it related to child pornography and its wider dissemination. There was no indication that this was part of a broader threat to 'the population as a whole' as in *Tsakouridis*, rather the harm done and the supposed threat posed was to an individual.

However, although targeted against an individual victim, it is important to note the social and public dimension of this wrong, a feature which appears to justify the Court's conclusion that such threats can in fact constitute a threat to *public* security. The direct harm and suffering is borne by the individual in question; however, it is framed by the Court in terms of an assault on the 'fundamental interests of the society' in question based on 'its particular values'.[58] These two positions can be reconciled by an appeal to the concept of 'shared wrongs'.[59] It is through the suffering of the individual that society, in this case the Member State's society, is wronged. Through common membership, the public as a whole shares the wrong arising from the harm suffered directly by the individual; by harming one in such a serious and wrongful manner the moral outrage is felt by all. This is different from a generalised threat of harm to the population but it does render the private harm a public wrong.

[55] Note this is to be distinguished from the origin of the threat: there must always be an individualized assessment of the threat posed by a particular individual. General measures of deterrence or general policies of deporting following a sentence of a particular length are not permitted. See *Bouchereau* (n 22).

[56] Case C-348/09 *PI v Oberburgermeisterin der Stadt Remscheid* (Opinion of AG Bot) EU:C:2012:123, para 44.

[57] *Tsakouridis* (n 43) para 46.

[58] Again see *E* (n 53) para 21.

[59] See SE Marshall and RA Duff, 'Criminalization and Sharing Wrongs' (1998) 11 *Canadian Journal of Law and Jurisprudence* 7.

These three points – defining public security in terms of the fundamental interest of society; defining seriousness in terms of the blameworthiness of the act; and allowing the derogation to be used in instances where the harm is to an individual rather than society – all point to a view of public security and the criminal law that is normative and defined in terms of values. It is not the harm or threat of harm caused to the state, its institutions or indeed the general population that is at stake. What is at stake is the offence caused by the perpetrator towards the host society by his wrongful acts and through the individual harm society as a whole is offended. It therefore appears to mark a shift from the previous conceptions of threats to public policy and public security and proportionality.[60]

This shift is confirmed in *K and HF*. In *K and HF* the place of values is made explicit both in the definition of a threat to public policy and public security, and secondly in the presence of such a threat in the past conduct of an individual. The Court notes that France and the UK (intervening) consider that excluding individuals from refugee status on the grounds found in the Geneva Convention and in Article 12(2) of Directive 2011/95/EC[61] 'contribute[s] … to ensuring the protection of the fundamental values of society in a Member State',[62] a position that is endorsed by the Court itself in its judgment, noting that:

> [I]t must be emphasised that the crimes and acts that are [the subject of exclusion orders] seriously undermined both fundamental values such as respect for human dignity and human rights, on which as stated in Article 2 TEU, the European Union is founded, and the peace which it is the Union's aim to promote, under Article 3 TEU.[63]

Furthermore, in its assessment as to whether such individuals, decades after the alleged incidents which formed the basis of the exclusion orders took place, continue to represent such a threat, the Court notes that while ordinarily past conduct alone is not sufficient to constitute a future threat, it can be the case that in extreme circumstances where the crimes committed were of an exceptional gravity, past conduct alone can, it seems, constitute sufficient grounds for a present threat, regardless of the propensity to act in a similar fashion in the future. This is due not to any threat or risk that the person poses to the security of the Member State but because of his 'mere presence … in the territory of the host Member State',[64] based on the fact that his past conduct demonstrates 'the persistence in him of a disposition hostile to the fundamental values enshrined in Articles 2 and 3 TEU'.[65]

[60] Again taking into account the limited existence of some cases of expulsion based on public morality. See *van Duyn* (n 19) and *Adoui and Cornuaille* (n 41). In the context of the free movement of goods, see Case 34/79 *Regina v Maurice Donald Henn and John Frederick Ernest Darby* EU:C:1979:295, [1979] ECR 3795.

[61] Directive 2011/95/EU on standards for the qualification of third-country nationals or stateless persons as beneficiaries of international protection, for a uniform status for refugees or for persons eligible for subsidiary protection, and for the content of the protection granted [2011] OJ L337/9.

[62] *K & HF* (n 24) para 44.

[63] ibid, para 46.

[64] ibid, para 51.

[65] ibid, para 60.

It would seem that the mere presence of such an individual, who has committed such wrongs and offended against the values of the host society in such a serious manner, is intolerable and in fact is a threat to the 'peace of mind' of the population of the host society, sufficient to constitute a threat to the public security.

It should be recognised that *K and HF* represents quite unusual circumstances that particularly lend themselves to an interpretation based on the underlying moral quality of the acts of the individuals concerned. As is evident from the very nature of war crimes, they are concerned with acts that are unlikely to recur in the future,[66] and are particularly abhorrent and contrary to a broad set of values endorsed by the international community as well as the Member States and the Union itself. However, while exceptional in its circumstances, the basic findings in *K and HF* – that criminal acts[67] represent a threat to the values of the host society and that the commission of such acts represent 'a disposition hostile to the values of the host society' – are based on findings dealing with the impact of imprisonment on the acquisition of rights under the Citizenship Directive analysed in the next section. The novelty in *K and HF* is the finding by the Court that such a disposition, and the mere presence of an individual who holds such a disposition, is sufficient, in certain circumstances to constitute a threat to the fundamental values of the host society, so as to justify expulsion. In doing so the Court imports the explicitly normative, value-based view on the criminal law adopted in the imprisonment cases into cases dealing with expulsion.

The consequence of defining imperative reasons of public security in such terms is that the acts of the individual are seen as an offence against the community and a violation of its particular normative code as reflected in its criminal law. As a result, that citizen can be expelled, or to use a more emotive language more appropriate to citizenship, exiled or banished.[68] That exile is only understandable by placing this understanding of crime within the concept of social integration. Implicit in the judgment, and explicit in the Opinion of AG Bot in *PI*, is a particular understanding of the relationship between integration and criminal acts. The threat posed by the individual is no longer weighed against his or her integration as two competing but separate interests such that one balances out the other as is implied by

[66] As recognised by the Court of Justice in response to a specific query from the national court regarding the specific political and historical circumstances within which the crimes took place. See ibid (n 24) para 60.

[67] It should be noted that there was no finding of criminal conduct in these cases. Rather the underlying decision was a decision adopted by asylum authorities on the basis of exclusion orders and on the grounds of serious suspicion rather than a criminal law standard.

[68] For Mancano, this represents a reversion for such individuals to the criminal law of the enemy as found in Jakobs rather than the criminal law of citizens. See Leandro Mancano, 'Punishment and Rights in European Union Citizenship: Persons or Criminals?' (2018) 24 *ELJ* 206. A similar view in relation to migrants generally (rather than EU specific) is found in Lucia Zedner, 'Is the Criminal Law only for Citizens? A Problem at the Borders of Punishment' in Mary Bosworth and Katja Franco Aas (eds), *The Borders of Punishment: Migration, Citizenship and Social Exclusion* (Oxford University Press, 2013).

the previous case-law of the Court of Justice and of the ECtHR. There is a closer, more causal relationship between integration and criminal activity rather than a mere accounting exercise. The implication is that his or her criminal acts evidence a failure to integrate in the first place or indeed undo any integration that may have been achieved.[69] If the individual's membership status is regulated according to his degree of integration, then by breaching the particular society's moral code and offending the host society, he or she demonstrates an attitude inimical to social integration. In the words of AG Bot: 'Mr I's conduct, which constitutes a serious disturbance of public policy, shows a total lack of desire to integrate into the society in which he finds himself and some of whose fundamental values he so conscientiously disregarded for years.'[70] Although the Court does not go so far as to draw that conclusion explicitly, its insistence on basing public security on the values of the host society and measuring seriousness in terms of blameworthiness reaches the same result. Rather than precluding a culpable individual from acquiring the status, as proposed by the AG, it simply allows his blameworthiness to overcome the protection that status supposedly offers.

Wrongdoing and Integration: Residence Rights

What was implicit in *PI* is explicit in cases dealing with the acquisition of residence rights by migrant EU citizens and in particular the effect of periods of imprisonment on the calculation of qualifying periods for permanent residence and the heightened protection found in Article 28(3) of the Citizenship Directive. In *Onuekwere*[71] the Nigerian husband of a migrant EU citizen sought permanent residence in order to benefit from the intermediate level of protection from expulsion contained in Article 28(2) of the Citizenship Directive. National authorities, however, refused his application on the grounds that periods he spent in prison not only did not count towards the qualifying period of five years for permanent residence,[72] but in fact broke the continuity of any such period.[73] In *MG*, decided on the same day, the Court made a similar finding in relation to an EU citizen seeking the heightened protection stemming from a ten-year residence period contained in Article 28(3) of the Citizenship Directive and relying on the reasoning of *Onuekwere*. Mrs MG, having spent time in prison for the physical

[69] Although note the need to assess the degree of integration of the individual concerned in *K & HF* (n 24) para 70.

[70] Case C-145/09 *Land Baden-Wurttemberg v Panagiotis Tsakouridis* (Opinion of AG Bot) EU:C:2010:322 para 60. Continuing to remain in a particular society while so flaunting its values amounts to a kind of abuse of rights or fraud according to the AG.

[71] Case C-378/12 *Nnamdi Onuekwere v Secretary of State for the Home Department* EU:C:2014:13.

[72] Citizenship Directive (n 6) Art 16.

[73] *Onuekwere* (n 71).

abuse of her children, was found not to be automatically eligible for the protection of Article 28(3) of the Citizenship Directive despite residence of more than ten years.[74] In *B and Vomero*,[75] decided a number of years later, the Court again dealt with the question of the relationship between periods of imprisonment and the ten-year period referenced in Article 28(3) of the Citizenship Directive, coming to the conclusion that an overall assessment of the integrative links of the individual is required at the time the expulsion decision is adopted in order to determine whether he or she benefits from the heightened protection contained in that article.

In *Onuekwere* the Court explicitly adopted a view of the criminal law as both normative (a code of values) and as communitarian (of the host society). Combining this with an understanding of the rights of EU citizenship as a reward for a prior experience of integration allowed the Court to come to the conclusion that criminal acts resulting in imprisonment either demonstrated a failure to integrate or undid or cancelled out any integration that may have taken place.[76] *B and Vomero*, while confirming the Court's finding in *Onuekwere* that the commission of an offence may have an impact on the degree of integration of an EU citizen in the society of the host Member State, nuances this with an assessment of the disintegrative and integrative effect of imprisonment itself.

Prompted by a strong opinion from AG Bot,[77] the Court in *Onuekwere* adopts an unambiguously normative view of the criminal law. The criminal law is seen as reflecting core values of a particular society and indicating the imperative rules of conduct individuals are expected to adopt in relation to each other and the community at large. There is no attempt to conceptualise the criminal law in terms of harm or risk posed by an individual. Indeed, the normative basis of criminal law informs not only the basis of criminalisation but also the justification for punishment – both retributive and rehabilitative goals reinforce each other within a normative paradigm of crime and punishment. For AG Bot, imprisonment is 'a period spent atoning for the crime committed',[78] a language remarkably close to Duff's account of punishment as 'secular penance'.[79] Rehabilitation is necessary precisely because the individual has disregarded the value system of the host society (and hence failed to integrate) – reflecting what Hart has termed the role of imprisonment to teach 'responsible citizenship'.[80]

[74] Case C-400/12 *Secretary for State for the Home Department v MG* EU:C:2014:9. The exact determination to be made by the national court.

[75] Joined Cases C-316/16 and C-424/16 *B v Land Baden-Württemberg and Secretary of State for the Home Department v Vomero* EU:C:2018:256.

[76] This section draws on a previous publication. See Stephen Coutts, 'Union Citizenship as Probationary Citizenship: *Onuekwere*' (2015) 52 *CML Rev* 531.

[77] Case C-378/12 *Nnamdi Onuekwere v Secretary of State for the Home Department* (Opinion of AG Bot) EU:C:2013:640.

[78] ibid, para 54.

[79] Antony Duff, *Punishment, Communication and Community* (Oxford University Press, 2003) 106.

[80] Henry Hart, 'The Aims of the Criminal Law' (1958) 23 *Law and Contemporary Problems* 401, 437.

This view of the criminal law is not only normative but is also communitarian. The criminal law is a public law and it is one given by the community to itself; a 'common law' in the literal sense of the word.[81] For the Court it represents 'the values expressed by the society of the host Member State'.[82] In the eyes of AG Bot the criminal law 'reflects the laws and values of … society'.[83] Moreover it is linked to the notion of citizenship in particular: 'Need it be recalled … that citizenship is for the citizen a guarantee of belonging to a political community under the rule of law?'[84] Criminal law reflects duties that individuals owe to each other as members of a political community governed by law, the content of which arises from shared values; a clear, if perhaps unconscious, endorsement of Duff's view of the criminal law.

This, then, is combined with a particular reading of EU citizenship and the role of integration in the acquisition of rights under the Citizenship Directive. On the one hand, the 'qualitative dimension' of integration is emphasised. On the other hand, the causal relationship between integration and rights is reversed. Integration is seen as not merely temporal and geographical – ie mere presence in the host Member State for a certain period of time[85] – but as also having 'qualitative elements'.[86] The term is borrowed from jurisprudence dealing with requirements of economic activity or self-sufficiency and arguably originally conceived of in the context of balancing the right of migrant EU citizens to equal treatment with the host Member State interest in them not becoming an 'unreasonable burden'.[87] What *Onukwere* does is take this material condition of economic contribution and transform it into a normative condition of respect for the values of the host society. There is also a shift in the relationship between integration and rights; whereas previously rights were seen as forming the basis for integration – allowing the migrant to participate fully in the life of the host Member State and hence become integrated – now rights, and in particular the rights associated with permanent residence, are seen as the *reward* for previously achieved integration; the acquisition of the heightened level of protection is 'subject to the integration of the citizen of the Union in the host Member State'.[88]

[81] In Duff's words a true 'common law'; see Antony Duff, *Answering for Crime: Responsibility and Liability in the Criminal Law* (Hart Publishing, 2007) 49.

[82] *Onuekwere* (n 71) para 26. See also *Secretary for State for the Home Department v MG* (n 74) para 31.

[83] *Onuekwere* (Opinion of AG Bot) (n 77), para 46.

[84] ibid, para 52.

[85] What Somek calls mere being and time. See Alexander Somek, 'Solidarity Decomposed: Being and Time in European Citizenship' (2007) 32 *EL Rev* 787.

[86] *Onuekwere* (n 71) para 24.

[87] Case C-325/09 *Secretary of State for the Home Department v Maria Dias* EU:C:2011:498, [2011] ECR I-6387. Recently significantly re-emphasised in the *Dano* line of cases. For an analysis, see the contributions in Thym, *Questioning EU Citizenship*, in particular Ferdinand Wollenschläger, 'Consolidating Union Citizenship: Residence and Solidarity Rights for Jobseekers and the Economically Inactive in the Post-*Dano* Era' and Paul Minderhoud and Sandra Mantu, 'Back to the Roots? No Access to Social Assistance for Union Citizens Who Are Economically Inactive' in Daniel Thym (ed), *Questioning EU Citizenship: Judges and the Limits of Free Movement and Solidarity in the EU* (Hart Publishing, 2017).

[88] *Onuekwere* (n 71) para 24.

The final piece of the reasoning of the Court is the link between integration and crime. Crime is seen as inimical to the values of the host society and represents a repudiation of its moral code, 'a transgression of the societal norms of the host Member State'.[89] In making this point, is important to highlight that it is not the period of imprisonment that concerns the Court or the Advocate General in *Onuekwere* but the underlying crime, ie the blameworthy act. The Court could have decided that imprisonment amounted to a form of 'internal exile', a place socially and to an extent geographically removed from society, literally a place apart, and in which normal links with the broader society would be undermined or fail to form. Indeed, this is the solution that was suggested implicitly by the German government who proposed that periods of imprisonment be treated analogously to periods spent abroad when deciding whether they break the continuous nature of the residence of an individual.[90] The Court waited until *B and Vomero* to analyse this possibility in detail. In *Onukwere* it is not the absence of the individual that is at stake, rather it is the underlying wrongful act and hence responsibility as a moral actor in his or her dealings with the community. Furthermore, not only does criminal activity prevent integration taking place, but in fact works to undo integration. This is evidenced by the finding that not only does criminal activity not count towards periods of residence, it in fact breaks the continuity of any such periods; in the word of AG Bot, any previously acquired integration is 'expunged' by the criminal conduct.[91]

B and Vomero[92] adopts this analysis but develops it in important ways, confirming the link between crime, integration and rights, while building on this by bringing in an analysis of imprisonment itself, in addition to the underlying criminal offence. *B and Vomero* reinforces the findings of *Onuekwere* in relation to the links between integration and protection against expulsion. In fact, the judgment is infused with an integration logic with the Court framing Article 28(3) of the Citizenship Directive and the question of its relationship with imprisonment around the integration motif, culminating in the main finding of the judgment that, rather than a bright-line rule applying, as might be implied by reference to a ten-year period, an 'overall assessment' of the integrative links of the individual taking into account a variety of factors should be conducted in order to determine if an individual benefits from the protection offered by Article 28(3).[93]

Furthermore, the link between integration and the enjoyment of the heightened protection is stressed in a secondary finding that enjoyment of the heightened

[89] *Onuekwere* (Opinion of AG Bot) (n 77) para 64.
[90] ibid, para 60.
[91] ibid, para 54.
[92] *B & Vomero* (n 75).
[93] For example: 'Directive 2004/38 … establishes a system of protection against expulsion measures which is based on the degree of integration of those persons in the host Member State, so that the greater the degree of integration of Union citizens and their family members in the host Member State, the greater the guarantees against expulsion they enjoy' (ibid, para 44).

protection in Article 28(3) is predicated on an individual first acquiring the right to permanent residence.[94] Importantly, this implies that in order to enjoy the heightened protection of Article 28(3) an individual must have spent at least the first five years of his residence in accordance with the conditions contained in the Citizenship Directive and in particular Article 7, a finding that is based in turn on the fact that integration has a 'qualitative', in addition to merely temporal and geographic, dimension.[95] Apart from ensuring that individuals who spend any time in prison during that period, such as the case of Mr Vomero, are necessarily excluded from permanent residence and therefore also the heightened protection of Article 28(3),[96] it also ensures that a condition of economic activity (or self-sufficiency) is imposed in order to obtain that protection. Thus, at least for the first five years of his or her residence an individual must not only be a good citizen in a normative sense, accepting the values of the host society, but must also be a good citizen in an economic sense, contributing in a material way to the host society, thereby neatly combining the restrictive and duty-orientated jurisprudence in the *Dano* line of case-law with that of *Onuekwere*.[97]

B and Vomero confirms the explicit endorsement of a normative view of crime first raised in *Onuekwere* with the finding that the nature of the underlying offence on which imprisonment is based is a relevant (but importantly not the only) factor in determining whether integrative links have been maintained or, on the contrary, broken at the time an expulsion decision is being taken. Thus the 'nature of the offence' and the circumstances in which it was committed' must be taken into account as they 'shed light on the extent to which the person concerned has … become disconnected from the society of the host Member State'.[98]

However, this assessment is complemented by a more realistic and nuanced assessment of the effect of imprisonment itself on the integration of the individual concerned. Contrary to the assessment in *Onukwere*, the Court importantly in its analysis separates out the underlying offence (and 'circumstances') from the period of imprisonment itself, and recognises the mixed effect any such imprisonment may have on an individual and their degree of integration. On the one hand, a side-effect of any such period is the forced removal of an individual from society and a weakening of their links with the social and economic environment. On the other hand, a stated aim of imprisonment, alongside punishment, is rehabilitation, a goal echoed in the Framework Decision on the Transfer

[94] ibid, para 61. Confirmed in *K & HF* (n 24) para 73.

[95] *B & Vomero* (n 75) paras 58–60.

[96] See the findings made by the national court in this regard: ibid, para 35.

[97] For a general assessment of this line of case-law and the restrictions and limitations on the rights of the economically inactive EU citizen, see the contributions in Thym (n 87) and in particular Wollenschläger and Minderhoud and Mantu. For an analysis including the expulsion cases, see Niamh Nic Shuibhne, 'Limits Rising, Duties Ascending: The Changing Legal Shape of Union Citizenship' (2015) 52 *CML Rev* 889.

[98] *B & Vomero* (n 75) para 74.

of Prisoners[99] and the *Wolzenburg* line of cases[100] referred to in the previous chapter. Thus a period of imprisonment, depending on the activities of the individual EU citizen, may both contribute to and/or undermine his or her degree of integration in the host society, always, however, against the backdrop of the underlying offence and the rejection of values it represents.[101] Finally, the disposition or attitude of the individual prisoner is important in this analysis, which should take account of the 'behaviour of the person concerned during the period of imprisonment' – another instance of the responsibilisation of the EU citizen through the concept of integration.[102]

The conclusion from these premises – rights are the reward for integration; integration requires respect for values; crime represents a disrespect for values – is that criminal activities preclude an individual from acquiring permanent residence in the case of *Onuekwere* or call into question the heightened protection in the case of *MG* and *B and Vomero*. There is an impact on membership and duties and the relationship between them. Permanent residence in particular 'goes beyond the mere right to reside and move within the territory of the European Union. It can create, for Union citizens, a feeling of being fully part of the society of the host Member State.'[103] That 'being fully part of society', however, is conditioned on a normative commitment, one that requires acceptance and respect for the values of that society, an identification with the morals of the host society and a sharing of their worldview – or at least those elements that are reflected in their criminal law.[104] Failure to respect those values results in exclusion, in a rejection of the membership promised by permanent residence and the maintenance of otherness. Imprisonment may offer the criminal EU citizen the opportunity to restore links previously forged with the host Member State or may alternatively 'reinforce that disconnection' depending on his or her conduct.[105] This exclusion of those deemed criminally deviant from membership in the community is not unique to EU law,[106] although perhaps the explicit, rather than implicit, manner in which it

[99] Framework Decision 2008/909/JHA on the application of the principle of mutual recognition to judgements in criminal matters imposing custodial sentences or measures involving deprivation of liberty for the purposes of their enforcement in the European Union [2008] OJ L327/27.

[100] Case C-66/08 *Proceedings concerning the execution of a European arrest warrant issued against Szymon Kozłowski* EU:C:2008:437, [2008] ECR I-6041. Case C-123/08 *Dominic Wolzenburg* EU:C:2009:616, [2009] ECR I-9621 and Case C-42/11 *Proceedings concerning the execution of a European arrest warrant issued against João Pedro Lopes Da Silva Jorge* EU:C:2012:517.

[101] See *B & Vomero* (n 75) para 74.

[102] For further discussion, see Stephen Coutts, 'The Absence of Integration and the Responsibilisation of Union Citizenship' (2018) 3 *European Papers* 761.

[103] *Onuekwere* (Opinion of AG Bot) (n 71) 44.

[104] See the view of the Bundesverfassungsgericht in *Ratification of the Treaty of Lisbon, Re (2 BvE 2/08)* [2010] 3 CMLR 13 (Bundesverfassungsgericht) para 331, discussed further in Chapter 7.

[105] *B & Vomero* (n 75) para 74.

[106] See Zedner (n 68) and Barbara Hudson, 'Punishing Monsters, Judging Aliens: Justice at the Borders of Community' (2006) 39 *Australian and New Zealand Journal of Criminology* 232.

operates is.[107] What it represents is the appropriation of a certain tendency and a view of criminal law, exclusion and the community, and imports it within the workings of EU citizenship through the use of a normative view of criminal law within the operation of the social integration paradigm.

Conclusion: A Supranational Duty of Respect towards National Communities

From this series of cases the Court has in fact used the concept of social integration inherent in EU citizenship and combined it with a normative and communitarian view of the criminal law to establish a set of duties for migrant EU citizens. However, although it may appear that the duty is of a passive and national character, it is in fact a more active, positive duty and one that is rooted in supranational law. There is therefore a combination of the transnational and supranational in constructing duties for EU citizens in this area. It is *through* national criminal law that the European Union constructs a supranational duty, which in turn is a duty of respect towards national communities.

National Communities

The content of the duties is to be found in national law and reflects national values. In both sets of cases the Court emphasises that it is national criminal law that is at stake. In *Onuekwere* there is no attempt on the part of either the Court or the Advocate General to impose any conditions flowing from EU law on what counts and what does not count as a 'wrong' for the purposes of deciding whether an individual has failed to integrate or otherwise.[108] In fact, it is very clear that the criminal law is a code that reflects the national society's set of values: 'The imposition of a prison sentence by the national court is such as to show the non-compliance by the person concerned with the values expressed by the society of the host Member State in its criminal law.'[109] Its wrongful character arises from the fact that it has been classified as such under *national* criminal law. The jurisprudence in the expulsion cases is also clear in emphasising the role of Member States in defining public policy and public security. These are seen as derogations

[107] Although see the recent turn towards denationalization for certain terror-related offences described by Audrey Macklin and Rainer Bauböck, 'The Return of Banishment: Do the New Denationalisation Policies Weaken Citizenship?' (2015) EUI Working Papers, RSCAS 2015/14.

[108] Except perhaps wrongs that result in custodial sentences, a requirement that flows more from the nature of the preliminary reference rather than anything inherent in the Court's reasoning.

[109] *Onuekwere* (n 71) para 26.

from Treaty obligations and exceptions that reflect particular national interests and values.[110] It is the 'fundamental interests of the host society' that may 'vary from one country to another and from one period to another'.[111] 'Member States essentially retain the freedom to determine the requirements of public policy and public security' and 'European Union law does not impose on Member States a uniform scale of values as regards the assessment of conduct which may be considered to be contrary to public security.'[112] This is particularly striking in the definition of public security, a concept one would imagine would be relatively objective and unchanging between societies. It is the international relations of the Member States and the integrity of their justice systems that is at stake in *K and HF*, and the values expressed in the exclusion clauses are relevant primarily because these are the values of the legal system of the Member States.[113]

Not only does the *content* of the duty of respect arise from national law but the *target* of the duty is also the national community. A crime is not a blameworthy act in a vacuum; it is committed against someone or something; it is a relational concept. Responsibility implies that we are answerable to someone for our actions.[114] In the cases analysed it is a crime committed against the national community. It is the relationship between the individual and the host society that is at stake;[115] the transnational relationship that stems from the primarily transnational character of EU citizenship. This is why it is perfectly logical to expel or exile an individual from one Member State to another for an act, such as rape or a drug offence, despite the fact that these acts may be criminalised throughout the Union. A risk- or harm-based assessment would not allow for this; the individual is a danger no matter where he or she may reside within the Union. Similarly, from a supranational perspective expulsion is also problematic; if the act is a wrong against the Union the exact location of the individual is of little relevance.[116]

[110] Although see certain critiques of the Court's jurisprudence in the broader question of public policy exceptions as not in fact leaving any autonomous space for Member States to define their own, distinctive public policy – see Catherine Kessedjian, 'Public Order in European Law' (2007–08) 1 *Erasmus Law Review* 25. However, it is submitted that there is a distinction between the Union exercising a certain negative control – ie ensuring that Member States do not invoke public policy reasons that would be contrary to the values of the Union – from a more positive control – ensuring that Member States can *only* invoke public policy reasons that conform to a Union-wide understanding of public policy. Indeed, such would seem to be the approach followed by the Court in, for example, Case C-36/02 *Omega Spielhallen- und Automatenaufstellungs-GmbH v Oberbürgermeisterin der Bundesstadt Bonn* EU:C:2004:614, [2004] ECR I-9609.

[111] *van Duyn* (n 19) para 18.

[112] *PI* (n 44) paras 21–23.

[113] *K & HF* (n 24) paras 43–44.

[114] See, in particular, Duff (n 81) ch 2.

[115] Note, for example, the characterisation of a threat to public security or policy as something which affects 'the peace of mind and physical security of the population of the Member State concerned' in *K & HF* (n 24) para 42.

[116] For a discussion of the problem in the case of the ECtHR jurisprudence, see P van Dijk, 'Protection of "Integrated" Aliens against Expulsion under the European Convention on Human Rights' in Elspeth

The expulsion only makes sense by conceiving of the crime as an offence against the national community.[117]

However, these national values and the particular normative choices made by the Member States are increasingly framed by a supranational law. Although there is no mention of EU criminal law instruments in cases dealing with the residence rights, in both *Tsakouridis* and in *PI* the Court does make reference to EU instruments that have been adopted in the areas of drug trafficking and the sexual exploitation of children.[118] In a sense EU law and particular EU normative choices, are employed to validate the national choices made by Member States and to leave open the possibility of using those particular values and normative choices to clarify the duty of respect imposed on EU citizens. In *K and HF* the fact that the underlying conduct justifying expulsion is seen as contrary to the values of the Union as expressed in Articles 2 and 3 TEU is explicit.[119] This is not quite the same thing as an EU value system, subsuming national determinations and replacing a national public policy with an EU public policy. It remains the national choice as reflected in national law, but there is a supranational presence in the field, not only in relation to controlling in a negative sense the discretion afforded Member States, but also in positively validating their choices, endorsing them on an EU level. The interaction between the national and supranational spheres in this area can be seen as a dialectic whereby national choices are reflected in EU instruments that in turn validate national choices, all the while leading to a greater convergence between individual, national communities while retaining those communities as distinct sites of self-determination that are seen as autonomous moral entities requiring respect.[120] It does not involve the gradual disappearance of a distinct national ground of public policy and hence the rationale for the exception in the first place.[121] In fact, once one accepts that

Guild and Paul Minderhoud (eds), *Security of Residence and Expulsion: Protection of Aliens in Europe* (Kluwer International, 2001) 38.

[117] I would like to thank Dmitry Kochenov for forcing me to articulate this point during useful comments on an earlier presentation of this chapter.

[118] *Tsakouridis* (n 43) para 46. *PI* (n 44) paras 25–26. The latter category of crimes appears to be a particular interest of the Union and sits within an increasing role for EU law in children's rights and victims in general. See Eleanor Drywood and Helen Stalford, 'Coming of Age? Children's Rights in the European Union' (2009) 46 *CML Rev* 143. It is worth noting also that the victims of MG's crimes were also her children.

[119] *K & HF* (n 24) para 46.

[120] See Floris de Witte, 'Sex, Drugs and EU Law: The Recognition of Moral and Ethical Diversity in EU Law' (2013) 50 *CML Rev* 1545.

[121] Some authors and indeed the Commission have floated the notion of a convergence in national notions of public policy. See Kessedjian (n 82); Maria Castillo and Régis Chemain, 'La Réserve d'Ordre Public en Droit Communautaire' in Marie-Joëlle Redor (ed), *L'ordre public: Ordre public ou ordres publics Ordre public et droits fondamentaux* (Bruylant, 2001) 161ff; and Commission, *Communication on the Special Measures concerning the Movement and Residence of Citizens of the Union* (n 33) 10: 'Member States have discretionary powers for interpretation. … Nevertheless, the national concepts of public policy, public security and public health may gradually approach each other as European integration advances.'

the 'threat to public policy' is in fact a wrong that concerns a distinct national community, there is no reason why Member States cannot share the same concept of public policy and the normative choices that go with it, and retain an ability to expel an EU citizen for a breach of the duty of respect, the target of the duty being as important as the content.

On its face this may seem as simply a negative duty to refrain from committing crimes. Nonetheless, one gets the impression from the Court's language in the expulsion and residence rights judgments that there is in fact a more positive, albeit rather inchoate, duty imposed on the citizen. It concerns the appropriate attitude the migrant citizen is expected to adopt vis-à-vis the host Member State.[122] In *K and HF* the Court speaks of the 'disposition' of the EU citizen.[123] This approach of seeing integration as partially a process of adopting a particular attitude is echoed in another area of the Court's case-law, in particular the imposition of integration requirements on TCNs.[124] To meet such requirements it is necessary that the individual in question 'make an effort' rather than meet some predefined linguistic or knowledge-based standard. What is important is the *attitude* the individual adopts towards the host society, their *willingness* to integrate. As guests seeking membership of the community, they are expected to reorientate their values in order to adopt the normative commitments of the host society. It is perhaps implicit and tacit but there is a positive requirement on the individual to at least demonstrate a certain attitude towards the host society. It is a deeper, thicker, normative and more social sense of integration.[125] Such a conclusion is implicit in the relationship between crime and integration discussed, particularly in AG Bot's Opinions in both *PI* and *Onukwere* and the judgment in *Onukwere*. The invocation of 'qualitative elements', drawing on the analogy of economic contributions from *Dias*,[126] appears to set up a positive and active dimension in the integration process on the part of the EU citizen, apparently in opposition to the rather passive 'territorial and temporal' dimensions cited by the Court.[127] Finally, specifically in the case of prisoners, it is clear from *B and Vomero* that what is at stake when assessing the extent to which they have or have not reintegrated is the behaviour or the prisoner while in custody and his or her conduct.[128]

[122] For a similar conclusion in the field of deportation in the UK and how such a practice facilitates the articulation of certain qualities of 'good citizenship', see Anderson, Gibney and Paoletti (n 30).

[123] *K & HF* (n 24) para 60.

[124] Case C-153/14 *Minister van Buitenlandse Zaken v K and A* EU:C:2015:453, para 56, in particular whereby under a proportionality analysis an individual who fails the test may nonetheless be granted a residence permit if he has demonstrated a 'willingness to pass the exam and have made every effort to achieve that objective'.

[125] The parallels with integration requirements increasingly imposed on TCNs (and permitted by EU law) as reflecting a more communitarian and integrationist (not to say assimilationist and exclusionary) approach towards migration cannot be ignored. See Rainer Bauböck and Christian Joppke, 'How Liberal are Citizenship Tests?' (2010) EUI Working Papers RSCAS 2010/41, and in the EU context Sergio Carrera (ed), 'The Nexus between Immigration, Integration and Citizenship in the EU' (25 January 2006) Immigration, Integration and Citizenship, CEPS, Brussels.

[126] *Dias* (n 69).

[127] *Onuekwere* (n 71) para 25.

[128] *B & Vomero* (n 75) paras 73 and 83.

A Supranational Duty

At the same time, there is a specifically *European* duty contained in EU citizenship, and in particular EU citizenship as a status of integration. Although the specific content of the duty is determined by reference to national criminal law and nationals are indeed subject to the same obligations, the nature of the duty and the consequences are different. For nationals it simply represents the duties co-citizens owe to each other in the context of a community of law, expressing particular moral choices, especially regarding appropriate mutual conduct.[129] In addition to the general duty under national law, it also represents a qualitative dimension to the integration process that they are subject to *qua* EU citizens. It is intimately linked to the integration process that itself is an integral part of EU citizenship. It is a duty imposed by EU law and with consequences in EU law, namely the temporary loss of rights of EU citizenship, in addition to whatever consequences may flow from national law.[130] Furthermore, the Union, by endorsing the expulsion of criminal citizens and validating Member State's normative choices in the area, can be said to be recognising the wrong done to that national community, and to be indirectly 'punishing' it by imposing consequences under EU law.

A similar dynamic becomes evident when considering expulsion cases not under Article 21 TFEU but under Article 20 TFEU and the *Zambrano* doctrine, founding derived rights of residence for TCN family members of non-mobile EU citizens.[131] In *Rendón-Marín*[132] and *CS*,[133] discussed in further detail in Chapter 3, the Court of Justice found that it was permissible to expel TCN family members even where to do so would lead to the denial of the genuine enjoyment of the rights attaching to the status of EU citizenship of the minor EU citizen child.[134] However, drawing on the rules developed under Directive 2004/38/EC, the Court likewise found that this possibility was subject to a sufficiently serious threat being established and the application of a proportionality analysis.[135] What is noteworthy about these cases, aside from resurrecting the Article 20 TFEU case-law, is the application of restrictions not to *transnational* rights – rights exercised vis-à-vis other Member States – but to *supranational* rights of non-mobile Union citizens

[129] See Duff (n 81) 49ff.

[130] For Mancano (n 68) this has the effect of rendering the individual an enemy rather than citizen in the scheme developed by Jakobs. It is possible to conclude that – in the context of a citizenship scheme based on a progressive and reinforcing relationship between rights and integration, a finding that criminal conduct is mutually exclusive with integration and hence rights – such persons are in some sense non-citizens. This is certainly the case vis-à-vis the host Member State at least temporarily [see Art 32 Citizenship Directive (n 6)]. Whether it is the case vis-à-vis the Union and other Member States is another question.

[131] See further Chapter 3.

[132] Case C-165/14 *Alfredo Rendón Marín v Administración del Estado* EU:C:2016:675.

[133] Case C-304/14 *Secretary of State for the Home Department v CS* EU:C:2016:674.

[134] *Rendón Marín* (n 132) para 81 and *CS* (n 133) para 36.

[135] *Rendón Marín* (n 132) paras 83–86 and *CS* (n 133) paras 40–42.

derived directly from the status of Article 20 TFEU. In a problematic move, the Court of Justice permits the expulsion of the EU citizen and his or her carer from the 'territory of the Union as a whole' on the basis of an offence committed against a single Member State.[136] Supranational rights are restricted by national criminal law, with the Court's endorsement.

A similar dynamic is evident in *Delvigne* in which the Court of Justice found a genuine, autonomous right to vote in European parliamentary elections existed, independently of movement and exercisable vis-à-vis a citizen's *home* Member State. However, it also found that this right could be limited for reason of serious criminal conduct.[137] Aside from the cursory proportionality analysis, the judgment is noteworthy for permitting the limitation of a directly effective, supranational right of political participation in the election of the European Parliament as an EU citizen, on the basis of an offence committed against a single Member State, namely France. As with *Rendón-Marín* and *CS*, it is national criminal law that is infringed, which leads to a limitation of a supranational right under EU law vis-à-vis the Union as a whole; the justification for the limitation of the supranational right is a national offence. Although the Court offers no detailed discussion of the possible justifications for prisoner disenfranchisement in the case,[138] one possible explanation for these is the concept of shared wrongs, explored in further detail in Chapter 6 in relation to the EAW FD. It is through offence to the Member State that the Union as a whole is concerned, and which justifies restrictions of an EU citizen's supranational rights.

What emerges from the cases considered in this chapter is a duty of respect towards the values of the host society peculiar to EU citizenship, reflecting both a rebalancing of the relationship of integration between the host-society and the individual, placing more emphasis on the role of the individual, and also a shift in the quality of that integration from an economic to a normative or indeed moral plane. Duties can be said to exist in EU citizenship but operate primarily at a transnational level; they become transnational obligations imposed by supranational law. More recently, this dynamic has shifted to the supranational domain, where national offences justify restrictions of supranational rights. It is through national criminal law that supranational duties are imposed on EU citizens and it is through primarily transnational processes that common normative choices are affirmed at the level of the Union in a dialectic between national and supranational law.

[136] Mancano (n 68) 220–21 notes the more favourable application of the proportionality assessment compared to *PI* and *Tsakouridis*, in *Rendón-Marín* in particular, and speculates that this may be due to the more severe consequences of expulsion in this case.

[137] *Delvigne* (n 13) paras 45ff.

[138] For an analysis of possible justifications for prisoner disenfranchisement, see Christopher Bennett, 'Penal Disenfranchisement' (2016) 10 *Criminal Law and Philosophy* 411.

PART III

An Area of Justice: Shared Enforcement and Shared Recognition of National Wrongs

The second transnational dimension of EU citizenship has been termed autonomy. It might be useful to add the addendum 'in a single legal space'. For that is what is at stake in the concept of autonomy in the context of EU citizenship. On one level it is an exercise in quasi-mutual recognition, simply obliging Member States, through the use of the principle of free movement in particular, to recognise legal situations that arise in other Member States even where they differ from how those situations are regulated under their own legal regimes. The implication, however, is somewhat broader. As recognised by AG Sharpston, it enables individuals to passport legal situations throughout the Union; to enjoy a single legal status, composed of rights acquired under different national legal orders, throughout the Union.[1] It generates a broader legal space, composed of different national legal orders, within which individuals can move. They do not remain tied to a particular national community but rather can travel throughout the territory of the Union. Their legal status is understood with reference to the wider Union as a whole.

Thus while primarily transnational in character it does generates a supranational reference point: the totality of the Member States' territory, that together form the Union territory. Indeed, a link between this transnational aspect of EU citizenship and the supranational status constructed by the Court in *Zambrano* can be discerned. Through autonomy EU citizens can be said to occupy and share the 'territory of the Union as a whole', a phrase that is particularly prominent in the Court's judgment in *Zambrano* and in subsequent cases.[2] Indeed, occupying this

[1] Joint Opinion of AG Sharpston in Case C-456/12 *O v Minister voor Immigratie, Integratie en Asiel and Minister voor Immigratie, Integratie en Asiel v B* EU:C:2014:135 and Case C-457/12 *S v Minister voor Immigratie, Integratie en Asiel and Minister voor Immigratie, Integratie en Asiel v G* EU:C:2014:136, para 95.

[2] Case C-34/09 *Gerardo Ruiz Zambrano v Office national de l'emploi (ONEm)* EU:C:2011:124, [2011] ECR I-1177; Case C-86/12 *Alokpa et al v Minstre du Travail de l'Emploi et de l'Immigration* EU:C:2013:645; Case C-87/12 *Ymeraga v Minstre du Travail, de l'Emploi et de l'Immigration* EU:C:2013:291; Case C-165/14 *Alfredo Rendón Marín v Administración del Estado* EU:C:2016:675; and Case C-133/15 *Chavez-Vilchez and Others v Raad van bestuur van de Sociale verzekeringsbank and Others* EU:C:2017:354.

composite, plural legal space amounts in the Court's eyes to the 'genuine enjoyment of the substance of the rights conferred by Union citizenship' that appears to lie at the heart of the Court's understanding of supranational citizenship.[3] As explored further in Chapter 3, through its Article 20 TFEU case-law, the Court of Justice appears to be constructing a place of rights.

Just as citizenship can be said to operate in a broader space of movement, criminal law has also been the subject of various efforts to create a single legal space. If anything the effort as creating a single 'area of justice' is even more explicit in the area of criminal law. Through the use of mutual recognition, a technique developed in the internal market and since exported (with various criticisms)[4] to the AFSJ,[5] the Union has attempted to ensure that crime, or more precisely, criminal enforcement, also operates with reference to the territory of the Union as a whole.

Two complementary aspects of this 'area of justice' are analysed in the following two chapters; the transnational enforcement of criminal law, in particular the operation of the European Arrest Warrant Framework Decision (EAW FD)[6] and the recognition of final judgments, most notably the operation of Article 54 of the Convention Implementing the Schengen Agreement (CISA).[7] Combined, they are designed to create a single area of justice for the enforcement and recognition of crime within the Union. Although the construction of the Area of Justice involves a far larger suite of mutual recognition instruments,[8] this study concentrates on these two as the most prominent examples that have been analysed by both judicial and academic writing,[9] those that are most closely connected with the free movement of persons[10] and finally as two complementary instruments;

[3] *Zambrano* (n 2) para 42.

[4] See, in particular, Steve Peers, 'Mutual Recognition and Crimial Law in the European Union: Has the Council Got it Wrong?' (2004) 41 *CML Rev* 5; and Markus Möstl, 'Preconditions and Limits of Mutual Recognition' (2010) 47 *CML Rev* 405.

[5] Particularly since the Hague Programme: *The Hague Programme: Strengthening Freedom, Security and Justice in the European Union* (2004) JAI 559. The prominence of mutual recognition as a technique for integration has since been formalized in the Treaty of Lisbon in Art 82(1) TFEU.

[6] Framework Decision 2002/584/JHA on the European arrest warrant and the surrender procedures between Member States (EAW FD) [2002] OJ L190/1.

[7] Convention on the Implementation of the Schengen Agreement.

[8] See Steve Peers, *EU Justice and Home Affairs Law*, 3 edn (Oxford University Press, 2011) ch 9.

[9] Indeed the EAW FD has been described as the Union's flagship instrument in this area and has been used as a template for other mutual recognition instruments, in particular other warrants such as the European Evidence Warrant (Framework Decision 2008/978/JHA on the European Evidence Warrant for the pupose of obtaining objects, documents and data for use in proceedings in criminal matters [2008] OJ L350/72) and its replacement the European Investigation Order (Directive 2014/41/EU regarding the European Investigation Order in criminal matters [2014] OJ L130/1). For the use of the structure and techniques (especially the abolition of the double criminality requirement) in other mutual recognition instruments see Peers (n 8) ch 9.

[10] Other instruments are undoubtedly frequently related to crime committed by individuals in circulation within the Union but not necessarily, whereas the EAW FD and Art 54 CISA directly relate to the situation of an individual who has moved to another Member State either before (in the case of the EAW) or after (in the case of Art 54 CISA) their prosecution and conviction/acquittal.

both are designed to ensure that an individual is called to account (and if necessary punished) for wrongs committed at least once within the Union, but only once.[11] They are two sides of the same coin of an area of justice: justice for the community in ensuring that an individual is punished; justice for the individual in ensuring that that punishment only takes place once.

The construction of this Area of Justice reinforces and complements EU citizenship. On the one hand, the free movement rights of EU citizens are directly reinforced by the existence of Article 54 CISA, a provision that is designed explicitly to maximise the opportunities of individuals to move throughout the Union. Indeed, this objective has been the main consideration to inform the interpretation of that provision by the Court of Justice. On the other hand, the EAW FD is a complement to EU citizenship. It is a shared enforcement mechanism for national criminal law and criminal judgments that complements the free movement of rights associated with EU citizenship with the free movement of responsibilities incurred under national criminal law. A combination of these two instruments ensures that an individual's status under criminal law, just as under civil law, is carried throughout the Union. Just as citizenship, crime is understood with reference to a broader legal space.

This shared space is, however, a composite legal space, composed of the various Member States and the national communities they represent. It is national criminal law and national judgments that travel throughout the Union. It is similarly clear that it is against the individual Member State that the individual is deemed to have offended, which judges that individual and to which he or she must return to be judged in the case of the EAW FD.

However, just as with the development of 'autonomy' within EU citizenship, the development of the single Area of Justice gives rise, in an even more explicit fashion, to broader supranational phenomena that focus around the idea of a shared space.[12] In the Area of Justice this shared space has been overlain with normative content that has arisen directly from transnational processes. Certain common rights have developed for use in transnational enforcement, a common citizenship justifies it and common understandings of wrongful conduct, ie crimes, are also assumed by the EAW FD in particular. A space of rights is complemented by a space of justice, including responsibilities vis-a-vis other Member States and

[11] For a particularly strong presentation of the complementarity of the EAW FD and Art 54 CISA, see Robin Lööf, 'Defending Liberty and Structural Integrity: A Social Contractual Analysis of Criminal Justice in the EU' (PhD thesis, Department of Law, European University Institute 2008).

[12] Starting from the very assertion of a single 'Area of Freedom, Security and Justice'. For a discussion of the representative and symbolic function of such a construction, see Patrick Twomey, 'Construcuting a Secure Space: The Area of Freedom, Security and Justice' in David O'Keefe and Patrick Twomey (eds), *Legal Issues of the Amsterdam Treaty* (Hart Publishing, 1999) and, in another sense, Hans Lindahl, 'Finding a Place for Freedom, Security and Justice: the European Union's Claim to Territorial Unity' (2004) 29 *EL Rev* 461. For a discussion in the context of Article 20 TFEU, see Chiara Raucea, 'European Citizenship and the Right to Reside: "No One on the Outside has a Right to be Inside"' (2016) 22 *ELJ* 470.

ultimately citizens.[13] But the supranational phenomenon goes further; by participating in a system of shared enforcement and by creating a system of shared recognition of national calling to account, Union law has implicitly assumed a shared supranational community.

In light of the national and transnational dimensions, it is argued here that that shared community is best understood as a composite community, whereby the wrong experienced by one Member State is shared by all and that the calling to account before one Member State counts as being called to account before all Member States. Crime, wrongful conduct and calling to account are experienced at a supranational level but through national communities.

[13] In this regard the increasing reference to the need to avoid impunity within the AFSJ as a principle of EU law is interesting. See, for example, Case C-129/14 PPU *Criminal proceedings against Zoran Spasic* EU:C:2014:586, paras 63–65 and Case C-182/15 *Aleksei Petruhhin v Latvijas Republikas Ģenerālprokuratūra* EU:C:2016:630, paras 36–37.

6

An Area of Justice – I. The European Arrest Warrant as a Transnational Calling to Account

Shared Citizenship, Shared Rights and Shared Wrongs

Introduction: Shared Enforcement

Criminal law has long been considered one of the prerogatives of the sovereign state and is intimately connected to the concept of territorial control and the legitimate use of force.[1] This nexus – between the legitimate use of force, territory and control – lies at the heart of the modern Weberian concept of the state[2] and is one of the fundamental aspects of statehood that is being challenged by the development of the former third pillar and now Title V of the TFEU. A particular lighting-rod for attention and no little criticism has been the 'flagship' instrument of mutual recognition in criminal law matters: the EAW FD.[3] It was accused of prejudicing the rights of individuals[4] and being based on a false analogy with the free movement of goods.[5] The use of mutual recognition – a governance technique developed in the internal market for the free movement of goods – in the AFSJ and especially in the area of judicial decisions in criminal matters has been viewed as generating

[1] See Christian Kaunert, 'The Area of Freedom, Security and Justice: The Construction of a 'European Public Order'' (2005) 14 *European Security* 459 and Maria Fletcher, Robin Loof and Bill Gilmore, *EU Criminal Law and Justice* (Edward Elgar, 2008) 5–6.

[2] Indeed, the provision of security as a (public) good founds the core of the justification of the state in the social contract tradition beginning (and most explicitly recognised) in Hobbes. See Ian Loader and Neil Walker, *Civilising Security* (Cambridge University Press, 2007) ch 2.

[3] Framework Decision 2002/584/JHA on the European arrest warrant and the surrender procedures between Member States (EAW FD) [2002] OJ L190/1.

[4] Markus Möstl, 'Preconditions and Limits of Mutual Recognition' (2010) 47 *CML Rev* 405.

[5] Steve Peers, 'Mutual Recognition and Criminal Law in the European Union: Has the Council Got it Wrong?' (2004) 41 *CML Rev* 5. Although see the response of Janssens who highlights the complexity and variability of mutual recognition instruments within the EU legal order. See Christine Janssens, *The Principle of Mutual Recognition in EU Law* (Oxford University Press, 2013), Conclusion.

instances of extraterritoriality in the area of criminal law and the use of force, a development that threatened the territorial integrity and sovereignty of Member States, the principle of legality, the fundamental rights of individuals, and the link between citizens and their states. It has been subject to a number of challenges and resistances by national constitutional courts.[6] Overall, it was said to challenge the traditional nexus between citizenship, territory, sovereignty and criminal law.[7]

Mutual recognition does challenge this traditional nexus, but not in a manner one might immediately assume. It is wrong to assume that there is a simple extension of territorial jurisdiction beyond the state,[8] allowing a Member State to exercise jurisdiction outside its own territory, imposing *its* law in the territory of other Member States, and hence raising problems of legality in particular. The territorial jurisdiction exercised by states in their criminal law is a part of criminal law that is (for the most part) defined by national law.[9] This is generally defined in accordance with the territory of the state but there are circumstances when the state seeks to exercise extraterritorial jurisdiction, largely based on personal jurisdiction.[10] Member States already claim extraterritorial jurisdiction in criminal law and the EAW FD does not change this in any way. It is certainly true that there is increasing change in traditional notions of territoriality in criminal law, linked to interrelated social, economic and technological developments,[11] and that the EAW FD is an element in the response to the globalisation of crime.[12] However, while it certainly facilitates the enforcement of extra-territorial offences the EAW FD does not, in and of itself, alter national territorial jurisdiction.

[6] See Jan Komarek, 'European Constitutionalism and the European Arrest Warrant: In Search of the Limits of "Contrapunctual Principles"' (2007) 44 *CML Rev* 9 and Valsamis Mitsilegas, 'The Constitutional Implications of Mutual Recognition in Criminal Matters in the EU' (2006) 43 *CML Rev* 1277.

[7] Valsamis Mitsilegas, *EU Criminal Law* (Hart Publishing, 2009) Conclusion.

[8] This view of mutual recognition may be considered implicit in Kalypso Nicolaidis and Gregory Shaffer, 'Transnational Mutual Recognition Regimes: Governance without Global Government' (2005) 68 *Law and Comtemporary Problems* 263.

[9] Some EU criminal law instruments that deal with substantive criminal law do oblige Member States to exercise extraterritorial jurisdiction in certain circumstances; see, for example, Framework Decision 2002/475/JHA on combating terrorism [2002] OJ L164/3 Art 9(1) and Directive 2011/93/EU on combating the sexual abuse and sexual exploitation of children and child pornography, and replacing Council Framework Decision 2004/68/JHA [2011] OJ L355/1, Art 17.

[10] The French Criminal Code, in particular, exercises so-called passive extraterritorial personal jurisdiction for serious crimes such as murder, meaning it claims authority to punish individuals for crimes committed against French citizens abroad. Irish law, on the other hand, exercises active extraterritorial jurisdiction, meaning it will prosecute Irish citizens for crimes committed outside the territory of the Republic of Ireland. The discrepancy between jurisdiction proved useful to the Irish Supreme Court when deciding not to surrender a British national sought in France for a crime committed in Ireland, with the Supreme Court requiring reciprocity between both the category of the crime (murder) and the precise form of jurisdiction; Ireland only exercised active extraterritorial jurisdiction (where the suspect is a national), whereas France was exercising passive extraterritorial jurisdiction (where the victim is a national). See *Minister for Justice, Equality and Law Reform v Bailey* [2012] IESC 16.

[11] See Lindsay Farmer, 'Time and Space in Criminal Law' (2010) 13 *New Criminal Law Review* 333.

[12] In particular terrorism, see Cian Murphy, *EU Counter-Terrorism Law: Pre-emption and the Rule of Law* (Hart Publishing, 2012) ch 7. Thus it may be characterised as an instance of transnational criminal law. For an account of the phenomena of transnational criminal law, see Neil Boister, *An Introduction to Transnational Criminal Law* (Oxford University Press, 2012).

Indeed, the EAW FD is at pains to ensure that Member States retain priority over the prosecution of crimes committed on their territory. Article 7(a) EAW FD provides that an EAW can be refused in cases where the crime took place principally in the territory of the executing Member State.[13] A requirement of reciprocity may also be imposed, allowing Member States to refuse to surrender where they do not themselves exercise extraterritorial jurisdiction in similar cases.[14] Similar provisions were found in other mutual-recognition instruments such as the European Evidence Warrant (EEW) and its replacement the European Investigation Order.[15] The question of extraterritorial jurisdiction is a sensitive one and treated as such by the EAW FD. Member States are quite simply not obliged under the mutual-recognition instruments to accept the jurisdiction of other Member States over acts committed on their territory. While not denying the existence of extraterritorial forms of jurisdiction, it nonetheless prioritises the claims of the Member State on whose territory a particular criminal act took place.

However, although EU mutual recognition instruments do not change the territorial jurisdiction of Member States' criminal law, there is a truth in the idea that traditional concepts of territoriality and sovereignty are disrupted. The mutual recognition instruments do imply a certain loss of control. But that loss of control is not over territorial jurisdiction per se; it does not imply that Member States are obliged to accept the jurisdiction of other Member States over their territory. What it does imply is a loss of control over how individuals on their territory are treated and the extent to which they are subject to the criminal justice system of other Member States. It obliges Member States to participate in the enforcement of other Member States' criminal laws on their territory. It is not extraterritorial *jurisdiction* that is at stake – indeed there are express provisions to prevent this occurring – but extraterritorial *enforcement*. And in being obliged to enforce other Member States' criminal law on their territory, Member States' traditional controls over how their citizens are treated and the principles of legality and of fundamental rights are applied on their territory are undermined. The EAW FD system, in establishing a system of shared enforcement, does raise serious questions regarding territoriality, the sovereignty of states and the legitimate use of force.

Legitimising Criminal Law: Three Dimensions

The legitimacy of a particular community holding an individual to account and potentially punishing him for wrongdoing depends on identifying a particular

[13] EAW FD (n 3) Art 7(a).

[14] ibid, Art 7(b). Exactly how narrowly the concept of type of extraterritorial jurisdiction is defined can lead to some surprising results. See *Bailey* (n 10).

[15] Framework Decision 2008/978/JHA on the European Evidence Warrant for the pupose of obtaining objects, documents and data for use in proceedings in criminal matters [2008] OJ L350/72, Art 13(f) and Directive 2014/41/EU regarding the European Investigation Order in criminal matters [2014] OJ L130/1 Art 11(e).

moral standing of that community vis-à-vis that individual.[16] For Duff this moral standing is assured through the status of citizenship and the link this creates between the individual and broader political community.[17] This relationship of citizenship (or 'guests' for non-citizens)[18] is a necessary but not a sufficient condition for the legitimacy of that community's actions in punishing an individual. Additionally, the wrong must be a public one – one that is of concern to the public. In other words it should be considered criminal by the community and reflected in the community's laws.[19] Finally, the community must ensure that by affording certain rights and complying with certain standards of procedural justice it does not forfeit its right to call individuals to account and potentially punish them; it owes basic duties in its conduct towards others in order not to undermine its own moral standing and hence legitimacy.[20]

All three elements are disrupted by the operation of the EAW system. Firstly, the EAW obliges Member States to recognise the authority of other Member States to punish their nationals; Member States can no longer claim any special responsibility for their nationals and hence refuse to recognise the claims of other Member States. Secondly, the EAW has (partly) abolished the rule against double criminality; Member States may now be asked to participate in the enforcement of another Member State's law even where the executing Member State does not consider the act to be criminal and hence wrongful. Thirdly and finally, on its face the EAW system prevents Member States from imposing any fundamental rights control on the process of surrender.

However, those elements of legitimacy that are disrupted at a national level – citizenship, legality and fundamental rights, all conferred by the system of transnational enforcement and usually protected in an extradition setting – *are* present in the operation of the EAW system, but at a supranational level. In their effort to create a more effective system of surrender[21] based on shared enforcement, Member States have perhaps undermined the traditional safeguards for individuals and for the sovereignty of states present in national legal orders.

[16] See Alejandro Chehtman, 'Citizenship v Territory: Explaining the Scope of the Criminal Law' (2010) 13 *New Criminal Law Review* 427.

[17] Antony Duff, *Answering for Crime: Responsibility and Liability in the Criminal Law* (Hart Publishing, 2007) ch 2. See also Farmer (n 11) 355.

[18] Duff (n 17) 54. Perhaps the most problematic aspect of Duff's theory; see Chehtman (n 16). In particular it has problems explaining not just the liability of non-nationals on the territory of the state but also certain forms of extraterritorial jurisdiction such as the passive extraterritorial jurisdiction exercised by France in *Bailey* (n 10).

[19] Duff (n 17) 49–50.

[20] ibid, 181–91.

[21] There is little doubt that effectiveness was a major motivating force behind the introduction of the EAW FD and indeed has informed to a considerable extent the subsequent interpretation of the FD by the Court of Justice. See Ester Herlin-Karnell, 'From Mutual Trust to the Full Effectiveness of EU Law: 10 Years of the European Arrest Warrant' (2013) 38 *EL Rev* 79. For a more recent restatement of the importance of effectiveness in the interpretation of the EAW FD, see Case C-514/17 *Ministère public v Marin-Simion Sut* EU:C:2018:1016, paras 27ff.

But in doing so they have at the same time both assumed and constructed a supranational normative framework for transnational enforcement. Citizenship, legality and fundamental rights, separated from national territory, are relocated within a supranational space. An analysis of the legitimacy of the EAW system of shared enforcement reveals a complex interaction between the national, transnational and supranational. The *transnational* enforcement of *national* law is justified and based on a common citizenship, supranational values and ultimately an indirect, composite supranational community.

Legitimising Shared Enforcement I: Shared Citizenship

Abolition of the Nationality Exemption

The nationality exemption was typically applied by states within the civil law tradition to shield their nationals from extradition to other states. Its justifications are many and varied and include a special relationship between the citizen and 'his' homeland, a general distrust of foreign jurisdictions, perceived biases against 'foreigners', a need to be judged by ones 'natural peers', or simply the practical difficulties that an individual might face in navigating a foreign legal system, often in a language he or she does not understand.[22] It does not necessarily imply that the state does not believe the individual should be punished for wrongful behaviour. Indeed, states frequently undertook to 'surrender or prosecute' in the context of extradition clauses if they exercised a nationality exception.[23] Within Duff's theory it can perhaps be understood as a claim by the state of nationality that *it* is the most appropriate entity to try and punish a particular individual. The calling to account of a particular individual should be before the community to which he belongs.

The nationality exemption was not carried forward within the EAW system. Instead it was replaced by a modified principle allowing Member States to refuse surrender or impose a guarantee that an individual, be it a national or resident, can serve their sentence in the executing Member State.[24] However, importantly, the individual remains subject to the issuing Member State's law and is still called to account before that Member State, the only difference being that the sentence is carried out closer to home.[25] The calling to account in the form of a trial still takes place before the issuing Member State; it is the punishment that is carried out by

[22] See generally Michael Plachta, '(Non-)Extradition of Nationals: A Neverending Story' (1999) 13 *Emory International Law Review* 70.

[23] In a related fashion extensive extraterritorial jurisdiction by such states ensured there was jurisdiction to prosecute in such cases. See ibid, 118ff.

[24] See EAW FD (n 3) Arts 4(6) and 5(3).

[25] See Chapter 4 and the judgments of Case C-579/15 *Openbaar Ministerie v Daniel Adam Popławski* EU:C:2017:503 and *Sut* (n 21).

the executing Member State.[26] Secondly, and as explored further in Chapter 4, the entire rationale and logic of the new article is different. It is based not on nationality but rather on the principle of social integration and the social links an individual may have with the executing Member State.[27]

The abolition of this exemption was subject to a significant degree of resistance from national constitutional courts. The German, Polish, Czech and Cypriot constitutional courts were all seized with constitutional challenges to the national implementing legislation, with all but the Czech court finding it in breach of national constitutional provisions preventing a national from being extradited. Characteristically, it was the German Constitutional Court (Bundesverfassungsgericht or BvfG) that provided the most trenchant criticism of the FD, and in doing so emphasised the special bond between the citizen and the state reflected in the prohibition on extradition. In its decision the BvfG highlighted the link between the nationality exception, the sovereign community and the individual. To be excluded from the state and subject to foreign laws was tantamount to an abrogation of the protection offered by the legal system of the state to a citizen when present on its territory. Indeed, such a procedure was equated to denationalisation or stripping an individual of rights inherent in citizenship and an analogy was drawn with the treatment of the Jewish community under National Socialism.[28]

Despite its perhaps dramatic rhetoric, in its remedy the BvfG showed itself more concerned with territorial effect of the EAW FD and the risk of foreign law being applied on German territory.[29] It therefore ordered the German government to implement the territorial exception in order to render the implementing legislation constitutional.[30] However, the link between citizenship, rights and territory

[26] A not unimportant feature giving rise to a certain shared responsibility for Member States for both the punishment and rehabilitation of individuals. See also the possibility that sentences be discounted to take into account sentences served in other Member States via Framework Decision 2008/675/JHA on taking account of convictions in the Member States of the European Union in the course of new criminal proceedings [2008] OJ L220/32.

[27] See further Chapter 4.

[28] *Re Constitutionality of German Law Implementing the Framework Decision on a European Arrest Warrant* [2006] 1 CMLR 16, paras 66–67.

[29] See, in particular, paras 85–86: 'There is a relevant connection to Germany when a significant proportion of the places where conduct or its effects have occurred lie in German territory. In this situation the responsibility of the State to avoid damage to its legal system, and the fundamental rights claims of the person against whom the arrest warrant is issued, coincide in such a way that usually there is an obstacle to extradition … the assessment is otherwise if the crime of which the person in question is accused has a decisive foreign connection. A person who does something under a foreign legal system must reckon with the possibility that he will be taken there to answer for it.'

[30] For a comment, see Nicolas Nohlen, 'Germany: The European Arrest Warrant Case' (2008) 6 *iCON* 153, arguing that the BvgG ignored the possibility of consistent interpretation as a possible means of rendering the impugned act compliant with EU law. It is possible that this misunderstands the problem, which was a possible lack of conformity of a national implementing law not with EU law (where the principle of consistent interpretation may and should play a role) but rather with the national constitution, in which case the extent to which any principle of consistent interpretation should play a role is surely a matter for domestic rules of statutory construction and interpretation.

drawn by the BvfG is not entirely without interest or foundation. Underlying the BvfG's concerns is not so much the obligation to subject the individual to the claims of other Member States, but doing so in the absence of the guarantees provided by the German legal order. It therefore highlights the territorially bound nature of normativity and the emplacement of both norms, including fundamental rights, and citizenship together within a particular territory and the degree to which the EAW disrupts this connection – a theme to which we return to below.[31]

Union Citizenship and a Single Area of Justice

The creation of a system of shared enforcement implies an altered relationship between the individual and both the executing and issuing Member States. The executing Member State must recognise the legitimate claims of other Member States over individuals located on its territory. The result is a certain weakening of the relationship between the executing Member State and its citizens as recognised by the BvfG. Conversely, the relationship between the *issuing* Member State and the community it represents (and potentially all Member States in the European Union) and the individual is also affected. Any individual may now be called to account directly anywhere in the Union for an offence committed against that Member State. These national responsibilities attach to an individual and may be enforced within a wider geographical area. Just as rights attach to individuals and are transported or passported throughout the Union, responsibilities are similarly placed in a broader space of movement and are enforceable anywhere in the Union.

There is a certain correspondence between the transnational rights associated with free movement and the transnational responsibilities, which is rooted in the status of EU citizenship. Both rights and responsibilities operate in a similar fashion of mutual recognition and both are justified by a similar membership structure based on transnational movement and multiple, potential memberships in a plural set of communities that together form a broader space of movement. Just as autonomy and choice lie at the heart of mutual recognition of rights associated with free movement, that same freedom and choice can be seen as legitimising responsibilities incurred in other Member States.[32] Individuals are given the opportunity to

[31] See Hans Lindahl, 'Finding a Place for Freedom, Security and Justice: The European Union's Claim to Territorial Unity' (2004) 29 *EL Rev* 461. For an account of the importance of the 'right to a place', see Alison Kesby, *The Right to Have Rights: Citizenship, Humanity and International Law* (Oxford University Press, 2012) ch 1.

[32] See Richard Bellamy, 'A Duty-Free Europe? What's Wrong with Kochenov's Account of EU Citizenship Rights' (2015) 21 *ELJ* 558, 563–65. Bellamy is not speaking specifically of responsibilities incurred through criminal law (in Duff's terms the responsibility to answer for wrongdoing) but rather civic responsibilities in the abstract. Nonetheless there is no reason such a reasoning cannot be applied in the current case. There are of course classic problems associated with legitimacy through consent and the contract tradition from which it emerges, a discussion of which lies outside the scope of this work. See Dudley Knowles, *Political Obligation: A Critical Introduction* (Routledge, 2010) chs 7–8.

move to other Member States and there enjoy certain rights as part of a broader status and in doing so subject themselves to responsibilities.

In opposition to the BvfG, this view of EU citizenship and the correlation with free movement and responsibilities was underlined by the Czech Constitutional Court. For the BvfG, EU citizenship is a status that merely supplements national citizenship with a set of extra rights, and does not alter the underlying national status in any fundamental way. It is simply an extension, a set of rights tacked on without affecting the nature of national citizenship itself and without changing the relationship with the state of nationality and the guarantees that go with it.[33] The Czech Constitutional Court, on the other hand, took a more symbiotic view of the relationship between EU citizenship and national citizenship. Not only is EU citizenship a set of additional rights – an extension of national citizenship rights – but it alters and changes certain aspects of national citizenship, in particular by recognising responsibilities to other Member States and thereby altering the relationship with the Member State of nationality. The link between free movement, EU citizenship and responsibilities is recognised by the Czech Constitutional Court for whom EU citizenship introduces

> [a] qualitatively new situation. … Citizens of the Member States enjoyed, in addition to rights arising from citizenship in their own State, also rights arising from EU citizenship, which guaranteed, among other things, free movement within the province of the entire Union. … If Czech citizens enjoyed certain advantages connected to the status of EU citizenship, then they had also to accept a certain degree of responsibility.[34]

It is important to note that in the Czech Constitutional Court's judgment it is the *status* of citizenship and the broader transnational membership relationship that is established by virtue of EU citizenship that justifies the transnational enforcement. Rights and responsibilities form the content of that status, and there is a connection and indeed complementarity between them in this context. That connection is not, however, found in some form of quid pro quo whereby an individual must have exercised or indeed be capable of exercising rights in order to hold responsibilities. There is not a direct correspondence between the exercise of some rights and incurring other responsibilities but rather in the broader membership status and structures that they imply. It is because of rights of free movement that an individual holds a relationship with other Member States, a relationship that in turn contains responsibilities justifying transnational enforcement. EU citizens stand in a particular form of moral and political relationship to other Member States of the Union; a relationship that for the Czech Constitutional Court legitimises their being directly subject to the criminal law of those states and justifies the removal of protections that states typically offered individuals who fell within

[33] *Re Constitutionality of German Law Implementing the Framework Decision on a European Arrest Warrant* (n 28) paras 74–75.

[34] *Re Constitutionality of Framework Decision on a European Arrest Warrant (Czech Constitutional Court)* [2007] 3 CMLR 24, para H6.

their jurisdiction.[35] EU citizenship is an integral part of national citizenship and changes the meaning of national citizenship. By virtue of being Czech one must also accept responsibilities towards France, Estonia, etc. This is why the exercise of some form of special protection vis-à-vis other states in the Union is no longer justified.

This link with the status of citizenship is important in Duff's account for founding authority to punish, and goes some way towards legitimising the more controversial aspects of the EAW FD. In order for a particular body to have the right to punish an individual it must have a particular moral standing vis-à-vis that individual.[36] That moral standing is based on a relationship of belonging to a particular community that generates a network of interactions and ties and ultimately rights and responsibilities. Due to the special bonds formed by EU citizenship, Member States therefore have the requisite moral standing in order to legitimately call individuals to account regardless of their place in the Union. And importantly, other Member States may not intervene to prevent that occurring. Just as Member States must respect the rights granted by other Member States, they must respect the responsibilities owed those Member States and the right of other Member States to enforce those responsibilities.

There is, however, a different structure in the enforcement of these responsibilities compared to rights acquired under EU law that emphasises the enduring national character of the wrong committed by an individual. The individual citizen typically acquires rights in a particular Member State, moves to another Member State and it is that, second, Member State that is under an obligation to enforce or respect those rights. The rights acquire a free-floating character. Thus an individual may move to Ireland, there be joined by his or her family members and subsequently move to France. France under those circumstances is obliged to recognise the right to family unification and take appropriate measures, such as the issuing of residence permits. Under the EAW system and the system of the free movement of responsibilities there is an additional stage involved, returning the individual to the original Member State and thereby rendering the process more circular. The responsibility is owed to the first Member State and remains owed to the first Member State; the obligation placed on the second Member State is merely transitory: to detain and surrender an individual and return him or her to the original Member State.[37] Thus the Court has underlined the fact that the EAW itself must

[35] Although it should be noted that the comment is largely academic; the Czech Constitutional Court did not find that the Czech Constitution prevented nationals from being surrendered in any case, the right to a homeland being largely a prohibition against forced exile such as occurred during the 'demolition' under the communist regime. See ibid, para 41.

[36] See Duff (n 17) ch 8.

[37] The Court has therefore emphasised that 'the decision of the executing authority it not intended to grant, in the present case, enforcement of a custodial sentence in the issuing Member State … that decision merely grants surrender of the person requested … so that the offence committed does not go unpunished. The basis for the enforcement of a custodial sentence lies in the enforceable judgment pronounced in the issuing Member State' in Case C-551/18 PPU *IK* EU:C:2018:991, para 56.

be based on an underlying national arrest warrant; it is the act under national law that lays the basis for liability and hence justifies the use of an EAW, which remains an ancillary step in the proceedings.[38] Unlike rights, responsibilities created under national criminal law remain clearly linked to a particular Member State. Not only are they created under a particular Member State's national law but they are owed, and remain owed, to that particular Member State; they do not detach from a particular community and float throughout the territory of the Union in the same manner as rights.[39]

Such an understanding fits with a conception of crime such as Duff's that is based on community and the links between a particular community, its criminal laws and the responsibilities held by an individual. A crime is an offence as created under the laws of a particular national community within the Union. It is before that community that an individual must return to be called to account and, in the event of a finding of guilt, be punished. Prosecution and punishment by another state not so wronged quite simply does not achieve the same goal.[40]

Responsibilities therefore play out in a broader space, which shifts between supranational, or Union-wide, and national. Furthermore, there is an underlying territorial element to this correspondence between rights and responsibilities; both are now emplaced in a broader geographic space composed of the territories of the Member States. The system of transnational enforcement of responsibilities established by the EAW is a reflection of this broader legal space, in part created by free movement rights. There is a link between free movement and crime but not only in the contested empirical claim that free movement leads to greater levels of cross-border crime and hence the need for so-called flanking measures.[41] EU citizens occupy a broader space of movement in which a status involving rights and responsibilities is established with separate national communities. It is a single Union-wide space of movement within which national responsibilities are enforced. The image of a single area of justice is not simply rhetorical but refers to a very real space with reference to which EU citizenship operates including both

[38] Case C-241/15 *Niculaie Aurel Bob-Dogi* EU:C:2016:385. Note the interesting characterisation of the EAW system as an intermediary system of mutual recognition by AG Bot: 'The Framework Decision represents, lastly, an intermediate stage in the gradual implementation and strengthening of the principle of mutual recognition, which is reflected in particular in the fact that a European arrest warrant is conceived as an instrument in national proceedings, the issue of which remains dependent on there being a pre-existing enforceable order at national level.' See Case C-241/15 *Niculaie Aurel Bob-Dogi* (Opinion of AG Bot) EU:C:2016:131, para 48.

[39] Like in the story of God and the thief, the EAW attaches 'an unseen hook and an invisible line which is long enough to let him wander to the ends of the world and still to bring him back with a twitch upon the thread'. Evelyn Waugh, *Brideshead Revisited* [1945] (Penguin 2000) part I, ch 5.

[40] Although note the ambiguity introduced by the operation of the *ne bis in idem* rule contained in Art 54 CISA. See further Chapter 7.

[41] As stated by Bruggeman 'the internationalisation of the major criminal organisations has come about regardless of the treaties on the free movement of goods and persons'. Willy Bruggeman, 'Policing in a European Context' in Joanna Apap (ed), *Justice and Home Affairs in the EU: Liberty and Security Issues after Enlargement* (Edward Elgar, 2004) 164.

rights and responsibilities. And it is in this single, supranational space that the issues of legality and rights, detached from national territory, re-emerge.

Legitimising Shared Enforcement II: Shared Wrongs

This moral standing between the issuing Member State and the individual established through EU citizenship justifies to some extent the obligation placed on the executing Member State to participate in a system of shared enforcement. However, it is not sufficient. The executing Member State must also stand in a particular relation with the wrongful act of that individual. For Duff, the justification for punishment emerges not just from the status of citizenship but also from the determination of conduct as publically wrongful in the eyes of that community. It must be a wrong that concerns the public and moreover it must concern that particular public or community.[42] Thus, while the wrongs we are concerned with in the system of shared enforcement remain fundamentally (trans)national that is not to say that there is not a certain shared dimension to them, both in conception and experience, that justifies shared enforcement and implies a broader supranational community.

Abolition of Double Criminality

Perhaps the most controversial aspect of the EAW FD was the abolition of the double-criminality rule. The EAW FD in principle abolishes the rule of double criminality; it may be reintroduced by Member States as an optional ground for refusal but this exception will not apply to a set list of thirty-two categories of core crimes, including murder, rape and theft, and acts subject to the Union's competence under Article 83(2) TFEU to criminalise certain acts.[43] Even where a requirement of double criminality is introduced, it is to be applied at a relatively high level of abstraction, thereby facilitating surrender even in these cases.[44] It therefore abolishes a strict rule of double criminality for potentially all crimes, and certainly for a list of thirty-two categories of core crimes. Furthermore, the criminal

[42] It is this concern to a particular community that underpins Duff's explanation of jurisdiction. See Duff (n 17) 49.
[43] EAW FD (n 3) Art 2(1) and (2).
[44] Case C-289/15 *Criminal proceedings against Jozef Grundza* EU:C:2017:4, para 36. *Grundza* concerned the interpretation of the double-criminality requirement in Framework Decision 2008/909/JHA on the application of the principle of mutual recognition to judgments in criminal matters imposing custodial sentences or measures involving deprivation of liberty for the purposes of their enforcement in the European Union [2008] OJ L327/27; however, there is no reason to believe that an interpretation of the double-criminality requirement that may be imposed in the implementation of the EAW FD would be interpreted differently.

nature and classification of the act is determined by the requesting Member State, a determination that must be accepted by the Member State of execution.[45]

The rule of double criminality can be described as an application of the general principle of legality in criminal law, namely that an act should not be punishable unless it is forbidden by sufficiently clear and validly adopted law or more specifically the principle of *nullum poena sine lege* (no punishment without law), the argument being that to arrest and detain an individual in a particular state for an act that that state does not in fact consider criminal would amount to an illegal deprivation of liberty in the absence of a crime and a violation of his or her right to liberty.

The EAW FD does not abolish the principle of legality but rather separates it from strict considerations of territory. The specific act for which the accused individual is being sought *is* a crime as defined by law. Indeed, it is defined as such by the most appropriate law, that where the act was committed or by the community whose interests were adversely effected. Crimes as wrongs are relational acts and take place with reference to a particular community; it is by reference to the law of that community that the legality or otherwise of the crime should be assessed.[46] This is precisely the position that has been adopted by the Court of Justice. In *Advocaten voor de Wereld* the plaintiffs, a Belgian NGO, raised a complaint based on the violation of fundamental rights, including the principle of legality.[47] The Court in its answer pointed out that the EAW FD does not classify an act as criminal or otherwise; that is for the national law of the issuing Member State. The EAW FD is merely an instrument of mutual recognition of a national act. The act is therefore validly classified as a crime under the appropriate national law, in this case the law of the requesting Member State.[48] It replaces national legality with a form of transnational legality.

What is really at stake is the participation of the executing Member State in the enforcement of another Member State's criminal law and its particular normative choices regarding what acts should be classified as criminal and the extent to

[45] For the residual category of offences for which Member States may make any mutual recognition subject to the double-nationality requirement, the Court has outlined a broad application of that principle in the sense that strict correspondence between the offence under the legal system of the issuing Member State and that of the executing Member State is not necessary. What is important is that the act would attract a criminal penalty in both Member States despite differences in the constituent elements of the crime or in the labelling of the crime. See *Grundza*. Note that *Grundza* concerned the Transfer of Custodial Sentences Framework Decision rather than the EAW FD. However, as noted by AG Bobek in that case the double-criminality rule in the former Directive was lifted from the latter and operates according to similar principles. One must assume that they would therefore be interpreted in a similar manner. Incidentally it is also interesting to note the interesting endorsement of a moral vision of the criminal law.

[46] Indeed, the question not only of whether the state has a right to punish but equally important *which* state has the right to punish is one that has largely been ignored by criminal law theory; see Chehtman (n 16) 430.

[47] Case C-303/05 *Advocaten voor de Wereld VZW v Leden van de Ministerraad* EU:C:2007:261, [2007] ECR I-3633.

[48] ibid, paras 52–54.

which the use of force on its territory must correspond with its understanding of wrongful conduct. As put by Peers:

> Since sovereign States are free to take different views as to what should be criminalized and to what extent, and these differences are rooted deeply in different cultures and national identities and represent different choices resulting from the democratic process in each State, why should States in principle be obliged to assist another State to apply its criminal law where the two States differ on whether the relevant act should be criminalized?[49]

Indeed this is precisely the rationale advanced by the Court of Justice for the identical provisions on double criminality included in the Framework Decision on the Transfer of Prisoners,[50] with the Court noting in *Grundza* that the option contained in that Framework Decision allowing Member States to subject any mutual recognition to the condition of double criminality 'enables Member States … to decline to recognise a judgment and enforce a sentence in respect of conduct which they do not consider to be morally wrong and which does not, therefore, constitute an offence'.[51]

Shared Conception of a Wrong

However, in truth the EAW FD does not entirely abolish the double-criminality rule; it establishes a presumption that it would be met in all relevant cases. The implication is that there is a shared conception of the wrongful character of certain actions throughout the European Union. As mentioned above, the requirement of double criminality is abolished definitively for a list of thirty-two categories of crimes.[52] This list is not random. The Court of Justice has claimed that the 'serious' character of these crimes justifies their placement on the list.[53] That may be somewhat misleading. There is a relationship with 'seriousness', as indicated by the *de minimis* rule contained in Article 1(3) EAW FD limiting the use of the EAW FD to offences that carry a certain minimum sentence.[54] However,

[49] Peers (n 5) 24–25. Indeed, originally the double-criminality rule was an expression of the rule of reciprocity in relation to criminal norms and only later came to be considered as an individual right. See Lech Gardocki, 'Double Criminality in Extradition Law' (1993) 27 *Israel Law Review* 288, 289.

[50] Transfer of Custodial Sentences Framework Decision (n 45). For further analysis of this Framework Decision, see Chapter 4.

[51] *Grundza* (n 45) para 45.

[52] EAW FD (n 3) Art 2(2).

[53] *Advocaten voor de Wereld* (n 47) para 57.

[54] The question of proportionality has also been used by some national courts as a reason to refuse surrender, considering detention and surrender for a minor offence a disproportionate interference with a suspect's rights (particularly if a family life is involved); see *Minister for Justice and Equality v Ostrowski* [2013] IESC 24, [2013] 5 JIC 1501. Although note this ruling was reversed on appeal to the Irish Supreme Court, see ibid. The Commission for its part does believe proportionality should play some role in the EAW system but is a matter to be assessed by the issuing Member State; the role of the executing Member State remains a formal one. See Report from the Commission on the implementation since 2007 of the Council Framework Decision of 13 June 2002 on the European arrest warrant and the surrender procedures between Member States COM(2011) 175 final, 7–8.

the 'seriousness' here is a label for their centrality to a common understanding of the core elements of a criminal justice system rather than any heightened level of harm or other moral transgression. After all, minor thefts that may fall within the scope of the EAW FD can hardly be considered 'serious' in terms of harm caused or inherent moral blameworthiness. Rather it is the centrality to a system of criminal law that protects the person and property that marks it as serious. These are acts against the person and against property that form the core of any system of criminal law concerned with protecting the liberty and interests of individuals and would generally be seen as falling within the category of *mala in se* – acts whose wrongful character arises independent of legal regulation and that form the basis of a shared common denominator regarding acts that should be criminal. Furthermore, other categories of crime on the list contained in Article 2(2) EAW FD are precisely those for which the Union has competence to enact approximation measures.[55] Again, the presumption is that by granting the Union approximating powers in such matters, a certain equivalence, or at least common understanding of the wrongful character of these acts, already exists. The double-criminality rule is not disapplied; it is simply presumed to have been met.

It is therefore the shared judgment of their wrongful character and the appropriateness of their criminalisation amongst Member States that justifies the abolition of a formal condition of double criminality in these instances. The abolition of the double-criminality rule does not mean that it is no longer necessary for these acts to be classified as criminal in all Member States. On the contrary, it is precisely because these acts are considered criminal by all Member States throughout the Union that there is no need to apply a rule of double criminality. These are acts that in the view of *all* Member States are wrongful and properly concern the public. This is precisely the understanding of AG Ruiz-Jarabo in *Advocaten voor de Wereld* when dismissing the requirement of double criminality. Such a requirement would be 'outmoded since the participants in the procedure (Member States) both regard the conduct which gives rise to the request as criminal … for the reasons stated, reciprocity and double criminality are presumed for certain offences'.[56]

Shared Experience of a Wrong?

However, in order for its punishment to be justified, a particular act must not only be considered a public wrong in the abstract by a particular community but it must concern that particular community; it must be a wrong against *that* community. Does this shared conception of a wrong translate into something

[55] For the link between the approximation competence contained in Art 83(2) TFEU and the expression of a supranational conception of wrongfulness, see Chapter 8. See also Anne Weyembergh, 'The Functions of Approximation of Penal Legislation within the European Union' (2005) 12 *Maastricht Journal of European and Comparative Law* 149.

[56] Case C-303/05 *Advocaten voor de Wereld VZW v Leden van de Ministerraad* (Opinion of AG Ruiz-Jarabo Colomer) EU:C:2006:552, paras 45–47.

deeper – a shared experience of the wrong and hence the reflection of a wider supranational community capable of being wronged in this sense?

For Lööf the EAW system assumes a single social contract throughout the Union.[57] The social contract is established as a mechanism for regulating relations between individuals *inter se* and in the field of criminal law amounts to a mutual commitment to restrict freedom for the promotion of liberty. The legitimacy of state action and the use of force arises from this network of horizontal relations established between citizens through the social contract and the implicit consent that goes with it.[58] For Lööf in order for the EAW system to be considered legitimate, the system of shared enforcement it involves implies that political relations are established not simply within a particular Member State but amongst individuals throughout the Union; in other words, the Union represents a single social contract.

The truth is perhaps somewhat more nuanced. The legal provisions and the responsibilities they establish imply not a single social contract, or rather not a single homogeneous and undivided social contract between EU citizens, but a plural, differentiated social contract mediated by national political communities. Within the operation of the EAW system the crime remains (trans)national and is directly experienced by national communities. It is in accordance with the issuing Member State's national criminal law that the act is considered wrongful and its seriousness is likewise assessed according to the same Member State's national criminal law.[59] The EAW must be based on an underlying national arrest warrant.[60] Furthermore, as described above, in contrast to the enjoyment of rights, in the enforcement of transnational responsibilities the role of the executing Member State is transitory. The individual is returned to the issuing Member State to stand trial or to serve punishment. The calling to account and the secular penance is served vis-à-vis the issuing Member State – the Member State against whom the wrong has been committed.[61] The executing Member State acts merely as an agent for the issuing Member State in a specific, intermediate role – that of detaining and returning the individual. The wrong is still considered primarily against the issuing Member State and the direct victim of the offence is the political community it represents; it remains a (trans)national rather than a supranational wrong.

[57] Robin Lööf, 'Defending Liberty and Structural Integrity: A Social Contractual Analysis of Criminal Justice in the EU' (PhD thesis, Department of Law, European University Institute 2008) Title II.

[58] For the consent basis for legitimacy, see Knowles (n 32) ch 7. It is therefore the original social contract between individuals *inter se* in forming a community rather than a subsequent social contract between the community and the government that is at stake for Lööf. See JW Gough, *The Social Contract: A Critical Study of its Development*, 2 edn (Clarendon Press, 1957), ch 1 for a distinction between the two stages of the social contract.

[59] See *Advocaten voor de Wereld* (n 47) and *Bob-Dogi* (n 38) underlining in different ways the national character of the offence underlying the EAW.

[60] *Bob-Dogi* (n 38).

[61] Although note the system of supranational responsibility established in the area of the transfer of sentences and EAW FD (n 3) Art 4(6). See further Chapter 4.

However, that is not to say that in addition to the wrong to the national community, there is no supranational wrong. The concept of a shared wrong, developed by Duff and Marshall in the national context in relations between individual citizens, may be applied by analogy.[62] For Duff and Marshall a wrong directly experienced by an individual becomes a matter of public concern not (simply) because of its potential effect on public order and the need to secure a law-abiding environment within which individuals can enjoy their rights.[63] The 'publicness' of the wrong is more fundamental. It is because of the direct victim's standing as a member of the community that the wrong is in fact shared by the community as a whole. It is because an individual has harmed one that he harms all; it is through the harm and suffering of the individual that the community is harmed vicariously.[64] The same logic could be applied between Member States who are members of the same meta-community; because you have directly wronged one community, you have indirectly wronged all communities. There is therefore a supplementary, indirect and vicarious supranational dimension to the wrong that involves the entire Union. The wronging of one national community is of public concern for the Union as a whole. It is through the commission of a national wrong that the supranational interest is engaged and hence the participation of all Member States in a system of shared enforcement is justified. This reconciles the undeniable national character of criminal wrongs – as seen not only by the structure of enforcement but also in the interaction of the principle of social integration with criminal law[65] – with the role of all other Member States in the enforcement of that wrong, and engages them and their citizens in a single space of public order and justice.

The wrong is now assessed with reference to the Union as a whole; it is in a sense experienced throughout the Union and the Member States collectively share a conception of the wrong. The act is considered wrongful and criminal throughout the territory of the Union. The national normative judgment regarding what acts are criminal that is detached from national territory through transnational enforcement re-emerges at a supranational level. The principle of legality is met in a twofold transnational and supranational sense. On the one hand, the

[62] See also Chapter 4.

[63] Although of course sufficiently serious perturbation of public order itself may be a sufficient reason to consider a particular wrong as something that concerns the public. There certainly is an effort on the part of EU institutions to legitimise the EAW and related mutual-recognition instruments in this light, claiming that in an area of free movement the maintenance of public order and the corresponding effective enforcement of criminal law throughout the Union justifies mutual-recognition instruments. See the assessment of the discourse surrounding the AFSJ by Kostakopoulou in Dora Kostakopoulou, 'The Area of Freedom, Security and Justice and the European Union's Constitutional Dialogue' in Catherine Barnard (ed), *The Fundamentals of EU Law Revisited* (Oxford University Press, 2007). See also the comments of Twomey regarding the Union's efforts to construct a 'secure space'. See Patrick Twomey, 'Construcuting a Secure Space: The Area of Freedom, Security and Justice' in David O'Keefe and Patrick Twomey (eds), *Legal Issues of the Amsterdam Treaty* (Hart Publishing, 1999).

[64] See SE Marshall and RA Duff, 'Criminalization and Sharing Wrongs' (1998) 11 *Canadian Journal of Law and Jurisprudence* 7.

[65] See Chapters 4 and 5.

formal legality of the criminal prohibition is assessed under the law of the issuing Member State through a transnational form of legality; it is under this law that the act is formally designated as criminal and the individual punished. However, that is supplemented by a supranational endorsement that implies a shared understanding of the wrongful character of the act throughout the Union and justifies the executing Member State's participation in the enforcement of that law. The common supranational conception and experience of the wrong supports the claim of transnational legality and underpins the transnational enforcement of national law.

There is therefore a complementarity between the operation of the EAW FD and the shared system of enforcement it creates and the operation of the *ne bis in idem* principle found in Article 54 of the Convention Implementing the Schengen Agreement (CISA).[66] As described in further detail in Chapter 7, through an interpretation of the principle contained in Article 54 CISA motivated by the need to secure the free movement of individuals, the Court of Justice has been led to construct a single status for individuals with reference to a single territory. This in turn implies that an individual's wrongful conduct is considered with reference to the Union as a whole, and that by being called to account before a single Member State he is called to account indirectly for the Union as a whole. Article 54 CISA therefore operates as a 'regulatory principle' for Lööf within the system of shared enforcement.[67] The transnational shared system of enforcement and the operation of a transnational *ne bis in idem* principle imply the unambiguous national nature of criminal law and hence wrongdoing but place them within a broader supranational framework of shared wrongs.

Legitimising Shared Enforcement III: Supranational Rights

Legitimacy and Rights

The final element of the legitimacy of criminal enforcement and punishment that is disrupted by the operation of the EAW FD relates not to the relationship of the community with the individual or the individual's actions but with its own conduct. Legitimacy is a function of the belief a particular actor has that power is exercised in conformity with accepted norms.[68] The legitimacy of the EAW system

[66] Convention on the Implementation of the Schengen Agreement (CISA).

[67] Lööf (n 57) Title II.

[68] For the relationship between belief, norms and legitimacy in the context of political regimes, see David Beetham, *The Legitimation of Power*, 1 edn (Humanities Press, 1991). Beetham's theory has the benefit of combining what Weiler terms social and normative legitimacy. See Joseph Weiler, 'In the Face of Crisis: Input Legitimacy, Output Legitimacy and the Political Messianism of European Integration'

therefore must also rest on a shared belief in the justice of the underlying criminal procedures. In order to participate in the system of shared enforcement, Member States and individual actors – judges, prosecutors and perhaps above all suspects – should be confident in the third element of the legitimacy of punishment – that of competence in protecting the rights of the accused and ensuring a just outcome;[69] because they are being asked to participate in the enforcement of another Member State's criminal justice system, their belief in its compliance with certain norms is also of relevance. It is this third element of legitimacy that has given rise to the problem that is mutual trust.

Mutual trust and its relationship with mutual recognition present a paradox: the greater the absence of equivalent measures, the greater the need of mutual trust, but it is precisely the absence of equivalence that renders the existence of trust less likely.[70] Mutual trust – either in the internal market or in the AFSJ – normally requires a certain degree of equivalence.[71] Commentators have underlined the lack of equivalence in the operation of the EAW FD and hold this up as the underlying basis for an absence of mutual trust and hence the problems of legitimacy associated with the EAW FD.[72] The accusation is that executing Member States

(2012) 34 *Journal of European Integration* 825, 827–28. See also Gráinne de Búrca, 'The Quest for Legitimacy in the European Union' (1996) 59 *MLR* 349, 349.

[69] The criminal process is a system of imperfect procedural justice in which the procedure is designed in order to secure a just outcome according to independent criteria of justice (ie guilt or innocence). The justice or otherwise of the procedure depends on the extent to which it is capable of arriving at the just outcome, ie criteria of accuracy. See John Rawls, *A Theory of Justice* (Harvard University Press, 1971) 85ff.

[70] See Miguel-Poiares Maduro, 'So Close and Yet So Far: The Paradoxes of Mutual Recognition' (2007) 14 *Journal of European Public Policy* 814. For its part the Court of Justice has recently underlined the need for trust between the different national judicial actors in particular, emphasizing in Case C-216/18 PPU *Minister for Justice and Equality v LM* EU:C:2018:586 the key role played by an independent judiciary in the implementation of EU law generally and mutual-recognition systems (in the instant case the EAW FD). In other cases, the Court has underlined the need for an EAW to be issued by a *judicial* authority, characterised by a position of constitutional independence. See, in particular, Case C-452/16 *Openbaar Ministerie v Krzysztof Marek Poltorak* EU:C:2016:858, Case C-453/16 PPU *Openbaar Ministerie v Halil Ibrahim Özçelik* EU:C:2016:860 and Case C-477/16 PPU *Openbaar Ministerie v Ruslanas Kovalkovas* EU:C:2016:861. Finally, in Case C-220/18 PPU *ML* EU:C:2018:589, the Court of Justice held that the duty of loyal cooperation exists as between the issuing and the executing judicial authorities, with the implication that when requesting information regarding prison conditions in the issuing Member State, the executing judicial authority should be reasonable in its requests (para 104) and accept assurances provided by or endorsed by the issuing judicial authority (paras 111–12).

[71] Although note that the absence of equivalence is precisely the exceptional characteristic of the operation of the *ne bis in idem* principle in Art 534 CISA. See chapter 7.

[72] See in particular Möstl (n 4), although see the discussion by Janssens of the heterogeneous character of mutual-recognition regimes in Janssens (n 5). For a discussion of the question of diversity between criminal justice systems in the Union and the manner in which this diversity impacts on the development of EU criminal law, see Renaud Colson and Stewart Field (eds), *EU Criminal Justice and the Challenges of Diversity: Legal Cultures in the Area of Freedom, Security and Justice* (Cambridge University Press 2016).

are being obliged to participate in the enforcement of the issuing Member State's criminal law but in the absence of any guarantees that the issuing Member State's procedures comply to the same extent with basic norms of procedural justice. However, while it is true that there has, until recently, been an absence of any explicit harmonised regime in the area of criminal justice in the area of rights, that situation is – albeit slowly – changing, as the Treaty of Lisbon introduces a legal basis for procedural harmonisation and the EU legislature responds to the criticisms levelled by scholars and practitioners. Furthermore, this ignores the presence of certain common standards of fundamental rights present at an EU level that emerge from the case-law of the Court of Justice.

Abolition of National Fundamental Rights Control

States may refuse to cooperate in extradition proceedings where they fear an individual's fundamental rights might be prejudiced.[73] Indeed, as we saw in Chapter 4, such an obligation arises from EU law where an EU citizen in another Member State is facing extradition to a third state.[74] The reasoning behind this is clear: the extradition of an individual to a state where he or she would be subject to violations of his or her fundamental rights would amount to complicity in a breach of the very standards that the extraditing state undertakes to uphold. It would in effect be co-responsible for a violation of fundamental rights, an act that according to its own legal order is forbidden. Again the link between the norms of a particular legal order and the territory of the state is clear; any use of force on the territory of the state must be in accordance with fundamental rights guarantees of that particular legal order.

Upon the adoption of the EAW FD it was unclear whether Member States could still impose a control based on fundamental rights, or, to put it another way, whether a potential breach of fundamental rights would constitute a valid reason for refusing to surrender an individual. Some authors claimed that Member States were indeed still subject to fundamental rights obligations and that consequently a possible breach could form a valid exception. They pointed in particular to obligations held by the Member States by virtue of Article 6 of the ECHR on the right to a fair trial.[75] The ECtHR has held that Contracting Parties are prohibited under Article 6 ECHR from extraditing an individual where there would be a real risk that

[73] And indeed may be obliged to in the context of the ECHR: see *Soering v United Kingdom* Series A no 161. A similar principle operates in respect of the Irish constitution: see *Attorney General v O'Gara* [2012] IEHC 179.

[74] See Case C-182/15 *Aleksei Petruhhin v Latvijas Republikas Ģenerālprokuratūra* EU:C:2016:630, paras 54–58 and Case C-473/15 *Peter Schotthöfer & Florian Steiner GbR v Eugen Adelsmayr* EU:C:2017:633, paras 22–26.

[75] For an example, see Susie Alegre and Marisa Leaf, 'Mutual Recognition in European Judicial Cooeration: A Step Too Far Too Soon? Case Study – The European Arrest Warrant' (2004) 10 *ELJ* 200.

his or her rights under Article 3 ECHR on the prohibition on torture or degrading treatment would be violated.[76] The strength of this argument would appear to be reinforced by Recital 12 of the EAW FD itself, which affirms the FD's compatibility with fundamental rights and Article 6 TEU and the Charter of Fundamental Rights (CFR) and Article 1(3) EAW FD, which states that the FD shall not modify fundamental rights obligations under Article 6 TEU.[77] On this basis, when implementing the EAW FD into national law, some Member States included an express provision allowing or requiring refusal to surrender an individual where to do so might violate his or her fundamental rights.[78]

However, the general rule of the EAW FD is that mutual recognition and surrender should be automatic. The only grounds for refusal are the mandatory and optional grounds listed in Articles 3 and 4. These grounds are exhaustive. Although there are guarantees and protections for specific violations of fundamental rights, eg for in absentia trials,[79] there are no grounds for refusal on a general fundamental rights ground. Recital 12 could be read simply as a reference to the general principle that all EU acts must comply with the fundamental rights standards of the Union in their operation, rather than founding a specific grounds for refusal to surrender. Indeed, in assessing the Member State's implementation of the FD, the Commission has argued that there is no right to refuse to surrender based on fundamental rights.[80] Furthermore, recital 12 of the EAW FD stresses the principle of mutual trust in the operation of the FD and its suspension may only take place after a determination by the Council that a serious and persistent breach of the ECHR has taken place with respect to a particular Member State.[81] The Court has confirmed that Member States may not refuse to surrender based on a fundamental right found in the national legal order based on the principles of effectiveness and primacy.[82] Thus Member States are not entitled to subject their participation in the EAW system, including in the use of force on their territory, to

[76] *Soering v United Kingdom* (n 73).

[77] EAW FD (n 3) recital 12 and Art 1(3).

[78] See Report from the Commission based on Article 34 of the Council Framework Decision of 13 June 2002 on the European arrest warrant and the surrender procedures between Member States COM(2006) 8 final, 6: 'Contrary to what certain Member States have done, the Council did not intend to make the general condition of respect for fundamental rights an explicit ground for refusal in the event of infringement.' For a specific national example, see the Irish European Arrest Warrant Act 2003 s 37. Ireland subsequently amended its implementing legislation on this, and indeed many other matters, reflecting the fact that it was a poorly drafted and ill-conceived piece of legislation. For an account, see Elaine Fahey, *EU Law in Ireland* (Clarus Press, 2010), 110–13.

[79] EAW FD (n 3) as amended by Framework Decision 2009/299/JHA amending Framework Decisions 2002/584/JHA, 2005/214/JHA, 2006/783/JHA, 2008/909/JHA and 2008/947/JHA, thereby enhancing the procedural rights of persons and fostering the application of the principle of mutual recognition to decisions rendered in the absence of the person concerned at the trial [2009] OJ L81/24.

[80] Report from the Commission on the implementation since 2005 of the Council Framework Decision of 13 June 2002 on the European arrest warrant and the surrender procedures between Member States COM(2007) 407 final, 6.

[81] EAW FD (n 3) recital 12.

[82] Case C-399/11 *Stefano Melloni v Ministerio Fiscal* EU:C:2013:107.

fundamental guarantees contained in the national legal order.[83] However, that is not to say that there is no fundamental rights protection. Instead, the fundamental rights that are set aside at a national level are replaced by a common, supranational conception of procedural and fundamental rights.[84]

Supranational Procedural Rights

The elaboration of EU criminal law and mutual recognition instruments in particular enjoyed a major boost following the terrorist attacks of 11 September 2011.[85] Like much criminal law of the period, EU criminal law was security driven and focused on effective enforcement.[86] The recently created AFSJ was accused of being heavy on security and light on freedom and justice,[87] with security being the key term in the discursive chain linking freedom, security and justice.[88] The balance began to shift somewhat with the coming into force of the Treaty of Lisbon and the introduction of the Stockholm Programme.[89] A new focus on procedural rights emerged to compensate for the perceived security bias. A procedural rights roadmap was adopted in which the institutions undertook to adopt measures in four key areas:[90] translation and interpretation; information regarding rights of accused persons; legal advice and the right to communicate with lawyers and third persons; and finally specific measures regarding particularly vulnerable accused persons. In addition, the roadmap promised a Green Paper on the issue of pre-trial detention. Legislation has been adopted with respect to three of these

[83] Although this has been contested by the German Bundesverfassungsgericht, in particular claiming that certain rights may form part of the national identity of Germany and therefore that their breach would not be permissible under the 'identity review' procedure established. See also the finding by the Italian Constitutional Court (Corte constituzionale) in *MB and MAS* that the respect for certain core fundamental rights, including the principle of legality with respect of criminal law, form part of the overriding principles of the Italian constitutional order. See Case C-42/17 *Criminal proceedings against MAS and MB* (Opinion of AG Bot) EU:C:2017:564, para 121.

[84] Whether this level is adequate or indeed respects the principle of constitutional identity are separate questions. See Leonard Besselink, 'EU Constitutionalism and National Parliaments: Insiders or Outsiders' in Davor Jančić (ed), *National Parliaments after the Lisbon Treaty and the Eurocrisis* (*Oxford University Press*, 2017).

[85] See generally Murphy (n 12).

[86] See, in particular, the security-focused Hague Programme: *The Hague Programme: Strengthening Freedom, Security and Justice in the European Union* (2004) JAI 559.

[87] Estella Baker, 'The European Union's "Area of Freedom, Security and (Criminal) Justice" Ten Years On' [2009] *Criminal Law Review* 833.

[88] Kostakopoulou (n 63) 174.

[89] The Stockholm Programme: An Open and Secure Europe Serving and Protecting Citizens [2010] OJ C115/01. See for the AFSJ more generally, Steve Peers, 'Justice and Home Affairs Law since the Treaty of Lisbon: A Fairy-Tale Ending?' in Diego Acosta Arcarazo and Cian Murphy (eds), *EU Security and Justice Law* (Hart Publishing, 2014). See also Valsamis Mitsilegas, 'The Limits of Mutual Trust in Europe's Area of Freedom, Security and Justice: From Automatic Inter-State Cooperation to the Slow Emergence of the Individual' (2012) 31 *Yearbook of European Law* 319.

[90] Resolution of the Council on a Roadmap for strengthening procedural rights of suspected or accused persons in criminal proceedings [2009] OJ C295/1.

measures: rights to interpretation and translation;[91] rights to information;[92] and the right to legal advice and to communicate with other parties.[93] In addition, a directive has been adopted establishing the presumption of innocence and providing for certain rules designed to ensure it is respected during criminal proceedings and a right to be present at trial.[94]

These measures are an explicit effort to strengthen mutual trust within the context of mutual recognition.[95] As with substantive criminal law competence under Article 81(2) TFEU,[96] there is no autonomous competence to develop a body of procedural rights for individuals; it is seen merely as an ancillary mechanism of underpinning the operation of mutual recognition instruments through reinforcing mutual trust. This ancillary function is stressed by the instruments themselves, all of which directly reference the problem of mutual trust in the context of the free movement of judicial decisions in their recitals.[97] The link with the problem of mutual recognition, and the EAW FD in particular, is further underlined by the existence of specific provisions for EAW FD proceedings.[98]

It will be noted that some of these directives, namely the right to information, interpretation and translation do not so much address core procedural rights but rather are targeted at the access of an individual to various procedural resources and information regarding their rights; they are primarily aimed at individuals not necessarily familiar with or able to navigate a particular legal system. They are designed with cross-border situations and the free movement of persons in mind.[99] It is a typical case of supranational harmonisation driven by cross-border processes and concerns.

[91] Directive 2010/64/EU on the right to interpretation and translation in criminal proceedings [2010] OJ L280/1. For an interpretation of these rights in the context of a simplified procedure, see Case C-216/14 *Criminal proceedings against Gavril Covaci* EU:C:2015:686.

[92] Directive 2012/13/EU on the right to information in criminal proceedings [2013] OJ L142/1. For an interpretation on the right to be informed of an accusation, see *Covaci* (n 91).

[93] Directive 2013/48/EU on the right of access to a lawyer in criminal proceedings and in European arrest warrant proceedings and on the right to have a third party informed upon deprivation of liberty and to communicate with thrid persons and with consular authorities while deprived of liberty [2013] OJ L294/1.

[94] Directive 2016/343/EU on the strengthening of certain aspects of the presumption of innocence and of the right to be present at the trial in criminal proceedings [2016] OJ L65/1. For a review of the legislative process that lead to its adoption and the positions of the different legislative actors, see Steven Cras and Anže Erbežnik, 'The Directive on the Presumption of Innocence and the Right to be Present at Trial: Genesis and Description of the New EU Measure' [2016] *EuCrim* 25.

[95] See generally Valsamis Mitsilegas, *EU Criminal Law after Lisbon* (Hart Publishing, 2016), chs 5–6.

[96] See further Chapter 8.

[97] Roadmap on Procedural Rights (n 90), Directive 2010/64/EU on the right to interpretation and translation in criminal proceedings [2010] OJ L280/1 (n 91) recital (3); Directive 2013/48/EU on the right of access to a lawyer (n 93) recital (4); Directive 2012/13/EU on the right to information in criminal proceedings (n 92) recital (4); and Directive 2016/343/EU on the Presumption of Innocence and the Right to be Present at Trial (n 94) recital (4).

[98] Directive 2010/64/EU on the right to interpretation and translation in criminal proceedings [2010] OJ L280/1 (n 91) Art 3(6); Directive 2012/13/EU on the right to information in criminal proceedings (n 92) Art 5; and Directive 2013/48/EU on the right of access to a lawyer (n 93) Art 10.

[99] Roadmap on Procedural Rights (n 90) recital (3) and Directive 2013/48/EU on the right of access to a lawyer (n 93) recital (8).

However, despite their ancillary nature, these measures nonetheless do both create and presume a certain common standard and even common content of procedural rights across the Union. On the one hand they create certain justiciable procedural rights under EU law, enforceable before the courts of Member States in a variety of key areas, most notably the right to a lawyer and right to access evidence.[100] Moreover, all these instruments refer to rights contained in the ECHR and in the ECtHR's jurisprudence and the CFR, and therefore considered common to the Member States. Furthermore, although concerned with information to rights and access to resources such as legal advice and translation, leaving the exact content of those rights to be determined by national law, in some areas these directives assume a common core of substantive rights. Thus in the Directive on the Right to Information Member States are obliged to inform suspects regarding rights to access a lawyer and the right to remain silent.[101] Suspects are subsequently to be provided with a Letter of Rights outlining rights to access the materials of the case and the length they can be detained before being brought before a judicial authority.[102] Similarly, the Access to a Lawyer Directive references not only the right to be able to access a lawyer, but also the consequences of not having access to a lawyer on legal proceedings and the admissibility of evidence obtained under such circumstances,[103] again assuming a certain common standard regarding circumstances under which evidence may be excluded in criminal proceedings.

More noteworthy is the directive establishing the presumption of innocence and the right to be present at trial, a remarkable piece of legislation marking a significant intervention into the criminal justice procedures of Member States.[104] This directive establishes the presumption of innocence, including significantly provisions relating to the burden of proof and its assignment to the prosecution in any particular case[105] and a right to remain silent.[106] Furthermore, it establishes a right to be present at trial, and additional exclusionary rules (albeit rather vague ones) regarding evidence that is obtained in breach of the right to remain silent.[107]

[100] These are clearly rights held by individuals and there is a case to be made for many of the provisions that they are sufficiently clear, precise and enforceable to enjoy the quality of direct effect. It will also be noted that unlike the EAW FD, they are Directives and hence capable (provided the above-mentioned conditions are met) of enjoying direct effect. See also Mitsilegas (n 95) 175. While noting the minimal nature of these directives, nothing in *Covaci* (n 91) or Case C-310/18 PPU *Criminal proceedings against Emil Milev* EU:C:2018:732 would imply these rights do not enjoy direct effect.

[101] Directive 2012/13/EU on the right to information in criminal proceedings (n 92) Art 3.

[102] ibid, Arts 3 and 4.

[103] Directive 2013/48/EU on the right of access to a lawyer (n 93) recital (50).

[104] Although the practical impact may be minimal in nature of the minimal nature of the harmonisation. See *Covaci* (n 91), para 48 and *Milev* (n 100).

[105] Directive 2016/343/EU on the presumption of innocence and the right to be present at trial (n 94), Art 6.

[106] ibid, Art 7.

[107] ibid, Art 10(2) which provides that it operates 'without prejudice to national rules and systems on the admissibility of evidence'. The presence of the exclusionary rule was subject to inter-institutional debate during the legislative process, leading to the current compromise. See Cras and Erbežnik (n 94) 34.

Finally, while, in light of their minimal nature,[108] the exact impact of these rights on national criminal procedural law may be more or less extensive,[109] perhaps the true impact of these measures is in the simple intervention of EU law into this field implying the jurisdiction of the Court of Justice and the application of the CFR in a sensitive area of national law.[110] Two aspects in particular stand out that may contribute to an increasing harmonisation of rights in this field: firstly, the tendency of the Court of Justice to interpret concepts as autonomous concepts of EU law;[111] and secondly, the ample scope for the application of the rights contained in the Charter to this field, which may in turn come to supplant or at least frame and condition the application of national fundamental rights systems in the operation of criminal justice systems.[112]

Although perhaps arriving somewhat late in the day and advancing in a piecemeal fashion, there is a certain harmonisation of certain procedural rights emerging through EU law as a direct consequence of mutual-recognition instruments. This is occurring both directly – as certain core rights, such as the right to access a lawyer, the right to remain silent, the right to be present at trial and the presumption of innocence are codified by EU law – and indirectly, as underlying rights of information and access contain assumptions regarding a common procedural tradition. It is through the need to legitimise a transnational system of shared enforcement of national law that certain supranational rights are emerging.

Supranational Fundamental Rights

The references of these procedural instruments to common standards of rights based in the ECHR and the CFR are not by accident and refer to the broader constitutional context of rights protection within the EAW system. Contrary to certain disappointed reactions to *Melloni*[113] and *Radu*,[114] the Court of Justice has not found that concerns regarding fundamental rights must be swept aside entirely in the interests of primacy and effectiveness of EU criminal law. What it

[108] *Milev* (n 100) para 47.

[109] And indeed may meet resistance in national legal cultures. See the example of the right to a lawyer during police questioning discussed in Chrisje Brants, 'What Limits to Harmonising Justice?' in Renaud Colson and Stewart Field (eds), *EU Criminal Justice and the Challenge of Diversity: Legal Cultures in the Area of Freedom, Security and Justice* (Cambridge University Press, 2016).

[110] Although note the absence of any consideration of the CFR by the Court in *Milev* (n 100) in contrast to the Opinion of AG Wathelet in the same case – see Case C-310/18 PPU *Criminal proceedings against Emil Milev* (Opinion of AG Wathelet) EU:C:2018:645, paras 50ff.

[111] Mitsilegas (n 95) 176–80.

[112] *Melloni* (n 82).

[113] ibid.

[114] Case C-396/11 *Ciprian Vasile Radu* EU:C:2013:39. For a comment, see Anita Davies, 'Radu – A Case of Failed Dialogue' (*eutopia law Blog*, 5 February 2013) http://eutopialaw.com/2013/02/05/radu-a-case-of-failed-dialogue/#more-1755, accessed 7 January 2019.

has unequivocally held is that Member States may not refuse to surrender an individual based on *national* standards of fundamental rights where to do so would compromise the operation of an EAW. Instead, in *Aranyosi and Căldăraru*,[115] further developed in *ML*,[116] it has replaced these domestic standards with common Union-wide standards, used to police a certain presumption of compliance by Member States.

Primacy, effectiveness and the unity of EU law[117] have always been linked to the development of fundamental rights in the Union and it would be naïve to assume that this dynamic would not operate in the field of AFSJ mutual recognition instruments. According to the accepted wisdom, fundamental rights were developed at a supranational level in order to allay the fears of national constitutional courts and head off any challenge from that quarter to the continued primacy of EU law.[118] What mutual recognition regimes in the AFSJ have brought to this equation is the additional element of a presumption of horizontal compliance between Member States with common standards of fundamental rights when operating within mutual-recognition regimes. Whether such presumptions are justified may be contestable, and the extent to which they are compatible with ECHR obligations remains an open question,[119] but it is undoubtedly the case that they are linked to the question of primacy and deemed necessary by the Court of Justice for the effective operation of these mutual recognition systems.[120] What this entails, in the area of criminal law, is a presumption of common standards of fundamental rights.

In *Radu* the Court of Justice found that Romania could not refuse to surrender one of its nationals to Germany on the basis that he was not informed of the German procedures issuing the EAWs. In its reference the referring court raised

[115] Joined Cases C-404/15 and C-659/15 *Pál Aranyosi and Robert Căldăraru v Generalstaatsanwaltschaft Bremen* EU:C:2016:198.

[116] *ML* (n 70).

[117] For a discussion of this new conceptual trinity that appeared in *Melloni* (n 82), see Leonard Besselink, 'The Parameters of Constitutional Conflicts after Melloni' (2014) 39 *EL Rev* 531, 543.

[118] Damian Chalmers, Gareth Davies and Giorgio Monti, *European Union Law*, 3 edn (Cambridge University Press, 2014) 252. See also Jason Coppel and Aidan O'Neill, 'The European Court of Justice: Taking Rights Seriously?' (1992) 29 *CML Rev* 669. Although for an alternative reading of the development of fundamental rights in the EU, see Gráinne de Búrca, 'The Road not Taken: the European Union as Global Human Rights Actor' (2011) 105 *American Society of International Law* 649.

[119] See Alexander Kornezov, 'The Area of Freedom, Security and Justice in Light of the EU Accession to the ECHR – Is the Break-up Inevitable?' (2012–13) 15 *Cambridge Yearbook of European Legal Studies* 227. See also recent jurisprudence of the Court of Justice in Case C-394/12 *Shamso Abdullahi v Bundesasylamt* EU:C:2013:813 and the ECtHR in *Tarakhel v Switzerland* App No 29217/12 (ECtHR) in the area of the transfer of asylum applications under the Dublin system.

[120] See Joined Cases C-411/10 and C-493/10 *NS v Secretary of State for the Home Dept* EU:C:2011:865, [2011] ECR I-13905. Indeed, the Court claimed that to allow suspension of mutual recognition regimes on a case-by-case basis would call into question the raison d'être of the European Union itself and the creation of an AFSJ (ibid, para 83). It clearly remains committed to this point of view as a consideration for any future accession to the ECHR. See Opinion 2/13 *Accession to the European Convention on Human Rights* EU:C:2014:2454.

a series of general questions regarding the status of fundamental rights in the EU legal order and in the operation of the EAW FD in particular. Avoiding the general questions, the Court in its reply limited itself strictly to the situation in hand, and found that a refusal to notify an individual when issuing EAWs was not a breach of their fundamental rights. Although some commentators read *Radu* as an implicit rejection by the Court of Justice of fundamental rights as a grounds for refusal in general,[121] in truth the *ratio* of the judgment is much narrower, simply refusing to find a breach in the circumstances of the case, and leaving open the broader question of the status of fundamental rights, and the possibility of them constituting a grounds for refusal.[122]

What became clear, however, in *Melloni* is that Member States may not refuse to surrender an individual based on their own, *domestic* standards of fundamental rights; at least where to do so would frustrate the effective application of the EAW, an almost inevitable outcome if the consequence of such an application would be the refusal to surrender an individual.[123] In *Melloni* an Italian national skipped bail and was convicted of fraud in absentia. He was later arrested in Spain and was subject to surrender proceedings based on an Italian EAW. Due to the fact that he was aware of his trial and was represented at all stages of the process he would not be granted a retrial upon return to Italy. The Spanish Constitution prohibited extradition in such circumstances, considering that to do so would breach the fundamental right to a fair trial. Article 53 CFR states that: '[N]othing in this charter shall be interpreted as adversely affecting human rights and fundamental freedoms as recognised, in their respective fields … by the Member States' constitutions.'[124] The Spanish Constitutional Court therefore referred a question to the Court of Justice, seeking in particular to know whether Article 53 CFR allowed the application of the Spanish constitution in this case. In its reply the Court rejected the possibility that the Spanish Court could apply its own constitutional provisions and refuse to surrender Mr Melloni. The Court of Justice based its argument on the principle of primacy and found that to allow the application of national provisions would allow Member States to disapply EU law and undermine its effectiveness.

Although some might read *Melloni* as a disappointment and further evidence of the lack of the Court's concerns for fundamental rights in criminal justice matters,[125] a careful reading of both *Radu* and *Melloni* does not exclude *any* form of fundamental rights control. Rather, *Radu* is silent on the general issue, merely finding that a breach of fundamental rights did not take place, and *Melloni* on the

[121] See Davies (n 114).

[122] For such an analysis, see Janssens (n 5) 207–10.

[123] *Melloni* (n 82). Although see Case C-168/13PPU *Jeremy F v Premier ministre* EU:C:2013:358 in which the French authorities were free to apply their rule regarding a right to appeal so long as the time limits contained in the EAW FD were respected.

[124] CFR Art 53.

[125] See, for example, Besselink (n 84).

contrary does subject the EAW system to a fundamental rights control but one based on *Union* provisions of fundamental rights, in particular the CFR.

Melloni makes two findings. Firstly, it finds that surrendering Mr Melloni in the circumstances of the case, namely where there was a verdict handed down in absentia but the accused appointed representatives who did in fact represent him throughout the trial, does not amount to a breach the right to a fair trial found in Article 47 CFR.[126] This is particularly the case in light of the adoption of Framework Decision 2009/299/EU amending the EAW FD to provide greater protection in the case of in absentia trials, ie a harmonisation of the conditions in which the right to trial is compromised by the absence of the accused.[127] The Court does assess the compliance of the EAW FD with fundamental rights but it is an assessment of an EU law instrument in light of EU fundamental rights. Secondly, it found that Spain may not apply its constitutional provisions where to do so would undermine the effectiveness of the EAW FD. But note that the Spanish Court's 'interpretation of Article 53 of the Charter would undermine the principle of the primacy of EU law inasmuch as it would allow a Member State to disapply EU legal rules *which are fully in compliance with the Charter* where they infringe the fundamental rights guaranteed by that State's constitution'.[128] Similarly, in the subsequent case of *Jeremy F* the Court was at pains to point out that the system of mutual trust on which the EAW system is based is founded on compliance by the Member States with 'fundamental rights recognised at Union level, particularly in the Charter'.[129] In *Lanigan* the Court, basing its judgment of Article 1(3) EAW FD, found that the operation of the EAW system must not lead to a breach of the fundamental rights standards found in the CFR.[130] Thus the continued detention of an individual, after substantial delays in the execution procedure, must be assessed in light of Article 6 CFR on the right to liberty.[131]

There is an implication that where Member States are *not* in compliance with the Charter, there is a possibility that the execution of an EAW may be refused. Indeed, this is precisely what occurred in *Aranyosi and Căldăraru*[132] in which the Court of Justice effectively transposed its jurisprudence developed in the field of

[126] *Melloni* (n 82) paras 49–50.

[127] Interestingly the Court describes this Framework Decision as reflecting a consensus amongst Member States regarding the appropriate criteria according to which one should assess the compatibility of an in absentia trial with fundamental rights. See ibid, para 62. Note, however, Besselink's point that this consensus was achieved amongst the governments of Member States, allowing executives to thereby circumvent national fundamental rights guarantees. See Besselink (n 84) 548.

[128] *Melloni* (n 82) para 58 (emphasis added).

[129] *Jeremy F* (n 123) para 47.

[130] See Case C-237/15 PPU *Minister for Justice and Equality v Lanigan* EU:C:2015:474.

[131] ibid, paras 53ff. See also Case C-640/15 *Minister for Justice and Equality v Tomas Vilkas* EU:C:2017:39.

[132] *Aranyosi & Căldăraru* (n 115). Although a full discussion lies outside the scope of this chapter it is important to note the broader debate regarding of mutual trust and the mutual recognition and the significant degree of judicial dialogue that has emerged between national constitutional courts, the

asylum transfers in *NS*[133] to mutual recognition of criminal judgments and in particular EAWs. In *Aranyosi and Căldăraru* two individuals, sought for prosecution in Hungary and to serve a sentence in Romania respectively, resisted their surrender on the grounds that there was a substantial risk of a breach of their rights if they were indeed surrendered. This was based on a number of judgments of the ECtHR finding substantial deficiencies in the penitentiary systems of this (and indeed other) Member States leading to a breach of Article 3 ECHR.[134] The Court of Justice noted that the operation of the EAW FD must comply with fundamental rights and that in exceptional circumstances could be suspended. This would be conditional on a finding of systemic deficiencies in relation to the prison system of the issuing Member State as a whole, followed by an assessment of the situation the individual concerned would face if surrendered in order to determine if there was in fact a real risk of a breach of his or her right to freedom from inhumane and degrading treatment found in Article 4 CFR.[135] Finally, in *LM* the Court of Justice has extended this to cover the right to a fair trial found in Article 47 CFR and the broader need for an impartial and independent judiciary in the context of a system built on mutual trust.[136]

There is certainly a tension between ensuring the effectiveness of the EAW system, which relies on notions of mutual trust between judicial actors that are perhaps problematic and the protection of fundamental rights, but it is incorrect to state that the EAW system contains no guarantees of fundamental rights. Surrender may be refused based on a potential violation of fundamental rights, but only where there is evidence of a persistent and systematic breach and only by reference to *EU* standards of fundamental rights. However, in such a situation the Member State would no longer be exercising an autonomous normative

Court of Justice and the ECtHR on the matter in recent times, particularly in light of *Opinion 2/13* (n 120) and *Aranyosi & Căldăraru* (n 115). For commentary, see Koen Lenaerts, 'La vie apès l'avis: Exploring the Principle of Mutual (Yet Not Blind) Trust' (2017) 54 *CML Rev* 805; Luisa Marin, '"Only You": The Emergence of a Temperate Mutual Trust in the Area of Freedom, Security and Justice and its Underpinning in the European Composite Constitutional Order' (2017) 2 *European Papers* 141; and Sacha Prechal, 'Mutual Trust before the Court of Justice of the European Union' (2017) 2 *European Papers* 75.

[133] *NS* (n 120).

[134] See Joined Cases C-4040/15 and C-659/15 *Pál Aranyosi and Robert Căldăraru v Generalstaatsanwaltschaft Bremen* (Opinion of AG Bot) EU:C:2016:140, paras 30–34.

[135] *Aranyosi & Căldăraru* (n 115) paras 89–94. There is thus a two-stage test requiring systemic deficiencies *in addition to* an individualised finding. During such an assessment the executing judicial authority is required to make full use of the information exchange mechanisms contained within the EAW system (see para 95). Furthermore, such a finding does not lead to the non-execution of the EAW but rather its postponement, during which the individual may be held or may have other restrictive conditions applied subject to the judgment in *Lanigan* (n 130) – see *Aranyosi & Căldăraru* (n 115) paras 98–102.

[136] *LM* (n 70). Although it should be noted that, contrary to the suggestion of the national court, the Court of Justice insisted on the need for the second element of the *Aranyosi* test, namely an assessment of the threat faced by the individual subject to the EAW, even in instances where systemic concerns have been found concerning the independence of the judiciary as a whole in the issuing Member State (see paras 68–69).

control, applying its own standards to prevent an individual from being surrendered, but would rather be acting as an agent under EU law. It would be applying EU law and EU fundamental rights in order to maintain the integrity of the EU legal order and in particular the system of shared enforcement established by the EAW FD. The rather exacting conditions that are applied to this may or may not be problematic, raising as they do a rather high threshold, and may be in tension with the ECtHR's rulings on the matter, but the fact remains that fundamental rights controls displaced at a national level are recreated at a supranational level in order to regulate the system of mutual recognition.

Conclusion: Transnational Enforcement in a Supranational Space

Criminal law is intimately connected to the concept of territorial control and the legitimate use of force. The establishment of a transnational system of enforcement and the subsequent loss of control entailed by Member States over how individuals on their territory are treated has significantly disrupted traditional understandings of citizenship, fundamental rights, questions of legality, and ultimately their relationship with the legal order and the territory of a particular Member State. It has above all called into question the traditional national framework for assuring the legitimate use of force on a particular territory.

The EAW is a transnational system of enforcing national wrongs. As the Court of Justice stated in *Advocaten voor de Wereld*, the EAW does not itself define or create crimes.[137] This is reflected in the underlying need for a national arrest warrant;[138] the EAW system is ancillary and supplemental to the prosecution of national crimes and the calling to account of those individuals accused of wronging national communities. Those crimes are defined by particular national communities and it is before those communities that individuals return to be called to account or to serve punishment. Indeed, the essentially national nature of crimes is in some respects strengthened by the EAW system; unlike extradition systems with their rule of double criminality it is exclusively under the law of the issuing Member State and at the discretion of the issuing Member State that an individual's conduct is assessed. It is a transnational system of enforcement, of calling citizens to account before particular national communities.

There is a complex interaction between transnational, national and supranational understandings of citizenship, wrongs and rights. The EAW system is above all a system for the transnational enforcement of national law. However, it is only by embedding national norms and values within the single supranational space

[137] *Advocaten voor de Wereld* (n 47) paras 52–53.
[138] See *Bob-Dogi* (n 38).

occupied by EU citizens that an effective system of transnational enforcement can be justified and legitimised. EU citizenship has given rise to a broader space of movement and set of political relations between individuals and Member States throughout the European Union. Above all, it has situated individuals in a broader space of rights and now responsibilities. This transnational space of movement and enforcement necessarily generates tensions regarding territory, norms and rights. However, these norms that are displaced at a national level re-emerge at a supranational level. This occurs through a process of both assuming pre-existing shared norms (such as the thirty-two categories of crimes) and through the active creation of supranational norms (such as the development of procedural rights). The wider geographic space of movement generated by EU citizenship corresponds to a single area of justice, not simply in allowing the 'free movement of judgments' or contributing to more effective law enforcement, but in being the location of certain, overarching, norms both in terms of the publicly wrongful nature of certain acts and fundamental rights and procedural guarantees. Indeed, not only are there certain supranational norms emerging through the EAW but a supranational community capable of sharing wrongs can also be detected. The legitimacy of the shared system of enforcement is therefore based on an assumption of shared citizenship, shared wrongs and shared rights that together are located in a shared space.

7

An Area of Justice – II. A Transnational *Ne Bis in Idem* Principle

Introduction

A German assaults a woman in Belgium, is apprehended and charged by authorities in Bonn, and settles the case by agreeing to pay a fine. Meanwhile, in Belgium the victim brings proceedings before the local criminal court. Can the Belgian prosecutor order the assailant to appear before the criminal court in Belgium?[1] In 1960 a German member of the French Foreign Legion attacks and kills a fellow German during the Algerian conflict and flees to the German Democratic Republic. He is convicted under French military law, but the sentence is later set aside under a general amnesty for acts committed in the Algerian conflict and in any case is time-barred. Later, after the fall of the Berlin Wall, Germany seeks to prosecute the by now aged ex-Legionnaire. Are German authorities prevented by the French amnesty and time-limits?[2] A Belgian is convicted and imprisoned in Norway for importing cannabis and other narcotics. He is later released and returned to Belgium where he is in turn prosecuted for exporting the same substances. Has he already paid his due to society? Is importing drugs the same act as exporting?[3] A woman receives the proceeds of crime in the Netherlands and later exchanges the same funds in a bureau de change in Belgium. Is the woman guilty of handling the proceeds of crime in the Netherlands, Belgium or both?[4]

The principle of *ne bis in idem* is a principle of law common to most legal systems and enjoys a long history.[5] Its principle purpose is to prevent an individual

[1] Joined Cases C-187/01 and C-385/01 *Criminal proceedings against Hüseyin Gözütok and Klaus Brügge* EU:C:2003:87, [2003] ECR I-1345.

[2] Case C-297/07 *Klaus Bourquain* EU:C:2008:708, [2008] ECR I-9425.

[3] Case C-436/04 *Criminal proceedings against Leopold Henri Van Esbroeck* EU:C:2006:165, [2006] ECR I-2333.

[4] Case C-367/05 *Criminal proceedings against Norma Kraaijenbrink* EU:C:2007:444, [2007] ECR I-6619.

[5] For a history in the common law and in particular American context, see Jay A Sigler, 'A History of Double Jeopardy' (1963) 7 *American Journal of Legal History* 283. See also the discussion (including the manifestation of the principle in contemporary international law) by Judge Pinto de Albuquerque in his separate opinion in *A and B v Norway* (Application Nos 24130/11 and 29758/11, 15 November 2016) (ECtHR) 55–62.

from being prosecuted or punished twice for the same act or crime. In general, it is designed to secure the rights of the individual vis-à-vis the state. However, as the above examples illustrate, in a single area characterised by multiple criminal justice systems, individuals can face prosecution from more than one state. Criminal acts are no longer limited by borders, if indeed they ever were, and Member States claim jurisdiction in different and sometimes overlapping ways. The possibility of multiple prosecutions in different parts of the European Union represents a major hindrance for anyone seeking to exercise their freedom of movement. In the EU legal order, the primary function of the *ne bis in idem* principle is therefore different from simply protecting the individual from a single abusive state: it is to secure the free movement of individuals, removing obstacles that may exist through the existence of multiple legal orders. In interpreting the principle in light of this particular goal, the Court of Justice has constructed a single status for individuals within a single area of justice, a development that in turn reflects a new understanding of the relationship between the individual and other Member States and indeed the Union as a whole.

The principle of *ne bis in idem* is, on its face, a relatively simple rule with clear rationales. It is designed to ensure that an individual is not prosecuted more than once for the same crime: its ultimate purpose is to ensure that the outcome of a criminal case is final. The reasons are well known. Firstly, it protects the individual from the possibility of vexatious prosecution; from being constantly hounded by vindictive or simply overzealous officers of the state. To allow continuous attempts at prosecution would place the individual in a persistent state of risk and fear of prosecution: a burdensome existence fraught with uncertainty. Secondly, it ensures balance in the criminal justice process between the two sides; the famed 'equality of arms' principle. It prevents the state from returning to court in an attempt to prosecute, a possibility that would give it multiple chances to amend and improve its case, an opportunity that is unavailable to the accused.[6] Finally, while for the most part the principle can be seen as protecting the rights of individuals vis-à-vis the state, there is also a broader public interest in securing finality in criminal judgments. It therefore is a specific manifestation of the general principle of *res judicita* and legal certainty.[7]

At the same time, the criminal justice process, in addition to protecting the rights and interests of the innocent and providing legal certainty, is concerned with ensuring that wrongful acts are prosecuted and punished in an appropriate manner that reflects the gravity of the offence. There is an interest in ensuring that the state has an adequate opportunity to call the individual to account and

[6] Described by Reed as 'heads-we-win, tails-lets-play-again' as quoted in Robin Lööf, '54 CISA and the Principles of *Ne Bis in Idem*' (2007) 15 *European Journal of Crime, Criminal Law and Criminal Justice* 309, 322.

[7] See Bas van Bockel, *The Ne Bis in Idem Principle in EU Law* (Kluwer, 2010) ch 1. See also Michiel Luchtman, 'The ECJ's Recent Caselaw on *Ne Bis in Idem*: Implications for Law Enforcement in a Shared Legal Order' (2018) 55 *CML Rev* 1717.

in a manner that reflects all the wrongful aspects of the act. There is a need to ensure that cases can be reopened if further evidence comes to light, that all crimes that a particular act might represent are prosecuted, and that an individual does not escape through a dismissal of his or her case on a technical matter without a proper assessment of the crime.

It is these counterveiling needs of the criminal justice system – those of the individual and those of the state – that render the interpretation of the *ne bis in idem* principle, so simple in theory, complicated in practice, with different jurisdictions interpreting what is ostensibly the same rule in opposing ways and with widely differing results for the individuals concerned.[8]

The principle has two dimensions, both of which have given rise to interpretative difficulties. Firstly, the definition of finality or *bis*; whether a particular case can be said to be finally settled or otherwise. Although some cases can clearly be considered to be finally settled – such as a judgment acquitting an individual following a full trial and deliberation that is no longer subject to appeal – there are other cases that fall short of a full trial of all aspects of the case, such as plea bargains. The application of the rule in these cases is less clear. A guiding principle that may be employed is that there should be a substantive assessment of the merits of the case.[9] However, judgments can vary as to what precisely a substantive assessment might entail and the test is not always simple to apply in practice. The second dimension of the principle relates to determining precisely for what an individual is not to be prosecuted twice (the *sameness* criteria).[10] The debate here tends to focus on whether an individual is to be protected from multiple prosecutions for the same act or series of acts or whether it is multiple prosecutions for the same crime that is at stake, ie whether sameness refers to crimes or to acts.

The *ne bis in idem* principle appears in the EU legal order in various provisions. It has long been a feature of the Court's jurisprudence in competition law sanctions. More recently it has appeared in Article 54 CISA, Article 3(2) EAW FD and Article 50 CFR. It is also contained in Article 4 of Protocol 7 of the ECHR.

The current chapter focuses on Article 54 CISA for two reasons. Firstly, there has been a convergence between the interpretation of the different legal provisions that contain the *ne bis in idem* principle in the European legal space both between the ECHR and the EU legal orders and the vertical and horizontal application of the principle. In both instances of convergence this has tended to use the interpretation developed in the context of Article 54 CISA. In *Zolotukhin* the ECtHR resolved the significant uncertainty and divergence that previously

[8] For an example of a particularly complicated interpretation of the double-jeopardy rule, see the US Supreme Court's interpretation of the Vth Amendment in Akhil Reed Amar, 'Double Jeopardy Law Made Simple' (1996–97) 106 *Yale Law Journal* 1807.

[9] See, for example, the Opinion of AG Sharpston in Case C-467/04 *Criminal proceedings against Giuseppe Francesco Gasparini and Others* (Opinion of AG Sharpston) EU:C:2006:406, [2006] ECR I-9199, para 75. See the discussion of the various solutions adopted by the ECtHR in different cases in *Zolotukhin v Russia* App no 14939/03 (ECrtHR, 10 February 2009) paras 70–77.

[10] van Bockel (n 7) ch 2.

existed in its jurisprudence on the interpretation of Article 4, Protocol 7 ECHR by effectively adopting the solution developed in the context of Article 54 CISA.[11] In *Mantello* the Court of Justice noted the shared objective of Article 3(2) EAW FD and Article 54 CISA and interpreted Article 3(2) EAW FD in the light of its jurisprudence based on Article 54 CISA.[12] In *M* the Court found that Article 54 CISA was merely a specific expression of the general principle found in Article 50 CFR, which itself is to be interpreted in light of Article 4, Protocol 7 ECHR.[13] Thus, through various chains of interpretation there appears to be a general convergence within the EU legal order between Article 54 CISA, Article 3(2) EAW FD, Article 50 CFR, and Article 4, Protocol 7 ECHR – all based primarily on the jurisprudence developed under Article 54 CISA.[14] The result is a uniform application of the principle in transnational, national and supranational situations that fall within the scope of the EU legal order,[15] corresponding to the protection found in the ECHR.[16]

Secondly, and more importantly, this chapter is concerned with the relationship between individual citizens, free movement and crime within what has been termed the single area of justice. It is therefore primarily concerned with the impact of multiple prosecutions from different jurisdictions on the movement of individuals within the Union. It deals with what has been termed 'horizontal' and geographic rather than a 'vertical' or temporal application of the principle, ie between legal orders in different places rather than within a single legal order over time.[17] Article 54 CISA is specifically a transnational and horizontal principle

[11] *Zolotukhin v Russia* (n 9).

[12] Case C-261/09 *Gaetano Mantello* EU:C:2010:683, [2010] ECR I-11477, paras 39–40. This was despite the fact that the situation at stake in *Mantello* was a 'vertical' one. Mr Mantello was resisting surrender from Germany to Italy by claiming he had already been punished under *Italian* law for the same act. Intervening Member States argued that Art 3(2) EAW FD only applied in transnational contexts, as a corollary to Art 54 CISA; see *Gaertano Mantello* (Opinion of AG Bot) EU:C:2010:501, [2010] ECR I-11477, para 7.

[13] Case C-398/12 *Criminal Proceedings against M* EU:C:2014:1057, para 35.

[14] More recently jurisprudence in the area of parallel administrative and criminal proceedings for various offences has developed significantly under both Art 50 CFR and Protocol 7, Art 4 ECHR, to some extent in parallel. Although, as pointed out by Luchtman the Court of Justice has arrived at the same conclusion by different means, finding a justified violation of the principle of *ne bis in idem* rather than a finding that the matter does not in fact engage the principle in the first place. See Luchtman (n 7) 1732. This does allow the Court of Justice greater scope in the future for specifying the application of the principle. See Case C-524/16 *Luca Menci* EU:C:2018:197, Case C-537/16 *Garlsson Real Estate SA, en liquidation and Others v Commissione Nazionale per le Società e la Borsa* EU:C:2018:193 and Joined Cases C-596/16 and C-597/16 *Enzo Di Puma v Commissione Nazionale per le Società e la Borsa and Commissione Nazionale per le Società e la Borsa v Antonio Zecca* EU:C:2018:192 for the interpretation of Art 50 CFR, and *A and B* (n 5) for the interpretation of Art 4, Protocol 7 ECHR. This has been occurred independently of Art 54 CISA. However, to this author's knowledge a transnational instance of parallel administrative and criminal proceedings, to which Art 54 CISA may apply, has not yet arisen.

[15] A set of situations that may prove to be expansive. See Case C-617/10 *Åklagaren v Hans Åkerberg Fransson* EU:C:2013:105.

[16] Although note the divergence in the interpretation of the sameness criteria in respect of administrative and criminal sanctions between the ECtHR and the Court of Justice as analysed in Luchtman (n 7).

[17] Lööf (n 6).

and has a particular relationship with free movement and citizenship of the Union. As put by AG Bot in *Kossowski*:

> The strength of the principle ... [found in Article 54 CISA] ... is justified by the importance of creating the area of freedom, security and justice for the creation of the European Union. This area is a supporting dimension of the single area of movement and economic activity, in that it provides that area with a legal framework containing the individual rights of citizens of the Union. In that regard it clearly relates to the concept of Union citizenship, and contributes towards giving that concept concrete reality.[18]

Article 4, Protocol 7 ECHR and Article 50 CFR are primarily concerned with a vertical application of the principle and are not directly related to the transnational dimension of EU citizenship.[19] Finally, the use of the principle in the context of competition law proceedings follows different principles and operates in a different legal context characterised by its quasi-administrative/criminal nature and the structure of the European Competition Network of competition law authorities applying overlapping legal provisions in a multilevelled context.[20]

On one level Article 54 CISA reads like any version of the *ne bis in idem* principle: '[A] person that has been finally judged may not be prosecuted ... for the same offences.' However, there is a crucial distinction relating to the scope of Article 54 CISA that differentiates it from other versions of the principle found in national and indeed international texts. The full article reads:

> A person who has been finally judged by a Contracting Party may not be prosecuted by *another* Contracting Party for the same offences provided that, where he is sentenced, the sentence has been served or is currently being served or can no longer be carried out under the sentencing laws of the Contracting Party.[21]

In contrast to traditional conceptions of the *ne bis in idem* principle, Article 54 CISA is not designed to protect the individual against multiple prosecutions within a single state. Rather it is designed to protect the individual against prosecutions from *other* states and in other legal orders. It is the first application of the principle in a *transnational* legal setting.[22]

[18] Case C-486/14 *Criminal Proceedings against Piotr Kossowski* (Opinion of AG Bot) EU:C:2015:812, para 44.

[19] It is, however, important in regulating the relationship between the individual and the Union when substantive EU criminal law (ie the capacity of the Union to define certain conduct as criminal) is enforced or where Member States imposing criminal sanctions are acting within the scope of EU law, eg *Åkerberg Fransson* (n 15).

[20] Luchtman (n 7) 1724–25.

[21] Convention on the Implementation of the Schengen Agreement, Art 54 (emphasis added).

[22] Some national legal orders, such as the Dutch, unilaterally take into account convictions in other states. See John Vervaele, 'Annotation of Cases C-187/01 and C-385/01 *Gözütok and Brügge*' (2004) 41 *CML Rev* 795, 804. An attempt to adopt a multilateral Convention by the Council of Europe failed for want of ratifications but later formed the basis for Art 54 CISA. See Christine van den Wyngaert and Guy Stessens, 'The International *Non Bis in Idem* Principle: Resolving Some of the Unanswered Questions' (1999) 48 *ICLQ* 779.

Not only is the scope of Article 54 CISA as a transnational principle different from other instances of the *ne bis in idem* principle, but its rationale is also different. Indeed, the different scope of Article 54 CISA quite logically flows from the different purpose of Article 54 CISA. Its purpose lies in the underlying goal of the Schengen Agreement itself, designed to secure free movement of individuals. The Schengen *acquis* is a body of law with a complicated history. Originally developed outside the scope of EU law amongst a select number of Member States, it has since been incorporated within the Treaties[23] and its scope has been extended, albeit on a phased-basis, to most Member States.[24] The UK and Ireland, reluctant to cede control over their borders have retained opt-outs of the *acquis*, exercised on a case-by-case basis, but have opted into Article 54 CISA.[25] Thus, when the Court of Justice refers to free movement in several Member States in the context of Article 54 CISA or indeed the European Union, it can be taken as referring to the Union as a whole. Nonetheless, the persistence of opt-outs in this area in particular does underline the continuing fragility of notions of EU territoriality and a single space of movement in a Union of variable geometry.[26]

The Court of Justice has been very clear that the objective of Article 54 CISA is 'to ensure that no one is prosecuted on the same facts in several Member States on account of his having exercised his right to freedom of movement'.[27] The primary purpose of Article 54 CISA is therefore not the protection of the individual from vexatious prosecution and to ensure legal certainty. That is not to say that Article 54 CISA does not protect individuals and ensure legal certainty; it does achieve these things. But it does so in the service of securing another goal: the free movement of individuals throughout the Schengen area. Legal certainty for the individual is necessary because it is necessary for free movement. The traditional rationale for the *ne bis in idem* principle is rendered instrumental to the *telos* of free movement.

If the scope of Article 54 CISA as a transnational principle reflects its *telos* as a measure designed to secure free movement, that same underlying goal has

[23] For a detailed account, see Eckart Wagner, 'The Integration of Schengen into the Framework of the European Union' (1998) 25 *Legal Issues of Economic Integration* 1.

[24] In addition to the UK and Ireland, Romania, Bulgaria, Cyprus and Croatia are not currently members of the Schengen Area, although it is envisaged that they will in time accede. See https://ec.europa.eu/home-affairs/what-we-do/policies/borders-and-visas/schengen_en (last accessed 13 April 2018). Note that the Common Travel Area (CTA) between the UK and Ireland will most likely persist after Brexit. As the CTA is the justification for the current opt-outs enjoyed by the UK and Ireland it is almost certain at the time of writing that Ireland will remain outside the Schengen Area and maintain its opt-outs in this area. Nonetheless Ireland has opted into that part of the Schengen *acquis* containing the *ne bis in idem* principle (see below).

[25] It should be pointed out that the United Kingdom and Ireland have both opted into this part of the Schengen Agreement: see Council Decision 2000/365/EC concerning the request of the United Kingdom of Great Britain and Northern Ireland to take part in some of the provisions of the Schengen *acquis* [2000] OJ L131/43 and Council Decision concerning Ireland's request to take part in some of the provisions of the Schengen *acquis* [2002] OJ L64/20.

[26] For an analysis, see Valsamis Mitsilegas, *EU Criminal Law after Lisbon* (Hart Publishing, 2016) 44–50.

[27] *Gözütok and Brügge* (n 1) para 38.

informed the interpretation of Article 54 CISA. As stated above, the *ne bis in idem* principle is notoriously difficult to apply and lends itself to various interpretations depending on the definition of sameness or finality. In the context of Article 54 CISA however, the various interpretative choices, normally available to a court when interpreting the principle of *ne bis in idem*, are conditioned and shaped by the underlying goal to secure free movement in a context of multiple jurisdictions. The interpretation of Article 54 CISA flows directly from the principle of free movement of persons. As with much in EU law,[28] this teleological perspective is key to understanding the reasoning of the Court.

If the technique has been teleological reasoning based on free movement, the consequence has been a reshaping the relationship between individuals and other Member States in the field of criminal law and between individuals, Member States and the Union as a whole. Directed by the need to secure free movement for individuals, the Court has been led to fashion a single status for individuals vis-à-vis the Union as a whole. Under this new regime, individuals are called to account by a single Member State but in the name of the Union as a whole. The result is that a crime against a Member State becomes a crime against the Union as a whole: that individual is called to account before the Union *through* the criminal justice of a single Member State. It is through the transnational process of the *ne bis in idem* that individuals are called to account in a plural, multilevelled political community.

Interpretation of Finality in Light of Free Movement: A Single Status

Strict Application of Mutual Recognition

The difficulty faced by the Court of Justice in interpreting the concept of finality in Article 54 CISA arises from unique situation of its application across different criminal justice systems with different and not always compatible means of settling cases. The solution is one frequently employed by EU law when faced with obstacles to free movement caused by differences in law or regulation between jurisdictions: that of mutual recognition.[29] It is the decision of the first Member State that determines the status of the individual and it is this decision that must be accepted by all other Member States. However, the principle of mutual recognition is not homogeneous in its application across the legal order of the Union. It varies in the degree to which other states are required to accept the decision

[28] Anthony Arnull, *The European Union and its Court of Justice* (Oxford University Press, 2006) ch 16.

[29] See generally Christine Janssens, *The Principle of Mutual Recognition in EU Law* (Oxford University Press, 2013).

of the original Member State, the legal order of which is to govern the particular decision, and, perhaps most importantly, if the second Member State is capable of exercising any controls, either regarding the validity of the original decision or in providing for exceptions, including the requirement of a sufficient degree of equivalence between the laws of the original Member State and its own laws. Through a desire to secure the maximum free movement for individuals and hence the maximum degree of certainty for such individuals, the Court of Justice in its elaboration of the principle of mutual recognition in Article 54 CISA has been led to adopt a particularly strict version of the principle of mutual recognition, albeit recently rendered more flexible through an insistence that there be a 'substantive assessment of the merits of a case' before it definitively forecloses prosecution throughout the Union.[30]

Firstly, the Court of Justice has insisted that the *ne bis in idem* principle operates in the absence of any equivalence. That a decision of a single Member State is to be applied in another Member State is not particularly novel.[31] In fact, this structure forms the definitional core of the principle of mutual recognition and lies at the heart of *Cassis de Dijon*.[32] However, unlike with other instances of the mutual recognition principle, in particular those found in both the case-law and legislation of the internal market, in the operation of Article 54 CISA, Member States are not entitled to subject their acceptance of a decision of another Member State to the condition that there exists a certain degree of similarity or functional equivalence between the laws of the respective Member States. There is no principle of 'mandatory requirements'[33] or 'public policy' derogations or equivalence test[34] that a Member State can invoke to prevent the operation of a decision to convict or acquit an individual, simply because in its own legal order it does not recognise similar decisions. Article 54 CISA implies that each Member State

> recognises the criminal law in force in the other Member States even when the outcome would be different if its own national law was applied. … The application by one Member State of the *ne bis in idem* principle as set out in Article 54 of the CISA, to procedures whereby further prosecution is barred, which have taken place in another Member State without a court being involved, cannot be made subject to a condition that the first State's legal system does not require such judicial involvement either.[35]

[30] Most clearly in Case C-486/14 *Criminal Proceedings against Piotr Kossowski* EU:C:2016:483. For a comment, see Stefano Montaldo, 'A New Crack in the Wall of Mutual Recognition and Mutual Trust: Ne Bis in Idem and the Notion of Final Decision Determining the Merits of the Case' (2016) 1 *European Papers* 1183.

[31] Indeed it may become a technique used increasingly frequently in transnational processes more generally; see Kalypso Nicolaidis and Gregory Shaffer, 'Transnational Mutual Recognition Regimes: Governance without Global Government' (2005) 68 *Law and Comtemporary Problems* 263.

[32] Case 120/78 *Rewe-Zentral AG v Bundesmonopolverwaltung für Branntwein* [1979] ECR 649.

[33] ibid. See also Case C-55/94 *Reinhard Gebhard v Consiglio dell'Ordine degli Avvocati e Procuratori di Milano* [1995] ECR I-04165. For a good example of the requirement of equivalence in legislation, see Directive 98/5/EC to facilitate practice of the profession of lawyer on a permanent basis in a Member State other than that in which the qualification was obtained [1998] OJ L77/36.

[34] See Janssens (n 29).

[35] *Gözütok and Brügge* (n 1) paras 33–34.

At stake in *Gözütock and Brügge* was the question of settlement decisions. Precisely the same logic has been applied to instances where cases have been disposed of due lack of evidence,[36] time-limits on prosecution[37] and findings of 'non-lieu' or absence of grounds.[38]

The strict version of mutual recognition in the context of the *ne bis in idem* principle was not uncontroversial and indeed prompted a response from certain Member States. Greece in particular tabled a proposal that, while not directly challenging the Court's judgment in *Gözütock and Brügge*, did include exceptions allowing a Member State to prosecute in certain situations, namely where the security or other 'equally essential interests' of the Member State was threatened, even where another Member State had already done so.[39] That proposal never gained sufficient support to make it into the Official Journal as a legislative instrument but it does underline the fact that alternatives existed to the interpretation of the Court of Justice in *Gözütock and Brügge*. Instead, the Court set aside the potential concerns of Member States in having some form of equivalence check and insisted on an interpretation that maximised the free movement of individuals.

In a complementary move the Court of Justice has found that not only must the decision of the authorities of the first Member State be recognised as valid, even in the absence of equivalence, but that for the purposes of the application of Article 54 CISA, the *effect* of that decision, and in particular whether it is considered final or otherwise, in the legal order of the second Member State, is to be determined by the law of the first Member State. In what can be called the *Turanský* principle the Court held that:

> [I]n order to assess whether a decision is "final" for the purposes of Article 54 of the CISA, it is necessary first of all to ascertain … that the decision in question is considered under the law of the Contracting state which adopted it to be final and binding, and to verify that it leads, in that State, to the protection granted by the *ne bis in idem* principle.[40]

It is by reference to the law of the issuing Member State that the effect of the decision is to be ascertained. Not only is the decision to acquit or convict to be adopted by the first Member State, but also the question of its finality – its ultimate effect in definitively regulating the status of the individual – is likewise to be determined by the law of the issuing Member State. Thus in *Turanksý* whether the decision of a Czech police officer discontinuing an investigation was final or not was to be determined according to Czech law. The outcome of that assessment under *Czech* law

[36] Case C-150/05 *Jean Leon Van Straaten v Staat der Nederlanden and Republiek Italië* EU:C:2006:614, [2006] ECR I-9327.

[37] Case C-467/04 *Criminal proceedings against Guiseppe Francesco Gasparini and Others* EU:C:2006:610, [2006] ECR I-9199 (n 9).

[38] *M* (n 13).

[39] Initiative of the Hellenic Republic with a view to adopting a Council Framework Decision concerning the application of the *ne bis in idem* principle [2003] OJ C100/24, Art 4(1). The proposal also concerned the related matter of dividing jurisdiction between Member States.

[40] Case C-491/07 *Criminal proceedings against Vladimir Turanský* [2008] ECR I-11039, para 35.

determined whether *Austrian* authorities could proceed with their own investigations and possible prosecution in Austria. The same formula has been employed by the Court in the subsequent cases of *Bourquain*[41] to the situation of general amnesties, and in *M*[42] to the situation of *non-lieu*, or dismissal for lack of grounds.

The result of both of the above interrelated rules – the acceptance of the decision in the absence of equivalence and ensuring that it is the law of the first Member State that determines the finality of the decision – is to grant maximum certainty to the individual. In other areas of mutual recognition, the legal position of an individual can be the result of a combination of the decision of the initial legal order and how that decision is accepted and applied in the second legal order. Thus in the area of the mutual recognition of diplomas the ability of the individual to practice a profession in a second Member State depends on a combination of the decision of the first Member State to grant a diploma and the conditions applied by the second Member State to the recognition of that diploma.[43] The precise status of the individual is therefore the result of the combined interaction of rules originating in two legal orders. The outcome is of course variable depending on precisely which two Member States are in question, although harmonising measures can reduce situations of legal uncertainty for individuals. The consequence is firstly greater or lesser free movement between those jurisdictions depending on the precise differences, and secondly a degree of variation in the extent of the freedom of movement throughout the Union. With Article 54 CISA, however, the Court is at pains to ensure the maximum degree of free movement for individuals, both between particular Member States but also across the Union as a whole. To secure such a result the decision of one Member State and only one Member State must be made applicable throughout the Union in the same manner. It is logical and necessary that this be the Member State that adopted the initial decision.[44] The result is a particularly strict interpretation of mutual recognition in Article 54 CISA. It aims at maximum recognition in an effort to achieve maximum free movement for individuals across all Member States.[45] As a

[41] *Bourquain* (n 2) para 48.

[42] Joined Cases 148/13-150/13 *A, B and C v Staatssecretaris van Veiligheid en Justitie* (Opinion of AG Sharpston) EU:C:2014:2111 (n 13).

[43] Janssens (n 29) 91ff using the example of driving licences.

[44] Logical because a decision to finally settle a case is part of an overall criminal justice *system* and the rules regarding its effect should take into account other elements of the criminal justice system. To transpose a decision and yet change its ultimate result may ignore this systemic quality. Necessary because once the decision of the first Member State is adopted by necessity any other result will result in variations.

[45] Such maximum recognition, and in particular the absence of equivalence, is dependent on what might charitably be termed the fiction of mutual trust between the legal orders of Member States. Maduro has lucidly pointed out the paradox of the operation of the twin principles of mutual recognition and mutual trust in the context of variations between legal orders: it is precisely when variation between legal orders is greatest and mutual trust less likely to exist that it needs to be relied and asserted by the Court to the greatest extent. If there was in fact real mutual trust between Member States, there would be no need to insist on it. See Miguel-Poiares Maduro, 'So Close and Yet So Far: The Paradoxes of Mutual Recognition' (2007) 14 *Journal of European Public Policy 814*.

result, the legal situation of an individual – the status of an individual with respect to a particular crime – is governed not by various combinations of two or even more Member States interacting but by the law of a single Member State and only that Member State. The outcome of this determination is in turn applicable in *all* other Member States in the exactly same fashion. Both the validity of a decision and its finality is determined by the law of one state and only one state.

A Substantive Assessment of the Merits of the Case

There is one instance in which a Member State may prosecute an individual who has already been subject to a final decision in another Member State, namely if the originally decision did not contain an assessment of the merits of the case. If a desire to secure maximum recognition of the individual's free movement is the principle goal of the Court of Justice in the interpretation of Article 54 CISA, this is not its *only* goal or concern. The Court is aware of the underlying tension in the *ne bis in idem* principle, namely to ensure that an individual is called to account properly for his actions once and only once, but that he should in fact be properly called to account. In line with jurisprudence in relation to the EAW FD,[46] the Court wishes to ensure that the European Union remains or indeed becomes, an area of *justice*, meaning that individuals should face justice for their wrongful actions and that they be properly called to account before a court. Article 54 CISA should not therefore be used as a mechanism to evade justice.[47]

The Court has accordingly insisted there be an 'examination of the merits of the case'.[48] There must occur in one Member State an assessment of the actions of an individual in light of all the relevant facts either during a trial or by a competent authority in relation to a decision whether to try or not. Thus a case discontinued for the simple reason that another Member State, better situated, commenced an investigation cannot be considered finally disposed of for the purposes of Article 54 CISA.[49] In *Miraglia*, in which Dutch authorities suspended their investigation because the Italian authorities had begun their own investigation, there was simply 'no assessment whatsoever of the unlawful conduct with which the defendant was charged'.[50] The Italian authorities were not therefore prevented

[46] Framework Decision 2002/584/JHA on the European arrest warrant and the surrender procedures between Member States (EAW FD) [2002] OJ L190/1. See Case C-306/09 *IB* EU:C:2010:626, [2010] ECR I-10341.

[47] See also Case C-182/15 *Aleksei Petruhhin v Latvijas Republikas Ģenerālprokuratūra* EU:C:2016:630, paras 36 and 37 in which the Court reads an object of 'preventing the risk of impunity for persons who have committed an offence' as part of the broader objective of the Union, found in Art 3(2) TEU, to offer an AFJS to its citizens. For further discussion, see Chapter 4.

[48] *Gasparini* (n 9).

[49] Case C-469/03 *Criminal proceedings against Filomeno Mario Miraglia* EU:C:2005:156, [2005] ECR I-2009.

[50] ibid, para 34.

from prosecuting. A decision 'where no determination has been made as to the merits of the case, cannot constitute a decision finally disposing of the case against that person within the meaning of Article 54 of the CISA.'[51] Similarly in *Spasic* the fact that an individual had only served the pecuniary and not the custodial element of his sentence had the result that his sentence was not in the process of being enforced within the meaning of Article 54 CISA.[52] To hold otherwise would mean an individual could evade justice. Finally, in *Kossowski* the Court combined the test contained in *Turansky*[53] with that in *Miraglia*[54] to produce a two-step test to determine if a case has been finally disposed of.[55] Firstly, and in accordance with *Turanksý*, the case must be definitively closed as determined by the law of the original Member State which adopted the decision.[56] Secondly, there must have been an assessment of the merits of the case.[57] Note that these two conditions are cumulative. Thus, in *Kossowski* German authorities were allowed to prosecute an individual whose case had been closed in Poland for lack of evidence due to the absence of key witnesses. The result, as Montaldo points out, is an attenuation of the strict principle of mutual recognition in this field, allowing the receiving Member State to subject recognition to some control.[58] Note, however, that this is not a control based on its own domestic law or standards, in ensuring protection of some domestic interests through imposing a requirement of equivalence. Or rather it is not only the domestic interest that is at stake. While certainly permitting a Member State to prosecute an individual where it deems its interests have been affected, it reflects a broader EU interest that an individual not escape punishment within the AFSJ. Importantly, due to the substantive nature of the control it should operate in a quasi-uniform manner across the Union; whether a substantive assessment of the merits of the case has taken place is a determination of fact and should not vary across the Union depending on jurisdiction. An individual remains open to prosecution throughout the Union or he does not.[59] The result is that an individual's status in relation to a particular crime vis-à-vis the Union as a whole remains uniform.

One further consequence of this concern to ensure that an individual be properly tried has been that Article 54 CISA can only operate to benefit the individual

[51] ibid, para 30.
[52] Case C-129/14 PPU *Criminal proceedings against Zoran Spasic* EU:C:2014:586, para 69.
[53] *Turanský* (n 40).
[54] *Miraglia* (n 49).
[55] *Kossowski* (n 30).
[56] ibid, para 36.
[57] ibid, para 42.
[58] Montaldo (n 30).
[59] There can of course be variations on the manner in which Member States will avail of an opportunity to prosecute an individual due to jurisdiction, substantive criminal law or prosecutorial policy. But this is simply a more specific manifestation of the fact that whether or not an individual will or will not be prosecuted in a particular Member State depends on the laws and practices of that state; a phenomenon that obtains in all areas of criminal law and one that is a necessary consequence of the (primarily) national nature of the criminal law competence.

who has in fact been judged or his case determined: it cannot benefit those who, while involved in the same situation, were not so judged. Its result cannot be applied as a precedent or by analogy to other similar cases. Unlike the operation of mutual recognition in regulatory matters, mutual recognition in the criminal law operates as an individualised principle – applicable only to the individual whose case has been dealt with. In *Gasparini* although the discontinuation of a case for being time-barred was in fact considered a decision that finally disposed of a case,[60] the decision could not be applied by analogy to the cases of other individuals involved in the same act.[61]

The result of interpreting the concept of finality in light of both the principle of free movement and the need to secure justice has been the creation of a single status for individuals. Through an especially strict application of the principle of mutual recognition, applicable in the absence of equivalence and governed solely by the law of the issuing Member State, the Court has been at pains to maximise certainty for the individual; this has been achieved by ensuring that his legal status vis-à-vis that crime is identical throughout the Union. At the same time, as indicated by *Gasparini* in particular, the Court is anxious to ensure that individuals do in fact face justice and that the principle of *ne bis in idem* does not operate to allow individuals to evade either being tried or serving their sentence. The result is that a substantive decision *relative to that individual* must be made. It is an individualised principle. The combination of these two moves has been the creation of a single, individual legal status attaching to individuals.

Interpretation of Sameness in Light of Free Movement: A Single Space

A single individual status, but in relation to what? If the use of a teleological interpretation of the notion of finality in Article 54 CISA has resulted in the creation of a unique legal status for individuals, not governed by multiple legal orders, a similar use of the same teleological interpretation focusing on free movement in defining *sameness* has resulted in the construction of a single space. It is again the existence of multiple legal orders combined with the need to secure free movement of persons that has determined the choice of the Court of Justice in its interpretation of the principle. In particular, it has forced the Court to opt for an interpretation of sameness based on the facts rather than the offence. Sameness for the purposes of Article 54 CISA is to be determined by the essential unity in space and time of the

[60] A not uncontroversial conclusion concerning the need to ensure a substantive assessment of the merits of the case. See *Gasparini* (Opinion of AG Sharpston) (n 9) para 75. Perhaps the decision can be understood as establishing a priority between the two goals contained in Art 54, the need to ensure legal certainty for individuals and the need to ensure that justice be done, with the priority being given to the former where they might conflict such as the present case.

[61] ibid, para 35.

acts of an individual. At the same time, the Court has insisted that this essential unity of factual elements is applied throughout the Union; it is not a concept that operates within a single Member State but extends across the borders of the Union.

A crime is the legal classification of a set of facts, generally the actions combined with the mental state of an individual. It exists by virtue of the law and the existence of a particular crime is the creation of a particular legal system. In other words, a crime is a legal construction of a particular legal system that enters into existence when a set of facts obtain. The *ne bis in idem* principle has long struggled with this essential duality between law and facts, in defining sameness. On the one hand a legal system might take the view that sameness is defined by reference to the offence; thus a single act may give rise to multiple offences[62] and the *ne bis in idem* principle does not prevent the state from prosecuting an individual for one of those offences despite a case having been heard and disposed of in relation to another. An alternative approach is to focus not on the definition of the offences but rather on the facts of the case. Under this approach an individual can only be prosecuted once for any act that resulted in wrongdoing. In this understanding sameness refers to the same act rather than the same crime.[63]

In a national legal system, or an international legal instrument that is applied in national contexts such as the ECHR, the choice of which approach to adopt will depend on the policy decisions and values contained in that particular legal order. In the context of a transnational legal order, one containing a *transnational ne bis in idem* principle concerned with maximising free movement in a space of multiple legal orders, that choice is quite simply not available. If the legal order wishes that rule to be effective in securing free movement, it must define sameness in terms of *facts* and not offences. The reason is clear: a crime is a creature of a legal order and the definition of crimes varies across legal orders. To require that a crime be defined in the same way across Member States in order for the principle to operate (and hence to ensure that individuals enjoy free movement) would be to radically reduce its application, if not to render it practically inoperable, at least in the absence of substantial harmonisation. In the words of the Court: 'Because there is no harmonisation of national criminal laws, a criterion based on the legal classification of the acts or on the protected legal interest might create as many barriers to freedom of movement within the Schengen territory as there are penal systems in the Contracting States.'[64]

[62] For example, a drunk driver who hits and kills an individual may be guilty of drunk driving, driving recklessly and a form of homicide such as manslaughter. Three crimes arising from a single act.

[63] The distinction between offence and act is a little too neat and in reality is likely to be coloured by the fact that facts are needed to substantiate an offence and similarly what facts are precisely relevant will be determined by the legal definition of the offence. Regardless of which approach is adopted it is impossible to exclude considerations of the other element. See van Bockel (n 7) ch 2. A further difficulty arises when states operate parallel administrative and criminal enforcement mechanisms for the same activity. This issue has been dealt with by the Court of Justice under Art 50 CFR: see *Åkerberg Fransson* (n 15) and more recently *Menci* (n 14).

[64] *Van Esbroeck* (n 3) para 34.

In the place of a definition based on legal classification, the Court has formulated a test based on the 'identity of the material acts, understood in the sense of the existence of a set of concrete circumstances which are inextricably linked together'.[65] The 'material acts at issue [must] constitute a set of facts that are inextricably linked together in time, in space and by their subject matter'.[66] Thus the legal classification of the offence is irrelevant; to hold otherwise, as indicated in the above quote from *Van Straaten*, would be to render the right of free movement nugatory.[67] The legal interest adversely affected by the crime is similarly irrelevant.[68] Finally, the assessment of 'sameness' is an objective rather than a subjective test – in determining whether acts are the same for the purposes of Article 54 CISA the subjective intention of the accused in relation to the various acts is not to be relied upon, instead an objective assessment of the facts should be undertaken.[69]

Not only has the Court of Justice found that it is the facts, and not the legal classification of those facts, that is at stake in defining sameness under Article 54 CISA but as a consequence of focusing on the facts, the principle can apply to cross-border acts, a possibility that would be excluded by a reliance on the legal classification of the acts. Thus a series of facts that involve the transporting of drugs between Member States are not to be conceived of as two separate offences of firstly exporting and secondly importing illegal substances, but rather may be seen as 'inextricably linked together in time, in space and by their subject-matter' and the same act for the purposes of Article 54 CISA.[70] This unity in time and space can even operate where there are variations in certain non-essential facts, such as the precise identity of persons involved and quantities of drugs at stake.[71] What is important is that the essential unity of the accused's individual act is maintained. Similarly, and even more tellingly, the mere presence of borders and different jurisdictions does not render a single act into multiple acts: an individual convicted of transporting contraband materials across various internal borders of the Schengen Area does not as a consequence commit several crimes.[72] It is an objective assessment of the fact seen in their essential unity, extending across the territory of various Member States, that is relevant, not the differing legal interests represented by the different Member States.[73] As put by AG Saugsmandsgaard Øe in *XC*:

> [A]lthough the scope of the *ne bis in idem* principle set out in Article 4(1) of Protocol No 7 to the ECHR is limited to the territory of each State considered separately, Article 50 of the Charter extends it to cover *the territory of the Union, regarded as one entity.*

[65] ibid, para 36.
[66] ibid, para 38.
[67] ibid.
[68] Case C-288/05 *Criminal proceedings against Jürgen Kretzinger* EU:C:2007:441, [2007] ECR I-6441. This is in contrast to the application of the principle in competition law proceedings. See Luchtman (n 7) 1724–25.
[69] *Kraaijenbrink* (n 4).
[70] *Van Esbroeck* (n 3) para 36.
[71] *Van Straaten* (n 36) para 49.
[72] *Kretzinger* (n 68) para 34.
[73] ibid, paras 34–36.

> Following the example of Article 50 of the Charter, the territorial scope of Article 54 of the CISA covers the territory of all the Member States participating in the Schengen area, *regarded as one entity.*[74]

The result of interpreting the sameness criteria in light of the need to secure free movement is therefore twofold. By disregarding the legal classification, the Court can ensure that it is the act itself that is at stake, and while laws vary across legal orders, facts do not. A single wrongful act can therefore be considered as such across the entire Union. It allows the possibility of understanding a particular wrongful act in a unified way across the various Member States of the Union. By focusing on acts rather than offences the Court has ensured that there is a commonality in terms of the subject matter of the principle: Member States are in effect considering the same thing. Secondly, in concentrating on the facts, and in particular ensuring that when considering the essential unity of time and space Member States are not to be limited to the territory of a single Member State, the Court has ensured that the *ne bis in idem* principle, and the wrongful act of the individual, is one that extends across Member States. Borders are irrelevant either in establishing separate crimes of importing and exporting in *Van Straaten*,[75] or in establishing multiple instances of the same crime, such as smuggling in *Kreitzinger*.[76] The point of reference is not the territory of individual Member States, rather the act is to be understood by reference to the EU territory as a whole. It ensures the essential territorial unity of the AFSJ with respect to criminal acts.

Consequences of an Interpretation in Light of Free Movement: A Multilevelled Calling to Account

We have seen how a strict application of the mutual recognition principle has led to a single status for individuals. Equally the effect of the decision is determined by a single Member State, by necessity the Member State that adopted the decision. The result is a maximisation of the free movement of individuals; not simply between two individual Member States but throughout the Union as a whole: an individual can be convicted in one Member State and move to a second Member State, a third and fourth and so on, secure in the knowledge that the determination of his case by the original Member State will follow him throughout the Union.[77] It mirrors the operation of mutual recognition in citizenship cases securing the

[74] Case C-234/17 *XC and Others v Generalprokuratur* (Opinion of AG Saugmandsgaard Øe) EU:C:2018:391, para 38.

[75] *Van Straaten* (n 36).

[76] *Kretzinger* (n 68).

[77] This is subject to the *Kossowski* proviso that an examination of the merits of the case has taken place, but unlike say a requirement of regulatory equivalence, this condition should apply in a uniform manner across the Union as discussed above.

autonomy of individuals throughout the Union.[78] Indeed, to quote again the comments of AG Bot in *Kossowksi*:

> The strength of the principle … [found in Article 54 CISA] … is justified by the importance of creating the area of freedom, security and justice for the creation of the European Union. This area is a supporting dimension of the single area of movement and economic activity, in that it provides that area with a legal framework containing the individual rights of citizens of the Union. In that regard it clearly relates to the concept of Union citizenship, and contributes towards giving that concept concrete reality.'[79]

At the same time, the Court is anxious to ensure that individuals do in fact face justice. This is evident from *Gasparini* in which individuals accused of participating in the same crime as Mr Gasparaini were not entitled to rely on the decision to dismiss in his case in order to face justice. In *Spasic*, interpreting Article 54 CISA in light of the principle contained in Article 52 CFR,[80] the Court found that the need to ensure that individuals do not evade justice rendered the requirement that sentences actually be enforced contained in Article 54 CISA a legitimate exception to the general rule that individuals do not face trial twice. The 'enforced' requirement in Article 54 CISA is therefore a legitimate exception to the right contained in Article 50 CFR. Thus because Mr Spasic had not in fact served the custodial element to his punishment received in Italy, he was liable to face trial for the same acts in Germany.[81] 'The execution condition laid down in Article 54 CISA is … intended … to prevent, in the area of freedom, security and justice, the impunity of persons definitively convicted and sentences in an EU Member State.'[82] Not to apply the execution condition in this case would lead mean Article 54 CISA 'would not be sufficient to prevent the impunity of persons definitively convicted and sentenced in the European Union'.[83] (Note the interesting shift from the Member States of the European Union to the European Union itself.) In *Kossowksi* the AFSJ becomes a key reference point and the interpretation of 'final … for the purposes of Article 54 of the CISA. … must be undertaken in the light not only of the need to ensure the free movement of persons but also of the need to promote the prevention and combatting of crime within the area of freedom, security and justice'.[84] A combination of these two points – that individuals enjoy a unique status with reference to the Union as a whole and that individuals do in fact face justice – is that individuals enjoy a unique status applicable throughout the Union with respect to a particular criminal act. To put it in the words of Duff, individuals are properly called to account for their wrongful actions in the European Union.

[78] See, for example, the 'name cases', Chapter 2.
[79] *Kossowski* (Opinion of AG Bot) (n 18) para 44.
[80] Providing for limitations on the rights contained in the Charter subject to certain conditions (necessary, provided for by law and not to affect the essence of the right in question).
[81] *Spasic* (n 52) para 55.
[82] ibid, para 63.
[83] ibid, para 63.
[84] *Kossowski* (n 30) para 47.

In a national context the concern is to ensure that an individual is called to account before the national community. It is the national community that one has offended, that has established through its criminal law the particular actions it deems wrongful in light of its own normative code. As we have seen in cases dealing with expulsion and periods of imprisonment, the Court of Justice has subscribed to this communitarian and normative view of crime.[85] A crime, beyond its immediate victim, is an offence against the community of citizens as a social collective[86] and it is on the authority of that community that an individual is called to account, tried and punished. Another state prosecuting an individual for a particular act quite simply does not suffice to answer for the wrong done that community.[87] It is precisely this reason that has made the establishment of a transnational *ne bis in idem* principle so difficult to achieve and why the taking into account of punishments administered by other states is seen as discretionary.

The relationship between the operation of the *ne bis in idem* principle and the community of citizens is well illustrated by its operation in federal systems. How a federation deals with the question of *ne bis in idem* reflects how it envisages the relationship between the different communities of which it is composed. The United States has long operated a doctrine of 'dual sovereignty' when it comes to the application of its double-jeopardy rule. Prosecution and indeed punishment for a particular act or crime by a state does not prevent prosecution by the federal authorities. A federal crime is a different thing from a state crime, even if it results from the same act.[88] An individual is accordingly not protected from being prosecuted separately by federal and state authorities. The ability to punish individuals is a reflection of the sovereign power. 'We have here two sovereignties, deriving power from different sources, capable of dealing with the same subject–matter within the same territory. … Each government in determining what shall be an offence against its peace and dignity is exercising its own sovereignty, not that of the other.'[89] This power has different origins and is exercised separately by different sovereigns: the state on the one hand, and the federation on the other. However, given the division of competences between the two levels of government, one might assume that a direct overlap, thereby creating the possibility of two crimes in two legal orders from one act, would not arise very frequently. Indeed, the dual-sovereignty rule could be justified on the basis that the different legal orders play a complementary role, protecting the same general interest in different instances.[90]

[85] See Chapter 4.

[86] See also Emile Durkheim, *The Division of Labour in Society*, trans George Simpson (The Free Press, 1933) ch 2.

[87] See, for example, the insistence by the Court of Justice in Case C-579/15 *Openbaar Ministerie v Daniel Adam Popławski* EU:C:2017:503, paras 44–45 that the exception to surrender contained in Art 4(6) EAW FD is in no way an *aud dedere aud judicare* rule, allowing the Netherlands to replace prosecuting by the issuing state with a willingness to prosecute the individual concerned in its own legal order. See further Chapter 4.

[88] *United States v Lanza* 260 US 377, 43 SCt 141.

[89] ibid, 382.

[90] See minority opinion of Brennan J in *Heath v Alabama* 474 US 82.

This 'interest-based' theory is, however, disproved by considering that the dual-sovereignty doctrine also applies *between states*, ie on a horizontal level. In such a case both states are exercising the same competence within their respective spheres. An application of the dual-sovereignty rule in this context implies that where an individual is tried and convicted in one state he can be tried and convicted for precisely the same act in a second state. Just as the federal and state levels reflect different sovereigns, each state represents a different sovereign.

> A State's interest in vindicating its sovereign authority through enforcement of its laws by definition can never be satisfied by another State's enforcement of *its* own laws. … In recognition of this fact, the [US Supreme] Court consistently has endorsed the principle that a single act constitutes an offence against each sovereign whose laws are violated by that act.[91]

Although phrased in terms of sovereignty, the language of the US Supreme Court could easily be translated into Duff's terms. Each sovereign in effect represents a separate community, each of which has the authority to both define what it deems wrongful conduct and to punish individuals accordingly. Two communities, each of which is wronged, reflect two crimes, both of which can be punished. The United States in its understanding of the application of the double-jeopardy rule between states thereby reflects a particular view of crime and of the communities that make up its federation.

The exact opposite situation obtains in the European Union with opposite implications for our understanding of its respective communities. Prosecution and punishment in one Member State means prosecution and punishment is impossible in another Member State. An individual is called to account before a national court and, if convicted, is punished by the sovereign power of that Member State. It is certainly an act of wrongdoing against that Member State and against the community that Member State embodies. However, the effect of that calling to account is Union-wide; it is valid and applicable throughout the Union vis-à-vis all Member States.

The result is that where two or more Member States claim jurisdiction, a race to prosecute can arise.[92] In an attempt to avoid the practical difficulties associated with parallel proceedings, the Union has attempted to institute rules for the coordination of criminal jurisdiction,[93] in effect formalising the delegation of the calling to account to a single Member State.[94] However, reflecting the inherent

[91] ibid, 93 (emphasis in original).

[92] See the case of *M* (n 13).

[93] Framework Decision 2009/948/JHA on prevention and settlement of conflicts of exercise of jurisdiction in criminal proceedings [2009] OJ L328/42.

[94] Note the interesting point raised by the Commission in relation to the operation of an obligation to prosecute that exists in certain Member States. When considering the operation of such a principle in light of a system of coordinating jurisdiction, the Commission noted that: '[I]t can validly be argued that in a common area of Freedom, Security and Justice this principle (the obligation to prosecute) is satisfied when another Member State prosecutes such a case.' See European Commission, *Green Paper on Conflicts of Jurisdiction and the Principle of Ne Bis in Idem in Criminal Proceedings* COM(2005) 696 final, 4.

national nature of the process and the sovereign power contained in the right to punish, the Framework Decision on Conflicts of Criminal Jurisdiction merely contains an obligation for consultation between national authorities. It does not establish binding rules allocating jurisdiction. The contrast with the ideas raised by the Commission in its Green Paper on the matter is notable. The Commission proposed certain objective criteria for allocation and even floated the idea of an EU body to eventually resolve conflicts of jurisdiction between national prosecutors, while noting such a move would involve 'complex questions'.[95] Such an institution was not created in the final instrument and in fact it was underlined that Member States would not be obliged to relinquish jurisdiction.[96] Eurojust does provide a coordinating function and has issues guidelines, which are, however, non-binding.[97] National communities jealously retain the authority to define wrongful behaviour, define when they consider themselves to be wronged and to call individuals to account for that wrong.

Yet once judged, all other Member States are prevented from prosecuting the same individual for the same act. The result is that crime has been punished, the wrongdoing expunged. It is by implication a single act of wrongdoing with reference to the Union as a whole that has been accounted for. No other acts of wrongdoing against other Member States remain to be punished. The individual Member State is, in addition to acting on its own interests, in a sense, acting on behalf of the Union as a whole. For Lööf this represents a 'regulatory principle' for the system of shared enforcement of criminal law established under the EAW, a system that in turn can only be justified by assuming the Union represents a single social contract as described in Chapter 6.[98] In Duff's words, the Union could be said to be a single community of citizens.

However, the supranational community that emerges is distinctly multilevelled and indeed paradoxical. It is not quite so simple as assuming a single, supranational social contract. It is through the wronging of the national community that an individual wrongs the supranational community, and it is through the punishment by the national community that the wrong is accounted for. In one sense the crime remains an offence against the national community. It is defined by national law and it is in some sense difficult thus to speak of it as a crime against the whole Union, especially if the act does not represent a crime in all parts of the Union. Yet this is precisely the implication of the transnational *ne bis in idem* principle. This supranational community has emerged through, and relies on, transnational (and therefore ultimately national) process and principles. It is through wronging

[95] Conflicts of Jurisdiction in Criminal Proceedings FD (n 93) Art 7.

[96] See ibid, recital point 11.

[97] There is, however, an interesting mediating role for Eurojust in the Framework Decision. See ibid, recital point 12 and Art 14. See Mitsilegas (n 26) 91–92.

[98] Robin Lööf, 'Defending Liberty and Structural Integrity: A Social Contractual Analysis of Criminal Justice in the EU' (PhD thesis, Department of Law, European University Institute 2008).

a national community that one wrongs the supranational community – as it is composed of other communities – and it is through being called to account on a national level that one is called to account supranationally. This national calling to account is transformed through the transnational *ne bis in idem* principle, interpreted in light of free movement into a supranational calling to account, that in turn reflects an ultimately composite supranational community of citizens.

PART IV

Supranational Wrongs

8

Supranational Public Wrongs: The Limitations and Possibilities of a European Community[1]

Introduction

There are a number of reasons why a community might wish to criminalise certain behaviour and hence deem it wrongful. The criminal law can be used to protect and promote a variety of interests, each of different social worth. Criminal law can be seen as a means of maintaining public order in society[2] and in particular maintaining freedom in conditions of security by minimising harmful or risky conduct between individuals.[3] Classic offences against the person, such as assault and murder, might be said to fall into this category. The criminal law can be seen as a means of expressing the values of a particular society – as an ongoing and reflexive process by which society makes manifest and reinforces its collective identity by proscribing conduct that offends against these values.[4] The criminal law may also be used to protect distinctly public goods – collective goods that bring benefit to society as a whole or that are seen as an aspect of the society's collective historical, economic or environmental patrimony, such as the environment, cultural heritage or a proper functioning market. These reasons for criminalisation are distinctive but they are also overlapping and are not mutually exclusive.[5]

[1] A previous version of this chapter was published in the (2017) 54 *CML Rev* 771–803. Reprinted here with the permission of Kluwer Law International.

[2] See, for example, Lacey's conception of the proper function of the criminal law in Nicola Lacey, *State Punishment: Political Principles and Community Values* (Routledge, 1987) ch 5, in particular: 'The criminal law is often understood as being concerned with the prevention and mitigation of *harms*: I have chosen to push the analysis back one stage to focus on the values and interests whose violation came to be identified as relevant harms' (101, emphasis in original).

[3] Thus the harm principle can in effect be dominant in providing a definition of wrongfulnes for the purposes of criminal law; see AP Simester and Andreas von Hirsch, *Crimes, Harms and Wrongs: On the Principles of Criminalisation* (Hart Publishing, 2011) ch 2.

[4] See, for example, Emile Durkheim, *The Division of Labour in Society*, trans George Simpson (The Free Press, 1933) ch 3, speaking of 'organic solidarity' in relation to criminal law.

[5] See Hart, who discusses the multivalued nature of the criminal law settling on a principal but not exclusive aim of the criminal law as expressing the needs of responsible citizenship with subordinate

Following Duff's account, the unifying characteristic of crimes is that they are public wrongs. They are wrongs shared by the community as a whole and experienced by the community, alongside and often through the wrong suffered by the individual citizen.[6] What constitutes wrongful conduct and publicly wrongful conduct is an open category, defined by the particular society in which the criminal law operates. It can therefore accommodate all of the above reasons for criminalisation, depending on the context-specific definition of wrongness. Acts may be deemed wrongful simply for breaching the shared morality of the community.[7] Serious harm to individuals may be considered wrongful, made public by its shared quality in which the group is offended on behalf of the individual.[8] Damage to certain public goods, shared by the community and seen as particularly valuable for intrinsic or instrumental purposes, can be seen as publicly wrongful. And although these can also be seen as manifesting a harm principle, it is because that harm is deemed a wrong and a wrong against the community that it is criminal.[9]

This chapter explores the extent to which EU criminal law is capable of articulating public wrongs on behalf of the European Union as a whole and of communicating the wrongful character of those actions (or omissions) to individual citizens. As crimes are wrongs classified as such by virtue of the particular values and nature of the community, they imply the existence of such a community of shared values. The Union's competence to criminalise, to identify conduct that attracts punishment, has been steadily growing over the past two decades, reaching a certain apogee in the Treaty of Lisbon. Can we therefore say that the Union now has the ability though its criminal law competence to identify common values and interests and to label them wrongful? Are there such things as European public wrongs and therefore a tentative European community expressed through its criminal law, and that calls individual citizens to account for wrongs done to the community and fellow citizens?

In the remainder of this chapter the activity of the Union in adopting substantive criminal law measures will be assessed for its capacity to give rise to or express the existence of a normative community at a Union-wide level in Duff's sense. In this assessment EU criminal law will be assessed for its capacity to make particular normative value judgments through its criminal law, to identify specifically supranational public wrongs, breach of which is considered an offence against the Union as a whole, to express those normative judgments through its substantive

goals of rehabilitation of the offender (presented as teaching responsibility). See Henry Hart, 'The Aims of the Criminal Law' (1958) 23 *Law and Contemporary Problems* 401, 401.

[6] Following the account of shared wrongs developed in SE Marshall and RA Duff, 'Criminalization and Sharing Wrongs' (1998) 11 *Canadian Journal of Law and Jurisprudence* 7.

[7] For the most vocal proponent of this purpose of the criminal law, see the discussion of Lord Devlin's views in HLA Hart, *Law, Liberty and Morality* (Oxford University Press, 1962).

[8] Marshall and Duff (n 6).

[9] For a discussion of the relationship between the harm principle and his own theory of crimes as public wrongs, see RA Duff, *Answering for Crime: Responsibility and Liability in the Criminal Law* (Hart Publishing, 2007) ch 4.

criminal law and finally to express its moral condemnation at the wrongful behaviour of its citizens. The claim is that the extent to which the Union is capable of fulfilling these functions is significantly conditioned by the multilevel nature of the Union as it is applied in the area of criminal law – it is severely limited in its ability to express and communicate norms and the existence of a political community at a supranational level – but that nonetheless such a capacity does in fact exist, albeit in a mediated and removed form. The next section details the significant limitations on the Union's ability to identify supranational public wrongs, express moral disapproval and to communicate that disapproval directly to individuals. The following section, on the other hand looks at those features of substantive criminal law adopted by the Union that do demonstrate at least some limited capacity to identify and express certain supranational public wrongs, either through the identification of supranational public values or supranational public goods, harm to which constitutes a wrong against the wider Union. The briefer final section returns to some of the findings of previous chapter and covers an alternative manner in which EU criminal legislation can give rise to a Union-wide sense of wrongdoing, this time not by articulating an autonomous supranational understanding but rather through identifying and framing national criminal law and the choices it entails, thereby giving rise to the concept of 'shared wrongs', conceptions of wrongful behaviour identified by the Union as shared amongst the Member States and endorsed by EU law.

Structural Limitations on an EU Supranational Community

The European Union is not a state; its competences are limited in various ways and are exercised through a multilevel framework.[10] The first point to note is that there are key differences between the manner in which the Union exercises its competence to criminalise behaviour and a state's ability to criminalise behaviour. Its authority to act is limited in scope, and in its decision-making structures, implementation and enforcement it relies on the political processes and legal systems of Member States to complete its work.[11] This is especially true in the area of criminal law.[12] These limitations frustrate the ability of the Union to both articulate and especially to communicate the publically wrongful character of particular conduct.

[10] For an account of the European Union as having a multilevel constitution, see Ingolf Pernice, 'Multilevel Constitutionalism in the EU' (2002) 27 *EL Rev* 511; and Ingolf Pernice, 'The Treaty of Lisbon: Multi-Level Constitutionalism in Action' (2009) 15 *Columbia Journal of European Law* 349.

[11] Luis María Díez-Picazo, 'What Does it Mean to Be a State within the European Union?' [2002] *Riv Ital Dir Pubbl Communitario* 651.

[12] For a more detailed account, see Stephen Coutts, 'The Lisbon Treaty and the Area of Freedom, Security and Justice as an Area of Legal Integration' (2011) 7 *Croatian Yearbook of European Law* 87.

Articulation of Public Wrongs – Limited Scope for EU Criminalisation

Post-Lisbon the European Union has two express legal bases for criminalisation: Article 83(1) TFEU, which replaces the old 'third pillar' competence of approximation; and Article 83(2) TFEU, allowing harmonisation of criminal law in order to better enforce other areas of law that have already been the subject of harmonising legislation at an EU level.[13] In different ways they are restricted in their ability to identify conduct as wrongful; in particular they are limited, ancillary and functional.

The Union's competence to criminalise is first and foremost an unusually *limited* competence. This does not necessarily prevent the Union articulating a common European public interest but it does limit its potential scope. The competence contained in Article 83(1) TFEU is limited both by the existence of certain preconditions and by the establishment of a closed list of areas in which the Union may legislate. It provides for legislation only in the case of 'particularly serious crime with a cross-border dimension resulting from the nature or impact of such offences or from a special need to combat them on a special basis'.[14] It is a limited and distinctly complementary role for the European Union dealing with transnational criminal phenomena.[15] Not content to limit the Union's competence by establishing preconditions, the drafters of the TFEU also identified the particular

[13] Dougan maintains that there remains a residual implicit criminalising competence from the earlier, pre-Lisbon caselaw of *Greek Maize*, *Environmental Crimes* and *Ship Source Pollution*; see Michael Dougan, 'From Velvet Glove to the Iron Fist: Criminal Sanctions for the Enforcement of Union Law' in Marise Cremona (ed), *Compliance and the Enforcement of EU Law* (Oxford University Press, 2012). It would appear that this view may be confirmed by the Court's judgment in *Taricco* in which the Court found that in fulfilling its duty to ensure effective and dissuasive penalties for VAT fraud under the relevant Directive – which did not call explicitly for criminal sanctions – 'criminal penalties may nevertheless be essential'. The matter is, however, complicated by the Court in the next paragraph citing the PIF convention on fraud against the Union's resources which does explicitly call for criminal penalties. See Case C-105/14 *Criminal proceedings against Ivo Taricco and Others* EU:C:2015:555, paras 39–40. If such a competence exists, its use is likely to be limited and in practice is largely taken over by the express competence contained in Art 83(2) TFEU. For the purposes of this chapter it is assumed that similar considerations would apply to a residual implicit competence as described by Dougan as applying to the competence contained in Art 83(2) TFEU. There remains the case of EU legislation whose enforcement may or may not be implemented via criminal legislation by Member States. For the purposes of the present discussion that is subsumed into the general regulatory criminal law competence of Art 83(2) TFEU.

[14] Art 83(1) TFEU.

[15] Sometimes termed 'Eurocrimes' in opposition to the Art 83(2) TFEU competence. See European Commission, *Towards an EU Criminal Policy: Ensuring the effective implementation of EU policies through criminal law* COM(2011) 573 final, 5. There are various criteria put forward to identify the common characteristic of these crimes; Mitsilegas, for example, cites them as an example of a securitisation impulse in EU law making [Valsamis Mitsilegas, *EU Criminal Law after Lisbon* (Hart Publishing, 2016) ch 3], whereas Chaves points out that these crimes are all related to conduct and forms of criminality that have either arisen or become more prominent in the late 20th and early 21st century due to changes in technology and globalisation more generally; see Mariana Chaves, 'EU's Harmonization of National Cirminal Law: Between Punitiveness and Moderation' (2015) 21 *EPL* 527, 544.

areas that do in fact meet those conditions; in addition to the requirements of transnationality and seriousness, EU action is limited to a closed list of ten areas. The competence contained in Article 83(2) TFEU, on the other hand, is not limited to a closed list of certain areas but is indirectly limited by the precondition of harmonisation in another EU policy area and the condition that criminalisation be necessary for its effective enforcement.[16]

Not only is Article 83(1) TFEU a limited competence, it was traditionally seen as an *ancillary* competence. Approximation in criminal law was historically justified by the need to secure confidence in a common area of movement. Such measures were first presented as mere flanking measures, designed to deal with any negative side-effects of free movement[17] and facilitating cooperation between judicial and police agencies in criminal matters. Indeed, as the criminal law competence of the Union developed, the competence of approximation became subservient to that of mutual recognition.[18] Thus the competence granted the Union under Article 83(1) TFEU was not originally envisaged as forming the basis for the Union to assert any autonomous understanding of public wrongs. It was traditionally viewed as ancillary and subservient to the goal of mutual recognition of national criminal law.

If the Article 83(1) competence is ancillary, Article 83(2) TFEU contains a *functional* criminal competence.[19] Although not limited in the same way as Article 83(1) TFEU to a closed list of measures, it is intended above all to be an effective enforcement tool rather than to express a determination of wrongful conduct by the Union. The competence now contained in Article 83(2) TFEU is directly descended from a doctrine designed to ensure the effective implementation of EU law. The characterisation of penalties as needing to be 'effective, proportionate and dissuasive' in *Greek Maize*,[20] the forerunner of *Environmental Crimes*,[21] is linked to the need for Member States to ensure that 'infringements of Community law are penalised under conditions, both procedural and substantive, which are analogous to those applicable to infringements of national law of

[16] See Jacob Öberg, 'Limits to EU Powers: A Case Study on Individual Criminal Sanctions for the Enforcement of EU Law' (PhD, European University Institute, 2014) and Ester Herlin-Karnell, *The Constitutional Dimension of European Criminal Law* (Hart Publishing, 2012) for a discussion on the limitations, potential or otherwise, on the EU's criminalisation competence under Art 83(2) TFEU.

[17] See Anne Weyembergh, 'The Functions of Approximation of Penal Legislation within the European Union' (2005) 12 *Maastricht Journal of European and Comparative Law* 149.

[18] Mutual recognition took prime place in the new system of competences in the Treaty of Lisbon, whereas in the Stockholm Programme the hierarchy between mutual recognition and approximation was made explicit: 'The approximation, where necessary, of substantive and procedural law should facilitate mutual recognition.' The Stockholm Programme: An Open and Secure Europe Serving and Protecting Citizens [2010] OJ C115/01, 12. Although not the subject of this chapter the competence to harmonise procedural rules is expressly made ancillary to the functioning of mutual recognition instruments in the Treaty of Lisbon ('to the extent necessary to facilitate mutual recognition of judgments and judicial decisions and police and judicial cooperation in criminal matters'). See Art 82(2) TFEU.

[19] See Mitsilegas (n 15) 60–62.

[20] Case 68/88 *Commission v Greece* EU:C:1989:339, [1989] ECR 2968 (*Greek Maize*), para 24.

[21] Case C-176/03 *Commission v Council (Environmental Crimes)* EU:C:2005:542, [2005] ECR I-7879.

a similar nature and importance and which, in any event, make the penalty effective, proportionate and dissuasive'.[22] That functional character is now enshrined in the wording of Article 83(2) TFEU which explicitly links its exercise to situations where 'the approximation of criminal laws and regulations of the Member States proves essential to ensure the effective implementation of a Union policy in an area that has been subject to harmonisation measures'. It is not a stand-alone competence but rather is something that complements for the purposes of *enforcement* another EU policy and goal, be it environmental, financial regulation, etc. It is quintessential regulatory criminal law.

This functional character can also be seen in the operation of the Article 83(2) TFEU competence as discussed by commentators and policymakers. Much discussion on Article 83(2) TFEU has centred on the criteria of necessity and effectiveness as limits to the competence of the Union.[23] These criteria, vague as they may be,[24] are seen as expressing the principles of subsidiarity and proportionality in the field of criminal law, regulating the relations and division of powers between the Union and the Member States. However, in addition to the competence question, in their understanding of these criteria, policymakers and commentators have adopted, both implicitly and explicitly, a distinctly functional and utilitarian vision of the criminal law competence contained in Article 83(2) TFEU. Deterrence provides the exclusive prism for understanding the criteria contained in Article 83(2) TFEU. The adoption of EU criminal law measures are only deemed to be 'effective' if they ensure compliance with the underlying policy by creating costs for individuals engaging in the conduct deemed to be prejudicial to the underlying policy. Similarly, they meet the 'necessity' criteria only if other, less onerous forms of sanctioning, such as administrative sanctions, would be incapable of achieving the same result.[25] It is an explicitly instrumental and utilitarian vision of the criminal law designed, through the application of sanctions and costs for individuals, to reduce harmful activities or promote particular behaviour in order to secure other goals or benefits.[26]

Even the capacity of the criminal law to express social disapproval, an aspect one imagines would be more closely linked to the forging of a Union-wide perspective on wrongfulness and the expressive dimension of criminal law, when it is

[22] *Greek Maize* (n 20) para 24, substantially mirroring the equivalence and effectiveness test applied by the Court in the area of national remedies. See Estella Baker, 'Criminal Jurisdiction, the Public Dimension to 'Effective Protection' and the Construction of Community–Citizen Relations' (2001) 4 *Cambridge Yearbook of European Legal Studies* 25.

[23] See Herlin-Karnell (n 16) ch 3; Öberg (n 16). For other possible meanings of the term effectiveness in this area see Annika Suominen, 'Effectiveness and Functionality of Substantive EU Criminal Law' (2014) 5 *New Journal of European Criminal Law* 388, who speaks of effectiveness in terms of the enforcement of the criminal law.

[24] For a critique of the use of the concept of 'effectiveness' as a competence conferring concept, see Herlin-Karnell (n 16) ch 4.

[25] Commission (n 15) 7–8.

[26] For a discussion of consequentialism and utilitarianism in criminal law theory, see Michael Moore, *Placing Blame: A Theory of Criminal Law* (Oxford University Press, 1997) 161–63.

acknowledged, is framed by the Commission in terms of its usefulness in deterring individuals; the connotations of social disapproval that come with designating a particular conduct as criminal are primarily seen as another 'cost' imposed on individuals in an attempt to dissuade them from a particular activity. '[C]riminal law sanctions may be chosen when it is considered important to stress *strong disapproval* in order to ensure deterrence. The entering of convictions in criminal records can have a particular *deterrent character*.'[27] It is viewing the expressive dimension of the criminal law through a purely utilitarian lens. The underlying goal of Article 83(2) TFEU, even when social disapproval is invoked, is not primarily to express social disapproval but to ensure better regulatory compliance for another EU policy through the imposition of costs. The goals of social disapproval and deterrence are of course not mutually exclusive and indeed, as recognised by the Commission and as shall be explored in more detail later in this chapter, are in a significant manner complementary. However, it is clear from the policy communications of EU institutions, and indeed the wording of Article 83(2) TFEU, that although these two goals may be complementary, there is a clear priority between these two reasons for criminalisation in the mind of the Commission.

The EU's competence to criminalise contained in Article 83(1) and (2) TFEU appears limited in its ability to express the values and hence communal identity of a Union-wide supranational normative community. Article 83(1) TFEU is exceptionally limited and ancillary, limited to so-called 'serious transnational crimes' that necessarily engage a cross-border interest. It is ancillary to national enforcement and has been justified primarily as a side-effect of free movement. From one perspective the competence contained in Article 83(1) TFEU could be seen as simply an institutionalised outgrowth of transnational processes of cross-border movement. Article 83(2) TFEU, on the other hand, is framed explicitly as a functional competence, parasitic on other EU competences. Both of these legal bases are limited and linked, in different ways, to other EU activities. Neither allows for a wide-ranging ability on the part of the Union to articulate conduct it deems to be wrongful in and of itself, independent of other concerns. And tellingly the question of the Union legislating in the core area of criminal law, those crimes deemed *mala in se*, has never even been raised, it being accepted uncritically as an area exclusively for the Member States.

Communication of Public Wrongs: EU Criminal Law as Multilevelled

Commentary on the limitations on the Union's competence to criminalise, particularly those contained in Article 83(2) TFEU, has focused on the adequacy or otherwise of those limitations from the point of the view of the constitutional

[27] Commission (n 15) 11 (emphasis in original).

balance between Member States and the Union.[28] Indeed there appears to be an insistence (no doubt linked to concerns regarding sovereignty)[29] on the need to retain a distinctly limited role for the Union in this area and a continued focus on the primacy of national actors in the field of criminal justice, not least of all national legislatures and governments. Although relevant, the institutional concerns and constitutional balance of powers between the Union and the Member States are not the focus of this chapter. However, they do point to another feature of criminal law in the Union: the necessity of EU criminal law to be mediated by national law. This in turn inhibits the communicative capacity of EU criminal law, ie to directly communicate to individuals, through prohibition of conduct and enforcement of the law, the wrongful character of certain acts and omissions. This is manifested in two points in particular: firstly, the inability of EU criminal law to directly establish criminal liability for individuals; and secondly, the persistent absence of an EU criminal justice system.

The Union Cannot Directly Impose Criminal Liability

The Union cannot itself impose criminal liability and under Article 83 TFEU is only capable of adopting directives in order to indirectly criminalise behaviour.[30] Directives are binding on Member States but cannot bind individuals with the result that the enactment of national law is required before individuals are subject to any obligations. This fact is well known and has been applied in the case of criminal law for some decades now. In *Pretore di Salo* the Court of Justice stated that the directive in question 'cannot, of itself and independently of a national law adopted by a Member State for its implementation, have the effect of determining or aggravating the liability in criminal law of persons who act in contravention of the provisions of that directive'.[31] This reasoning was explicitly based on the Court's prior jurisprudence on the absence of direct effect of directives.[32]

The straightforward application of the inability of directives to directly impose liability on individuals has evolved into a general principle that EU law cannot aggravate the criminal liability of individuals. Unlike in other areas of law, the

[28] See, for example, Jacob Öberg, 'Do We Really Need Criminal Sanctions for the Enforcement of EU Law?' (2014) 5 *New Journal of European Criminal Law* 370.

[29] See Jannemieke Ouwekerk, 'Criminal Justice beyond National Sovereignty: An Alternative Perspective on the Europeanisation of Criminal Law' (2015) 23 *European Journal of Crime, Criminal Law & Criminal Justice* 11.

[30] Under Art 83 TFEU the Union may only adopt directives. Thus under Art 83(1) TFEU 'the European Parliament and the Council may, *by means of directives* adopted in accordance with the ordinary legislative procedure' (emphasis added). Similarly, under Art 83(2) 'if the approximation of criminal laws and regulations of the Member States proves essential to ensure the effective implementation of a Union policy … *directives* may establish minimum rules' (emphasis added).

[31] Case 14/86 *Pretore di Salò* EU:C:1987:275, [1987] ECR 2545, para 20.

[32] ibid, para 19.

indirect effect of directives has been explicitly set aside in the area of criminal liability. Thus in *Kolpinghuis* the Court accepted that the principle of sincere cooperation would normally imply a duty of consistent interpretation and an obligation to interpret national law in light of EU law. However, if the fulfilment of such a duty led to the aggravation of criminal liability, its application would have to be set aside.[33] In contrast to *Pretore di Salo*, the judgment in *Kolpinghuis* was based not only on the nature of directives, but also on the general principles of EU law and in particular the principle of legality and non-retroactivity of criminal law. This move from an argument based on the lack of direct effect to one based on general principles allowed the Court to subsequently extend the principle to regulations, at least those requiring some degree of national implementing measures.[34]

That the EU legal order recognises the principle of legality is not in and of itself particularly controversial and indeed is to be welcomed.[35] However, the real question at stake in the case-law is not whether criminal liability should be laid down in a legal instrument validly adopted, ie that it should enjoy the quality of 'legality', but rather *which* level of a multilevel legal order is competent to do so, ie the question is *whose* legality.

The answer from the Court's jurisprudence is that the principle of legality operates at the national level.[36] Mere adoption by the Union of measures criminalising conduct is not sufficient to meet the requisite standard of legality. Of course, the criminal prohibition does in a sense originate at an EU level, it is after all on foot of an EU law instrument that the Member State adopts a national criminal law, but this should not be confused with legality in the sense of the criminal law principle of legality, ie be adopted by a competent and legitimate legislature in a sufficiently clear and public manner such that individuals can be said to placed under a legitimate and binding obligation. EU law is certainly binding but it is binding on the Member States; prior to implementation there is no legal obligation, be it direct or indirect, placed on individuals. EU law in the criminal field quite simply does not enjoy that quality.

This deficiency is revealed by the contrasting reasoning and conclusions reached by the Advocate General and the Court in *Berlusconi*.[37] AG Kokott found

[33] Applied similarly in the case of Framework Decisions. See Case C-105/03 *Criminal proceedings against Maria Pupino* EU:C:2005:386, [2005] ECR I-5285.

[34] Case C-60/02 *Criminal proceedings against X* EU:C:2004:10, [2004] ECR I-651 (*X*). In *X* the Court accepted that although the principle of conforming interpretation would apply to create possible civil remedies (and by implication obligations), it could not operate to impose criminal obligations in the absence of national implementing legislation.

[35] For a detailed analysis of the theoretical underpinnings and the operation of the principle across three member states and the Union as a whole, see Christina Peristeridou, *The Principle of Legality in European Criminal Law* (Intersentia, 2015).

[36] It will be noted that this is consistent with the finding of both the AG and the Court regarding the principle of legality in the challenge to the EAW FD. See Case C-303/05 *Advocaten voor de Wereld VZW v Leden van de Ministerraad* EU:C:2007:261, [2007] ECR I-3633.

[37] Joined Cases C-387/02, C-391/02 and C-403/02 *Criminal Proceedings against Silvio Berlusconi, Sergio Adelchi and Marcello Dull'Utri et al* EU:C:2005:270, [2005] ECR I-3565.

that the offending piece of national legislation rendered a situation that was previously in compliance with EU law into a situation that breached EU law and should therefore be set aside, leaving the original, more stringent, regime in place. According to the Advocate General, the principle of the retroactive application of the more lenient criminal sanction or regime was not relevant. The retroactive application of the more lenient sanction allows an individual to benefit from an altered assessment of the conduct on the part of the legislature. However, in the Advocate General's opinion the legislature had not in fact altered its opinion because the relevant legislature was *the EU legislature*.[38] The Court, on the other hand, applied the principle of the application of the more lenient sanction. The subsequent national measure did breach EU law, but was not set aside as in normal circumstances it should be. The Court's reasoning was largely based on the nature of the directive and its inability to bind individuals or impose obligations. In this sense it marks a return to the classic 'direct effect' reasoning of *Pretore di Salo*.[39] But considering it in light of the Advocate General's reasoning, implicit in the Court's rather technical judgment is the fact that it is not the EU legislature that ultimately imposes criminal liability. It is an affirmation of the multilevel nature of the process of criminalisation in the EU legal order and the inability of the EU legislature to identify offending conduct that would bind individuals directly or even indirectly. Any imposition of criminal liability must be mediated by national law.[40]

That conclusion was re-emphasised in a pair of judgments dealing with the question of limitation periods in Italian criminal law, and in particular the extent to which those periods should be set aside in the event that the enforcement of the underlying EU law was rendered ineffective. In the first case, *Taricco*, the Court found that Italian law should in principle be set aside, relying on ECtHR judgments to the effect that the principle of legality is not affected by changes in limitation periods.[41] Indeed, the Court insisted on the fact that disapplying the national rule on limitation periods in this case

> would in no way lead to a conviction of the accused for an act or omission which did not constitute a criminal offence under *national* law at the time when it was committed … nor to the application of a penalty which, at that time was not laid down by *national* law.[42]

After contestation on the part of the Italian Constitutional Court, which considered the question of limitation periods to go to the substantive definition of the core elements of a crime under its national legal order and thereby engaging the principle of legality,[43] the Court found that the national court was free to continue

[38] ibid, paras 61–62.
[39] *Pretore di Salò* (n 31).
[40] Dougan (n 13).
[41] *Taricco* (n 13), para 57.
[42] ibid, para 56 (emphasis added).
[43] Case C-42/17 *Criminal proceedings against MAS and MB* (Opinion of AG Bot) EU:C:2017:564, para 39.

to apply the – in theory non-compliant – national rules if to do otherwise would in fact lead to a breach of the principles of legality and non-retroactivity.[44] This was in light of the fact that within the *Italian legal order*, limitation periods formed part of the substantive part of criminal law and therefore attracted the application of those principles.[45]

The general principle that EU law cannot aggravate criminal liability is true, but is not the whole truth. The truth is that EU law cannot even *create* criminal liability for individuals. Criminal law must enjoy a certain quality of 'legality', adopted by a competent and legitimate legislature, in a sufficiently clear manner and enjoy such legality at the time of the offending conduct.[46] But that process, by which an offence acquires that quality of legality, takes place at a national level, not at the EU level. Thus the accusations sometimes levelled at EU instruments for being too vague[47] and hence breaching the principle of legality miss the mark. The EU instrument is not the legal instrument that renders the conduct criminal. It is the national implementing legislation that definitively binds the individual, and it is that legislation that must conform to the principle of legality.[48]

Operating within National Criminal Justice Systems

The systemic nature of criminal justice is often raised in general discussions on criminal law.[49] Criminal justice involves a variety of actors and institutions, at different stages of the process and with varying levels of discretion.[50] Putative criminal acts need to be defined, detected, enforced, judged and sanctions applied,

[44] Case C-42/17 *Criminal proceedings against MAS and MB* EU:C:2017:936, paras 45 and 58.

[45] ibid. The case of *MAS and MB* concerned more than mere limitation periods and is in fact an instance of constitutional tension between the Italian Constitutional Court and the Court of Justice with the Corte Costituzionale raising the prospect of engaging its 'counter-limits' procedure and disapplying EU law in the event of an unfavourable response from the Court of Justice. See *MAS and MB* (Opinion of AG Bot) (n 43), para 10.

[46] For a general assessment of the various elements of the principle, see Peristeridou (n 35) ch 1.

[47] See Cian Murphy, *EU Counter-Terrorism Law: Pre-Emption and the Rule of Law* (Hart Publishing, 2012) 51 specifically in relation to the Framework Decision on Combating Terrorism: '[T]he FDCT [Framework Decision on Combatting Terrorism] has resulted in broad legal rules that run contrary to the principle of legality.' Similarly, accusations that vagueness in the definition of the Union's competence, cited in relation to the effectiveness criteria under Art 83(2) TFEU, as breaching the principle of legality [see Perrine Simon, 'The Criminalisation Power of the European Union after Lisbon and the Principle of Democratic Legitimacy' (2012) 3 *New Journal of European Criminal Law* 242] are similarly misplaced; it is not the competence of the enacting legislative body that must be precisely defined (indeed national legislatures are subject to far fewer constraints on their ability to criminalise behaviour) but the obligations imposed on individuals at any given time.

[48] Note that this is echoed in the Court's pronouncement on the application of the principle of legality in the context of EAW proceedings; legality is assured not by the quality of the EAW FD but rather by the national legislation of the issuing Member State. See *Advocaten voor de Wereld* (n 36) para 52.

[49] For a treatment of the criminal justice system as such, see Lucia Zedner, *Criminal Justice* (Oxford University Press, 2004).

[50] See a related discussion of the concept of effectiveness in the context of multiple national systems by Suominen (n 23).

all in a context that respects the rights of the accused and the need for an effective and fair process. The legislature, the police, prosecutors, the judiciary, prison services and probationary bodies are all involved. Various aspects of the system interact, complementing and compensating for each other; obligations to prosecute may be alleviated by greater discretion in relation to conviction; a lesser degree of detection and prosecution may be compensated by a higher sanction; and so on.[51]

There is no EU criminal justice *system* in the proper sense. EU criminal law is applied in the context of national criminal justice systems and must take account of their particular features and characteristics, which are generally a product of divergent and distinct historical experiences.[52] There is a distinct absence of an institutional structure for the enforcement of substantive EU criminal law. There is no EU police force, criminal courts or prisons. Above all there is no EU trial. The trial is the central forum in which the individual is called to account before his or her fellow citizens. It is a public and communicative process involving a rule-governed and symbolically loaded dialogue between the different parties determining and assessing the wrong to the community, and an opportunity for the accused to answer for their potentially wrongful conduct before that community.[53]

A European Public Prosecutor's Office (EPPO) has recently been established to prosecute crimes against the financial interests of the Union.[54] This is, without doubt, a significant development, not because of the importance of the office itself, but simply by virtue of the fact that there is now in fact a Union-level institution involved in the administration of criminal law and in particular in the prosecution of crimes. Its importance, which is certainly not to be understated from a constitutional point of view, therefore arises from the prior absence of the Union from this field of state activity rather than any features of the Office itself. Indeed, two aspects of the creation of the EPPO underline the primarily national nature of both criminal liability and the criminal justice system within the European Union even after its establishment. Firstly, its decentralised structure. After an initial and highly contested Commission proposal proposing a vertically integrated and centralised institution,[55] a version, heavily amended by the Council, was adopted establishing a collegiate structure, with representatives from the Member States and locating

[51] See generally Zedner (n 49).

[52] For an overview of the usefulness and difficulties of comparing national criminal justice systems, see David Nelkin, 'Comparing Criminal Justice' in Mike Maguire, Rod Morgan and Robert Reiner (eds), *The Oxford Handbook of Criminology*, 5 edn (Oxford University Press, 2012). For contributions analysing the application of EU criminal law in national legal systems, see Renaud Colson and Stewart Field (eds), *EU Criminal Justice and the Challenges of Diversity: Legal Cultures in the Area of Freedom, Security and Justice* (Cambridge University Press, 2016).

[53] See Antony Duff, *Answering for Crime: Responsibility and Liability in the Criminal Law* (Hart Publishing, 2007) ch 8. See also RA Duff, *Punishment, Communication and Community* (Oxford University Press, 2001) 80.

[54] Regulation 2017/1939/EU implementing enhanced cooperation on the establishment of the European Public Prosecutor's Office ('the EPPO') [2017] OJ L283.

[55] See Mitsilegas (n 15) 104–05.

main responsibility for the management of prosecutions in 'Permanent Chambers', the key figure of which will be the nationally appointed European prosecutor of the Member State affected.[56] Secondly, all prosecutions will take place within national criminal justice systems and be governed by national law. This fact indeed has justified the exclusion of the Court of Justice from judicial review of much of the EPPO's activity, that function falling to national judicial systems. In the words of the Commission in its proposal: '[I]t is ... appropriate to consider the European Public Prosecutor's Office as a national authority for the purpose of the judicial review of its acts of investigation and prosecution.'[57] The process of establishing the EPPO has been characterised by a continual dilution of its supranational elements and the emergence of a distinctly decentralised institution operating within national legal systems.[58]

Furthermore, EU law only specifies the punishment to a certain extent and certainly does not enforce the punishment of any individual, be it custodial, monetary or some form of alternative sanction. Under the old *Environmental Crimes* jurisprudence the competence to specify sanctions was explicitly denied the then Community,[59] whereas under the old third pillar sanctions were imposed but were of a minimum nature, typically providing for a minimum–maximum sentence (the so-called min–max solution) in order to facilitate the operation of mutual recognition instruments.[60] Although there have been some efforts at developing a sanctioning policy,[61] sanctioning still remains to a large extent the purview of the national legal system and subject to their various systems, and must operate within that system, leading to potential variations in their elaboration and enforcement through prison and probation authorities.[62] Of course, the Union generally

[56] Tommaso Rafaraci, 'Brief Notes on the Euopean Public Prosecutor's Office: Ideas, Project and Fulfilment' in Rosanna Belfiore and Tommaso Rafaraci (eds), *EU Criminal Justice: Fundamental Rights, Transnational Proceedings and the European Public Prosecutor's Office* (Springer 2018) 160.

[57] Quoted in Mitsilegas (n 15) 114.

[58] As put by Rafaraci: 'The national link between the decentralised and central levels therefore remains decidedly – and intentionally – prominent, with a significant shift in the decision making centre of EPPO towards a national one' (n 55, 159).

[59] Since remedied by the Treaty of Lisbon: see Art 83(2) TFEU. See also the concerns of AG Mazak arguing against the ability of the Union to specify sanctions in *Ship Source Pollution* raising the issue of the consistency of each national penal system. See Case C-440/05 *Commission v Council (Ship Source Pollution)* (Opinion of AG Mazák) EU:C:2007:393, para 104.

[60] Although indirectly this activity does declare a certain common consideration of the seriousness of these acts. Additionally, it appears that in certain cases the imposition of these minimum sentences in Framework Decisions, and in particular in the more recent directives adopted since the introduction of the Treaty of Lisbon, has led to increased penalisation under certain national law. See Chaves (n 15).

[61] Steve Peers, *EU Justice and Home Affairs Law*, vol II: *EU Criminal Law, Policing and Civil Law*, 4 edn (Oxford University Press, 2016) 206–09.

[62] The problematic nature of this situation has been acknowledged by the European Commission in considering the effectiveness of EU criminal law, noting that simply defining the different components of offences is not sufficient, but rather that similar attention needs to be paid to detection, prosecution rules, the levels and indeed the application of sanctions. See generally European Commission, *Green Paper on the approximation, mutual recognition and enforcement of criminal sanctions in the European Union* COM(2004) 334 final.

lacks an enforcement capacity and relies on national agencies and institutions to ensure that all EU law is applied. The Union is not a state and lacks core features of the state, including the ability to exercise force. For this it relies on the Member States.[63] However, the enforcement of a particular sanction and the infliction of 'hard treatment' in the furtherance of expressing disapproval is absolutely central to the concept of criminal law. The very purpose of the criminal law as a communicative exercise is tied to its application and the imposition of sanctions. Indeed, it is this feature that for some scholars *defines* criminal law in contradistinction to other forms of legal sanction that merely prospectively seek to guide behaviour.[64] It is through the sanction, and in particular the imposition of 'hard treatment',[65] that the community communicates its moral disapprobation, underlines the wrong it considers has been done both to the individual victim and the community as a whole, and facilitates the reform, reconciliation and repentance of the offender through a system of 'secular penance'.[66] As part of a multilevel system that is necessarily mediated by national law, EU law explicitly (and for very good reasons) does not have capacity to engage in a meaningful communicative activity with wrongdoers directly through the imposition and enforcement of sanctions. For all the talk on the part of the Commission of criminal sanctions demonstrating social disapproval,[67] this is only very weakly manifested and communicated to the convicted as the social disapproval of a supranational community at Union level. The individual is not called to account within a European forum; instead it is before a national court, representing the national community, that he or she is judged and censure pronounced.

The Emergence of Supranational Public Wrongs

EU criminal law is therefore reliant in both a legislative and an administrative sense on national actors. It is national legislators that must intervene in order to definitively bind individuals under a national law that alone enjoys the quality of legality. Similarly, it is national law enforcement agencies that must investigate, prosecute, try and punish an individual. National law and national criminal justice actors are the direct intermediaries faced by individuals; the presence of the

[63] Díez-Picazo (n 11) 657 discussing the application of EU law in the context of national institutional autonomy, ie the principle that in the application of EU law national rules and procedures are to apply, so long as they conform to the principles of effectiveness and equivalence; see Trevor Hartley, *The Foundations of European Union Law*, 8 edn (Oxford University Press, 2014) ch 7.

[64] Joel Feinberg, 'The Expressive Function of Punishment' (1965) 49 *The Monist* 397.

[65] See Duff (n 9) 82.

[66] ibid, 106. See also the general theory of punishment put forward by Bennett in which through the process of punishment an individual is given an opportunity to atone for his or her wrongs and to re-establish the bonds of citizenship severed by his or her criminal conduct. See Christopher Bennett, *The Apology Ritual: A Philosophical Theory of Punishment* (Cambridge University Press, 2008).

[67] Commission (n 15).

Union as a political community either through its laws or its actions is manifested in a limited manner, if at all. EU law's expressive and communicative capacity is certainly limited. However, it is not non-existent; the fact remains that the Union does in fact adopt criminal law that ultimately results in individuals being subject to sanctions, a fact that necessarily requires some consideration of its capacity to express and communicate values through its criminal law.

As a preliminary point the cooperative and complementary roles of national and supranational institutions in the development, implementation and application of EU law should be noted, a dynamic that applies just as much in the field of criminal law. The interactive relationship of national and supranational actors in the field of criminal law clearly place it in the category of fields structured according to cooperative federal principles.[68] Both national and supranational actors are involved in the elaboration, implementation and enforcement of the body of law we call EU criminal law with distinct but complementary and cooperative roles. The multilevel nature of EU criminal means that it is *mediated* by national criminal justice systems and legalisation, not that it is absent.

Thus, in a certain sense when acting on foot of EU criminal legislation Member States can be said to be acting within the broad field of EU criminal law, giving substance to and applying in practice normative choices made at a Union level. By analogy with the manner in which national courts can be said to be 'European' courts when applying EU law, national legislators and law enforcement personnel can perhaps be said to be acting in a 'European' capacity when implementing and enforcing EU criminal law. Just as the Union's legal order is the outcome of a productive and cooperative endeavour in which both national courts and supranational courts play a role,[69] European criminal justice may be viewed as a broader field encompassing national and supranational criminal justice actors acting in a collective manner generating norms and expressing the values of the wider EU community.[70]

And the Union itself, by the very act of adopting *criminal* law necessarily articulates such values. Behind the actions of national legislators and law enforcement actors implementing EU criminal law lies a common normative source expressing the values and choices of a supranational community. And behind the structural limitations imposed on the Union both in its regulatory competence, now found in Article 83(2) TFEU, and its 'Eurocrimes' competence found in Article 83(1) TFEU, lies an ability, limited and indirect, to identify certain acts or conduct deemed wrongful by the Union and hence to give expression to certain values and normative choices. This appears to have taken place in two broad categories: firstly

[68] See Robert Schütze, *From Dual to Cooperative Federalism: The Changing Structures of European Law* (Oxford University Press, 2009).

[69] See generally Karen Alter, *Establishing the Supremacy of European Law: The Making of an International Rule of Law in Europe* (Oxford University Press, 2001).

[70] For a similar point, see Christopher Harding and Joanna Banach-Gutierrez, 'The Emergent EU Criminal Policy: Identifying the Species' (2012) 37 *EL Rev* 758.

the identification of common European public goods, harm to which constitutes a wrong; and secondly the expression of distinctly European public values.

European Public Goods

It is perfectly open to a society to consider respect and protection for certain public goods of the community as elements of its normative code, breach of which constitutes not simply a harm but a wrong against the community (albeit it a wrong by virtue of the harm). Indeed for Duff 'wrongful violations of public goods seem to be strong candidates for criminalisation'.[71] This purpose, while linked, exists alongside the purely functional or instrumental view of criminal law. Criminal law may be seen as a deterrent and perform an ancillary role of preventing and minimising harm to a collective good. However, that is not its primary goal and indeed other forms of regulatory law may more effective in this regard.[72] Rather it is intended to express the moral condemnation of the community for the violation of a public good. It is to identify certain interests of the community, damage or harm to which constitutes a wrong against the community and to call individual citizens to account for that harm or damage.[73]

EU law identifies a number of public goods, the violation of which constitutes a crime and therefore a wrong. Although, as described above, a functional reasoning justified the attribution of competences to the Union in *Environmental Crimes*, amongst the discussion of effective enforcement the Court of Justice also highlighted the specificity of the environment as an objective of the Union as one that is particularly important and transversal: '[I]n the words of Article 6 EC "[e]nvironmental protection requirements must be integrated into the definition and implementation of the Community policies and activities", a provision which emphasises the fundamental nature of that objective and its extension across the range of those policies and activities'.[74] The specifically public and collective nature

[71] Duff (n 9) 126.

[72] ibid, 87.

[73] Thus Öberg's claim, reflected in the Commission's own communications, that before the Union exercise its competence under Art 83(2) TFEU it must first demonstrate through an impact assessment the effectiveness of criminal law in reducing harm or ensuring compliance, misunderstands the nature of criminal law as distinct from regulatory law. Under a moralist view of criminal law, its *primary* purpose is not to ensure compliance (although this may be a useful added benefit) but to declare and punish wrongdoing. It involves a fundamentally different purpose. See Öberg (n 28) 347–76. Adopting a moralist view of the criminal law does raise the question of the appropriateness of including terms such as 'essential' and 'effective implementation' in the text of Art 83(2) TFEU or indeed the conceptual coherence of Art 83(2) TFEU, which seems to ignore completely (or at least sideline) the distinctive moral character of criminal law.

[74] *Environmental Crimes* (n 21) para 42. Indeed, one of the main concerns of commentators following *Environmental Crimes* was whether it was in fact, by virtue of the importance of the policy area, limited to the environment, or whether the new competence extended beyond to other areas of EU action. *Ship Source Pollution* did little to clarify this question, which, while in theory being a policy based on transport policy, had clear overlaps with the environment, a fact that was highlighted by the Court of Justice when identifying the Framework Decision in question as relating to 'conduct which is likely to cause particularly serious environmental damage'. See Case C-440/05 *Commission v Council (Ship*

of the environment as a good was highlighted by AG Ruiz-Jarabo Colomer: 'There thus emerges a right to enjoy an acceptable environment, not so much on the part of the individual as such, but as a member of a group, in which the individual shares common social interests.'[75] A number of other European public goods can be identified alongside the environment, the violation of which constitutes a wrong. Baker has noted the internal market has been identified as a public good to be protected (at least implicitly) by criminal law.[76] Unlike in the case of *Greek Maize*,[77] in *Spanish Strawberries*[78] the Court was concerned not just with the rights of the individuals concerned but the collective interests of the then Community.[79] The protests of farmers and the inaction of the state authorities was framed as a threat not simply to the importers directly concerned but as threatening the 'integrity' of the market and its future availability to the Community as a whole, to whom it belonged as 'a collective asset'.[80] Thus Member States were obliged to ensure, through their criminal justice system, that this collective asset was protected and preserved. Related to the internal market, the financial system is also a concern of EU criminal law with a recent directive adopted mandating specific and tough sanctions for market abuse.[81] In both legislation[82] and case-law[83] the need to protect the 'integrity' of the financial system has been stressed and is now protected by criminal law. The financial resources of the Union is another public good protected by criminal law,[84] complete with an EU institution to prosecute such fraud.[85] Currency, and in particular the euro, is also a good protected by supranational criminal law.[86] Finally, the provision of security itself and the wide range of measures that have been adopted, and in particular the constitution of the EU as a

Source Pollution) EU:C:2007:625, [2007] ECR I-9097 para 67. See Steve Peers, 'The European Community's Criminal Law Competence: The Plot Thickens' (2008) 33 *EL Rev* 399, 406.

[75] See Case C-176/03 *Commission v Council (Environmental Crimes)* (Opinion of AG Ruiz Jarabo Colomer) EU:C:2005:311, para 67.

[76] Baker (n 22).

[77] *Greek Maize* (n 20).

[78] Case C-265/95 *Commission v French Republic (Spanish Strawberries)* EU:C:1997:595, [1997] ECR I-6959.

[79] Baker (n 22).

[80] ibid, 41.

[81] Directive 2014/57/EU on criminal sanctions for market abuse [2014] OJ L173/179 (Market Abuse Directive). See, in particular, the preamble and Art 1(1). See also Framework Decision 2003/568/JHA on combating corruption in the private sector [2003] OJ L192/54, which in its preamble speaks of the threat posed by such corruption to 'law abiding society as well as distorting competition … and impeding sound economic development' (point 9 of preamble).

[82] Market Abuse Directive (n 81).

[83] See Case C-45/08 *Spector Photo Group v Commissie voor het Bank-, Financie en Assuranctiewezen (CBFA)* EU:C:2009:806, [2009] ECR I-12073.

[84] See Directive 2017/1371 on the fight against fraud to the Union's financial interests by means of criminal law [2017] OJ L189/29. Indeed, in a different context, it was the direct implication of the Union's own resources that triggered the application of the CFR in Case C-617/10 *Åklagaren v Hans Åkerberg Fransson* EU:C:2013:105.

[85] EPPO Regulation (n 54). Although note the decentralised nature of the institution described above.

[86] Directive 2014/62/EU on the proctection of the euro and other currencies against counterfeiting by criminal law and replacing Framework Decision 2000/383/JHA [2014] OJ L151/1 (Counterfeiting Directive).

'secure space',[87] can be seen as a public good 'offered' to the citizens of the Union.[88] Indeed, in this regard it is interesting to note the increasing reference by the Court of Justice to the goal of ensuring the absence of impunity within the AFSJ,[89] as has been noted in earlier chapters.

Although there is no explicit pronouncement that would appear to definitively identify the criteria the Union uses to identify public goods worthy of protection by criminal law it would appear that the examples identified above fall into two categories.[90] On the one hand there is the category of classic public goods that correspond to policy domains that have (to varying extent) been appropriated by the Union either through a functionalist spillover effect and/or in its ever-expanding quest to secure output legitimacy. Under these criteria a clean environment and public security would be considered public goods par excellence. In the language of economists they are non-excludable (individuals cannot be excluded from their enjoyment) and non-rivalrous (the use by one individual does not diminish its use by another).[91] These qualities mean they typically will not be adequately or efficiently provided by private market operators and must therefore be provided by the public, in this case the European Union. In these areas the Union represents a typical public authority ensuring the protection of a classic public good.

The other group of public goods identified above are similarly public goods in the economic sense of being non-excludable and non-rivalrous but have an additional quality that appears to be linked more specifically to the nature of the Union itself as a polity and which explains the particular language used by the Court and the legislature in identifying them. Those other public goods appear to be more clearly associated with the Union's traditional vocation of generating prosperity through creating market institutions at a European level, namely the internal market itself, the financial system and the currency. These are institutional facts

[87] Patrick Twomey, 'Construcuting a Secure Space: The Area of Freedom, Security and Justice' in David O'Keefe and Patrick Twomey (eds), *Legal Issues of the Amsterdam Treaty* (Hart Publishing, 1999).

[88] For security as a public good, see Ian Loader and Neil Walker, *Civilising Security* (Cambridge University Press, 2007) ch 6. Indeed, Loader and Walker's claim goes further to argue that public security is a public good in an even stronger sense, in that the provision of the good goes someway to *constituting* the community: '[W]e may understand public goods as having a constitutive dimension, as being in some measure implicated in the very dynamic through which particular publics become conceived and self-conceived as publics' (145). There is an argument to be made that the treaties, and the concept of an AFSJ in particular, offer some support for this in the context of the European Union in particular, with Art 3(2) TEU, stating that '[t]he Union shall offer its citizens an area of freedom, security and justice without internal frontiers' and Art 67 TFEU stating that '[t]he Union shall constitute an area of freedom, security and justice'.

[89] Case C-129/14 PPU *Criminal proceedings against Zoran Spasic* EU:C:2014:586, paras 63–64 and Case C-182/15 *Aleksei Petruhhin v Latvijas Republikas Ģenerālprokuratūra* EU:C:2016:630, para 37.

[90] With the exception of the Union's own financial resources which would appear to be a public good in the most literal sense.

[91] For a description of the classic account of public goods produced by economist Mancur Olsen, see Alun Howard Gibbs, *Constitutional Life and Europe's Area of Freedom, Security and Justice* (Ashgate, 2011) 48.

in Searle's term; systems of rules.[92] These European-wide market institutions are systems of rules that govern market participation by individuals in such a way as to secure prosperity, institutions that are to a large extent reliant on trust generated by the anticipated enforcement of a body of rules. Their protection lies specifically in the maintenance of the 'integrity' of the body of rules that constitute the institutional fact. Similarly, in the case of currency counterfeiting the Union is specifically concerned with ensuring 'trust in the genuine character' of the currency.[93] Hence, perhaps, an explanation for the use of the language of integrity and the references to the systemic nature of these particular 'public goods' by both the legislature and the Court.

The Union has not simply identified certain public goods as worthy of protection but has, by insisting on the use of criminal rather than administrative or regulatory law, indicated that it views an attempt to undermine or cause harm to such public goods as wrongful in a public sense, ie an offence against the community. Although much of the discussion on the use of the criminal law has focused on the utilitarian and instrumental purpose in enforcing EU objectives, there are some indications that the EU institutions are aware of the condemnatory function of the criminal law and are anxious to use the criminal law for this precise purpose. Behind much of the struggle over competence in the *Environmental Crimes* saga lay the ability of the Community itself (now Union) to prescribe criminal law measures rather than rely on the traditional formula of 'effective and equivalent' measures and leave the decision to criminalise in the hands of Member State governments. Although for the most part emphasising the instrumental nature of these measures as deterrents, the Commission has not been ignorant of the condemnation and social disapproval that is communicated via criminal law[94] and in its arguments before the Court in *Ship Source Pollution* it stressed the fact that the conduct concerned 'must be regarded as reprehensible' and hence requiring criminal rather than civil sanctions.[95] Similarly, AG Mazak described the criminal law as 'a barometer of the importance attached by a community to a legal good or value'.[96]

By insisting on the competence of the *Union* to criminalise such conduct EU law is by implication identifying certain public goods as *European* public goods,

[92] As described by Neil MacCormick, 'Law as Institutional Fact' (1974) 90 *LQR* 102, 105ff.

[93] Counterfeiting Directive (n 86) recital 15.

[94] See Commission (n 15) 11.

[95] *Ship Source Pollution* (n 74) para 31.

[96] *Ship Source Pollution (Opinion of AG Mazák)* (n 59) para 95. See also the comments of AG Ruiz Jarabo-Colomer in *Environmental Crimes*, noting that: '[I]n academic thinking a degree of consensus has emerged that ecosystems should be regarded as particularly important legal interests, and that their protection is vital for the very existence of humankind, with the consequence that their conservation and maintenance fully justify the intervention of criminal law with a specific safeguard … the ethical dimension of criminal punishment must not be overlooked. When an act is sanctioned in criminal terms, it is held to merit the most severe reproach because it transgresses the fundamental tenets of the legal system.' Case C-176/03 *Commission v Council (Environmental Crimes)* (Opinion of AG Ruiz-Jarabo Colomer) EU:C:2005:311, paras 73–74.

harm to which constitute a *European* public wrong. In *Ship Source Pollution* the Advocate General stressed the fact that:

> It must be recalled that upholding Community (now Union) law is the responsibility of the Community institutions. … if the legal interests protected in such offences were one of the objectives of the Community, no one would dispute the ability of its law-making bodies to require the Member States to prosecute in criminal law.[97]

In a somewhat different context, in *Åkerberg Fransson* it was the Union's interest in the protection of its own resources and the treaty obligation placed on Member States to ensure their protection that rendered it a matter of EU law, thereby ensuring the application of the CFR to the criminal proceedings in question.[98] A similar reasoning and insistence on the Union's interest in the prosecution of VAT fraud can be found in *Taricco*.[99]

European Public Values

All law involves valuation; a judgement of how we stand in relation to acts, relationships and objects.[100] The criminal law is the judgement of the community of certain acts, or in more limited cases omissions, it deems to be publically wrongful. It therefore involves an assessment of conduct according to its wrongfulness and necessarily involves a normative valuation of that act. Although Article 83(1) TFEU has been justified primarily in terms of its ancillary role in facilitating mutual recognition and police and judicial cooperation in a space of free movement,[101] it cannot entirely obscure the valuative or expressive character of declaring a particular act or activity criminal. Indeed, for some areas of activity it would appear to be the principal function of the Union's legislative activity. Two categories of EU law substantive criminal law measures with expressive characteristics appear to have emerged. Firstly, a number of measures reference the core values of the Union as expressed in the classical liberal democratic list of values contained in Article 2 TEU, namely 'respect for human dignity, freedom, democracy, equality, the rule of law and respect for human rights'. The expression of these values is used as a means of justifying certain measures criminalising behaviour such as racist or

[97] *Environmental Crimes* (n 21) paras 49–50.
[98] *Åkerberg Fransson* (n 84).
[99] *Taricco* (n 13).
[100] Cass Sunstein, 'Incommensurability and Valuation in Law' (1994) 92 *Michigan Law Review* 779, 783 speaking of 'kinds of valuation': '[T]he term is meant to draw attention to our diverse stances towards relationships or prospects or to the disparate theories of valuation through which we conceive and evaluate relationships, events or prospects. Every kind of valuation embodies a qualitatively distinctive judgment or response.'
[101] See, in particular, Mitsilegas (n 15) ch 3 and Weyembergh (n 17).

xenophobic crimes. A second instance of the Union using criminal law measures to adopt a particular moral or valuative judgement appears to arise in the case of particularly vulnerable people or victims; the Union appears to have taken a particular interest in the protection of weaker members of society and in deploying its competence in the field of criminal law in order to promote their protection.

Turner has described in detail the expressive nature of the Framework Decision on Combating Racism and Xenophobia.[102] She has convincingly demonstrated that the ostensible justifications for the measure in harmonising national legislation to facilitate judicial cooperation are either not achieved or unnecessary, particularly following the abolition of double-criminality requirements for the majority of mutual recognition instruments and in particular the EAW FD.[103] The preparatory legislative documents contain various assertions of the particular values of the Union, in particular democracy, the rule of law and non-discrimination, and how these in fact motivate and inform the legislation.[104] These values make their way into the preamble of the framework decision that speaks of the principles of 'liberty, democracy, respect for human rights and fundamental freedoms and the rule of law, principles upon which the European Union is founded and which are common to the Member States'.[105] Indeed, given the failure to properly harmonise the most contentious aspect of racist speech, Holocaust denial, and the failure to impose any requirements of enforcement and prosecution, its practical impact either as a harmonising instrument or an enforcement tool at a national level is likely to limited,[106] leading to the conclusion that 'the expressive value of the Framework Decision is greater than its practical impact … [and that] … the European Union is using the Framework Decision primarily to make a statement about the values for which it stands'.[107]

Finally, attention should be drawn to a number of instruments that have been adopted that appear to display a particular concern with vulnerable individuals. EU criminal law appears to be particularly concerned with weak or vulnerable members of society and instruments adopted to achieve this appear to go well beyond minimal harmonisation measures. The Directive on the Sexual Exploitation of Children is a remarkable piece of legislation and is notable for its

[102] Jenia Iontcheva Turner, 'The Expressive Dimension of EU Criminal Law' (2012) 60 *American Journal of Comparative Law* 555. Although an alternative perspective would be that it is precisely because of the existence of an EU competence that the abolition of the double-criminality rule is justified. See the discussion on this matter in Chapter 6.

[103] ibid, 572.

[104] ibid, 571.

[105] Framework Decision 2008/913/JHA on combating certain forms and expressions of racism and xenophobia by means of criminal law [2008] OJ L328/55 preamble point (1).

[106] Turner (n 102) 572. Although see the contrary opinion expressed by Chaves (n 15) 534–35.

[107] Turner (n 102) 572.

breadth, comprehensiveness and its value-laden language.[108] It offers a marked contrast to other harmonisation instruments, in particular the Framework Decisions, which tended to be terse and minimal in nature. Alongside the elements of various offences,[109] it lays down penalties,[110] regulates certain defences available,[111] limitation periods,[112] territorial jurisdiction rules,[113] reporting requirements,[114] and measures for the subsequent treatment of offenders both in terms of their rehabilitation but also criminal records and disqualification from various activities.[115] In its application, and in particular in aggravating sanctions for particularly vulnerable victims and for crimes that take place in the context of a relationship of responsibility,[116] it has a clear expressive and communicative function, articulating a particular judgement about the how to classify, not simply the harm, but the culpability and wrongfulness of particular acts.[117] There is little or no attempt to justify the measure on the basis of a disparity between the legislation of Member States or the need to secure enhanced judicial cooperation, and certainly no attempt to justify the comprehensive nature of the harmonisation effort on these grounds. There is no attempt to justify the replacement of the Framework Decision by the Directive. The sole reason for the new, much more comprehensive Directive is the question-begging assertion that 'serious criminal offences such as the sexual exploitation of children and child pornography require a comprehensive approach'.[118] Although this is no doubt true, it does not justify action by the European Union. Rather its depth, comprehensiveness and inclusion of key choices regarding the normative assessment and appropriate response to the phenomenon of the sexual exploitation of children can only be said to manifest a desire to appropriate a particular policy area, one that deals with particularly vulnerable individuals, and to express and give voice to a condemnation at a supranational level.[119] According to its proposal the legislation is aimed

[108] Directive 2011/93/EU on combating the sexual abuse and sexual exploitation of children and child pornography, and replacing Council Framework Decision 2004/68/JHA [2011] OJ L355/1 (Directive on the Sexual Exploitation of Children).

[109] ibid, Arts 3–5.

[110] ibid, Art 3.

[111] ibid, Art 8 relating to consensual activity.

[112] ibid, Art 15.

[113] ibid, Art 17, obliging Member States to exercise active personal extraterritorial jurisdiction.

[114] ibid, Art 16.

[115] ibid, Arts 10 and 24.

[116] ibid, Art 9, alongside the usual aggravating circumstances such as recidivism.

[117] Although it is certainly true that the extent of harm suffered is related to the relationship in which the offence took place.

[118] Directive on the Exploitation of Children (n 108) preamble point (6).

[119] Note this concern with children is not limited to this particular piece of legislation and indeed extends beyond the realm of the criminal law. It is worth noting that various EU criminal law cases figure children as victims [see *Pupino* (n 33), Case C-348/09 *PI v Oberburgermeisterin der Stadt Remscheid* EU:C:2012:300, Case C-193/16 *E v Subdelegación del Gobierno en Álava* EU:C:2017:542 and Case C-400/12 *Secretary for State for the Home Department v MG* EU:C:2014:9]. The European Union has been particularly active in developing children's rights and child-protection measures. See Eleanor

at combating acts that undermine 'the core values of modern society relating to the special protection of children' and are justified by the fact that '[n]ational legislation covers some of these problems, to varying degrees. However, it is not strong or consistent enough to provide a vigorous social response to this disturbing phenomenon.'[120] The justification for EU action is simply the fact that in the judgment of the EU legislature, or at least the proposing institution within that legislature, these are particularly serious and 'disturbing'[121] wrongs and Member States do not do enough to identify and punish them as such.

The Directive on the sexual exploitation of children is one example of the European Union intervening in a comprehensive fashion in order to criminalise harm to a particularly vulnerable class of individuals. Another example of this concern with vulnerable victims can be seen in the Directive on Combating Human Trafficking.[122] The Directive demonstrates a particular concern with the victims of human trafficking, mandating specific measures to ensure their protection in any investigation and proceedings[123] and general assistance.[124] Again, particularly vulnerable victims, especially children, are to enjoy enhanced protection,[125] and again, crimes against particularly vulnerable victims are to attract aggravated sanctions.[126] Although not a substantive criminal law provision, in the sense that it does not seek to criminalise any particular behaviour, similar concern with vulnerable individuals can be seen in the Victims' Rights Directive.[127] Aside from a measure that is generally aimed at a vulnerable group of individuals, the Victims' Rights Directive has specific provision for particularly vulnerable individuals,[128] especially children.[129] It would appear that the European Union through various instruments has shown a particular concern for vulnerable groups of individuals and especially vulnerable victims of crime,

Drywood and Helen Stalford, 'Coming of Age? Children's Rights in the European Union' (2009) 46 *CML Rev* 143.

[120] Proposal for a Directive on combating the sexual abuse, sexual exploitation of children and child pornography repealing Framework Decision 2004/38/JHA COM(2010)94 final 2.

[121] Echoing efforts to justify retributivism in punishment by Michael Moore, who argues for a return to sentiment and feeling as legitimate grounds for justifying punishment. See Moore (n 26).

[122] Directive 2011/36/EU on preventing and combating trafficking in human beings and protecting its victims and replacing Council Framework Decision 2002/629/JHA [2011] OJ L101/1.

[123] ibid, Art 12.

[124] ibid, Art 11.

[125] ibid, Arts 13–16.

[126] ibid, Art 4(2)(a).

[127] Interestingly for Moore moral outrage based on sympathy with victims is one of the justifications for the morality of a retributive approach to punishment: '[S]uch revulsion [at particularly heinous crimes] is the only tolerable response to serious wrong-doing.' See Moore (n 26) 144. Similarly, for Duff and Marshall it is through the suffering of fellow members of the community (ie citizens) that individual harms become public wrongs. See Marshall and Duff (n 6).

[128] Directive 2012/29/EU establishing minimum standards on the rights, support and protection of victims of crime, and replacing Council Framework Decision 2001/220/JHA [2012] OJ L315/57, Arts 22–23 designating such persons as those with 'specific protection needs'.

[129] ibid, Art 24.

either generally or through an intense interest in the protection of children. Through its measures in this field it appears to be taking a principled stance and articulating a set of values it believes are, or should be, central to the identity of the European Union.

Framing National Criminal Law: Supranational Wrongs and Shared Wrongs

But perhaps to focus on the function of supranational approximation and harmonisation measures adopted by the Union as expressing an autonomous normative judgement at a supranational level is to miss an important role that this competence plays in the broader context of criminal law and its operation in the Union.

It is in the interaction with national criminal law and transnational processes and by framing national criminal law that supranational criminal law reveals one of its major purposes. This is particularly relevant for the competence under Article 83(1) TFEU, the so-called 'Eurocrimes', the ancillary nature of which has already been noted above. In this context the Union does not need to create criminal liability or to communicate the wrongful character of an action directly to individuals. EU criminal law, in order to perform its function of *complementing* national law and providing a common supranational framework for the choices made at national level, does not and indeed need not have these characteristics. In this manner EU substantive criminal does not express some form of autonomous value judgement detached from the choices made at a national level, rather it acknowledges and endorses normative choices made in the context of national criminal law.

Weyembergh points out the relationship between double criminality and approximation of criminal law; approximation will result in a situation where the double-criminality rule is automatically met, enabling easier and more effective mutual recognition of national judgments.[130] As described in Chapter 6 the abolition of the double-criminality rule is premised on a shared conception of wrongs. The justification for the list of 32 categories of core crimes for which double criminality is abolished in the EAW FD is found in the fact that 'the participants in the procedure (Member States) both regard the conduct which gives rise to the request as criminal … reciprocity and double criminality are presumed for certain offences'.[131] By firstly attributing competence to the Union and then by enacting

[130] Weyembergh (n 17) 158. Hence Turner's accusation that the Framework Decision on Xenophobia and Racism is unnecessary partially because of the abolition of double criminality in the EAW FD perhaps misunderstands the relationship between double criminality and approximation; it is because of approximation that the abolition of the rule is then justified; see Turner (n 102) 571–72.

[131] Case C-303/05 *Advocaten voor de Wereld VZW v Leden van de Ministerraad* (Opinion of AG Ruiz-Jarabo Colomer) EU:C:2006:552, paras 45–47.

legislation, the drafters of the Treaty, who it must be remembered are ultimately the Member States,[132] have explicitly endorsed a certain shared vision of certain wrongful actions, particularly those that operate on a transnational level. Thus they are at the same time acknowledging at a Union level the normative judgement of these actions and the tendency of these actions to afflict more than one Member State; a shared conception and a shared experience of a wrong.

A more curious, and certainly not inevitable, use of supranational criminal law is the use of substantive criminal law measures to endorse national choices and conceptions of public policy and value judgements in the field of EU citizenship, explored in Chapter 4.[133] Here, the interaction between national and EU normative judgements is more nuanced and would appear to lead to a certain convergence, if not identity, between national and a European conception of public policy. Public policy remains an inherently national concept, a fact that is still stressed by the Court of Justice. At the same time in both *Tsakouridis*[134] and *PI*[135] the Court has used legislation adopted at a Union level to endorse and validate the choices made by Member States in exercising their prerogatives under the public policy exception, in *Tsakouridis* the Framework Decision on Drug Trafficking[136] and in *PI* the Directive on the Sexual Exploitation of Children.[137] By allowing Member States to expel EU citizens, they are depriving them (temporarily) of EU law rights; that deprivation is justified not only by national conceptions of public policy but also under European law.[138] It indirectly results in a communicative process with the individual concerned – through endorsing national law as applied in a particular case, the Union speaks to the individual and communicates its own understanding

[132] And it must be remembered that any extension to the list of 32 crimes is by unanimity in Council.

[133] See Loïc Azoulai and Stephen Coutts, 'Restricting Union Citizens' Residence Rights on Grounds of Public Security' (2013) 50 *CML Rev* 553 and Mitsilegas (n 15) ch 8.

[134] Case C-145/09 *Land Baden-Wurttemberg v Panagiotis Tsakouridis* EU:C:2010:708, [2010] ECR I-11979.

[135] *PI* (n 119).

[136] Framework Decision 2004/757/JHA laying down minimum provisions on the constituent elements of criminal acts and penalties in the field of illicit drug trafficking [2004] OJ L335/8. See *Tsakouridis* (n 134) para 46.

[137] Directive on the Exploitation of Children (n 108). See *PI* (n 119) para 26.

[138] It is worth noting that the correctness and desirability of the Court's interpretation of Art 28 of the Citizenship Directive (Directive 2004/38/EC on the right of citizens of the Union and their family members to move and reside freely within the territory of the Member States [2004] OJ L158/77) has been questioned. On the one hand it appears to go beyond the scheme of the directive, which appears to intend a specific meaning for public security, narrower than the general category of public policy. In *PI* (n 119), in particular, the Court appears to conflate the terms. The result is a more restrictive interpretation of the Directive, limiting EU citizens' rights and facilitating their expulsion and hence exclusion from the host Member State. For a critical account of the judgment, see Georgios Anagnostaras, 'Enhanced Protection of EU Nationals against Expulstion and concept of internal Public Security: Comment on the PI Case' (2012) 37 *EL Rev* 627; Dora Kostakopoulou, 'Co-Creating European Union Citizenship: Institutional Process and Crescive Norms' (2012–2013) 15 *Cambridge Yearbook of European Legal Studies* 255, 277ff; and Dimitry Kochenov and Benedikt Pirker, 'Deporting the Citizens within the European Union: A Counter-Intuitive Trend in Case C-348/09 PI v Obergurgermeisterin der Stadt Remscheid' (2012–13) 19 *Columbia Journal of European Law* 369.

of the wrongful character of his act, adding to the expression of moral disapproval on the part of the Member State.[139]

A series of incidents therefore highlights the role substantive EU criminal law plays in endorsing value judgements made in national criminal law. This takes place in either the operation of approximation instruments, whose stated goal is to support or facilitate the application of national criminal law, through identifying shared conceptions (and possibly experiences)[140] of wrongs amongst national criminal laws; and secondly though endorsing choices made at a national level in determinations of what constitutes public policy, a category that is supposed to correspond with the fundamental interests and common values of a particular national community. EU criminal law therefore gives rise not simply to supranational expressions of moral evaluation but, to a certain extent, the confirmation of shared conceptions of wrongs amongst Member States.

Conclusion

All law is expressive to some extent and embodies an exercise in communal valuation. The criminal law is perhaps particularly explicit in this regard, identifying as it does wrongful conduct, communicated to the individual through a process of trial and judgment, often by peers in a jury, and the serving of a 'penance' in (aptly termed) penitentiaries. It therefore has an especially pertinent expressive function in articulating and communicating the community's values to its individual members.

EU criminal law is clearly limited in its capacity to articulate public wrongs. This is a function of its limited and conferred competence and the manner in which this is exercised. In its conferred nature it is by necessity limited to certain core areas, predefined by Member States on the one hand and by the action of the Union in other areas (indirectly conferred) on the other. Moreover, its criminal competence does not even appear to have been created with an expressive function in mind. It is seen as ancillary and regulatory or functional. It is similarly limited in its ability to communicate disapproval or condemnation on the part of the supranational community. It is multilevel and requires transposition. Importantly, this necessarily excludes the ability to impose criminal liability. Finally, it lacks the important institutional context for the communication of public wrongs in individual cases. The symbolism of the criminal law is intimately bound up

[139] See also Joined Cases C-331/16 and C-366/16 *K v Staatssecretaris van Veiligheid en Justitie and HF v Belgische Staat* EU:C:2018:296 as discussed in Stephen Coutts, 'The Expressive Dimension of the Union Citizenship Expulsion Regime: Joined Cases C-331/16 and C-366/16, *K and HF*', European Papers Forum, www.europeanpapers.eu/en/system/files/pdf_version/EP_EF_2018_I_039_Stephen_Coutts_0.pdf, accessed 2 November 2018.

[140] See Robin Lööf, 'Defending Liberty and Structural Integrity: A Social Contractual Analysis of Criminal Justice in the EU' (PhD thesis, Department of Law, European University Institute 2008).

with its institutional processes, a symbolism that the Union lacks. EU criminal law is therefore extremely limited in its ability to articulate and communicate public wrongs to its individual citizens on behalf of the supranational community.

However, it remains the case that, for all its limitations, the Union does enjoy an explicit criminal competence and one that necessarily carries with it an independent expressive and evaluative function linked to the capacity to articulate public wrongs. It is limited and intervenes only in specific instances. Although obscured by the technical and functional manner in which EU criminal law is discussed and justified by commentators and the institutions, its mere enactment and the values used to guide the choices imply a certain set of supranational public wrongs, albeit at times ill-defined and implicit. In employing the criminal law, EU law is implicitly classifying certain goods as European public goods, which engage a European public interest, violation of which constitutes not only material damage but also a wrong to the European community.

However, although EU criminal law taken *by itself* is limited, when placed in the broader context of the European criminal justice field it does nonetheless play an expressive and communicative role. Firstly, the cooperative relationship that obtains between Member States and the Union at both a legislative and administrative level in the implementation of EU law in general and in criminal law in particular should not be ignored, leading to a certain co-responsibility amongst national and supranational actors for the enforcement of what is ultimately *European* criminal law. Secondly, it is in the interaction with national norms and in transnational processes that the approximating competence of the Union under Article 83(1) TFEU reveals an important role in endorsing national criminal law. Both the legislature and the Court of Justice have used supranational criminal law in this fashion. The legislature has used these instruments to justify a shared conception in national law of these wrongful conducts in the abolition of double criminality in mutual recognition instruments, and the Court has used these instruments to endorse national choices under the public policy exception in the area of social integration and EU citizenship – thus revealing the multilevel and composite nature of the Union as a political community and the presence of shared conceptions of wrongs.

Criminal law articulates *public* wrongs, a fact that points to the link between collective identity and the expressive dimension of the criminal law. Without necessarily subscribing to the extreme version of ontological identification between the moral code of a community and the community itself,[141] it is the case that the political community is, at least partially, constructed through the relations it established between its constituent members, expressed by its norms and formally by its laws. Choice is a means of affirming identity, a fact as true

[141] See the characterization of Lord Devlin's position by Hart (n 7) 51: '[A] society is identical with its morality as that is at any given moment of its history, so that a change in its morality is tantamount to the destruction of the society.'

in law as in other dimensions of human action.[142] Criminal law as a set of laws is more normative than most, implying explicit valuations and viewing them as rules of imperative public conduct guiding behaviour between individuals. As an expression of social values, it can be said to some extent perform a constituent function for the political community, binding individuals together through shared conceptions of wrongfulness and playing a role in its self-determination. As put by the Bundesverfassungsgericht: 'By criminal law, a legal community gives itself a code of conduct that is anchored in its values and whose violation according to the shared convictions on law, is regarded as so grievous and unacceptable for social co-existence in the community that it requires punishment.'[143] The European Union's criminal law competence is certainly limited in its ability to make choices about 'shared convictions' and to communicate those choices directly to individuals. Nonetheless by necessity it does just that in a number of cases, and if legislation like the Directive on the Sexual Exploitation of Children is any indication, will do so in an increasing manner in the future. Moreover, in its choices it interacts with the choices made by national political communities, reflecting and endorsing national criminal law. The criminal law competence of the Union, and in particular its ability to articulate and communicate public wrongs, is limited, multilevel and composite, restricted in scope and requiring mediation by national legal orders. Nonetheless it does express the existence of an interacting, composite and plural community of communities at a supranational level.

[142] See the discussion by Somek of the importance of choice for the purposes of collective self-determination in the context of cosmopolitanism: 'It is through choice that a subject constitutes itself into the cause of an end and thus creates its appearance in the social world'; see Alexander Somek, 'The Cosmopolitan Constitution' in Miguel Maduro, Suvi Sankari and Kaarlo Tuori (eds), *Transnational Law: Rethinking European Law and Legal Thinking* (Cambridge University Press, 2014) 118. See also Sunstein (n 100) 823: '[T]he expression of the appropriate evaluative attitude should be understood as a human good, constitutive of desirable characteristics. By making certain choices and not others, people express various conceptions both of themselves and of others.'

[143] *Ratification of the Treaty of Lisbon, Re (2 BvE 2/08)* [2010] 3 CMLR 13 (Bundesverfassungsgericht) para 328.

Conclusion: EU Citizenship, Criminal Law and the Restructuring of Community

In *Answering for Crime*[1] and other writings Duff has elaborated a comprehensive theory of criminal law that allows us to view criminal law in a new light. By approaching criminal law from a perspective based on a relational conception of responsibility and citizenship and community, he has provided us with a theory of criminal law that is both analytical and normative. His theory is analytical in that it allows us to make sense of the main features of criminal law: the types and sources of criminal wrongs, the trial, defences, excuses and punishment. It is normative in providing a basis for the legitimacy of restricting the liberty of individuals and of inflicting punishment.

Duff's main purpose is to provide an adequate theory of criminal law and in doing so he relies on the concepts of citizenship and political community. However, conversely, Duff's account of criminal law can inform and enrich our understanding of citizenship. In particular it adds a new perspective to a status that in law is typically analysed in terms of rights and liberties, especially those related to migration issues,[2] and political participation.[3] It provides a specific context to explore notions of duties, values and community and how they relate to citizenship. Following Duff's account, the criminal law is a basis for a set of duties

[1] Antony Duff, *Answering for Crime: Responsibility and Liability in the Criminal Law* (Hart Publishing, 2007). See also Antony Duff, *Punishment, Communication and Community* (Oxford University Press, 2003); RA Duff, 'Law, Language and Community: Some Preconditions for Criminal Liability' (1998) 18 *OJLS* 189; Richard Dagger, 'Republicanism and the Foundations of Criminal Law' in RA Duff and Stuart P Green (eds), *Philosophical Foundations of Criminal Law* (Oxford University Press, 2011); SE Marshall and RA Duff, 'Criminalization and Sharing Wrongs' (1998) 11 *Canadian Journal of Law and Jurisprudence* 7. See most recently RA Duff, *The Realm of Criminal Law* (Oxford University Press, 2018) and RA Duff and SE Marshall, 'Crimes, Public Wrongs, and Civil Order' (2019) 13 *Criminal Law and Philosophy* 27.

[2] In the case of the EU, see in particular Dora Kostakopoulou, *Citizenship, Identity and Immigration in the European Union; Between Past and Future* (Manchester University Press, 2001). For a US-based example, see Linda Bosniak, *The Citizen and the Alien: Dilemas of Contemporary Membership* (Princeton University Press, 2006).

[3] See, for example, Jo Shaw, *The Transformation of Citizenship in the European Union: Electoral Rights and the Restructuring of Political Space* (Cambridge University Press, 2007). There is a rich literature on the political theory of EU citizenship that has significant relevance for legal studies. See especially the work of JHH Weiler, in particular Joseph Weiler, 'To Be a European Citizen: Eros and Civilisation' in Joseph Weiler (ed), *The Constitution of Europe* (Cambridge University Press, 1999); and Habermas, eg Jurgen Habermas, 'Citizenship and National Identity: Some Reflections on the Future of Europe' in Ronald Beiner (ed), *Theorizing Citizenship* (State University of New York Press, 1995).

that flow from the status of citizenship; it is as fellow members of the political community that we are called to account for our wrongful action. Similarly, what precisely defines a public wrong is variable and context specific and is rooted in the common understandings and values of the particular community. Criminal law has an expressive quality, giving voice and meaning to certain norms of the community. Finally, through the institution of criminal law the community is manifested in a very real way and directly relates to the individual as a collective. It is a public wrong; a wrong that concerns the community. The individual is called to account before the community through prosecution and trial in the name of 'the people'. Criminal law can therefore add a new perspective on citizenship, bringing a more value-infused, duty-orientated and community-situated notion of citizenship to the fore.

The present study is an attempt to bring this perspective to bear on EU citizenship. This is particularly appropriate for a number of reasons. Firstly, it is a timely exercise: both EU citizenship and in particular the role of the Union in criminal law matters has seen rapid growth over the past two decades. Secondly, these two areas have been associated in the policy language and rhetoric of the EU institutions; the activity of the EU in criminal law is increasingly phrased in terms of security, a public good that is then 'offered' to EU citizens.[4] Thirdly, an observation that occasionally surfaces in relation to EU citizenship is the lack of duties associated with the status,[5] despite the Treaty's assertion to the contrary.[6] This study argues that there are in fact duties associated with EU citizenship and that at least some of them can be found in criminal law. Fourthly, another complaint levelled at EU citizenship is its rootless, liberal conception of the individual, devoid of a meaningful sense of community and norms.[7] Although not denying that some truth may lie behind these sentiments, this study argues that the concept of community and norms may in fact be present in EU law, in the area of criminal law. Finally, many legal studies of EU law have focused on free-movement rights on the one hand

[4] See especially The Stockholm Programme: An Open and Secure Europe Serving and Protecting Citizens [2010] OJ C115/01, but rhetorical associations can also be discerned in earlier institutional statements. For an account, see Stephen Coutts, 'Citizenship of the European Union' in Cian Murphy and Diego Acosta Arcarazo (eds), *EU Security and Justice Law: After Lisbon and Stockholm* (Hart Publishing, 2014).

[5] Dmitry Kochenov, 'EU Citizenship without Duties' (2014) 20 *ELJ* 482. See response from Richard Bellamy, 'A Duty-Free Europe? What's Wrong with Kochenov's Account of EU Citizenship Rights' (2015) 21 *ELJ* 558. See also Richard Bellamy and Joseph Lacey, 'Balancing the Rights and Duties of European and National Citizens: A Demoicratic Approach' (2018) 25 *Journal of European Public Policy* 1403 for responsibilities primarily relating to economic activity. See also Stephen Coutts, 'The Absence of Integration and the Responsibilisation of Union Citizenship' (2018) 3 *European Papers* 761.

[6] 'Citizens of the Union shall enjoy the rights and be subject to the duties provided for in the Treaties', Art 20(2) TFEU.

[7] See Michelle Everson, 'The Legacy of the Market Citizen' in Jo Shaw and Gillian More (eds), *New Legal Dynamics of European Union* (Clarendon Press, 1995) and more recently Michelle Everson, 'A Very Cosmopolitan Citizenship: But Who Pays the Price?' in Michael Dougan, Niamh Nic Shuibhne and Eleanor Spaventa (eds), *Empowerment and Disempowerment of the European Citizen* (Hart Publishing, 2012). See also Päivi Johanna Neuvonen, 'Retrieving the Subject of European Integration' [2018] *ELJ* 1, https://doi.org/10.1111/eulj.12301.

and on the political rights of citizens on the other, or some combination of both. This study is an exercise in exploring how another distinct, substantive area of EU law can contribute to our understanding of EU membership and EU citizenship.[8]

Complementing Union Citizenship

Citizenship is a status that carries with it rights and duties and is located within a political community, normally associated with a set of underling common values.[9] The treatment of criminal law in EU law contributes to all three aspects of EU citizenship.

Rights

Although the focus of this work has been how norms expressed in criminal law, both national and supranational, can contribute towards the imposition of certain duties on EU citizens and give rise to the expression of common values, a consideration of the interaction of EU citizenship and criminal law does reveal some new rights associated with EU citizenship and how existing rights are strengthened and reinforced.[10]

Rights associated with the social integration and with the free movement of EU citizens are extended and reinforced in the context of criminal law. Although the criminal law has been used to restrict EU citizens' residence rights in host Member States, certain aspects of criminal law, in particular the goal of rehabilitation, have led to the further inclusion of EU citizens under certain circumstances. Thus the concept of rehabilitation has bolstered the right to equal treatment enjoyed by EU citizens in the context of the serving of sentences, both under the EAW FD[11] and the Framework Decision on the Mutual Recognition of Custodial Sentences.[12] A sufficiently integrated EU citizen may also be protected by the operation of a

[8] To the extent that this exercise could be repeated in other areas of law is a question for further research. For the reasons expressed above, especially taking Duff's theory into account, criminal law would appear to be an especially appropriate candidate.

[9] For the different components of citizenship, see Rainer Bauböck, *Recombinant Citizenship* (1999) Political Science Series 67, Institute for Advanced Studies, Vienna. See generally the contributions in *The Oxford Handbook of Citizenship*, ed Ayelet Shachar et al (Oxford University Press, 2017).

[10] Aside from the general consideration that criminal law is a law that imposes duties on citizens in an effort to secure greater liberty rights for all. See Etienne Picard, 'La fonction de l'ordre public dans l'ordre juridique' in Marie-Joëlle Redor (ed), *L'ordre public: Ordre public ou ordres publics? Ordre public et droits fondamentaux* (Bruylant, 2001).

[11] Framework Decision 2002/584/JHA on the European arrest warrant and the surrender procedures between Member States (EAW FD) [2002] OJ L190/1.

[12] Framework Decision 2008/909/JHA on the application of the principle of mutual recognition to judgements in criminal matters imposing custodial sentences or measures involving deprivation of liberty for the purposes of their enforcement in the European Union [2008] OJ L327/27.

Member State's nationality exemption, shielding him or her from expulsion to a third state.[13] Secondly, the right to free movement is clearly and directly reinforced by the operation of the transnational *ne bis in idem* principle located in Article 54 CISA. The interpretation of the Court of Justice has principally, if not exclusively, been focused on maximising the free movement of individuals and reducing burdens, and its interpretative choices, imposing strict mutual recognition of the original Member State's laws and developing a rule based on facts rather than crimes, have contributed a great deal to this effort. There is a parallel to be drawn between the manner in which a single civil status, such as a legal name, is created and rendered portable throughout the Union and the manner in which a status under national criminal law is similarly rendered applicable Union-wide.

Criminal law has also given the Union the opportunity to develop a set of supranational fundamental rights and procedural rights. Civil rights and fundamental rights are closely linked with the historic development of national citizenship.[14] Additionally, in both their selection and the manner in which they are elaborated and applied, fundamental rights express the norms and political values of a political community.[15] The development of a *ne bis in idem* principle, while primarily orientated at securing free movement, is nonetheless an important safeguard for the individual faced with the community's sanctioning powers and is one clear example of a supranational fundamental right.[16] More generally, through the imposition of a common space of movement and the consequential setting aside of national fundamental rights guarantees in certain areas, the Union has been obliged to further develop its own set of fundamental rights.[17] Finally, the necessity

[13] Case C-247/17 *Oikeusministeriö v Denis Raugevicius* EU:C:2018:898.

[14] See TH Marshall, *Citizenship and Social Class* [1950], ed Robert Moore (Pluto Press, 1992). The precise relationship between fundamental rights and citizenship is a question of debate. For a view arguing for a conceptual separation, see Martijn van den Brink, 'EU Citizenship and Fundamental Rights: Empirical, Normative and Conceptual problems' (2019) 25 *ELJ* 21. Without engaging in the broader debate, the present author does believe in at least a historical link between the development of fundamental rights and citizenship and some conceptual affinity.

[15] See, for example, Cass Sustein, 'Incommensurability and Valuation in Law' (1994) 92 *Michigan Law Review* 779, 802ff speaking of the US First Amendment relating to the right to free speech.

[16] Indeed as pointed out in Chapter 7, there is convergence between the supranational and the transnational application of the principle under the rubric of Art 50 CFR. See Case C-261/09 *Gaetano Mantello* EU:C:2010:683, [2010] ECR I-11477 for its application in the context of the EAW FD and Case C-617/10 *Åklagaren v Hans Åkerberg Fransson* EU:C:2013:105 for a supranational application.

[17] See Case C-396/11 *Ciprian Vasile Radu* (Court of Justice, 29 January 2013) and Case C-399/11 *Stefano Melloni v Ministerio Fiscal* EU:C:2013:107 both of which considered the operation of the EAW FD in light of the CFR. It is notable that in *Melloni* what was at stake was the operation of an amendment to the EAW FD which had effectively harmonised national conceptions of the right to a fair trial in the context of in absentia trials, ie Framework Decision 2009/299/JHA amending Framework Decisions 2002/584/JHA, 2005/214/JHA, 2006/783/JHA, 2008/909/JHA and 2008/947/JHA, thereby enhancing the procedural rights of persons and fostering the application of the principle of mutual recognition to decisions rendered in the absence of the person concerned at the trial [2009] OJ L81/24. See also Joined Cases C-404/15 and C-659/15 *Pál Aranyosi and Robert Căldăraru v Generalstaatsanwaltschaft Bremen* EU:C:2016:198, and relatedly regarding the development of the rule of law as a key operative principle in the Union's legal system, Case C-216/18 PPU *Minister for Justice and Equality v LM* EU:C:2018:586.

to secure 'mutual trust' has resulted in a process of rolling out a pan-European set of procedural rights, which, while limited and reliant on national procedures, do form the nucleus of European criminal procedural rights, a development no doubt remarkable to many.[18]

Duties

When the question is considered, EU citizenship is generally considered bereft of duties. It is certainly true that only rights figure in the list contained in Article 21 TFEU. Nonetheless, one of the major arguments of this work is that duties of EU citizenship can be located in criminal law and operate in all three areas of EU citizenship: social integration; free movement or autonomy, and the supranational.

Firstly, through linking integration, crime and the status of the criminal offender in the host Member State and placing them in a communitarian account of both integration and crime, the Court of Justice has imposed a duty of respect for the norms of host societies on individual EU citizens as a condition for their continued enjoyment of membership in that community. This has occurred both in suspending rights of free movement and residence through the exercise of the public policy exception,[19] and in acquiring rights through the treatment of periods of imprisonment on the acquisition of rights under the Citizenship Directive.[20] And although the object of such a duty of respect, in terms of values and norms, is provided by national law, the duty itself, it is suggested, is one that is imposed by EU law as an element of EU citizenship. In *Rendón Marín*,[21] *CS*[22] and *Delvigne*[23] this respect for national criminal law entails consequences for the enjoyment of supranational rights.

However, the concept of duties of EU citizenship through criminal law goes beyond the dimension of social integration of EU citizens but is also found in the concept of a free area of movement. It is suggested that a duty to respect the laws

[18] This study has only dealt in passing with the concept of victims' rights, a new area for many Member States that points to a more fundamental change in the structure of criminal justice systems and one that the Union appears to be at the forefront of championing. See Directive 2012/29/EU establishing minimum standards on the rights, support and proction of victims of crime and replacing Council Framework Decision 2001/220/JHA [2012] OJ L315/57 and Directive 2004/80/EC relating to compensation to crime victimes [2004] OJ L261/1. For a general account of victims in the criminal process, see Lucia Zedner, *Criminal Justice* (Oxford University Press, 2004) 143ff.

[19] Case C-145/09 *Land Baden-Wurttemberg v Panagiotis Tsakouridis* EU:C:2010:708, [2010] ECR I-11979, Case C-348/09 *PI v Oberburgermeisterin der Stadt Remscheid* EU:C:2012:300 and Joined Cases C-331/16 and C-366/16 *K v Staatssecretaris van Veiligheid en Justitie and HF v Belgische Staat* EU:C:2018:296.

[20] Directive 2004/38/EC on the right of citizens of the Union and their family members to move and reside freely within the territory of the Member States [2004] OJ L158/77.

[21] Case C-165/14 *Alfredo Rendón Marín v Administración del Estado* EU:C:2016:675.

[22] Case C-304/14 *Secretary of State for the Home Department v CS* EU:C:2016:674.

[23] Case C-650/13 *Thierry Delvigne v Commune de Lesparre Médoc and Préfet de la Gironde* EU:C:2015:648.

of other Member States exists also in the area of justice and is represented by the system of shared enforcement established by the EAW FD in particular. Both of these developments – rights of free movement and the area of justice – are linked by the notion of a single space or area occupied by EU citizens and with reference to which wrongs are enforced. Free movement has established a relationship with various Member States carrying with it rights. That relationship also entails responsibilities, which likewise are enforced transnationally through a Union-wide system of enforcement.

Finally, the Union can be said to establish a number of duties at a supranational level, imposed on EU citizens. Here, however, it should be pointed out that, aside from its limited and ancillary scope, in the multilevel context of the EU legal system, the capacity of the Union to directly bind individuals is distinctly limited. As *Berlusconi*[24] in particular indicates, EU law cannot directly impose criminal liability on individuals and does not enjoy the quality of legality in the criminal-law sense of being a validly adopted and binding act imposing criminal obligations on individuals. This is even more evident in *MAS and MB*,[25] with the national definition of what constitutes the substantive core of a crime prevailing over EU-level considerations of effectiveness. However, it is suggested that an important role for supranational criminal law is in justifying the use of national criminal law in a transnational setting. It therefore indirectly affects individuals through endorsing national criminal law in the restriction of EU citizens' rights or in facilitating transnational enforcement of national criminal law.

Values

Finally, a word should be said regarding values. Values and norms are central to the identity of a particular political community, particularly one that is not modelled on the nation,[26] and can form an important aspect of the concept of belonging, which is frequently considered a constituent element of citizenship.[27] The Union was originally designed as a technocratic institution, albeit one with a political vocation, and its values have frequently seemed distant and/or ill-formed.[28] This book argues that regardless of what one may think concerning the desirability of the particular values and normative choices made in the

[24] Joined Cases C-387/02, C-391/02 and C-403/02 *Criminal proceedings against Silvio Berlusconi, Sergio Adelchi and Marcello Dull'Utri et al* EU:C:2005:270, [2005] ECR I-3565.

[25] Case C-42/17 *Criminal proceedings against MAS and MB* EU:C:2017:936.

[26] For a developed account and possible application to the European Union, see Jurgen Habermas, 'The European Nation-State: On the Past and Future of Sovereignty and Citizenship' in Jurgen Habermas (ed), *The Inclusion of the Other* (MIT Press, 1998).

[27] Shaw (n 3) 19.

[28] See, for example, Andew Williams, 'Taking Values Seriously: Towards a Philosophy of EU Law' (2009) 29 *OJLS* 549.

context of EU criminal law,[29] the fact remains that one of the principal functions of criminal law is to express certain norms and that one of the principal functions of punishment is to communicate the public condemnation for breach of those norms. Although indirect and often phrased in terms of instrumental or technical goals of compliance, EU criminal law does have the capacity to express certain normative choices on behalf of the Union as a whole, either in designating certain goods, often those associated with market institutions, as public goods, harm to which constitutes a wrong against the Union as a whole, or in more select areas expressing certain values and norms adopted by the Union as guiding principles in criminalising certain conduct. More importantly, perhaps, is the endorsement function of supranational criminal law and its validation of national criminal law and the application of national criminal law in transnational settings. Again, the cases of *PI*,[30] *Tsakouridis*,[31] and especially *K and HF*,[32] are most striking in this regard, but a similar operation be seen in the certain of the 32 categories for which double criminality is typically abolished.[33]

The Restructuring Political Community in the European Union: Between National, Transnational and Supranational

Duff's account of the criminal law is intimately linked with the notion of community. Starting from the premise that criminal law is *public* law, he identifies a significant role for the political community in explaining and justifying criminal law. It is therefore a communitarian account of both criminal law and of citizenship.[34] Crimes are public wrongs, wrongs that concern the public. There must therefore be a public capable of being concerned. At the same time it is the norms and values of the community collectively that determine the content of the non-derogable norms of conduct that comprise the criminal law, its 'civil order'.[35]

[29] EU criminal law has, until recently, been heavily criticised for a security-orientated focus that compromised fundamental rights; see, for example, Sionaidh Douglas-Scott, 'The EU's Area of Freedom, Security and Justice: A Lack of Fundamental Rights, Mutual Trust and Democracy?' (2008–2009) 11 *Cambridge Yearbook of European Legal Studies* 53 and Estella Baker, 'The European Union's "Area of Freedom, Security and (Criminal) Justice" Ten Years On' [2009] *Crim LR* 833. For an overview of the concept of security and its history see Lucia Zedner, *Security* (Routledge, 2009).

[30] *PI* (n 19).

[31] *Tsakouridis* (n 19).

[32] *K & HF* (n 19).

[33] Anne Weyembergh, 'The Functions of Approximation of Penal Legislation within the European Union' (2005) 12 *Maastricht Journal of European and Comparative Law* 149.

[34] While noting that a clean-cut distinction between the two is not particularly plausible. See Duff, *Punishment, Communication and Community* (n 1) ch 2.

[35] See Duff and Marshall (n 1). Hence the association of criminal law with public order; see Agnes Cerf, 'Ordre public, droit pénal et droits fondamentaux' in Redor (n 10). See also Nicola Lacey, *State Punishment: Political Principles and Community Values* (Routledge, 1987) 100–01 speaking of the fundamental interests and values of the community.

Similarly, although many acts that result in crimes might directly be harms or wrongs against individuals, crimes themselves are wrongs against the public; they are shared wrongs experienced vicariously by the community at large via the membership of the victim, and by taking place amongst the community those acts become of concern to that community. Criminal law therefore necessarily presupposes a public, a community, and is a legal context within which the relationship of the individual citizen to that community operates. Viewing citizenship through the lens of criminal law can therefore reveal certain aspects of the broader community.

Much like the Union itself, the community that emerges from this study on the interaction between criminal law and EU citizenship is not simple or clear-cut but plays out in a complex interaction of the national, transnational and supranational in what is ultimately a composite polity: a 'community of communities'.[36] To look for the emergence of a complete, distinct European supranational community through top-down efforts at harmonisation and integration is to look in the wrong place. It is not the operation of a supranational competence of criminalisation that is the main engine behind the emergence of a supranational community in this context. Rather, such an entity emerges in a more organic fashion through the transnational processes triggered by free movement and social integration and their interaction with criminal law. Supranational norms certainly play a role but are limited and ancillary. Of more immediate relevance is the manner in which they reinforce transnational processes, confirming and endorsing national criminal law as they do so.

The Primacy of National Communities

Although recent times have seen a rapid growth in the role of the Union in criminal law, it remains an area of law tied to national sovereignty and remains largely in the hands of national legislators. This picture of the national community as the primary locus of the articulation, application and experiencing of crimes is similarly visible in instances where criminal law interacts with EU citizens.

Crimes as wrongs are primarily articulated at a national level. The determination of what conduct should be subject to criminalisation takes place at a national level. The Union's competence to criminalise through approximation measures is limited in scope by its functional nature in the context of Article 83(2) TFEU and the closed list contained in Article 83(1) TFEU. EU law cannot directly create crimes but must rely on the mediating actions of Member States and only national criminal law enjoys the quality of legality. The vast majority of substantive criminal law, including the core crimes known as *mala in se*, remains in the hands of the Member States, a situation that is unlikely to change in the near future.

[36] Dora Kostakopoulou, 'European Citizenship: Writing the Future' (2007) 13 *ELJ* 623, 628.

A similar privileging of the national is seen in transnational contexts. It is the fundamental interests and values of the host society that determine the content of public policy in expulsion cases, even when those cases concern expulsion from the Union as a whole. The element of national choice has been underlined by the Court of Justice, for whom public policy and public security represent the fundamental interests of (the national) society, including where supranational rights are at stake. A similar privileging of the national community is identifiable in the system for allocating individuals to particular Member States for the purposes of imprisonment. The principle of social integration only supplements, it does not replace, the principle of nationality. At the same time both the EAW FD and Article 54 CISA concern the mutual recognition of national crimes and national judgments, defined by reference to the issuing Member State or Member State of final judgment.

Not only is the wrong articulated at a national level but the wrong is also experienced at a national level; it is the national community that experiences the wrong through the violation of its norms. Clearly, it is not the Union that holds individuals to account, arrests, prosecutes, tries and punishes individuals; all of these functions, so central to the criminal law and reflecting the response of the community that is wronged, are carried out by the institutions of the Member States. The recent controversy over the establishment of the European Public Prosecutor's Office and its eventual decentralised structure is testimony to the sensitivities of the matter, even in an area where the Union's institutional interest is most directly implicated, namely its own financial resources. The national nature of the experience of the wrong is most clearly evident the case of expulsion and acquisition of residence rights treated in Chapter 5. Crimes are wrongs against the national community that justify the limitation of rights vis-à-vis that community. However, even in matters of mutual recognition certain features of the legal practice serve to highlight the continued national nature of the wrong. In the operation of the EAW FD, although the executing Member State contributes to the enforcement of the crime, ultimately the individual is returned and tried by the issuing Member State, the community that experienced the wrong. Similarly, Member States are reluctant to cede the right to punish wrongs they see themselves as having experienced as is proved by the absence of binding rules for allocating jurisdiction and the explicit insistence on inviolability of the national right to prosecute in the Framework Decision on Coordinating Criminal Jurisdiction.[37]

National Wrongs in Transnational Processes

However, those national wrongs are located within transnational processes closely linked to the operation of EU citizenship. The Court has made use of national criminal law to regulate the status of individual Union citizens in host

[37] Framework Decision 2009/948/JHA on prevention and settlement of conflicts of exercise of jurisdiction in criminal proceedings [2009] OJ L328/42.

Member States leading to their greater inclusion and greater exclusion, and has used national criminal law to impose a transnational duty of respect. At the same time, national wrongs are now recognised and enforced transnationally. National criminal law now operates within a single 'area of justice' that corresponds to the area of movement offered EU citizens through rights of free movement; rights and responsibilities, generated from national law, are enjoyed with reference to a broader geographical space.

Supranational Implications – Shared Rights, Shared Wrongs and Shared Punishment

These transanational processes, however, while respecting the essentially national nature of wrongs and the communities that experience them, necessarily engage EU law and give rise to a common framework or norms, wrongs and community.

Firstly, there is much evidence to suggest that the treatment of criminal law within EU law gives rise to a shared conception of wrongdoing and hence a shared moral framework under which citizens' duties towards each other within the broader community are evaluated. The EAW FD in its abolition of double criminality for certain core crimes presupposes a common characterisation of those acts as wrongful across the Union. Similarly, acts that form the object of an approximation competence by the Union are similarly presumed to be wrongful for all Member States. Under the operation of the public policy exception, national criminal law and the wrongful characterisation they entail can be endorsed by EU law and the normative choices made by the supranational community. Furthermore, offences against national communities entail the limitation or suspension of transnational, and possibly supranational, rights. Although the Union lacks any direct means of punishing and thus directly communicating its condemnation of individuals who breach certain norms, it may do so *indirectly*, not (only) through the implementation of substantive EU criminal law but also through endorsing national criminal law when it arises in transnational processes.

Not only is there a common supranational conception of certain wrongs but there is evidence that a community exists at a supranational level capable of experiencing those wrongs.[38] The legitimacy of the EAW system as a shared system of enforcement may be seen as reflecting a shared experience of the wrong by the Union as a whole. More evident is the operation of the *ne bis in idem* principle; once called to account for wrongdoing in one Member State, the wrong is expunged vis-à-vis all Member States, the implication being that only one such wrong exists. Even the scheme adopted through the EAW FD and the Framework

[38] See Robin Lööf, 'Defending Liberty and Structural Integrity: A Social Contractual Analysis of Criminal Justice in the EU' (PhD thesis, Department of Law, European University Institute, 2008).

Decision on the Transfer of Custodial Sentences[39] could be seen in this light; there is an embryonic shared system of punishment, allowing Member States to collectively communicate condemnation to the individual. In *Rendón Marín*,[40] *CS*[41] and *Delvinge*[42] national criminal law is used to restrict EU-level rights, a phenomenon that can be explained through the concept of a wrong shared by the Union as a whole. Finally, the rise in the principle of the need to avoid impunity[43] gives rise to the impression of a joint supranational interest in condemnation; avoidance of impunity for a crime committed is evidently a Union-wide concern.

But note that those wrongs are experienced *through* the wrongs suffered by national communities. It is the wrong suffered by the national community that is enforced within the EAW system but the legitimacy of that system of shared enforcement is premised on the sharing of that wrong by the executing Member State and potentially by all Member States. Similarly, the individual is called to account before the *national* courts for a national wrong and that calling to account is valid Union-wide. The paradox is that crime remains resolutely national and yet collectively the Member States participate in its enforcement and recognise any subsequent calling to account for that crime. The answer, it is submitted, lies in the shared nature of the wrong.[44] It is through wrongs done to individual Member States that one wrongs the Union as a whole.

The result is a composite, multilevel polity that operates along both a transnational and/or horizontal axis and a supranational or vertical axis. However, the connections between national and supranational communities and the relationship between transnational and supranational processes are complex than this simple vertical–horizontal picture would suggest. National, transnational and supranational processes interact and reinforce each other. The national remains privileged but operates in transnational contexts, these transnational contexts are facilitated by a supranational criminal law, which in turn endorses national normative choices. Meanwhile, the assumptions behind transnational systems of enforcement and recognition manifest a supranational community. It is through transnational processes that supranational rights, wrongs and ultimately a community emerge.

[39] Transfer of Custodial Sentences Framework Decision (n 12).
[40] *Rendón Marín* (n 21).
[41] *CS* (n 22).
[42] *Delvigne* (n 23).
[43] See, for example, Case C-129/14 PPU *Criminal proceedings against Zoran Spasic* EU:C:2014:586 and Case C-182/15 *Aleksei Petruhhin v Latvijas Republikas Ģenerālprokuratūra* EU:C:2016:630.
[44] Marshall and Duff (n 1).

BIBLIOGRAPHY

Acosta Arcarazo D, *The Long-Term Residence Status as a Subsidiary Form of EU Ctizenship: An Analysis of Directive 2003/109*, vol 23 (Martinus Nijhoff, 2011).

Adam S and Elsuwege V, 'EU Citizenship and the Federal Challenge through the Prism of Family Reunification' in Kochenov D (ed), *EU Citizenship and Federalism: The Role of Rights* (Cambridge University Press, 2017).

Alegre S and Leaf M, 'Mutual Recognition in European Judicial Cooperation: A Step too Far too Soon? Case Study – The European Arrest Warrant' (2004) 10 *ELJ* 200.

Alter K, *Establishing the Supremacy of European Law: The Making of an International Rule of Law in Europe* (Oxford University Press, 2001).

Anagnostaras G, 'Enhanced Protection of EU Nationals against Expulsion and Concept of Internal Public Security: Comment on the PI Case' (2012) 37 *EL Rev* 627.

Anderson B, *Imagined Communities*, 2nd edn (Verso, 2006).

Anderson B, Gibney MJ and Paoletti E, 'Citizenship, Deportation and the Boundaries of Beloning' (2011) 15 *Citizenship Studies* 547.

Anon, Editorial Comments: 'EU Law as a Way of Life' (2017) 54 *CML Rev* 357.

Ashworth A, *Principles of Criminal Law*, 2 edn (Clarendon Press, 1995).

Azoulai L, 'La Citoyenneté Européenne, un Statut d'Intégration Sociale' in Cohen-Jonathan G et al (eds), *Chemins d'Europe: Mélanges en l'honneur de Jean Paul Jacqué* (Dalloz, 2010).

——, '"Euro-Bonds": The Ruiz Zambrano Judgment or the Real Invention of EU Citizenship' (2011) 3(2) *Perspectives on Federalism*.

——, 'L'autonomie de l'individu européen et la question du statut' (2013/14) EUI Working Papers LAW.

——, 'Transfiguring European Citizenship: From Member State Territory to Union Territory' in Kochenov D (ed), *EU Citizenship and Federalism: The Role of Rights* (Cambridge University Press, 2017).

Azoulai L and Coutts S, 'Restricting Union Citizens' Residence Rights on Grounds of Public Security' (2013) 50 *CML Rev* 553.

Baker E, 'Taking European Criminal Law Seriously' [1998] *Crim LR* 361.

——, 'Criminal Jurisdiction, the Public Dimension to "Effective Protection" and the Construction of Community-Citizen Relations' (2001) 4 *Cambridge Yearbook of European Legal Studies* 25.

——, 'The European Union's "Area of Freedom, Security and (Criminal) Justice" Ten Years On' [2009] *Crim LR* 833.

Barbou des Places S, 'The Integrated Person in EU Law' in Azoulai L, Barbou des Places S and Pataut E (eds), *Constructing the Person in EU Law: Rights, Roles, Identities* (Hart Publishing, 2016).

Barrett G, 'Introduction – A New Improved Formula? The Treaty of Lisbon and National Parliaments' in Barrett G (ed), *National Parliaments and the European Union: The Consitutional Challenge for the Oireachtas and other Member State legislatures* (Clarus Press, 2008).

Bauböck R, 'Recombinant Citizenship' (1999) Political Science Series 67, Institute for Advanced Studies, Vienna.

——, *Transnational Citizenship: Migration and Rights in International Migration* (Edward Elgar, 1994).

——, 'Why European Citizenship? Normative Approaches to Supranational Union' (2007) 8 *Theoretical Inquiries in Law* 453.

Bauböck R and Joppke C, 'How Liberal are Citizenship Tests?' (2010) EUI Working Papers RSCAS 2010/41.

Beetham D, *The Legitimation of Power*, 1 edn (Humanities Press, 1991).

Bellamy R, 'A Duty-Free Europe? What's Wrong with Kochenov's Account of EU Citizenship Rights' (2015) 21 *ELJ* 558.
Bellamy R and Lacey J, 'Balancing the Rights and Duties of European and National Citizens: A Demoicratic Approach' (2018) 25 *Journal of European Public Policy* 1403.
Bennett C, *The Apology Ritual: A Philosophical Theory of Punishment* (Cambridge University Press, 2008).
Besselink L, 'The Parameters of Constitutional Conflicts after Melloni' (2014) 39 *EL Rev* 531.
——, 'EU Constitutionalism and National Parliaments: Insiders or Outsiders' in Jančić D (ed), *National Parliaments after the Lisbon Treaty and the Eurocrisis* (Oxford University Press, 2017).
Boister N, *An Introduction to Transnational Criminal Law* (Oxford University Press, 2012).
Böse M, 'Mutual Recognition, Extradition to Third Countries and Union Citizenship: *Petruhhin*' (2017) 54 *CML Rev* 1781.
Bosniak L, *The Citizen and the Alien: Dilemas of Contemporary Membership* (Princeton University Press, 2006).
Bouza Garcia L, 'The European Citizen's Initiative: A New Institution for Empowering Europe's Citizens?' in Dougan M, Níc Shuibhne N and Spaventa E (eds), *Empowerment and Disempowerment of the European Citizen* (Hart Publishing, 2012).
Braithwaite J and Pettit P, *Not Just Deserts: A Republican Theory of Criminal Justice* (Oxford University Press, 1992).
Brants C, 'What Limits to Harmonising Justice?' in Colson R and Field S (eds), *EU Criminal Justice and the Challenge of Diversity: Legal Cultures in the Area of Freedom, Security and Justice* (Cambridge University Press, 2016).
Brubaker R, *Citizenship and Nationhood in France and Germany* (Harvard University Press, 1992).
Bruggeman W, 'Policing in a European Context' in Apap J (ed), *Justice and Home Affairs in the EU: Liberty and Security Issues after Enlargement* (Edward Elgar, 2004).
Burri T, T*he Greatest Possible Freedom: Interpretive Formulas and their Spin in Free Movement Caselaw* (Nomos 2015).
Caney S, 'Liberalism, Communitarianism: A Misconceived Debate' (1992) 40 *Political Studies* 273.
Carrera (ed) S, 'The Nexus between Immigration, Integration and Citizenship in the EU' (25 January 2006) Immigration, Integration and Citizenship, CEPS, Brussels.
Castillo M and Chemain R, 'La réserve d'ordre public en droit communautaire' in Redor M-J (ed), *L'ordre public: Ordre public ou ordres publics? Ordre public et droits fondamentaux* (Bruylant, 2001).
Cerf A, 'Ordre public, droit pénal et droits fondamentaux' in Redor M-J (ed), *L'ordre public: Ordre public ou ordres publics? Ordre public et droits fondamentaux* (Bruylant, 2001).
Chalmers D, 'The Persona of EU Law' in Azoulai L, Barbou des Places S and Pataut E (eds), *Constructing the Person in EU Law: Roles, Rights, Identities* (Hart Publishing, 2016).
Chalmers D, Davies G and Monti G, *European Union Law*, 3 edn (Cambridge University Press, 2014).
Chaves M, 'EU's Harmonization of National Cirminal Law: Between Punitiveness and Moderation' (2015) 21 *European Public Law* 527.
Chehtman A, 'Citizenship v Territory: Explaining the Scope of the Criminal Law' (2010) 13 *New Criminal Law Review* 427.
Cloots E, *National Identity in EU Law* (Oxford University Press, 2015).
Colson R and Field S (eds), *EU Criminal Justice and the Challenges of Diversity: Legal Cultures in the Area of Freedom, Security and Justice* (Cambridge University Press, 2016).
Coppel J and O'Neill A, 'The European Court of Justice: Taking Rights Seriously?' (1992) 29 *CML Rev* 669.
Costello C, '*Metock*: Free Movement and "Normal Family Life" in the Union' (2009) 46 *CML Rev* 587.
Council of the European Union, 'The Hague Programme: Strengthening Freedom, Security and Justice in the European Union' (2004) JAI 559.
Coutts S, 'The Lisbon Treaty and the Area of Freedom, Security and Justice as an Area of Legal Integration' (2011) 7 *Croation Yearbook of European Law* 87.
——, 'Union Citizenship as Probationary Citizenship: *Onuekwere*' (2015) 52 *CML Rev* 531.

——, 'Delvigne: A Multi-Levelled Political Citizenship' (2017) 42 *EL Rev* 867.
——, 'The Absence of Integration and the Responsibilisation of Union Citizenship' (2018) 3 *European Papers* 761.
——, 'The Expressive Dimension of the Union Citizenship Expulsion Regime: Joined Cases C-331/16 and C-366/16, *K and HF*', European Papers Forum, www.europeanpapers.eu/en/system/files/pdf_version/EP_EF_2018_I_039_Stephen_Coutts_0.pdf (accessed 2 November 2018).
Cras S and Erbežnik A, 'The Directive on the Presumption of Innocence and the Right to be Present at Trial: Genesis and Description of the New EU Measure' [2016] *EuCrim* 25.
Dagger R, 'Republicanism and the Foundations of Criminal Law' in Duff R and Green SP (eds), *Philosophical Foundations of Criminal Law* (Oxford University Press, 2011).
Davies A, 'Radu – A Case of Failed Dialogue' (*eutopia law Blog*, 5 February 2013) http://eutopialaw.com/2013/02/05/radu-a-case-of-failed-dialogue/#more-1755, accessed 7 January 2019.
Davies G, '"Any Place I Hang my Hat?" or: Residence Is the New Nationality' (2005) 11 *ELJ* 43.
——, 'Has the Court Changed, or Have the Cases? The Deservingness of Litigants as an Element in Court of Justice Citizenship Adjudication' (2018) 25 *Journal of European Public Policy* 1442.
Dawes A and Lynskey O, 'The Ever-Longer Arm of EC Law: The Extension of Community Competence into the Field of Criminal Law' (2008) 45 *CML Rev* 131.
de Bruycker P, 'La libre circulation des citoyens européens entre codification et reforme' in Carlier J-Y and Guild E (eds), *L'Avenir de la libre circulation des personnes dans l'UE* [*The Future of Free Movemenet of Persons in the EU*] (Bruylant, 2006).
de Búrca G, 'The Road not Taken: The European Union as Global Human Rights Actor' (2011) 105 *American Society of International Law* 649.
——, 'The Quest for Legitimacy in the European Union' (1996) 59 *MLR* 349.
de Lobkowicz W, 'L'Europe et la sécurité intérieure: Une elaboration par étapes' (décembre 2001) La documentation française, no 5144–45.
de Witte F, 'Sex, Drugs and EU Law: The Recognition of Moral and Ethical Diversity in EU Law' (2013) 50 *CML Rev* 1545.
Díez-Picazo LM, 'What Does it Mean to be a State within the European Union?' [2002] *Rivista Italiana di Diritto Pubblico Comunitario* 651.
Dougan M, 'The Spatial Restructuring of National Welfare States within the European Union: The Contribution of Union Citizenship and the Relevance of the Treaty of Lisbon' in Neergaard U, Nielson R and Rosebury L (eds), *Integrating Welfare Function into EU Law: From Rome to Lisbon* (Djøf Forlag, 2009).
——, 'What Are We to Make of the Citizens' Initiative' (2011) 48 *CML Rev* 1807.
——, 'From Velvet Glove to the Iron Fist: Criminal Sanctions for the Enforcement of Union Law' in Cremona M (ed), *Compliance and the Enforcement of EU Law* (Oxford University Press, 2012).
——, 'The Bubble that Burst: Exploring the Legitimacy of the Case Law on the Free Movement of Union Citizens' in Adams M et al (eds), *Judging Europe's Judges: The Legitimacy of the Case Law of the European Court of Justice* (Hart Publishing, 2013).
——, 'Judicial Review of Member State Action under the General Principles and the Charter: Defining the "Scope of Union Law"' (2015) 52 *CML Rev* 1201.
Douglas-Scott S, 'The EU's Area of Freedom, Security and Justice: A Lack of Fundamental Rights, Mutual Trust and Democracy?' (2008–09) 11 *Cambridge Yearbook of European Legal Studies* 53.
Drywood E and Stalford H, 'Coming of Age? Children's Rights in the European Union' (2009) 46 *CML Rev* 143.
Duff A, *Punishment, Communication and Community* (Oxford University Press, 2003).
——, 'Theorizing Criminal Law: A 25th Anniversary Essay' (2005) 25 *OJLS* 353.
——, *Answering for Crime: Responsibility and Liability in the Criminal Law* (Hart Publishing, 2007).
——, *Theories of Criminal Law*, Stanford Encyclopedia of Philosophy (Summer 2013).
——, 'Law, Language and Community: Some Preconditions for Criminal Liability' (1998) 18 *OJLS* 189.
——, Punishment, Communication and Community (Oxford University Press, 2001).

——, *Answering for Crime: Responsibility and Liability in the Criminal Law* (Hart Publishing, 2007).
——, 'Responsibility, Citizenship and Criminal Law' in Duff R and Green SP (eds), *Philosophical Foundations of Criminal Law* (Oxford University Press, 2011).
——, *The Realm of Criminal Law* (Oxford University Press, 2018).
Duff R and Marshall S, 'Crimes, Public Wrongs, and Civil Order' (2019) 13 *Criminal Law and Philosophy* 21.
Durkheim E, *The Division of Labour in Society*, trans G Simpson (The Free Press, 1933).
Düsterhaus D, 'EU Citizenship and Fundamental Rights: Contradictory, Converging of Complementary?' in Kochenov D (ed), *EU Citizenship and Federalism: The Role of Rights* (Cambridge University Press, 2017).
Eleftheriadis P, 'Citizenship and Obligation' in Dickson J and Eleftheriadis P (eds), *Philosophical Foundations of European Union Law* (Oxford University Press, 2012).
European Commission, Communication on the Special Measures concerning the Movement and Residence of Citizens of the Union which are Justified on Grounds of Public Policy, Public Security or Public Health COM(1999) 372 final.
——, Green Paper on the approximation, mutual recognition and enforcement of criminal sanctions in the European Union COM(2004) 334 final.
——, Communication from the Commission to the European Parliament and the Council on guidance for better transposition and application of Directive 2004/38/EC on the right of citizens of the Union and their family members to move and reside freely within the territory of the Member States COM(2009) 313 final.
——, Towards an EU Criminal Policy: Ensuring the effective implementation of EU policies through criminal law COM(2011) 573 final.
Everson M, 'The Legacy of the Market Citizen' in Shaw J and More G (eds), *New Legal Dynamics of European Union* (Clarendon Press 1995).
——, 'A Very Cosmopolitan Citizenship: But Who Pays the Price?' in Dougan M, Níc Shuibhne N and Spaventa E (eds), *Empowerment and Disempowerment of the European Citizen* (Hart Publishing, 2012).
Fahey E, *EU Law in Ireland* (Clarus Press. 2010).
Farmer L, 'Time and Space in Criminal Law' (2010) 13 *New Criminal Law Review* 333.
Feinberg J, 'The Expressive Function of Punishment' (1965) 49 *The Monist* 397.
——, *The Moral Limits of the Criminal Law: Harm to Others*, vol I (Oxford University Press, 1984).
——, *The Moral Limits of the Criminal Law: Offense to Others*, vol II (Oxford University Press, 1985).
——, *The Moral Limits of the Criminal Law: Harm to Self*, vol III (Oxford University Press, 1986).
——, *The Moral Limits of the Criminal Law: Harmless Wrongdoing*, vol IV (Oxford University Press, 1988).
Ferrera M, *The Boundaries of Welfare: European Integration and the New Spatial Politics of Social Protection* (Oxford University Press, 2005).
Fletcher M, Loof R and Gilmore B, *EU Criminal Law and Justice* (Edward Elgar, 2008).
Gardocki L, 'Double Criminality in Extradition Law' (1993) 27 *Israel Law Review* 288.
Gibbs AH, *Constitutional Life and Europe's Area of Freedom, Security and Justice* (Ashgate, 2011).
Gough J, The Social Contract: A Critical Study of its Development, 2 edn (Clarendon Press, 1957).
Habermas J, 'Human Rights and Popular Sovereignty: The Liberal and Republican Versions' (1994) 7 *Ratio Juris* 1.
——, 'Citizenship and National Identity: Some Reflections on the Future of Europe' in Beiner R (ed), *Theorizing Citizenship* (State University of New York Press, 1995).
——, 'The European Nation-State: On the Past and Future of Sovereignty and Citizenship' in Habermas J (ed), *The Inclusion of the Other* (MIT Press, 1998).
——, 'The Postnational Constellation and the Future of Democracy' in Habermas J (ed), *The Postnational Constellation* (Polity Press, 2001).
Hailbronner K, 'Union Citizenship and Access to Social Benefits' (2005) 42 *CML Rev* 1245.
Hailbronner K and Thym D, 'Case Note C-34/09: Zambrano v ONEm' (2011) 48 *CML Rev* 1253.

Hammar T, *Democracy and the Nation State: Aliens, Denizens and Citizens in a World of International Migration* (Ashgate, 1990).
Harding C and Banach-Gutierrez J, 'The Emergent EU Criminal Policy: Identifying the Species' (2012) 37 *EL Rev* 758.
Hart H, 'The Aims of the Criminal Law' (1958) 23 *Law and Contemporary Problems* 401.
——, 'The Aims of the Criminal Law' (1958) 23 *Law and Contemporary Problems* 401.
Hart H, *Law, Liberty and Morality* (Oxford University Press, 1962).
——, 'Are There Any Natural Rights?' (1955) 64 *Philosophical Review* 175.
Hartley T, *The Foundations of European Union Law*, 8 edn (Oxford University Press, 2014).
Harvey C, 'Promoting Insecurity: Public Order Explusion and the ECHR' in Guild E and Minderhoud P (eds), *Security of Residence and Expulsion: Protection of Aliens in Europe* (Kluwer International, 2001).
Herlin-Karnell E, *The Constitutional Dimension of European Criminal Law* (Hart Publishing, 2012).
——, 'The Swedish Supreme Court and the European Arrest Warrant: Comment on the Decision of 21 March 2007, Surrending of Polish National (Ö 430-07)' [2007] *Europarättsligtidskrift* 885.
——, 'From Mutual Trust to the Full Effectiveness of EU Law: 10 Years of the European Arrest Warrant' (2013) 38 *EL Rev* 79.
Hudson B, 'Punishing Monsters, Judging Aliens: Justice at the Borders of Community' (2006) 39 *Austrialian and New Zealand Journal of Criminology* 232.
Iliopoulou Penot A, 'The Transnational Character of Union Citizenship' in Dougan M, Níc Shuibhne N and Spaventa E (eds), *The Empowerment and Disempowerment of the European Citizen* (Hart Publishing, 2012).
Janssens C, *The Principle of Mutual Recognition in EU Law* (Oxford University Press, 2013).
Karydis G, 'L'ordre public dans l'ordre juridique communautaire: un concept à contenu variable' [2002] *Revue trimestrielle de droit européen* 1.
Kaunert C, 'The Area of Freedom, Security and Justice: The Construction of a "European Public Order"' (2005) 14 *European Security* 459.
Kesby A, *The Right to Have Rights: Citizenship, Humanity and International Law* (Oxford University Press, 2012).
Kessedjian C, 'Public Order in European Law' (2007–08) 1 *Erasmus Law Review* 25.
Knowles D, *Political Obligation: A Critical Introduction* (Routledge, 2010).
Kochenov D, 'A Real European Citizenship: A New Jurisdiction Test: A Novel Chapter in the Development of the Union in Europe' (2011) 18 *Columbia Journal of European Law* 55.
——, 'EU Citizenship without Duties' (2014) 20 *ELJ* 482.
——, 'On Tiles and Pillars: EU Citizenship as a Federal Denominator' in Kochenov D (ed), *EU Citizenship and Federalism: The Role of Rights* (Cambridge University Press, 2017).
Kochenov D and Pirker B, 'Deporting the Citizens within the European Union: A Counter-Intuitive Trend in Case C-348/09 PI v Obergurgermeisterin der Stadt Remscheid' (2012-2013) 19 *Columbia Journal of European Law* 369.
Komarek J, 'European Constitutionalism and the European Arrest Warrant: In Search of the Limits of "Contrapunctual Principles"' (2007) 44 *CML Rev* 9.
Kornezov A, 'The Area of Freedom, Security and Justice in Light of the EU Accession to the ECHR – Is the Break-up inevitable?' (2012–13) 15 *Cambridge Yearbook of European Legal Studies* 227.
Kostakopoulou D, *Citizenship, Identity and Immigration in the European Union; Between Past and Future* (Manchester University Press, 2001).
——, 'Ideas, Norms and European Citizenship: Explaining Institutional Change' [2005] 68 *MLR* 233.
——, 'The Area of Freedom, Security and Justice and the European Union's Constitutional Dialogue' in Barnard C (ed), *The Fundamentals of EU Law Revisited* (Oxford University Press, 2007).
——, 'European Citizenship: Writing the Future' (2007) 13 *ELJ* 623.
——, 'The Anatomy of Civic Integration' (2010) 73 *MLR* 933.
——, 'Co-Creating European Union Citizenship: Institutional Process and Crescive Norms' (2012–13) 15 *Cambridge Yearbook of European Legal Studies* 255.

Kramer D, 'From Worker to Self-Entrepeneur: The Transformation of Homo Economicus and the Freedom of Movement in the European Union' (2017) 23 *ELJ* 172.
Kuipers J-J, 'Cartesio and Grunkin Paul: Mutual Recognition as a Vested Rights Theory Based on Party Autonomy in Private Law' (2009) 2 *European Journal of Legal Studies* 66.
Kymlicka W, *Multi-Cultural Citizenship: A Liberal Theory of Rights* (Oxford University Press, 1995).
——, 'Liberal Nationalism and Cosmopolitan Justice' in Benhabib S (ed), *Another Cosmopolitanism* (Oxford University Press, 2006).
Lacey N, *State Punishment: Political Principles and Community Values* (Routledge, 1987).
Lenaerts K, 'EU Citizenshp and the European Court of Justice's "Stone-by-Stone" Approach' (2015) 1 *International Comparative Jurisprudence* 1.
——, 'La vie apès l'avis: Exploring the Principle of Mutual (Yet not Blind) Trust' (2017) 54 *CML Rev* 805.
——, 'Constitutionalism and the Many Faces of Federalism' (1990) 38 *American Journal of Comparative Law* 205.
Lindahl H, 'Finding a Place for Freedom, Security and Justice: The European Union's Claim to Territorial Unity' (2004) 29 *EL Rev* 461.
Loader I and Walker N, *Civilising Security* (Cambridge University Press, 2007).
Lööf R, 'Defending Liberty and Structural Integrity: A social contractual analysis of criminal justice in the EU' (PhD thesis, Department of Law, European University Institute, 2008).
Lyon-Caen G, 'La réserve d'ordre public en matiere de liberé d'etablissement et de libre circulation' (1966) *Revue trimestrielle de droit européen* 693.
MacCormick N, 'Law as Institutional Fact' (1986) 90 *LQR* 102.
——, 'Reconstruction after Deconstruction: A Response to CLS' (1990) 10 *OJLS* 539.
Macklin A and Bauböck R, 'The Return of Banishment: Do the New Denationalisation Policies Weaken Citizenship?' (2015) EUI Working Papers, RSCAS 2015/14.
Maduro M-P, 'So Close and Yet So Far: The Paradoxes of Mutual Recognition' (2007) 14 *Journal of European Public Policy* 814.
Magnette P, *La citoyennéte européenne* (Editions de l'Université de Bruxelles, 1999).
Mancano L, 'Punishment and Rights in European Union Citizenship: Persons or Criminals?' (2018) 24 *ELJ* 206.
Marin L, '"A Spectre is Haunting Europe": European Citizenship in the Area of Freedom, Security and Justice' (2011) 17 *European Public Law* 705.
——, '"Only You": The Emergence of a Temperate Mutual Trust in the Area of Freedom, Security and Justice and its Underpinning in the European Composite Constitutional Order' (2017) 2 *European Papers* 141.
Marshall S and Duff R, 'Criminalization and Sharing Wrongs' (1998) 11 *Canadian Journal of Law and Jurisprudence* 7.
Marshall T, *Citizenship and Social Class* [1950], ed R Moore (Pluto Press, 1992).
Mendes J, 'Participation and the Role of Law after Lisbon: A Legal View on Article 11 TEU' (2011) 48 *CML Rev* 1849.
Mendéz AJ, 'European Citizenship after Martiníz Sala and Baumbast: Has European Law Become More Human but Less Social?' in Poirias Maduro M and Azoulai L (eds), *The Past and Future of EU Law* (Hart Publishing, 2010).
Mill JS, *On Liberty and Other Essays* [1859] (Oxford University Press, 1991).
Minderhoud P and Mantu S, 'Back to the Roots? No Access to Social Assistance for Union Citizens Who Are Economically Inactive' in Thym D (ed), *Questioning EU Citizenship: Judges and the Limits of Free Movement and Solidarity in the EU* (Hart Publishing, 2018).
Mitsilegas V, *EU Criminal Law* (Hart Publishing, 2009).
——, 'The Limits of Mutual Trust in Europe's Area of Freedom, Security and Justice: From Automatic Inter-State Cooperation to the Slow Emergence of the Individual' (2012) 31 *Yearbook of European Law* 319.
——, 'European Criminal Law and Resistance to Communautarisation after Lisbon' (2010) 1 *New Journal of European Criminal Law* 458.

——, EU Criminal Law after Lisbon (Hart Publishing, 2016).
——, 'The Constitutional Implications of Mutual Recognition in Criminal Matters in the EU' (2006) 43 *CML Rev* 1277.
Monar J, 'The Area of Freedom, Security and Justice' in Bast J and von Bogdandy A (eds), *Principles of European Constitutional Law*, 2 edn (Hart Publishing and Verlag CH Beck, 2010).
——, 'The Dynamics of Justice and Home Affairs: Laboratories, Driving Factors and Costs' (2001) 39 *Journal of Common Market Studies* 747.
Moore M, *Placing Blame: A Theory of Criminal Law* (Oxford University Press, 1997).
Möstl M, 'Preconditions and Limits of Mutual Recognition' (2010) 47 *CML Rev* 405.
Murphy C, EU Counter-Terrorism Law: Pre-Emption and the Rule of Law (Hart Publishing, 2012).
Nelkin D, 'Comparing Criminal Justice' in Maguire M, Morgan R and Reiner R (eds), *The Oxford Handbook of Criminology*, 5 edn (Oxford University Press, 2012).
Neuvonen PJ, 'Retrieving the Subject of European Integration' (2010) 25 *ELJ* 6.
Níc Shuibhne N, 'Derogating from the Free Movement of Persons. When Can EU citizens Be Deported?' (2005–06) 8 *Cambridge Yearbook of European Legal Studies* 187.
——, 'The Resilience of EU Market Citizenship' (2010) 47 *CML Rev* 1597.
——, '(Some) of the Kids are All Right' (2012) 49 *CML Rev* 349.
——, 'The Third Age of EU Citizenship' in Syrpis P (ed), *The Juriciary, the Legislature and the EU Internal Market* (Cambridge University Press, 2012).
——, 'Limits Rising, Duties Ascending: The Changing Legal Shape of Union Citizenship' (2015) 52 *CML Rev* 889.
——, 'Seven Questions for Seven Paragraphs' (2011) 36 *EL Rev* 161.
Nicolaidis K, 'Trusting the Poles? Constructing Europe through Mutual Recognition' (2007) 14 *Journal of European Public Policy* 682.
Nicolaidis K and Shaffer G, 'Transnational Mutual Recognition Regimes: Governance without Global Government' (2005) 68 *Law and Comtemporary Problems* 263.
Nohlen N, 'Germany: The European Arrest Warrant Case' (2008) 6 *iCON* 153.
Norrie A, *Crime, Reason and History: A Critical Introduction to Criminal Law*, 1 edn (Weidenfeld & Nicolson, 1993).
O'Brien C, 'I Trade, therefore I Am: Legal Personhood in the European Union' (2013) 50 *CML Rev* 1643.
——, '"Civis Captialist Sum": Class as the new Guiding Princple of EU Free Movement Rights' (2016) 53 *CML Rev* 937.
——, 'The ECJ Sacrifices EU Citizenship in Vain: *Commission v United Kingdom*' (2017) 51 *CML Rev* 209.
O'Leary S, *The Evolving Concept of Community Citizenship: From the Free Movement of Persons to Union Citizenship* (Kluwer, 1996).
——, 'Putting Flesh on the Bones of European Union Citizenship' (1999) 24 *EL Rev* 68.
——, 'The Past, Present and Future of the Purely Internal Rule in EU Law' in Dougan M, Níc Shuibhne N and Spaventa E (eds), *Empowement and Disempowerment of the European Citizen* (Hart Publishing, 2012).
Öberg J, 'Do We Really Need Criminal Sanctions for the Enforcement of EU Law?' (2014) 5 *New Journal of European Criminal Law* 370.
——, 'Limits to EU Powers: A Case Study on Individual Criminal Sanctions for the Enforcement of EU Law' (PhD, European University Institute, 2014).
Olsen ED, 'Transnational European Citizenship: Tracing Conceptions of Citizenship in the European Integration Process' (PhD thesis, European University Institute, Florence, 2008).
Ouwekerk J, 'Criminal Justice beyond National Sovereignty: An Alternative Perspective on the Europeanisation of Criminal Law' (2015) 23 *European Journal of Crime, Criminal Law & Criminal Justice* 11.
Pataut E, 'A Family Status for the European Citizen' in Azoulai L, Barbou des Places S and Pataut E (eds), *Constructing the Person in EU Law: Rights, Roles and Identities* (Hart Publishing, 2016).

Peers S, 'Mutual Recognition and Criminal Law in the European Union: Has the Council got it Wrong?' (2004) 41 *CML Rev* 5.
——, 'The European Community's Criminal Law Competence: The Plot Thickens' (2008) 33 EL Rev 399.
——, *EU Justice and Home Affairs Law*, 3 edn (Oxford University Press, 2011).
——, 'The European Arrest Warrant: The Dilemas of Mutual Recognition, Human Rights and EU Citizenship' in Rosas A, Bot Y and Leits E (eds), *The Court of Justice and the Construction of Europe: Analyses and Perspectives on Sixty Years of Case-Law* (Asser Press, 2013).
——, 'Justice and Home Affairs Law since the Treaty of Lisbon: A Fairy-Tale Ending?' in Acosta Arcarazo D and Murphy C (eds), *EU Security and Justice Law* (Hart Publishing, 2014).
——, *EU Justice and Home Affairs Law*, vol I: *EU Immigration and Asylum Law* and vol II: *EU Criminal Law, Policing and Civil Law*, 4th edn (Oxford University Press, 2016).
Peristeridou C, *The Principle of Legality in European Criminal Law* (Intersentia, 2015).
Pernice I, 'Multilevel Constitutionalism in the EU' (2002) 27 *EL Rev* 511.
——, 'The Treaty of Lisbon: Multi-Level Constitutionalism in Action' (2009) 15 *Columbia Journal of European Law* 349.
Picard E, 'La fonction de l'ordre public dans l'ordre juridique' in Redor M-J (ed), *L'ordre public: Ordre public ou ordres publics? Ordre public et droits fondamentaux* (Bruylant, 2001).
Plachta M, '(Non-)Extradition of Nationals: A Neverending Story' (1999) 13 *Emory International Law Review* 70.
Plender R, 'An Incipient Form of European Citizenship' in Jacobs F (ed), *European Law and the Individual* (North-Holland, 1976).
Prechal S, 'Mutual Trust before the Court of Justice of the European Union' (2017) 2 *European Papers* 75.
Preuß U, 'Problems of a Concept of European Citizenship' (1995) 1 *ELJ* 267.
Rafaraci T, 'Brief Notes on the Euopean Public Prosecutor's Office: Ideas, Project and Fulfilment' in Belfiore R and Rafaraci T (eds), *EU Criminal Justice: Fundamental Rights, Transnational Proceedings and the European Public Prosecutor's Office* (Springer, 2018).
Raucea C, 'European Citizenship and the Right to Reside: "No One on the Outside has a Right to be Inside?"' (2016) 22 *ELJ* 470.
Rawls J, *A Theory of Justice* (Harvard University Press, 1971).
Raynor P and Robinson G, *Rehabilitation, Crime and Justice*, ed J Campling (Palgrave Macmillan, 2005).
Réveillère V, 'Family Rights for Naturalised EU citizens: *Lounes*' (2018) 55 *CML Rev* 1855.
Ritz C and Vasconcelos B, 'Extradition Discrimination? Pisciotti's Legal Battle Continues as Regional Court of Berlin Refers Questions of Fundamental EU Law Principles to the CJEU' (2016) 37 *European Competition Law Review* 277.
Rock P, 'Sociological Theories of Crime' in Reiner R, Maguire M and Morgan R (eds), *The Oxford Handbook of Criminology*, 5 edn (Oxford University Press, 2012).
Rosenfeld M, *The Identity of the Constitutional Subject: Selfhood, Culture and Community* (Routledge, 2010).
Šadl U and Sankari S, 'Why Did the Citizenship Jurisprudence Change?' in Thym D (ed), *Questioning EU Citizenship: Judges and the Limits of Free Movement and Solidarity in the EU* (Hart Publishing, 2017).
Schiltz C, '*Akrich*: A Clear Delimitation without Limits' (2005) 12 *Maastrict Journal of European and Comparative Law* 241.
Schönberger C, 'European Citizenship as Federal Citizenship: Some Citizenship Lessons of Comparative Federalism' (2007) 19 *European Review of Public Law* 61.
Schütze R, *From Dual to Cooperative Federalism: The Changing Structures of European Law* (Oxford University Press, 2009).
Shaw J, 'Citizenship of the Union – Towards Post-National Membership' (1997) 06/97 Jean Monnet Working Papers, http://centers.law.nyu.edu/jeanmonnet/archive/papers/97/97-06-.html, accessed 14 March 2013.
——, *The Transformation of Citizenship in the European Union: Electoral Rights and the Restructuring of Political Space* (Cambridge University Press, 2007).
——, 'The Political Representation of Europe's Citizens: Developments' (2008) 4 *EuConst* 162.

Shaw J and Wiener A, 'The Paradox of the European Polity' in Green Cowles M and Smith M (eds), *The State of the European Union: Risks, Reforms, Resistance and Revival*, vol 5 (Oxford University Press, 2000).
Simester A and von Hirsch A, *Crimes, Harms and Wrongs: On the Principles of Criminalisation* (Hart Publishing, 2011).
Simon P, 'The Criminalisation Power of the European Union after Lisbon and the Principle of Democratic Legitimacy' (2012) 3 *New Journal of European Criminal Law* 242.
Somek A, 'Solidarity Decomposed: Being and Time in European Citizenship' (2007) 32 *EL Rev* 787.
——, *Individualism: An Essay on the Authority of the European Union* (Oxford University Press, 2008).
——, 'The Cosmopolitan Constitution' in Maduro M, Sankari S and Tuori K (eds), *Transnational Law: Rethinking European Law and Legal Thinking* (Cambridge University Press, 2014).
Spaventa E, 'Case C-109/01 Secretary of State for the Home Department v H Akrich' (2005) 42 *CML Rev* 225.
——, Free Movement of Persons in the European Union: Barriers to Movement in their Constitutional Context (Kluwer Law International, 2007).
——, 'Seeing the Woods despite the Trees? On the Scope of Union Citizenship and its Constitutional Effects' (2008) 45 *CML Rev* 13.
——, 'Earned Citizenship: Understanding Union Citizenship through its Scope' in Kochenov D (ed), *EU Citizenship and Federalism: The Role of Rights* (Cambridge University Press, 2017).
Streit M and Mussler W, 'The Economic Constitution of the European Community: From "Rome" to "Maastrict"' (1995) 1 *ELJ* 5.
Sunstein C, 'Incommensurability and Valuation in Law' (1994) 92 *Michigan Law Review* 779.
Suominen A, 'Effectiveness and Functionality of Substantive EU Criminal Law' (2014) 5 *New Journal of European Criminal Law* 388.
Tadros V, The Ends of Harm: Moral Foundations of the Criminal Law (Oxford University Press, 2011).
Thym D, 'The Elusive Limits of Solidarity: Residence Rights of and Social Benefits for Economically Inactive Union Citizens' (2014) 52 *CML Rev* 17.
—— (ed), *Questioning EU Citizenship: Judges and the Limits of Free Movement and Solidarity in the EU* (Hart Publishing, 2017).
Tryfonidou A, *The Impact of Union Citizenship on the EU's Market Freedoms* (Hart Publishing, 2016).
Turner JI, 'The Expressive Dimension of EU Criminal Law' (2012) 60 *American Journal of Comparative Law* 555.
Twomey P, 'Constructing a Secure Space: The Area of Freedom, Security and Justice' in O'Keefe D and Twomey P (eds), *Legal Issues of the Amsterdam Treaty* (Hart Publishing, 1999).
van den Brink M, 'EU Citizenship and (Fundamental) Rights: Empirical, Normative and Conceptual Problems' (2019) 25 *ELJ* 21.
van Dijk P, 'Protection of "Integrated" Aliens against Expulsion under the European Convention on Human Rights' in Guild E and Minderhoud P (eds), *Security of Residence and Expulsion: Protection of Aliens in Europe* (Kluwer International, 2001).
van Middelaar L, *Passage to Europe: How a Continent became a Union*, trans L Water (Yale University Press, 2013).
von Bogdandy A et al, 'Reverse Solange – Protecting the Essence of Fundamental Rights against EU Member States' (2012) 49 *CML Rev* 489.
Walker N, 'Denizenship and Deterritorialisation in the European Union' in Lindahl H (ed), *A Right to Inclusion and Exclusion: Normative Faultlines of the EU's Area of Freedom, Security and Justice* (Hart Publishing, 2009).
——, 'The Place of Territory in Citizenship' in Bauböck R and others (eds), *The Oxford Handbook of Citizenship* (Oxford University Press, 2017).
Walters W, 'Deportation, Expulsion and the International Police of Aliens' (2000) 6 *Citizenship Studies* 265.
Waugh E, *Brideshead Revisited* [1945] (Penguin, 2000).
Weiler J, 'To Be a European Citizen: Eros and Civilisation' in Weiler J (ed), *The Constitution of Europe* (Cambridge University Press, 1999).

Weiler J, 'In the Face of Crisis: Input Legitimacy, Output Legitimacy and the Political Messianism of European Integration' (2012) 34 *Journal of European Integration* 825.
Weiner A, *European Citizenship Practice* (Westview Press, 1998).
Weyembergh A, 'The Functions of Approximation of Penal Legislation within the European Union' (2005) 12 *Maastricht Journal of European and Comparative Law* 149.
White RC, 'Conflicting Competences: Free Movement Rules and Immigration Laws' (2004) 29 *EL Rev* 385.
Williams A, 'Taking Values Seriously: Towards a Philosophy of EU Law' (2009) 29 *OJLS* 549.
Wollenschläger F, 'A New Fundamental Freedom beyond Market Integration: Union Citizenship and its Dynamics for Shifting the Economic Paradigm of European Integration' (2011) 17 *ELJ* 1.
——, 'Consolidating Union Citizenship: Residence and Solidarity Rights for Jobseekers and the Economically Inactive in the Post-*Dano* Era' in Thym D (ed), *Questioning EU Citizenship: Judges and the Limits of Free Movement and Solidarity in the EU* (Hart Publishing, 2017).
Zedner L, *Criminal Justice* (Oxford University Press, 2004).
——, 'Is the Criminal Law Only for Citizens? A Problem at the Borders of Punishment' in Bosworth M and Franco Aas K (eds), *The Borders of Punishment: Migration, Citizenship and Social Exclusion* (Oxford University Press, 2013).

INDEX

www.ingramcontent.com/pod-product-compliance
Ingram Content Group UK Ltd.
Pitfield, Milton Keynes, MK11 3LW, UK
UKHW021908150926
475560UK00003B/254

9 781509 915361